GAYOSO

GAYOSO AS GOVERNOR-GENERAL

GAYOSO

*The Life
of a Spanish Governor
in the Mississippi Valley
1789-1799*

JACK D. L. HOLMES

PUBLISHED BY
Louisiana State University Press

FOR

The Louisiana Historical Association

To

Miss Irene F. Barrow

and

Mrs. Hallette Mary Barrow Cole

Who showed that Gayoso's *noblesse oblige*,

warmth, friendliness, and hospitality

live on in his descendants.

PREFACE

BIOGRAPHIES of great men rarely require a statement from the authors justifying their work. But what factors determine a man's greatness or his place in history? Douglas Southall Freeman once wrote, "A man's place in history depends, in large part, on care and fortune—care in preserving essential records, and good fortune in having a biographer who uses those records sympathetically." It is my belief that Manuel Gayoso de Lemos was a great man, and this biography hopes to illustrate his importance. In a larger sense, however, this is more than a biography of a man. It is a story of the critical decade, 1789–1799, in the Lower Mississippi Valley.

Few local and regional studies of Spanish Louisiana have examined the rich archives of Spain and Mexico. American history texts do not mention Gayoso; neither do Latin American history books. For the most part the Lower Mississippi Valley is a lacuna in our knowledge of the history of both the United States and Latin America. Louisiana was for almost four decades a Spanish borderlands province on New Spain's northern frontier. With Cuba it shared a role in defending Spain's American *Mare Nostrum*—the Gulf of Mexico. Its proximity to the nascent settlements of the early American West would shape the direction of United States expansion a generation before Manifest Destiny.

Because the Spaniards insisted on extensive and accurate records

of virtually every day-by-day detail and because they have preserved millions of documents in libraries and archives, historians
are able to piece together the eighteenth-century Mississippi Valley
story with accuracy and meaning. Sociologists and anthropologists
may study acculturation and ethnic data; demographers have detailed census reports from which to make observations; geographers
can study the detailed explorations and reconnaissances made by
military and civilian personnel on the vast, unexplored frontier;
political scientists can examine the interesting phenomenon of a
Spanish colonial government, founded on the notion of centralization
of power, forced to adapt to a non-Spanish people living in an in-
dividualistic, decentralized frontier atmosphere. Virtually every
aspect of economic, social, political, and military history can be
recaptured by reading the numerous documents.

Gayoso was, during this final decade of the eighteenth century,
the central figure in waning Spanish power. By focusing attention
on his administration as governor of the Natchez District, one
can see in sharp contrast the weakness and strength of Spanish
colonial power in the Mississippi Valley.

For the past six years I have been uncovering documents con-
cerning Gayoso in libraries and archives of America and Europe.
During the course of my research, writing, and rewriting, numerous
persons have given me invaluable assistance. Mrs. Margaret Francis
Shaw, former secretary to the manager of the Gayoso Hotel in
Memphis, Tennessee, first put me on the trail of the governor by
compiling a scrapbook based on years of correspondence with
Gayoso's descendants. From this scrapbook I learned of Mrs. C.
Grenes Cole, the governor's great-great-granddaughter whose
charming New Orleans home and collection of Gayoso papers were
opened to my research. Her encouragement and moral support
throughout these years were always an inspiration. José Mancebo
Benfield of Mexico City, another lineal descendant of the Spanish
Gayosos, supplied me with family histories.

Dr. Alfred B. Thomas of the University of Alabama has led me
into the Spanish borderlands with his keen insight into the true
scope of American history and his numerous helpful suggestions.
Dr. Lewis U. Hanke of Columbia University directed the doctoral

thesis at the University of Texas which was my first attempt at a biography of Gayoso. Dr. Raleigh A. Suarez, dean of the Humanities Division at McNeese State College, first read the revised version and made numerous excellent suggestions to improve the manuscript, as did Dr. A. P. Nasatir of San Diego State College, whose own important research in Spanish Louisiana history, sympathetic suggestions, and careful and critical reading of the manuscript aided me greatly. Dr. A. P. Whitaker of the University of Pennsylvania and Dr. Irving A. Leonard of the University of Michigan sent me valuable tips when I first began my study of Gayoso. Dr. Lawrence Kinnaird, formerly of the University of California, kindly suggested I look into the Segovia archives where I was able to solve a number of questions surrounding Gayoso.

Members of the Publications Committee of the Louisiana Historical Association, and particularly the chairman, Dr. Joe Gray Taylor of McNeese State College, rendered invaluable service by reading the entire manuscript and by offering many helpful suggestions. All errors are, however, my own.

For the many librarians, archivists, clerks, and helpers in the United States, Spain, Portugal, Cuba, and Mexico I have nothing but praise. I wish to mention in particular the following: Dr. Vergil L. Bedsole, head of the Department of Archives at Louisiana State University; Dr. Garland F. Taylor, former director of libraries of the Howard-Tilton Memorial Library of Tulane University; Dr. Connie Griffith, head of the Archives Department at Tulane University; Winston DeVille, former head of Special Collections of the Mobile Public Library; Miss Pollyanna Creekmore, head of the McClung Collection of the Lawson McGhee Library in Knoxville, Tennessee; Miss Rose Oliver, former librarian at the Louisiana State Museum Library of New Orleans; Miss Katherine Bridges, Louisiana librarian at Northwestern State College in Natchitoches, Louisiana; Dr. José M. de la Peña, director, and his able staff at the Archivo General de Indias in Seville; the directors and staff of the Archivo General de Simancas, the Biblioteca Nacional of Madrid, and the Archivo Histórico Nacional in Madrid; Admiral Julio F. Guillén Tato, director, and his competent staff at the Museo Naval and the Archivo Museo D. Álvaro de Bazán Marina de Guerra in El Viso del Marqués; and Sr. D. A. Zapatero, chief of the Overseas Section of the Archivo Histórico Militar in Madrid.

I am grateful for the friendship and historical acumen of Juan José Andreu of the University of Zaragoza, whose own research on the Spaniards in the Mississippi Valley has made the hours in which we discussed our mutual interests both valuable and happy.

Because of the nature of this study, a great deal of money was expended during the past six years in traveling to distant archives and on all the various expenses of historical research. I wish to thank the following individuals and institutions for help at various times: Miss Irene F. Barrow; Mrs. Hallette Mary Barrow Cole; the University of Texas for a graduate fellowship, 1958–1959, under which my first research on Gayoso was initiated; the American Philosophical Society for a research grant in 1960 to study the New Orleans Cabildo; the Fulbright Commission for a research grant and renewal during 1961 and 1962 for research on the defenses of the Mississippi Valley; and the University of Alabama for a faculty research grant during the summer of 1964, during which I gathered a few more documents concerning the career of Manuel Gayoso de Lemos.

J.D.L.H.

CONTENTS

LIST OF TABLES

ABBREVIATIONS

AGI   Archivo General de Indias (Seville)

AGMS   Archivo General Militar de Segovia

AGN   Archivo General de la Nación (Mexico)

AGS   Archivo General de Simancas

AHN   Archivo Histórico Nacional (Madrid)

AM   Department of Archives and History, State of Mississippi

ASHM   Archivo y Biblioteca del Servicio Histórico Militar (Madrid)

BN   Biblioteca Nacional (Madrid)

MN   Museo Naval (Madrid)

PC   Papeles de Cuba (AGI, Seville)

SD   Audiencia de Santo Domingo (AGI, Seville)

JOURNALS

ETHS   East Tennessee Historical Society *(Publications)*

HAHR   Hispanic American Historical Review

MVHR   Mississippi Valley Historical Review

WTHS   West Tennessee Historical Society *(Papers)*

GAYOSO

CHAPTER I

A New Governor for Natchez

THE SMALL group of Natchez planters who milled uneasily about the square opposite the New Orleans Cabildo should have been joking and laughing. It was April and the Louisiana sun spread its warmth over the Lower Mississippi Valley. But the Natchez tobacco planters were unhappy and restless; the coffee seemed extra bitter to them. Already deeply in debt, facing possible financial ruin, and worried over the sale of their next crop, they had come to New Orleans for two reasons: to plead with the governor-general to intercede on their behalf with King Charles IV to continue buying their tobacco for the government factories, and to meet the officer who had been appointed governor of the newly constituted Natchez District.

Hearts quickened as a shout rang out, "There she comes!" The small brig tacked easily, showing her name, *La Industria*, and the superstitious murmured that this was a good omen. On board was the new governor, Lieutenant-Colonel Manuel Gayoso de Lemos. The voyage had been a long and dangerous one; illness and storms almost robbed the Natchez planters of their governor before his delayed arrival on April 12, 1789. The new governor hid his nervousness and his concern over his wife's fever as he waved to the

3

expectant crowd on the levee. The planters wondered about the experience and training of this stocky, amiable officer. If they had seen a dossier on him, they would have been greatly reassured.

Manuel Luis Gayoso de Lemos y Amorín was born May 30, 1747, at Oporto, the charming coastal town in Portugal to which Douro River boats bring their loads of world famous wine. His father, Manuel Luis Gayoso de Lemos y Sarmiento, was Spanish consul in the Portuguese port; and his mother, Theresa Angelica Amorín y Magallanes was a native of Oporto.[1] Little is known about young Manuel's early life; it is possible he was educated at Westminster College in England.[2] On July 7, 1771, however, he entered the Spanish army as a cadet in the Lisbon Regiment. Because of his natural friendliness and skill in languages and diplomacy, he earned promotions to sub-lieutenant in 1772, sub-lieutenant of grenadiers in 1779, and lieutenant on April 4, 1781.[3] Esteban Miró, who was governor-general of Louisiana when Gayoso arrived at New Orleans in 1789, wrote of his early acquaintance with the new Natchez governor: "This officer served four years with me in the Lisbon Regiment from 1773, and even then he had distinguished himself

[1]Baptismal record of Manuel Gayoso de Lemos, Nostra Senhora de Asunção (Sé Catedral), Oporto (Portugal), June 21, 1747, original in the Arquivo do Distrito do Porto, folio 205. A certified copy is in Gayoso's *expediente matrimonial* (1797), Archivo General Militar de Segovia. His father was born in Pontevedra, August 30, 1721. See Gayoso's last will and testament, New Orleans, July 18, 1799, copies in Notarial Archives, Parish of Orleans (New Orleans), Acts of Notary Pedro Pedesclaux, XXXV, folios 612–15; and in Gayoso's *causa mortuoria* (1799–1801), AGI, PC, legajo 169; Jack D. L. Holmes, "Gallegos notables en la Luisiana," *Cuadernos de Estudios Gallegos* (Santiago de Compostela, Spain), No. 57 (1964), 103-104. Without exception, the published accounts of Gayoso's life give the wrong date or place or both.
[2]Col. John Pope, *A Tour through the Southern and Western Territories* (reprint ed.; New York, 1888), 29, states that Gayoso was brought up at the Court of London. Arthur P. Whitaker, "Gayoso de Lemos, Manuel," *Dictionary of American Biography*, ed. Allen Johnson and Dumas Malone (20 vols.; New York, 1928–1936), VII, 201; and Irving A. Leonard, "A Frontier Library, 1799," HAHR, XXIII (February, 1943), 24, both state that Gayoso was educated in London. A contemporary of Gayoso, Andrew Ellicott, wrote, "He was educated in Great Britain, and retained in a considerable degree the manners, and customs, of that nation until his death, especially in his style of living." *Journal of Andrew Ellicott* (Philadelphia, 1803; reprint ed.; Chicago, 1962), 215.
[3]Gayoso's service records, Natchez, June 30, 1794, and New Orleans, June 30, 1795, AGI, PC, legs. 161-a, 1443-b, respectively.

through his talent, knowledge of various languages, and excellent conduct. . . ." [4]

For more than a year during 1781 and 1782, Gayoso served on the Spanish warship *La España,* one of the many vessels in the squadron of Francisco de Borja. His ship, which boasted between sixty and sixty-four cannons and had made the Atlantic crossing to Veracruz in 1774,[5] cruised between Cádiz and Cape Finisterre, keeping vigilance over the western coast of the Iberian Peninsula. He later joined the large squadron of Luis de Córdoba, one of Spain's most brilliant naval commanders.[6]

In the 1780–81 siege of Gibraltar, a combined Franco-Spanish squadron of more than fifty ships met at Cádiz, and Gayoso had an opportunity to watch some of the commanders in action. There were Buenaventura Moreno, who led the naval forces, and Luis de Berton de Balbe de Quiers, Duque de Crillon, who commanded the army. The governor of Cádiz was General Alejandro O'Reilly, whose military ability had been demonstrated in Louisiana in 1769. Cádiz was crowded with such royal personages as the Count of Artois (later Charles X) and the Duke of Bourbon from France. O'Reilly needed a bilingual adjutant, and he chose Gayoso, who had been appointed captain on June 25, 1782.[7]

This early naval experience was to prove invaluable to the governor of Natchez when he sought to organize a squadron of galleys on the Mississippi River.[8] A good governor, however, was expected

[4]Esteban Miró to Father Bailío Antonio Valdés y Bazán (Minister for the Indies), No. 40, Confidential, New Orleans, May 20, 1789, AHN, Sección de Estado, leg. 3901.

[5]"Estado de la Armada Española," in Casareo Fernández Duro, *Armada española desde la unión de los reinos de Castilla y de Aragón* (10 vols.; Madrid, 1902), VII, 227, 292–93.

[6]Gayoso's service sheets. Córdoba (1706–1796) and Borja (1726–1808) were both captains general of the Spanish Armada who achieved great distinction. Julio F. Guillén y Tato, *Iconografía de los capitanes generales de la Armada, 1750–1932* (Madrid, 1934), 13–14, 31–32. Oil portraits of the two hang in Madrid's Museo Naval.

[7]Gayoso's service sheets. On the naval campaigns directed from Cádiz against Gibraltar, 1779–1782, see Adolfo de Castro, *Historia de Cádiz y su provincia desde los remotos tiempos hasta 1814* (Cádiz, 1858), 513–27; Fernández Duro, *Armada española,* VII, 293.

[8]Gayoso's role in the organization and direction of the Mississippi Squadron will be discussed below, chapter 4. Gayoso acknowledged the utility of his

to be more than a brilliant military commander; and Gayoso learned even more in the field of public administration from the Conde de O'Reilly, governor of the province of Cádiz, under whom he served from 1782 to 1785. Born in Beltrasna, near Dublin, Ireland, in 1722, O'Reilly fled to Spain and joined the Irish Brigade along with so many of his contemporaries. He rapidly rose through the ranks and is credited with many of Spain's reforms in the New World, particularly his reorganization of the defenses and military organization of Cuba, Mexico, and Louisiana following the Seven Years' War. Although he is execrated in the memory of Louisiana's francophile historians, his contributions to the sound administration of that province in 1769 and 1770 cannot be overemphasized.[9]

As governor of Cádiz from 1779 to 1786, O'Reilly achieved even more distinction as a political administrator, and his government was noted as the greatest in that province's history. Upon his retirement in 1786, the municipal council memorialized his accomplishments in city improvement, public welfare, and municipal finance.[10] Gayoso was fortunate to work with O'Reilly, and he undoubtedly learned much about the general problems of government as well as the particular situation of the province of Louisiana.[11]

Gayoso undoubtedly distinguished himself as O'Reilly's aide; and in 1785 the Spanish ambassador to Portugal, the Conde de Fernán Núñez, "borrowed" the young captain for six months. Leave was

---

early naval training: "As for my nautical knowledge, including the ability to command such a squadron, His Excellency Joseph de Mazarredo can inform you of this aspect of my ability." Gayoso to the Conde de Santa Clara (captain-general of Cuba), No. 11, Very Confidential, New Orleans, June 5, 1798, AGI, PC, leg. 1502-B.

[9]O'Reilly's role in Louisiana history is discussed in Jack D. L. Holmes, "Some Irish Officers in Spanish Louisiana," *The Irish Sword,* VI (Winter, 1964), 234–40.

[10]The cabildo's memorial of April, 1786, and O'Reilly's answer, dated Cádiz, April 27, 1786, are in the *Actas de Cabildo* of the Archivo Municipal de Cádiz, Vol. CXLII, folios 98, 99–100, 101–110. An excellent discussion of O'Reilly's government of Cádiz is in Castro, *Historia de Cádiz,* 510–13.

[11]Gayoso later claimed that his understanding of how to treat royalty in New Orleans was based on his observations of how the Conde de O'Reilly treated the French princes in 1782. Gayoso to the Príncipe de la Paz (Manuel Godoy, Minister of State), No. 18, Confidential, New Orleans, April 18, 1798, AHN, ESTADO, leg. 3900.

extended to Gayoso on several occasions to remain at the Lisbon embassy, and he performed numerous important duties for his ambassador.

Don Carlos José Gutiérrez de los Ríos, sixth Count of Fernán Núñez, was the scion of a distinguished Andalucian family, whose ancestry went at least as far as the thirteenth-century conquest of Córdoba by San Fernando. His diplomatic success in Portugal earned him the appointment as ambassador to France, succeeding the famous Conde de Aranda in 1787. The Conde de O'Reilly had informed the Conde de Fernán Núñez that Gayoso's services as adjutant in Cádiz met with his complete satisfaction, and the ambassador to Lisbon soon found Gayoso was as useful to him.[12]

Three of Gayoso's activities indicate the varied nature of the task he was expected to perform. The first might come under the modern-day term, public relations. Juan Bautista Muñoz, last of the Spanish historical chroniclers, was engaged in the arduous task of assembling documents dealing with Spain's discovery and conquest of the New World. In the spring of 1785, he proposed to visit the various Portuguese archives and libraries and obtained permission for such a visit. Although the Conde de Fernán Núñez was unable to meet the historian, Captain Manuel Gayoso took him to various private and public libraries and archives, including the Arquivo do Torre do Tombo in Lisbon. When Muñoz expressed his thanks to the Spanish ambassador, he especially remarked on the many kindnesses of Gayoso.[13]

Of even more ceremonial nature was the famous double marriage between the prince, Gabriel Antonio, third son of Charles III, and

[12]The Conde de Fernán Núñez to the Conde de Floridablanca (Minister of State), Lisbon, July 9, 1785, AHN, ESTADO, leg. 4492-*bis*. A brief sketch of the sixth count of Fernán Núñez is found in the biography of his illustrious son, by the Marqués de Villa-Urrutia, *Fernán Núñez el embajador* (Madrid, 1931), 9-13.

[13]Muñoz to Fernán Núñez, Lisbon, May 20, 1785, AHN ESTADO, leg. 4541-II. Additional data on the Muñoz project is in Juan Bautista Muñoz, *Historia del Nuevo Mundo* (Madrid, 1793), v; Real Academia de la Historia (Madrid), *Catálogo de la collección de Don Juan Bautista Muñoz* (3 vols.; Madrid, 1954-56), III, lxviii-lxxx; Floridablanca to Fernán Núñez, Aranjuez, May 6, 1785; and Fernán Núñez, to Muñoz, Villaviciosa, May 17, 1785, AHN, ESTADO, leg. 4541-II.

Mariana Victoria, eldest daughter of the Portuguese monarchs; and between Don Juan, brother of the Portuguese princess, and Carlota Joaquina, firstborn daughter of the Prince of Asturias. The weddings took place on March 27 and 28, 1785, amid the pomp and splendor of costly banquets and fireworks. In all the tedious details of arranging such a complicated ceremony, the ambassador was ably assisted by Gayoso. In gratitude, Fernán Núñez wrote to the Spanish Minister of State, Floridablanca, "This officer has carried out his duties with tremendous zeal, activity and brilliance, which correspond to his honor, manner of thinking, and his expressed desires for the best service to the Royal monarch." [14]

A more serious aspect of Gayoso's duties involved the shipwreck of the *San Pedro de Alcántara* off the rockbound coast just north of Lisbon on February 2, 1786. In addition to the many boxes of flora and fauna intended for the Museum of Natural History which Charles III had created, the *San Pedro* carried a crew and passenger list in excess of four hundred persons, and a treasure consisting of $8,000,000 in gold, silver, and copper bars bound from Peru to Cádiz.

Fernán Núñez immediately sent Captain Gayoso to the site to help with the survivors and supervise the initial recovery of the treasure. Gayoso knew the language and was familiar with the coast, having sailed along it many times. Moreover, Fernán Núñez was confident that Gayoso's zeal, activity, and intelligence would all be combined in his best efforts to provide the necessary assistance. Within two months, approximately 98 per cent of the gold and silver had been recovered; and a grateful merchants' association in Cádiz voted Gayoso $2,500 in cash and a garnished sword in token of its appreciation for his efforts. [15]

Because of his excellent record, O'Reilly and Fernán Núñez both recommended Gayoso for promotion; and on September 20, 1786, he was named lieutenant colonel. [16] Important ministers in Spain took

[14]Fernán Núñez to Floridablanca, Lisbon, July 9, 1785, AHN, ESTADO, leg. 4492-*bis*. According to Fernán Núñez's passport, dated December 26, 1784, his primary function in Lisbon was to arrange this marriage; and his expense account was increased by 10,000 doubloons (about $160,000). Documents *ibid*.

[15]Details on Gayoso's operations at Peniche are in AHN, ESTADO, legs. 4467–1, 4475–1,2.

[16]Gayoso's service sheets. Fernán Núñez to Floridablanca, Lisbon, September 7, 1786, AHN, ESTADO, leg. 4360.

notice of the young man's demonstrated abilities, and Gayoso's family obviously supported him for greater services to his king. Gayoso's father was consul of Oporto until his death on March 16, 1787. Gayoso's brother, Francisco Gayoso de Lemos, exercised the functions of vice-consul during his father's illness and shortly after his death.[17] Father Mayne, confessor to Charles III, was also a relative of Gayoso.[18] Additional support came from another kinsman, Josef Caamaño, former Spanish *charge d'affaires* in Lisbon who succeeded Fernán Núñez as ambassador.[19] In a country and age when family influence was taken for granted in determining the political and military future of the younger children, Gayoso had reason to be proud of his many contacts.

Perhaps his heart would have been contented in Lisbon, for Gayoso met and wooed a beautiful Lisbon belle, Theresa Margarita Hopman y Pereira. As he finished up his accounts and the details of the *San Pedro* salvage at Peniche, he requested six months extension of his leave in July, 1787.[20] His plans for marriage received unexpected acceleration that fall when he learned he was being considered for an assignment in America.

On November 2, the Minister of the Indies, Fray Bailío Antonio Valdés, wrote his monarch that he had been looking for an officer

[17]Gayoso's father worked steadily to protect Spanish merchants and sailors and to thwart smuggling attempts at Oporto. For his correspondence, see AHN, ESTADO, leg. 4492. About his death and the activities of his son, Francisco, see Francisco Gayoso de Lemos to Fernán Núñez, Oporto, March 24, 1787; Fernán Núñez to Francisco Gayoso de Lemos, Lisbon, April 7, 1787, AHN, ESTADO, leg. 4516-II. Francisco later served as Cabinet courier and in other ministerial positions at the Court in Madrid. Caamaño to Floridablanca, Lisbon, November 8, 18, 1787, AHN, ESTADO, leg. 4537-II; Gayoso's Last Will and Testament. He was granted Manuel's power of attorney. Statement of change in power of attorney, New Orleans, October 9, 1798, Notarial Archives of New Orleans, Pedro Pedesclaux, Vol. XXXII, folios 787–90.
[18]Fernán Núñez to Floridablanca, Lisbon, February 15, 1785, AHN, ESTADO, leg. 4541-II.
[19]Appointment as *charge d'affaires*, Madrid, January 27, 1785, AHN, ESTADO, leg. 4492-*bis;* commission as ambassador, Madrid, July 1, 1787, *ibid.,* leg. 4402; list of his services, *ibid.,* leg. 4541-II. Numerous letters between Gayoso and Caamaño were cited in his *causa mortuoria.* His relationship to Gayoso is mentioned in Gayoso to the Baron de Carondelet (governor-general of Louisiana), New Madrid, December 3, 1795, AGI, PC, leg. 43.
[20]Caamaño to Floridablanca, Lisbon, July 5, 1787; Floridablanca to Caamaño, San Ildefonso, July 24, 31, 1787, AHN, ESTADO, leg. 4537-II. The requests for extension were approved.

skilled in prudence and diplomacy and who spoke fluent English to take command of the fort of Natchez in the Spanish Province of Louisiana. "I have learned," he said, "that all the necessary qualities for this task are combined in the person of Lieutenant-colonel and Adjutant of the Plaza of Cádiz, Don Manuel Gayoso de Lemos, who is presently in Lisbon, and recently commissioned by the Conde de Fernán Núñez in the shipwreck of the ship *San Pedro Alcántara* at Peniche and its treasure recovery." Valdés had spoken with the Conde de Floridablanca about Gayoso's proposed appointment, and the Minister of State had concurred.[21]

On September 17, Valdés had written Gayoso about a possible new appointment and suggested that he come to the Court for verbal discussions.[22] Gayoso had replied, "With a short delay of three or four days, which I can later make up on the road, I shall leave this city in compliance with your orders. I am filled with recognition of the confidence which His Majesty has seen fit to express in me and his kindness will inspire in me the most ardent desire to sacrifice myself in his service. . . . " [23]

On October 4, Gayoso left Lisbon to receive his orders from the Court.[24] As was customary, all pertinent correspondence from the governor-general of Louisiana, Esteban Miró, and the captain-general of Cuba, José de Ezpeleta y Galdiano, was shown to Gayoso. The entire history of the Natchez District was sketched to the man who was expected to carry out Spain's new policy in the Mississippi Valley.

The Natchez District embraced a huge extent of territory in West Florida, from Punta Cortada (Pointe Coupée) in the south, to the mouth of the Yazoo River in the north. The Old Tunica stream was later established as the proper southern boundary between Punta Cortada and Natchez. Although the Mississippi River formed the western border, the district had rather vague eastern

---

[21] (Valdés to the king), (San Ildefonso), November 2, 1787, AHN, ESTADO, leg. 3889.

[22] Valdés to Gayoso, San Ildefonso, September 17, 1787, *ibid.*

[23] Gayoso to Valdés, Lisbon, September 30, 1787, *ibid.*

[24] Caamaño to Floridablanca, Lisbon, October 4, 1787, AHN, ESTADO, leg. 4537-2.

boundaries and actually extended only a few leagues inland, depending on the extent of Indian settlement.[25]

First visited by Europeans under the command of Pierre Le Moyne, Sieur d'Iberville, Natchez soon boasted Fort Rosalie, named for the Countess of Pontchartrain.[26] From 1700 until the close of the French and Indian War, the Natchez District was sparsely settled, particularly after the so-called Natchez massacre in 1729, when an Indian slaughter of some two hundred colonists was followed by the virtual annihilation of the Natchez Tribe in 1732.[27]

After the British gained control of West Florida in 1763, large land grants were awarded to individuals in an effort to settle the vast hinterland. One block of land in the vicinity of Homochitto River, consisting of 25,000 acres, was granted to Amos Odgen of New Jersey in 1767. He subsequently sold his property to Richard and Samuel Swayze for twenty cents per acre. When the Swayzes moved to the Natchez District, they induced a number of their friends to accompany them and organized the "Jersey Settlement." Another large grant served as a reward to Major General Phineas Lyman of Connecticut for his services against the French in Canada.

[25]Gayoso to William Dunbar, New Orleans, June 7, 1790, AGI, PC, leg. 41; Gayoso to (Duque de Alcudia), Natchez, March 31, 1795, AGI, PC, leg. 2354; Gayoso to Conde de Aranda, Natchez, July 5, 1792, AGI, PC, leg. 2353, 177, and translated as "Political Condition of the Province of Louisiana," in James A. Robertson (ed.), *Louisiana under the Rule of Spain, France, and the United States, 1785–1807* (2 vols.; Cleveland, Ohio, 1911), I, 269–89; a portion of this highly revealing document, based on a copy in AHN, ESTADO, leg. 3883, is printed in Manuel Serrano y Sanz, *El Brigadier Jaime Wilkinson y sus tratos con España para la independencia del Kentucky, años 1787 a 1797* (Madrid, 1915), 43–45; cf. Miró to Alcudia, Aranjuez, March 18, 1793, printed as "Representaciones upon the Limits of Louisiana" Louisiana Historical Society's *Publications*, IX (1916), 82-83.

[26]Alcée Fortier, *A History of Louisiana* (4 vols.; Paris, 1904), I, 45; Richebourg G. McWilliams (ed. & trans.), *Fleur de Lys and Calumet, being the Pénicaut Narrative of French Adventure in Louisiana* (Baton Rouge, 1953), 28–30.

[27]John W. Monette, *History of the Discovery and Settlement of the Valley of the Mississippi* (2 vols.; New York, 1846), I, 254-77; François-Xavier Martin, *The History of Louisiana, from the Earliest Period* (New Orleans, 1882), 156-68.

Lyman was less successful than the Swayze brothers in colonizing the land.[28]

Although the British system of issuing large land grants of 1,000 to 25,000 acres proved a failure in providing for actual settlement and cultivation, there were enough people in West Florida in 1778 to cause a party of British surveyors to explore the region. They placed the boundary line at Bayou Pierre, some twelve miles east of a Grindstone Fort, but when the Choctaws protested that this line extended through their hunting and ball game grounds on the banks of the Yazoo, Governor Chester authorized the surveyors to move the line six leagues further north near the mouth of the Yazoo River. The line ran across the Big Black and Bayou Pierre, snaked a winding course to Standing Pines Creek, and broke out of the woods at the Homochitto River.[29]

When the family quarrel between American colonists and Great Britain intensified in the 1770's, many worried merchants and farmers looked to the Natchez District, especially when the Proclamation of 1763 encouraged veterans of the French and Indian War to settle on generous land grants in West Florida. Clusters of cabins soon appeared along the banks of streams and bayous which flowed into the Mississippi—Big Black, Bayou Pierre, Cole's Creek, Fairchild's Creek, St. Catherine Creek, Homochitto River, Buffalo Creek, Sandy Creek, and Bayou Sara. The Indian nations inhabiting the Natchez District, which included the Choctaws, Chickasaws, and Talapoosa, determined the future course of expansion to the white settlers.[30]

The Big Black—often called the Loosa Chitto—had a course which rose between the headwaters of the Yazoo and Pearl Rivers before meandering two hundred miles into the Father of Waters.

[28]Benjamin L. C. Wailes, *Report on the Agriculture and Geology of Mississippi, Embracing a Sketch of the Social and Natural History of the State* (Philadelphia, 1854), 59–61; Dunbar Rowland (ed.), *Encyclopedia of Mississippi History* (Atlanta, 1907), II, 760–61.

[29]Gayoso to Floridablanca, No. 4, Confidential, New Orleans, January 26, 1792, AHN, ESTADO, leg. 3902. Part of this letter is printed in Serrano y Sanz, *El Brigadier Jaime Wilkinson*, 11–12.

[30]Francis Baily, *Journal of a Tour in Unsettled Parts of North America in 1796 and 1797* (London, 1856), 292; Gayoso to Aranda, No. 1, July 5, 1792; Miró to Alcudia, March 18, 1793.

NATCHEZ DISTRICT SETTLEMENTS, 1785–1795

Big

Black

32°

Bayou

Pierre

Cole's Creek

31° 45'

Fairchild's
Creek

NATCHEZ

SECOND CREEK

SANDY CREEK

31° 30'

Fort

St. Catherine
Creek

White Cliffs

31° 15'

Homochitto

Red
River

River

31°

Buffalo Creek

Bayou Sara

```
0    7    14
|————|————|
   Miles
```

Chafalaya
River

Rolling hills stretched lazily toward the Mississippi near the Grand Gulf where the mouth of the Big Black was just forty yards wide. The soil here was excellent, and the high, fertile land seemed to welcome settlers. Abundant quantities of building stone in the vicinity were soon utilized to build homes and mills.[31]

As the travelers descended the Mississippi, they noted the settled areas, passing in succession Bayou Pierre, Cole's Creek, Fairchild's Creek, St. Catherine Creek, and the Homochitto River. The Homochitto followed a southwest course for half the length of the Big Black before splitting into two forks. A few miles before it entered the Mississippi, it passed through a lake which was later surrounded by fertile settlements.[32]

The fort at Natchez stood near the bluffs, which presented a wide panorama of the winding Mississippi. The location was observed at 31° 33′ 46″ North Latitude and was encircled by Fairchild's Creek and St. Catherine Creek, along both banks of which the early settlers had established their cabins and farms.[33] Nestled in the highlands which faced the Mississippi delta, Natchez presented a hilly appearance, which contrasted markedly with the flat, sandy, sterile coast to the south. These hills extended inland for twelve to fifteen miles.[34]

The most striking feature of the Natchez topography was the formidable bluffs which rose from one hundred to one hundred and fifty feet above the river. William Bartram admired their remarkable beauty in 1777: "From eight or nine feet below the loamy vegetative mould at top, to within four or five feet of the water, these cliffs present to view strata of clay, marle and chalk,

[31]Timothy Flint, *The History and Geography of the Mississippi Valley, to which is Appended a Condensed Physical Geography of the Atlantic United States, and the Whole American Continent* (Cincinnati, 1833), 230.
[32]*Ibid.*
[33]Andrew Ellicott to Secretary of State (Timothy Pickering), Natchez, April 1, 1797, in Southern Boundary, United States and Spain, Andrew Ellicott (3 vols., MSS.; 1796–1804; U.S. National Archives, Department of State, Record Group 76), I (hereinafter cited as Southern Boundary MSS).
[34]Baily, *Journal*, 346–47; C. F. Volney, *A View of the Soil and Climate of the United States of America*, trans. C. B. Brown (Philadelphia, 1904), 18–19; W. H. Sparks, *The Memories of Fifty Years* (Philadelphia, 1870), 245–46.

of all colours, as brown, red, yellow, white, blue and purple; there are separate strata of these various colours, as well as mixed or particoloured." [35]

Because the Mississippi flowed a tortuous course through the delta bordering the Natchez District, the distance to a given point by water was almost twice that by horseback. The lack of roads and trails through the dense thickets and forests virtually prevented land travel except by horseback or foot. From the Yazoo River in the north to the Tunicas Cut in the south, the great river flowed an estimated one hundred thirty miles. [36]

In general, Natchez weather was mild. Temperatures in the winter rarely dropped to permit snow or ice. Although the summer heat sometimes raised the mercury to 107°, the hot spells were usually of short duration. Rainfall was moderate to heavy, but the well-watered highlands were more salubrious than the southern settlements. [37]

The rich black soil extended for a depth of almost two feet and covered a clay base. By the judicious planting of cane and ground-holding shrubbery and trees, soil leeching was avoided. Wild hops and strawberries dotted the meadows, and stately live oaks and thickets of cane reached for the skies. Rye, oats, and wheat—three desirable crops which grew poorly in Lower Louisiana and West Florida—flourished in the favorable climate and soil of Natchez. [38]

Animals abounded in the area. Bear hunts were a successful frontier amusement in which Natchez settlers engaged. On one such hunt, an early British colonist, John Hutchins, killed more than one hundred bears during the space of one winter. Shorter hunts produced larders and pelt racks full of beaver and otter. For the com-

[35]Mark Van Doren (ed.), The Travels of William Bartram (New York, 1940), 346–47. One traveler was even more impressed by the spectacular white Ellis Cliffs, located twenty miles south of Natchez: Joseph Holt Ingraham, The South-west by a Yankee (2 vols.; New York, 1835), II, 15.

[36]George H. V. (Victor) Collot, A Journey in North America (2 vols. and atlas; Paris, 1826; reprint ed., Florence, 1924), II, 55–71.

[37]Ibid., II, 64; Baily, Journal, 283; Wailes, Report, 299–308; Carondelet to Las Casas, No. 136, New Orleans, July 20, 1792, AGI, PC, leg. 178.

[38]Gilbert Imlay, Topographical Description of the Western Territory of North America (3rd ed.; London, 1797), 423; Wailes, Report, 341–56.

petent angler, trout and perch lay waiting in the many streams.[39] Opossum, mole, raccoon, polecat, squirrel, rabbit, deer, and mink filled the forests; and a large variety of birds, snakes, and alligators were also found. Although wolves and "tigers" (the Southern panther) were a constant danger to cattle herds,[40] Natchez and its district must have seemed an ideal place to live: its population at the beginning of the American Revolution must have exceeded fifteen hundred.[41]

The Spanish banner flew over the British fort at Natchez shortly after the lightning-like thrusts of Bernardo de Gálvez, Spain's youthful governor and general commanding the Louisiana troops. Lieutenant Colonel Alexander Dickson, commanding his Britannic Majesty's Sixteenth Regiment on the Mississippi, surrendered the fort at Baton Rouge on September 21, 1779. Part of the surrender terms included the delivery of Fort Panmure de Natchez by Captain Forster into the hands of Captain Juan de la Villebeuvre.[42]

Loyalties of the various settlers in Natchez were divided about

[39]Charles S. Sydnor, *A Gentleman of the Old Natchez Region, Benjamin L. C. Wailes* (Durham, North Carolina, 1938), 9–10.

[40]Wailes, *Report*, 310-14; Baily, *Journal*, 269 and *passim;* proclamation of Gayoso, Natchez, February 28, 1793, Hicky Papers, Louisiana State University Archives. This last document, with additional notes on wild animals and their danger to herds in Natchez, is in Jack D. L. Holmes, "Livestock in Spanish Natchez," *Journal of Mississippi History,* XXIII (January, 1961), 28.

[41]The first Spanish census, taken in 1784, indicated 616 white men, 505 white women, 275 male Negro slaves, and 223 female Negro slaves, or a total population of 1,619. Padrón general del Distrito de Natchez, 1784, AGI, PC, leg. 116. Another interesting description of the Natchez district in 1776 is W. M. Carpenter (ed.), "The Mississippi River in the Olden Time, a Genuine Account of the Present State of the River Mississippi and of the Land on its Banks to the River Yasous, 1776," *The Commercial Review of the South and West [DeBow's Review],* III (February, 1847), 115–23, based on the notes of the editor's grandfather, Caleb Carpenter.

[42]The exact date of the surrender of Fort Panmure de Natchez to the Spaniards is controversial. John W. Caughey, *Bernardo de Gálvez in Louisiana, 1776–1783* (Berkeley, 1934), 158; and Albert W. Haarmann, "The Spanish Conquest of British West Florida, 1779–1781," *The Florida Historical Quarterly,* XXXIX (October, 1960), 113, both accept October 5. A statement of Juan de la Villebeuvre, Natchez, September 21, 1779, enclosed in Miró to Valdés, No. 39, Confidential, New Orleans, May 20, 1789, AHN, ESTADO, leg. 3888 *bis,* and AGI, PC, leg. 2352, indicates an earlier date for Spanish occupation; see also, Justin Winsor, *Narrative and Critical History of America* (8 vols.; Boston, 1889), VI, 740.

the war between Spain and England. The Tories, including Colonel Anthony Hutchins, brother of the American geographer-general Thomas Hutchins, favored the British. The pro-patriot settlers, on the other hand, welcomed the dashing "Captain" James Willing, an American who raided the Tory settlements along the Mississippi.[43]

Although the Natchez fort had been occupied by the Spaniards in 1779, on April 22, 1781, Captain John Blommart, a Natchez mill owner acting under orders from the governor of Pensacola, initiated a revolt which gave control of the Natchez fort to the British and loyalist settlers. The revolt was short-lived, however, for the following month Bernardo de Gálvez lay siege to Pensacola; and news of the British capital's fall soon after discouraged their partisans at Natchez. Captain Carlos de Grand-Pré—destined to play a major role in Natchez history—moved his militia into position from Baton Rouge and Punta Cortada. There was no showdown at Natchez, however, and on July 23, 1781, a militia captain from Opelousas, Estevan Roberto de la Morandier, raised the Spanish flag over the Natchez fort without opposition.[44]

Juan de la Villebeuvre, who may be considered the first Spanish

---

[43]Hutchins, a native of New Jersey who first emigrated to North Carolina before exploring the Natchez District in 1772, finally settled at White Apple Village, twelve miles from Natchez. Note by Lyman C. Draper in Samuel S. Forman, *Narrative of a Journey down the Ohio and Mississippi in 1789-90* (Cincinnati, 1888), 56. His activities during the Willing raid of 1778 are mentioned in Ellicott, *The Journal of Andrew Ellicott*, 130–32; his role during the Natchez revolt is in Anthony Hutchins to [Esteban Miró], New Orleans, July 10, 1785, AGI, PC, leg. 198. The best treatment of Willing's raid is John W. Caughey, "Willing's Expedition down the Mississippi, 1778," *The Louisiana Historical Quarterly*, XV (January, 1932), 5–36. For an account of his senseless destruction of personal papers of known Tory sympathizers, see deposition of Stephen Watts (Gayoso's future father-in-law), Natchez, March 5, 1796, in Gayoso's *expediente matrimonial*, Archivo General Militar de Segovia.

[44]Documents on the Natchez revolt and its recapture are located in AGI, PC, legs. 9, 170, 173, 175, 193, 196, 684, 1304, 1376, 2359. Additional data is in the deposition taken from various witnesses at New Orleans in May, 1781, Archivo Nacional de Cuba, Floridas, leg. 2; John W. Caughey, "The Natchez Rebellion of 1781 and its Aftermath," *The Louisiana Historical Quarterly*, XVI (1933), 57–83. On its recapture, see service sheet of de la Morandier, New Orleans, August 31, 1788, AGI, PC, leg. 161-A; Articles of Capitulation, Juan de la Villebeuvre to Blommart, Natchez, May 4, 1781, and Blommart to Estevan de Lamorandiere, Fort Panmure, June 28, 1781, AGI, PC, leg. 170-A.

commander of the Natchez fort, issued a set of regulations governing the district in 1780, prior to the revolt.[45] Thereafter, a confusing succession of commandants exercised power for varying terms. They were all military officers. Captain Carlos de Grand-Pré took command in 1781; but the following year Colonel Esteban Miró, interim governor-general of Louisiana, exercised command over Natchez. Lieutenant Colonel Pedro Joseph Piernas, who had exercised command of Louisiana during the Gálvez expeditions, was military commander of Natchez from 1782 to 1783. He was succeeded for several months in 1783 by Francisco Collell. Captain and brevet lieutenant colonel Phelipe Treviño gained the command from 1783 until July, 1785. He was replaced by Lieutenant Colonel Francisco Bouligny, a former lieutenant-governor of Louisiana, from July, 1785, until March, 1786, when Grand-Pré, who had been promoted to lieutenant colonel, again took command.[46]

The powers of these military commandants were generally the same as those enjoyed by other Spanish commandants in Louisiana and West Florida. "The duty of commandants," according to one source, "is to superintend the police, preserve the peace of the district, examine the passports of travellers, and to suffer no strangers to settle within the limits of their command, without regular leave obtained from government. They are to prevent smuggling, to certify that all lands petitioned for by the inhabitants are vacant before they are granted, and when required put the owner in possession. They are besides notaries public, and in their offices it is necessary to register all sales of lands and slaves, and even to make the contracts for those purposes before them. They act as sheriffs, levy executions on property, attend and certify the sale, and collect the proceeds. They also take inventories of the property of intestates." [47]

[45]Juan de la Villebeuvre, Good Government Decree, Fort Panmure de Natchez, October 10, 1780, AGI, PC, leg. 113. The decree covered such matters as hunting, Negro slaves, law, and order.

[46]The basis for the terms of these commandants was an analysis of the records in the Chancery Court of Natchez (Mississippi) and the following printed works: May Wilson McBee (ed.), *The Natchez Court Records, 1767-1805, Abstracts of Early Records* (Ann Arbor, 1953), 1-33 and *passim;* Rowland (ed.), *Encyclopedia of Mississippi History,* II, 311-12.

[47]*An Account of Louisiana* (Providence, 1804), 57. There is another edition

Daniel Clark added the following comment on the duties of the commandants:

> The Commandants hear & determine all causes in pecuniary matters not exceeding 100 Dollars, when the suit is for a larger sum, they begin the process, collect the evidences & proofs & remit the whole to the Governor to be decided here by the Competent tribunal, they can inflict no corporal punishment except on Slaves, but have the power of arresting & imprisoning when they think necessary, advice of which & of their motives for so doing must be transmitted to the Governor. . . . He has no salery [sic] as commandant unless he receives no other pay or pension in which case he is intitled [sic] to 100 $ P annum. . . .[48]

Following the transfer of Natchez to the Spaniards, immigration from the United States continued. In May, 1782, thirteen American families representing seventy-two white people and eighty-eight Negro slaves were admitted as settlers. Included in the number were such outstanding men in later Mississippi and Louisiana affairs as Thomas Green, Cato West, David Smith, and James White.[49] By the summer of 1785, Francisco Bouligny could write about the population, "The greater part of the inhabitants of this town are natives of North America, others are English royalists, a few are French, and very rarely there is a Spaniard. Almost all of them are occupied in cultivating the land, with the exception of a few merchants who reside in the small growing town of Natchez." [50] The Natchez commandant, supported by a

---

of this valuable pamphlet published in Washington in 1803 and reprinted in *Old South Leaflets* (Boston, 1900), V, No. 105. A portion regarding the powers of the commandants is in Robertson, *Louisiana*, I, 217. Cf. Jack D. L. Holmes, "Law and Order in Spanish Natchez, 1781–1798," *The Journal of Mississippi History*, XXV (July, 1963), 188.

[48]Daniel Clark to James Madison (Secretary of State), New Orleans, September 8, 1803, printed in Clarence E. Carter (ed.), *The Territorial Papers of the United States*, Vol. IX: *The Territory of Orleans, 1803–1812* (Washington, 1940), 39.

[49]Grand-Pré's account of American families arriving in Natchez, Natchez, July 6, 1782, AGI, PC, leg. 193-B.

[50]Francisco Bouligny to Miró, Fort Panmure de Natchez, August 22, 1785, in Lawrence Kinnaird, (ed.), *Spain in the Mississippi Valley* (3 parts; Washington, 1946–49), Part II, 136.

garrison of sixty men, a quartermaster, and a surgeon, had a small hospital and a warehouse for supplies. Annual expenses of the post for supplies and medicines were approximately six thousand pesos; the captain commanding was paid sixty-two pesos per month.[51]

A conservative estimate of the population, by families, of the Natchez District made in 1785 showed St. Catherine Creek, 180; Second Creek, 55; Cole's Creek, 40. Bouligny estimated an average of four persons per family, giving a white population of 1,100. There were about nine hundred Negro slaves.[52] Beginning in 1787, the residents of Natchez were obliged to appear before the commandant, Lieutenant Colonel Carlos de Grand-Pré, and sign their names (or marks) to an oath of allegiance. The text of the oath varied, but in general was similar to the first one of January 4, 1787:

> We, the undersigned, freely and spontaneously, without bribe or threat, and only in recognition of the generous protection which has been granted them by the Spanish Government, desirous of living in this province, and with permission granted by the Governor, swear by God our Lord, placing the hand on the Holy Bible, do pledge our word of honor and promise by all means which serve to keep faith among men, in conformity with the royal order which was read by the commandant, not to offend, directly or indirectly, nor to conspire against the Spanish nation; but on the contrary, to defend and assist it to the best of our ability, might and means; revealing to its leaders any plot, conspiracy or enterprise which might be directed against it, of which we may have news, subjecting ourselves completely to the Spanish laws, keeping faith and inviolable the orders, decrees and edicts of the Kingdom and of this Government, and obeying them all with the same exactness and loyalty of His Catholic Majesty's other vassals, in which character and class henceforth they will be considered.[53]

[51]Last Regulation of Employees and Other Obligations of the Province of Louisiana, approved by Royal Order of December 7, 1785, [without date or signature], AHN, ESTADO, leg. 3888 bis.

[52]Bouligny to Miró, August 22, 1785. This is a reasonable estimate in view of the total population as listed in the census of 1784, which was 1,619. See supra, note 41.

[53]Loyalty Oath, Natchez, January 4, 1787, AGI, PC, leg. 13. Slightly different versions are found in Loyalty Oath, Natchez, January 12, 1790, AGI, PC, leg. 2362; and Charles Gayarré, History of Louisiana, the Spanish Domination (New York, 1854), 202–203.

Even as Gayoso discussed these historical details with Valdés and Floridablanca, there were new rumblings of discontent in Natchez. In 1785 the Georgia assembly passed a bill creating the County of Bourbon, which included territory lying between the mouth of the Yazoo River and the thirty-first parallel. Among the proposed officers of a new land speculation company whose interests were directed against the Spanish in the Natchez District was Thomas Green, who had settled in Natchez in 1782 and had taken an oath to defend the province against exactly this type of threat. The Georgia commissioners failed to make their claims on the Natchez District. Disapproval of their actions by the United States Congress and the viceroy of New Spain, Bernardo de Gálvez, caused the commissioners to retire from Natchez. They left behind an uneasy feeling of discontent and insecurity for Spanish officials and American settlers alike.[54]

The following year, acting on orders from Louisiana's intendant, Martín Navarro, Commandant Grand-Pré confiscated the cargoes of two American flatboats belonging to Thomas Ormis and Joseph Calvert. Ormis escaped arrest and returned to the western American settlements where he condemned the Spanish seizures.[55] Apparently in retaliation, the "hero of Vincennes," George Rogers Clark, seized the cargoes of three Spanish Louisiana traders at Vincennes. According to one report, Clark was recruiting an expedition of filibusters to invade Louisiana and capture Natchez.[56]

Another threat was posed in 1787 by Captain John Sullivan, a French soldier of fortune who had served during the American Revolution. Upon his being refused a post in the Spanish service, he

[54]Bouligny to Miró, No. 8, Fort Panmure de Natchez, July 24, 1785, AGI, PC, leg. 2352, translated in Duvon C. and Roberta Corbitt (trans. & eds.), "Papers from the Spanish Archives relating to Tennessee and the Old Southwest, 1783–1800," *Publications* of the ETHS, IX (1937), 125–28 (this continuing series will henceforth be abbreviated as Corbitt, "Papers from the Spanish Archives," with the appropriate volume, year, and pages); Edmund C. Burnett (ed.), "Papers relating to Bourbon County, Georgia," *American Historical Review*, XV (1909-1910), 68–69.
[55]Kinnaird (ed.), *Spain in the Mississippi Valley*, Part II, xviii.
[56]James Alton James, *The Life of George Rogers Clark* (Chicago, 1928), 359–60; Miró to Campo de Alange, August 11, 1792, in Jack D. L. Holmes (ed.), *Documentos ineditos para la historia de la Luisiana, 1792–1810* (Madrid, 1963), 51.

plotted with dissidents from the State of Franklin to invade Louisiana and take possession of New Orleans. The Spanish *charge d'affaires* in the United States, Diego de Gardoqui, complained to the American secretary of war; and orders were issued to stop Sullivan.[57]

These threats against Natchez and Louisiana were serious enough to call attention to Spain's age-old problem in the New World—lack of population. If, as the Conde de Aranda averred, a deserted province attracted foreigners as flies to honey, Natchez and Louisiana were in potential peril. Spain's changing policy toward Natchez can only be understood in the historical context of her previous experience with the province of Louisiana.

When Louisiana belonged to France, its population failed to increase in proportion to the visionary hopes predicted by the famous John Law. A census of 1721 indicated 684 white people and 514 Negro Slaves.[58] Forty-five years later, at the end of the French domination, there were 6,987 whites and 5,940 Negro slaves.[59] Under the Spaniards the population fared somewhat better, at least as far as its increase is concerned. The first Spanish census in 1769 showed a total population of 13,538, about evenly divided between whites and Negroes.[60] By 1788 Louisiana boasted 36,235 inhabitants.[61] While this increase was admirable by Spanish standards, Louisiana was still virtually a "desert" by comparison with the United States. North Carolina alone had 393,751 people in the census of 1790.

[57]*Ibid.*; Juan Baptista Muñoz to Antonio Porlier, March 30, 1788, BN, and printed in Manuel Serrano y Sanz (ed.), *Documentos históricos de la Florida y la Luisiana, siglos xvi al xviii* (Madrid, 1912), 320–21; John Sullivan to Major William Brown, Charleston, September 24, 1787; War Office to Brig. Gen. Josiah Harmar, October 16, November 14, 1787, in *American State Papers, Foreign Relations*, I, 281–82.

[58]Récensements 1706–1741, Ministere des Colonies, Paris, published by William Beer (ed.), "Early Census Tables of Louisiana," *Publications* of the Louisiana Historical Society, V (1911), 93,

[59]*Resúmen general de la colonia de la Luisiana*, New Orleans, 1766, MN, Tomo 569, folio 107.

[60]Martin, *Louisiana*, 206.

[61]*Ibid.*, 251. This figure includes only upper and lower Louisiana. In the seven West Florida posts of Manchac, Galvez-Town, Baton Rouge, Feliciana, Natchez, Mobile, and Pensacola, the population was 6,376.

Spain's failure to populate the province came not from turning her back on the problem. As early as 1765, Louisiana opened its deserted lands around the Attakapas and Opelousas prairies to displaced Acadians, who came from forced exile in the United States by the hundreds to settle along the bayous and streams of Louisiana. By a special decree of April 5, 1786, temporary asylum was granted to certain American and British loyalists who had fled to Louisiana as a result of the American Revolution. In 1787 Pierre d'Arges Wouves was appointed immigration agent in Kentucky, and advertising broadsides invited the industrious to settle in Louisiana. The archives are filled with dozens of petitions: from Irishmen such as Pedro Bryan Bruin and Agustín Macarty; from Hollanders such as Peter Paulus living in Philadelphia; from Prussians the stature of the famous Baron von Steuben; and from Americans such as Colonel George Morgan of New Jersey. All had a common theme—give us large land grants, freedom of worship, navigation of the Mississippi, and an outlet for our goods; and we will introduce settlers by the thousands.

The early plans were not completely satisfactory. Land speculation with the get-rich-quick expectation guided the motives of many applicants. But many saw in Governor-General Miró's relaxation of the commercial restrictions on river trade in 1786 a means of improving their lot by the sweat and blisters of honest work. With conditions in the United States apparently leading to disaster—1786 was the low point in America's depression with farm wages declining as much as 20 per cent from the 1780 levels—many felt a new start in Spanish Louisiana was more than desirable.[62]

[62]There has been much written on the Louisiana immigration: Clarence E. Carter (ed.), "A Projected Settlement of English-Speaking Catholics from Maryland in Spanish Louisiana, 1767, 1768," *American Historical Review*, XVI (January, 1911), 319–26; Fernando Solano Costa's two articles, "La emigración acadiana a la Luisiana española (1783–1785)," and "La fundación de Nuevo Madrid," in *Cuadernos de Historia Jerónimo Zurita*, II (1954), 85–125, IV–V (1956), 91–108; Gilbert C. Din, "Colonización en la Luisiana española: proyectos de emigración en la Luisiana del siglo xviii," (Ph.D. dissertation, Historia de América, Facultad de Filosofía y Letras, Universidad de Madrid, 1960); and Lawrence Kinnaird, "American Penetration into Spanish Louisiana," in George P. Hammond (ed.), *New Spain and the Anglo-American West* (2 vols.; Lancaster, Pennsylvania, 1932), I, 211–37. The best over-all accounts of the population movement and its importance are in Mattie Austin Hatcher,

Spanish engineers from Havana, intendants in Louisiana, and historians in Spain all agreed that Spain would have to populate Louisiana or lose it.[63] The alternative lay between having Americans outside the frontiers, where, unobserved, they might work all sorts of mischief, or bringing them in as presumably loyal vassals where they could be watched. When Luis de Las Casas, captain general of Cuba from 1790 through 1796, argued against allowing Americans to settle in Louisiana because of their close ties with their former brethren,[64] Governor-General Miró replied, "We ought to consider them already within the house." If they attacked and captured New Orleans from Ohio, added Miró, they would earn glory; if they revolted as subjects of Spain, they would reap nothing but the title, "traitors." [65]

The sentiment in favor of allowing the Americans to enter Louisiana as industrious settlers was already held by the major Spanish officials in New Orleans when an incident occurred in 1787 which

---

"The Louisiana Background of the Colonization of Texas, 1763–1803," *Southwestern Historical Quarterly*, XXIV (January, 1921), 169–94; and Arthur P. ✔Whitaker, *The Spanish-American Frontier, 1783–1795, the Westward Movement and the Spanish Retreat in the Mississippi Valley* (Boston, 1927). A somewhat jingoistic version of the American frontiersman's role in westward expansion at the expense of Spain ("almost imbecile in its fatuity"), is Theodore Roosevelt, *The Winning of the West* (4 vols.; New York, 1894), III, 131–48.

[63]Pedro Gatell's Memorial, Havana, October 11, 1780, BN, Tomo 19,247, folios 101–107, and printed in Serrano y Sanz (ed.), *Documentos de la Luisiana*, 353–60, connected the importance of populating the province with improving its fortifications. Martín Navarro, Louisiana's intendant, expressed his agreement that population was necessary to stop foreign movements toward the Province: Reflections of Navarro, New Orleans (1782–1784), BN, Tomo 19,247, folios 152–66, and printed *ibid.*, 361–82. It is translated from a copy in AGI, PC, in Robertson (ed.), *Louisiana*, 1, 235–61, with date of *c.* 1785. In Madrid, Spain's last great chronicler of America, Juan Bautista Muñoz, called the Mississippi the "key to North America," the preservation of which should be the major concern of Spain: Muñoz to Antonio Porlier (representing the Council of State), Madrid, March 30, 1788, BN, and printed in Serrano y Sanz (ed.), *Documentos de la Luisiana*, 316–20.

[64]Las Casas to Campo de Alange, Havana, February 17, 1791, transcript in Mississippi Territorial Archives, Spanish Dominion (9 vols.; 1759–1820; Department of History and Archives, Jackson, Mississippi), III, 800–808.

[65]Miró to Alange, August 11, 1792, in Holmes (ed.), *Documentos de la Luisiana*, 26–27.

was to have far-reaching repercussions on Spanish policy in the
Mississippi Valley. On July 2, General James Wilkinson unexpected-
ly arrived in New Orleans with a boat filled with merchandise.
Behind him he left a rather broken trail of questionable activities;
in the future he modestly beheld himself as the "George Washington of the West." Born in 1757 near the present-day town of Bene-
dict, Maryland, Wilkinson had studied and practiced medicine before enlisting in the American Revolution. He fought and ran from
Boston to Montreal. He was with "Mad" Anthony Wayne and
Washington and fought a duel with General Horatio Gates. He left
the seaboard after the war with a large number of bills outstanding.
A contemporary described this magnificent scoundrel: "A person
not quite tall enough to be perfectly elegant, compensated by
symmetry and appearance of health and strength; a countenance
open, mild, capacious, and beaming with intelligence; a gait firm,
manly, and facile; manners bland, accomodating and popular; an
address easy, polite and gracious, invited approach, gave access,
assured attention, cordiality and ease. By these fair terms, he con-
ciliated; by these he captivated." [66]

Generously bestowing gifts from his boat on Spanish commandants from St. Louis to New Orleans, Wilkinson astounded Miró by
his self-assured demeanor. Another shock came in the form of the
"First Memorial," in which Wilkinson proposed a vast trade empire
covering the western frontier settlements and New Orleans. With
Spain in control of the Mississippi since 1784, special privileges
might be extended to those who had Wilkinson's recommendation to
trade in the capital of Louisiana.

Miró was not as naïve as Wilkinson presumed. While stalling
Wilkinson on his proposals, Miró considered the profits to be made
personally from a connection with the popular Kentuckian. Moreover, considering the benefits to Louisiana, the governor-general
envisioned the day when there might be a vast, independent western
nation, linked economically to Spanish Louisiana, which would
serve as a strong barrier against further United States expansion.

Wilkinson received several thousand dollars in credit and the

[66]Quoted from Marshal's *History of Kentucky,* in James Ripley Jacobs,
Tarnished Warrior, Major-General James Wilkinson (New York, 1938), 71.

privilege of bringing up to $60,000 worth of Kentucky produce to
New Orleans *sans* duty. He returned to the cheering Kentuckians
who promptly elected him to the Assembly in 1788. Januslike,
Wilkinson secretly wrote to Miró to keep the Mississippi River
closed, while at the same time he demanded in the Kentucky
legislature its opening. Wilkinson was to be disappointed, however; when he returned to New Orleans in June, 1789, he found
the Spanish court had rejected his proposals but had decided on a
bold new tack in its Mississippi policy.[67]

Miró embarked on a twofold program. The first was to populate
Louisiana in such a way that its settlers would be able to defend
it from any attacks, even, presumably from former countrymen. The
second goal was to form surreptitious connections with Kentucky
and other western settlements in an effort to create an additional
barrier toward any American aggression. As the plan developed, the
Natchez District would be the scene of the first goal; its new governor, the instrument of the second.[68]

These were the historical facts and future plans explained to Gayoso during his briefing at Madrid in the fall of 1787. On November
3, Gayoso's confidential orders were drafted. He was named governor of the Fort of Natchez and equipped with verbal and written instructions on the object of his mission. He was ordered to Cádiz

[67]Of the vast literature on Wilkinson, the best biography, utilizing Spanish
and American sources, is Jacobs, *Tarnished Warrior*. An adequate sketch is
Isaac J. Cox, "James Wilkinson," in the *Dictionary of American Biography* (20
vols.; New York, 1928–1936), XX, 222–26. On the early stage of the so-called
"Spanish Conspiracy" featuring Wilkinson's role, see also, Serrano y Sanz,
El Brigadier Jaime Wilkinson; Arthur P. Whitaker (ed.), "James Wilkinson's
First Descent to New Orleans in 1787," *HAHR*, VIII (February, 1928), 82–97;
and José Navarro Latorre and Fernando Solano Costa, *¿Conspiración
española? 1787–1789, contribución al estudio de las primeras relaciones históricas
entre España y los Estados Unidos de Norteamérica* (Zaragoza, Spain, 1949).
General James Wilkinson, *Memoirs of my own Times* (3 vols.; Philadelphia,
1816), while useless for an understanding of the "conspiracy," is a remarkably
audacious example of prevarication at its best!

[68]Miró and Navarro to Valdés, No. 13, Confidential, New Orleans, September
25, 1787, AHN, ESTADO, leg. 3888 *bis.*, and translated from the AGI, PC, in
Corbitt, "Papers from the Spanish Archives," XII (1940), 102–109; *cf*. Miró to
Alange, Madrid, August 11, 1792, in Holmes (ed.), *Documentos de la Luisiana,*
22–23.

where, accompanied by his wife and servants, he was to embark on the first merchant vessel or warship for Havana. In Havana he was expected to discuss the nature of his mission with the captain-general, Brigadier Joseph de Ezpeleta. His intructions concluded with the roseate words, "The King having been informed of the way you have fulfilled all matters heretofore charged to you with the zeal and efficiency you devote to all matters of the Royal Service, trusts you will display equal vigor toward that with which you are now charged and that you will be ever more worthy of the sovereign's pleasure and continued gratitude." [69]

Gayoso was married to Theresa Margarita Hopman y Pereira in 1787.[70] The birth of the couple's first child, whom they named Manuel Gayoso Hopman, occurred in 1788 and the departure of the new governor was thus delayed.[71] Valdés had written the president of the *Contratación* in Cádiz that Gayoso should leave with his family and servants, but not take a cargo of flint with him to Louisiana, as the new governor requested. The brigantine *Nuestra Señora del Carmen*, which Gayoso was supposed to take, sailed without him; and the departure was delayed until September, 1788. On the sixth of the month he was granted permission to sail on the packet boat *San José alias el Afortunado*, commanded by Captain Francisco de Alfalla. Accompanying Gayoso and his wife

[69]Royal order, confidential, San Lorenzo, November 3, 1787, draft, AHN, ESTADO, leg. 3889. Valdés communicated similar orders to Miró on the same date, *ibid*.

[70]Gerónimo Cavallero to Valdés, San Lorenzo, November 14, 1787, *ibid*., grants Gayoso royal permission to contract matrimony with Miss Hopman. It is possible the couple was already married in 1786 prior to receiving royal permission, but no documents substantiating this supposition have been located.

[71]According to statements made by Gayoso in his marriage contract with Margaret Cyrilla Watts, Natchez, January 14, 1796, owned by Mrs. C. Grenes Cole of New Orleans (cited hereinafter as Cole Papers); Gayoso's last will and testament, 1799; and a letter from Maria Hopman to (Theresa Margarita), Lisbon, January 9, 1789, *ibid*., young Manuel remained in Lisbon with a maternal aunt. He never again saw his father. One of his descendants, Pedro de Lemos, late director of the Museum of Fine Arts and Art Gallery of Stanford University, painted a portrait of Gayoso, the governor, and wrote a short, if inaccurate, sketch of the governor in the Natchez (Mississippi) *Democrat*, Pilgrimages Edition (March, 1942), 10, 12.

were two servants from Galicia, Francisco Antonio Sánchez Gixón, 20, and Josef Antonio Mayo, 21.[72] The voyage was a long one, and Gayoso undoubtedly became well-acquainted with Juan Ventura Morales, comptroller of the army and royal treasury in Louisiana, who was returning to the province with a Negro slave.[73] In less than a decade Gayoso and Morales would be bitter enemies.

Gayoso reached Havana, probably in December, 1788. During the several months he waited for another ship to carry him and his family to New Orleans, he accomplished two important goals. He discussed Louisiana affairs with the captain-general and he met a stranger from Tennessee, Dr. James White. White had spoken with Gardoqui in New York about the possible separation of Franklin from its American ties with the aid of Spain. Gardoqui had sent him to Havana, where, under the assumed name, Jacques Dubois, he met the Natchez governor before going to New Orleans. White suggested that Gayoso make an inspection of Franklin, the Cumberland settlements, and Kentucky as the best way of knowing their exact situation and sentiments. Gayoso was taken with the idea; and he wrote Valdés, enclosing a hastily-drawn map of the Old Southwest and asking permission to make the journey.[74]

It is doubtful if Gayoso accepted White's glowing tales of rampant rebellion in Franklin at face value. Perhaps the picture of John Sevier drinking toasts to the Spanish king was too much for Gayoso's penetrating mind. He wrote, "Before now I had believed they wear two faces, and even White paints things with

[72]Valdés to President of the Real Audiencia de Contratación, Aranjuez, April 29, 1788; Royal order, San Lorenzo, November 9, 1787; Petition of Gayoso, Cádiz, September 4, 6, 1788, AGI, Contratación, leg. 5532; Francisco Gómez de Grijalba, Marqués del Surco's certification, Cádiz, September 6, 1788, AGI, PC, leg. 538-A.

[73]Petition of Morales, Cádiz, September 2, 1788, AGI, Contratación, leg. 5532; Valdés to Intendant of Louisiana, San Ildefonso, September 13, 1787, AGI, PC, leg. 2317-b.

[74]Gayoso to Valdés, Havana, January 3, 1789, AHN, ESTADO, leg. 3888 *bis.;* Gayoso to the Conde de Floridablanca, May 8, 1789, AHN, ESTADO, leg. 3902. The map which Gayoso drew is in the map collection of AHN, and is printed in Miguel Gómez del Campillo, *Relaciones diplomáticas entre España y los Estados Unidos según los documentos del Archivo Histórico Nacional* (2 vols.; Madrid, 1944–1945), I, opposite 352; and Navarro Latorre and Solano Costa, *¿Conspiración española?,* opposite 72.

enough appearance of sincerity which does not dispel my distrust; one of the faces I believe is honestly what they propose, but I also believe that the second is . . . to find a better outlet to the Gulf . . . by way of the Mobile River." [75] Gayoso promised to take advantage of the voyage that lay ahead of him and White to study the man and his ideas further.[76]

On January 7, 1789, a royal decree explained Gayoso's mission. Charles III wrote, "Inasmuch as I have been informed of the necessity that in the Plaza of Natchez there be established a Governor of distinguished zeal, prudence, activity, and a knowledge of foreign languages employed by the inhabitants of its district, and, in order that he may attend in time of war to the defense of that important post on the Mississippi River, and in time of Peace to the discharge of the commissions and commands that may be issued, and to take charge of its security," he was appointing Gayoso to that post with an annual salary of two thousand pesos.[77] Although his initial appointment stated that Gayoso's salary was not to begin, as was customary, until after he had taken possession of his post at Natchez, Minister of the Indies Valdés had authorized the pay to begin on Gayoso's arrival in New Orleans, thus giving the new governor time in which to consult Miró about the security of the province.[78] In addition to his written instructions, Gayoso evidently

[75] Gayoso to Valdés, January 3, 1789.
[76] On the White mission, see also Gardoqui to Floridablanca, Nos. 12, 13, Confidential, New York, September 18, October 28, 1786, AHN, ESTADO, leg. 3893; Samuel Cole Williams, *History of the Lost State of Franklin* (Johnson City, Tennessee, 1924), 230, 294–96; Albert V. Goodpasture, "Dr. James White," *Tennessee Historical Magazine*, I (December, 1915), 282–91; Gayarré, *Louisiana*, 261–64; and two monographs by A. P. Whitaker, "The Muscle Shoals Speculation, 1783–1789," MVHR, XIII (December, 1926), 365–86; and "Spanish Intrigue in the Old Southwest: an Episode, 1788–1789," *ibid.*, XII (September, 1925), 155–76.
[77] Royal decree of appointment for Gayoso, Madrid, January 7, 1789, copy in Archivo Nacional de Cuba (Havana), Reales Cédulas, IX, 63. A typed copy was provided by the courtesy of the director of the Cuban National Archives.
[78] Valdés to Intendant of Louisiana, Madrid, September 8, 1789, AGI, PC, leg. 2317-b; royal order of September 8, 1789, cited in Gayoso to Miró, New Orleans, November 4, 1791, AGI, PC, leg. 41. In addition to his annual salary, Gayoso was granted $500 annually for table expenses, in view of the special nature of his post. These salaries are generally misleading because it was common practice

had extensive oral orders which gave him unusual freedom and latitude in governing his new post, including the rare privilege of corresponding directly with Spanish ministers instead of the usual custom of following the chain of command through New Orleans and Havana.

On February 21, 1789, Dubois, Gayoso, and his family embarked on the brigantine *San Juan Bautista,* commanded by Captain Bautista Favie. At some point after leaving Cádiz, Doña Gayoso gave birth to her second child, a daughter who was named Henriqueta.[79] The trip almost proved disastrous. A violent Gulf storm blew the ship off course and for nine days they were in danger of sinking. The *San Juan Bautista* seemed about to live up to its namesake. They put in at the Yucatecan port of Campeche in New Spain. After a month's delay, a small brig, *La Industria,* carried the exhausted Gayoso and his fever ridden wife to New Orleans, where they arrived on April 12, 1789.[80]

---

to take out a number of deductions. Gayoso was specifically exempt from paying the *media annata,* usually equivalent to one-half the first year's salary, taken in advance. Royal order, January 7, 1789. There were charges, however, for the *Inválidos* (a disabled veterans' fund), the *Monte Pío* (pension fund for veterans and widows of veterans), discounts, draft fees, and numerous minor costs. Gayoso drew $1,000 in Cuba, $400 in Campeche, and drafts to cover table expenses while on the journey. In addition, he received $200 to cover expenses for Dr. James White, who traveled with him. It was common practice for salaries to be delayed several years in Louisiana, and by the end of 1791, Gayoso found himself in dire financial straits. See the salary adjustment for Gayoso by José de Orué, New Orleans, November 9, 1791, AGI, PC, leg. 538-A; Gayoso to Miró, New Orleans, December 7, 1790, and November 4, 1791, AGI, PC, leg. 41. Gayoso was also authorized $365 annually to rent a suitable house for his quarters, as was approved for his predecessor. Valdés to Miró, Madrid, July 1, 1789, copy, AGI, PC, leg. 184-A.

[79]*Fé de bautismo* (baptismal record) of Henriqueta, cited in the inventory of Gayoso's estate, *causa mortuoria,* AGI, PC, leg. 169. When the Gayosos left Cádiz he did not have a child; when he arrived at Campeche he owed table expenses for his child: adjusted costs of Orué, November 9, 1791, AGI, PC, leg. 538-A. She is never mentioned again, except indirectly when Gayoso refers to his "loved ones" buried in the Natchez cemetery. Gayoso to Stephen Minor, New Orleans, January 18, 1798, Gayoso de Lemos Correspondence, Louisiana State University Archives.

[80]Gayoso to Valdés, No. 1, Confidential, New Orleans, May 8, 1789, AHN, ESTADO, leg. 3902; Miró to Ezpeleta, No. 43, New Orleans, April 20, 1789, AGI, PC, leg. 1394.

Gayoso spent the next few weeks at Government House with Miró. Less time was spent discussing their past military activities in the Lisbon Regiment than in deciding the policy Gayoso would carry out in Natchez. The long journey had taken its toll on Gayoso and his wife. Having recently given birth to Henriqueta, she was too weak to fight the fever that seized her. After a short illness, she died and one of Gayoso's first duties in Natchez was to bury her there.[81]

While he was still in New Orleans, however, Gayoso had an opportunity to meet the Natchez planters who had come to the city with their tobacco. Despite his illness, Gayoso evidently made an excellent first impression. Miró wrote Valdés that "the planters evidenced great pleasure in having such a governor, many of them adding that his appointment proved the great interest which His Majesty has in the well-being of that District's settlers." Miró also requested that, in view of the importance of Natchez in the new Spanish program, Gayoso should be raised from lieutenant-colonel to full colonel. The Supreme Council of State agreed, and on October 25, 1789, Gayoso was made a colonel.[82]

On May 19, 1789, Gayoso took official possession of his Natchez command by swearing to support the Holy Church and the laws of Spain. Miró administered the oath of office a week later, and on June 1st Gayoso left New Orleans for Natchez to take up the reins of his first American government.[83]

In analyzing Spain's Louisiana policy, the longtime minister of state, Manuel de Godoy, stated that Charles IV attempted to send "special men, who, because of their knowledge of colonial government, would employ great moderation toward those inhabitants." [84]

[81]Miró to Domingo Cabello, New Orleans, January 18, 1790, AGI, SD, leg. 2553.
[82]Miró to Valdés, No. 40, Confidential, New Orleans, May 20, 1789, AHN, ESTADO, leg. 3901; Gayoso's Service Records.
[83]Valdés to Ezpeleta, Madrid, February 7, 1789, in Kinnaird (ed.), *Spain in the Mississippi Valley*, Part III, 266–67; Miró to Valdés, No. 212, New Orleans, June 12, 1789, AGI, SD, leg. 2553; Porlier to Gayoso, Madrid, July 31, 1789, AGI, PC, leg. 176-B; *Auto*, New Orleans, May 25, 1789 (act of possession by Gayoso, witnessed by Miró), AGI, PC, leg. 140.
[84]Carlos Seco Serrano (ed.), *Príncipe de la Paz, Memorias* (2 vols.; Madrid, 1956), I, 296–97.

Gayoso was such a special administrator. In the best tradition of Spanish colonial policy he had been carefully selected to perform a special mission. His fluency in languages employed in his new command gave him a decided advantage over his predecessor, the commandant Grand-Pré. Gayoso had theoretical and practical knowledge in military and naval affairs and a gregarious disposition which was to win the support and admiration of men on the frontier. Red, black, or white; American, French, or English; harmless cranks, explorers, soldiers, and sailors; visiting royalty and diplomats from Paris to London, from Madrid to Philadelphia; scientists, botanists, and surgeons—all would remember the name of Manuel Gayoso de Lemos, first governor of the Natchez District.

CHAPTER II

Administration of the Natchez District

W HEN GAYOSO arrived in Natchez in June, 1789, he found a bewildering variety of tasks confronting him. His district was located on the frontier and had to be defended from Indian attacks and foreign aggression. The population, scattered along the streams and rivers and linked to Natchez only by the tortuous Mississippi, was Anglo-American and accustomed to self-government, independence, and self-reliance. Insufficient adminstrative funds and the dearth of capable colonial officials were ineluctable elements of Spanish colonial government in Natchez as elsewhere in Spanish America. In the eight years of his government at Natchez, Gayoso was forced by circumstance to adjust to many republican features of government. The manner in which he met these challenges shows he was a good administrator, able to steer a smooth course between autocracy and democracy, between the divine right paternalism of Spain and the individualism of the frontier.

At first he was guided by Miró's instructions in addition to those he had received at Court and from the captain-general. Miró's proc-

33

lamation of April 20, 1789, which shows the influence of the new Spanish policy as well as suggestions by Gayoso and petitions of James White, set forth the basic policy which the Natchez governor was to pursue. The governor-general's proclamation stated:

> It will be permitted to every good Inhabitant to come down & settle in the Province of Louisiana either at Natchez or any other place of both Misisipi's shores, they will not be molested on religious matters, although no other public worship will be permitted to be publickly exercised than that of Roman catholic Church: Land shall be granted to them at their arrival in proportion of the hands, or facultys each Family should have; they will have the liberty of importing all their property in any produce whatsoever of the Country without paying any duty whatever, with the absolute freedom to dispose of the said property in the Posts they should pass by or in this town. Immediately after their arrival they shall enjoy the same franchises & privileges as the other subjects of his most Catholic Majesty, under the condition they shall at the same time take the due oath of allegiance & bound themselves only to take up arms in defence of this Province against whatsoever enemy who could attempt to invade it." [1]

On July 30, 1789, Gayoso signed a land petition of Dennis Collins for 240 arpents,[2] and during the next few months he spent a good

[1]Miró's concessions to Westerners, New Orleans, April 20, 1789, AGI, PC, leg. 2370, printed in Corbitt, "Papers from the Spanish Archives," XX (1948), 104–105. Royal orders establishing the means and rules to be employed toward the American immigrants are dated July 14, 1788, and seven orders dated May 14, 1789. Valdés to Miró, Aranjuez, May 14, 1789, AGI, PC, leg. 176-B; Marqués de Casa-Calvo to Ramón de López Ángulo, New Orleans, May 5, 1801, AGI, PC, leg. 70-B; Miró to Grand-Pré, No. 506, Confidential, New Orleans, February 28, 1789, AGI, PC, leg. 2362.

[2]The arpent's exact size is somewhat difficult to ascertain because it tended to vary from place to place. The *arpent de face*, or arpents front, was a tract of one arpent upon the river bank, which extended away from the river for a depth sufficient to embrace a total area of forty arpents. The arpent is .85065 of the acre. The basis of my figures are early plats of the Arkansas post near present-day Marion, Crittenden County Clerk's Office, Plats Vol. I, survey No. 2317, which shows 320 arpents as 272.21 acres. According to William O. Scroggs, "Rural Life in the Lower Mississippi Valley about 1803," *Proceedings* of the Mississippi Valley Historical Association, VIII (1914–1915), 271–72, a plantation of 20 arpents front would have an area of 800 arpents or 680 acres.

deal of his official time in approving additional grants for other new settlers.[3] Spanish laws and customs guided the practice of land grants. "The Land titles emanate from the Crown some by grants direct from it, the Major part by grants from the Governor, & in distant Posts from the Commandants who were authorized to make them,—They are all held in fee Simple . . . . There are no Feudal rights whatever & no Noblesse."[4] The history of Spanish land grants in Louisiana dates back to Governor Alejandro O'Reilly's proclamation of February 18, 1770. To each newly arrived family wishing to settle on the river banks, six to eight arpents of frontage by forty arpents in depth would be granted free of all costs save that of the surveyors' and secretarial fees. During the first three years of possession, the settler was required to build and maintain levees of an established size and construction and to clear the frontage of their grants to a depth of at least two arpents. Failure to fulfill any of these conditions resulted in the grant's reversion to the royal domain. Grants could neither be sold nor alienated by the proprietors until after three years of possession and the fulfillment of the requirements. Guardians were responsible for supervising the lands of their minor charges. Lands were also required to be fenced along the frontage during the first three years of occupancy. Land grant applications had to be witnessed by the prospective grantee, a judge of the district, and two adjoining settlers. Copies of the document were placed in the government secretary's office and in the governor-general's files; a third went to the proprietor to be annexed to the titles of his grant.[5]

A book of old Natchez maps, compiled by county surveyor Charles W. Babbitt (Natchez, 1902) and kept in the Natchez Chancery Court Records, indicates that the French acre or arpent used at Natchez was 4,095 square yards or 69 yards square. *An Account of Louisiana*, 44-45, says the Parisian arpent was 180 feet square! Most writers customarily use acres interchangeably with arpents.

[3]Land petition of Dennis Collins and others, Natchez, July 30, 1789, MSS., Louisiana Miscellaneous MSS., 1763–1789, Manuscript Division, Library of Congress.

[4]Clark to Madison, September 8, 1803, in Carter (ed.), *The Territorial Papers of the United States*, IX: *Orleans*, 34.

[5]O'Reilly's regulation, New Orleans, February 18, 1770, translated in *Appendix to an Account of Louisiana* (n.p., n.d.), lxiii–lxvii. A copy of this valuable pamphlet containing various regulations in Spanish Louisiana is in the

These original instructions were modified but slightly when Valdés informed Miró in 1789 of the following regulation:

> In order that conditions be more convenient and opportune for the development of agriculture and that the families arriving there to settle on the estuaries and bayous will be granted sufficient subsistence and protection—objects necessary to the security of the Province—to each family which has no Negro slaves, will be granted land six arpents frontage on the Bayou or Estuary by forty in depth; those who have four or six large children or field hands with them will be granted ten arpents of frontage by forty in depth. . . .⁶

Although these were the regulations in theory, in actual practice the governor of Natchez had wide latitude in determining the actual size to be granted. An analysis of the numerous land grants indicates considerable variation in the size. Numerous individuals also petitioned for and received additional land grants. Thus, Anthony Hutchins, the irascible old Tory who had sworn his allegiance to Spain almost as many times as he had conspired against her, owned 8,510 arpents in the Second and Sandy Creek section. William Dunbar, a Scot who served as surveyor for the Spanish government on occasion, possessed two thousand arpents in 1792. On April 19, 1797, however, Governor Gayoso granted him a highly desirable lot measuring twenty-six arpents and nine perches of land square

---

library of the Louisiana State Museum (New Orleans). The king approved of O'Reilly's ordinance. Marqués de Grimaldi to Luis Unzaga, San Ildefonso, August 24, 1770, translated in *Documents Relative to Louisiana and Florida Received at the Department of State* (Washington c. 1834), 2. A copy of this valuable pamphlet dealing with land grants by the governors and intendants of Louisiana is in the U.S. National Archives, General Records of the State Department, Record Group 59.

⁶Valdés to Miró, May 14, 1789. An interesting discussion of land claims in Upper Louisiana (present-day Missouri) is found in Louis Houck, *History of Missouri* (3 vols.; Chicago, 1908), II, 214–30. The immigration decree of Bernardo de Gálvez, New Orleans, February 19, 1778, is printed in Louis Houck (ed.), *The Spanish Régime in Missouri* (2 vols.; Chicago, 1909), I, 155–57. *Cf.* Eugene M. Violette, "Spanish Land Claims in Missouri," *Washington University Studies*, VIII (1921), 167–200; Francis P. Burns, "The Spanish Land Laws of Louisiana," *Louisiana Historical Quarterly*, XI (October, 1928), 557–81.

measure in the heart of Natchez—a land grant which later caused Dunbar considerable litigation with the city of Natchez.[7]

Inasmuch as the objective of granting land was to populate the Natchez District with "desirable" inhabitants, Gayoso used a personal rule of reason in deciding who was to get how much and when. Those immigrants who brought their friends and large families, such as Pedro Bryan Bruin, were particularly favored with large grants. Bruin received 1,450 arpents when he settled at Bayou Pierre in 1788 with twenty-three men, five women, seven children, and thirty-one Negro slaves. Because of his many services to the Spanish government, he was given an additional 500 arpents located three miles from the mouth of Bayou Pierre and 1,800 arpents in the triangular section of land formed by Bayou Pierre and the Mississippi.[8]

When young Samuel S. Forman of New Jersey descended the Mississippi and reached Natchez in 1790, he was suddenly surprised by Gayoso's generous grant of eight hundred acres of choice land "including a beautiful stream of water, with a gravelly bottom. . . near the White Cliffs." The only cost to Forman was a sixty-dollar surveyor's fee.[9] Perhaps this action of Gayoso was an effort to please the youth's uncle, Ezekiel Forman, a prosperous Natchez planter who had living on his plantation seventy-four slaves and two mulattoes.[10]

[7]Natchez census (Padrón), 1792, AGI, PC, leg. 2353; Eron Rowland, Life, Letters, and Papers of William Dunbar (Jackson, Mississippi, 1930), 76–78; Dunbar's Memorial to Congress, November 14, 1804, printed in Clarence E. Carter (ed.), The Territorial Papers of the United States, V: Mississippi (Washington, 1937), 346–50. When Dunbar died in October, 1810, he had two large plantations near Natchez, The Forest and Duck Pond Plantation. He owned an additional thousand acres on Thompson's Creek and various scattered pieces of real estate in Mississippi and Louisiana. Last Will and codicil of Dunbar, dated The Forest, October, 1810, and proved on January 8, 1816. Natchez Chancery Court Records, Will Books, I (1802–1812), 129–32.

[8]Natchez census of 1792; land grants signed by the Baron de Carondelet, July 20, 1796, AGI, PC, leg. 2364. For a sketch of Bruin, see Holmes (ed.), Documentos de la Luisiana, 81 n. An extended treatment is in the same author's "Some Irish Officers in Spanish Louisiana," 245–46.

[9]Samuel S. Forman, Narrative of a Journey down the Ohio and Mississippi in 1789–90 (Cincinnati, 1888), 54–55; Grand-Pré to Miró, Natchez, April 16, 1790, in Kinnaird (ed.), Spain in the Mississippi Valley, Part II, 326–27.

[10]Natchez Census of 1792. On the Formans in Natchez, see Holmes (ed.), Documentos de la Luisiana, 189 n.

Although Gayoso had the authority to take away land as well as grant it, he seems not to have exercised this power without just cause.[11] On the contrary, he employed his discretionary powers in keeping with his instructions to build up a loyal, numerous, and prosperous population capable and willing to fight for Louisiana and their homes. Those individuals who applied for land primarily for speculative purposes were discouraged from settling in Natchez. Gayoso favored the return of lands granted to settlers who declined to cultivate them for the purpose of giving the plots to true settlers and farmers. Thus, when Robert Stark petitioned in 1793 for permission to sell the land he had been granted and return to the United States, Gayoso felt that Stark was not entitled to sell the lands in question and he recommended to Carondelet that the land revert to the crown for distribution to someone else.[12]

Groves Morris received a typical land grant on Cole's Creek. Following his petition in 1794 Gayoso issued instructions for its survey by Dunbar, which was accomplished on November 26, 1794. By February 24, 1795, Morris had received his grant with the condition that he make a road and regular clearing, take possession within one year, and build houses and plant the land within three years.[13] The requirement of actually developing the land grants was strictly enforced in most cases; and if planters petitioned for additional grants of land, the governor took into consideration whether they had made proper use of what they already had. Those who obviously intended to speculate in lands were refused additional grants.[14]

In 1789 Gayoso's administrative duties received a setback when his wife, ill since her arrival at New Orleans, died. The governor was beside himself with grief: he had also lost his infant daughter, Henriqueta; and with his only son Manuel still in Europe, he must have felt desperately alone. He was also struck by the fever; and

[11]George Willey, "Natchez in the Olden Times," in appendix of John F. H. Claiborne, *Mississippi as a Province, Territory and State* (Jackson, Mississippi, 1880), 529.

[12]Gayoso to Carondelet, No. 338, Natchez, August 6, 1793, AGI, PC, leg. 42.

[13]Land grant to Groves Morris, New Orleans, February 24, 1795, AGI, PC, leg. 22.

[14]Petition of Nathaniel Tomlinson, Natchez, December 11, 1795, AGI, PC, leg. 33; Grand-Pré to Carondelet, No. 38, Natchez, July 9, 1795, AGI, PC, leg. 32; Carondelet to Grand-Pré, New Orleans, June 25, 1795, AGI, PC, leg. 22.

he gave interim command of the Natchez District to the former commandant, Carlos de Grand-Pré, who was military commander of the Louisiana Regiment's troops at Natchez. Gayoso remained in New Orleans where he occupied an apartment belonging to Captain Elías Beauregard.[15]

While he was in New Orleans in 1789 and 1790, Gayoso had an opportunity to discuss plans for his district with Miró at length. Having already become acquainted with the major facets of his duties, he was able to talk more intelligently with his governor-general on specific matters. One subject of discussion was undoubtedly the most significant diplomatic mission which Gayoso ever attempted to fulfill: the so-called "Spanish" conspiracy.

Gayoso had already met Dr. James White of Tennessee on the journey from Havana to New Orleans and had made tentative plans to visit the Cumberland, Kentucky, region and other Western settlements as soon as he was settled. The long delay occasioned by his illness and the loss of his wife enabled too many Westerners to know or hear about the Spanish governor to allow him to make the journey without arousing suspicion in the Western settlements. Moreover, Gayoso had committed an error in judgment by writing directly to Spain for permission to make the journey without first discussing it with Miró.[16] Most Spanish officials were jealous of their prerogatives, and Miró was no exception. He wrote a caustic letter to Gayoso in which he complained:

> I am displeased with your operations in this matter. . . .If someone had said to me, "A month and a half will not pass without your having to complain of Gayoso for something," I would have answered him with a thousand words

[15]Miró to Valdés, No. 46, Confidential, December 31, 1789, AHN, ESTADO, leg. 3886; Miró to Domingo Cavello, Confidential, New Orleans, January 18, 1790, AGI, SD, leg. 2553, and a copy in AHN, ESTADO, leg. 3888 *bis.;* Joseph Xavier Pontalba to Miró, (New Orleans), May 12, 1792, in Heloise Hulse Cruzat (trans.), "Letters, in Journal Form, written to Don Estevan Miro, ex-Governor of Louisiana, by Don Joseph Xavier de Pontalba in 1792," *Louisiana Historical Quarterly,* II (October, 1919), 416.

[16]Gayoso to Valdés, Havana, January 3, 1789; Minutes of the Supreme Council of State (Madrid), March 16, 1789; Miró to Cavello, New Orleans, January 18, 1790, AHN, ESTADO, leg. 3888 *bis.;* Miró to Gayoso, Confidential, New Orleans, July 10, 1789, AGI, PC, leg. 6.

of wrath . . . [but] by your actions you make it seem
that you were the organ of the Ministry, and therefore I
have no further function in matters of this nature. In spite
of everything I am far from desiring to break with you,
hoping you will accept this as a fraternal correction. . . .
Friend, in this world we cannot live without disappoint-
ments, but I hope that similar occurrences will not repeat
themselves.[17]

While in New Orleans Gayoso had an opportunity to mend his
fences, and he seems to have succeeded admirably. Perhaps the
loss of Gayoso's wife and his obvious grief and disappointment
softened the governor-general's temper. The best proof we have
that Miró's confidence was fully restored is his unqualified recommendation of Gayoso to conduct the undercover work with Wilkinson and the Western settlers who threatened to break away from
the United States.[18] In 1791 Miró wrote about Gayoso, "He speaks
French and English fluently; he has learned how to earn the
love and general esteem [of his people]; he has great talent and an
extraordinary capacity; for these reasons and because he is already
acquainted with the confidential matters regarding this Province,
I consider him apt to succeed me in its command." [19]

Thoughts of provincial command, however, were necessarily
reserved for the future in Gayoso's mind. Although he did exercise
temporary command of the province when Miró made a voyage to
Havana on top secret business,[20] Gayoso's primary concern from
1790 to 1792 was the political administration of the Natchez District.

There was much to do. He returned from New Orleans to re-
sume command at Natchez and found a myriad of duties facing him.

Grand-Pré had initiated a town plan for Natchez before Gayoso
arrived in 1788. The previous year Miró had written to the Minister
of the Indies, the Marqués de Sonora, describing the settlements
along the three Natchez bayous, Santa Catalina, Second Creek,

[17]Miró to Gayoso, "Mr. Conway's House," July 14, 1789, AGI, PC, leg. 6.
[18]Miró to Campo de Alange, August 11, 1792, in Holmes (ed.), *Documentos de la Luisiana*, 38–39.
[19]Miró to Antonio Porlier, No. 51, New Orleans, March 20, 1791, AGI, SD, leg. 2588.
[20]Valdés to Miró, Madrid, February 22, 1790, AGI, PC, leg. 176-B.

and Cole's Creek. He suggested the establishment of parishes for the first two combined and for Cole's Creek, the construction of a church, *presbytere*, guardhouse, and a commandant's residence for both parishes. Miró felt that the combination of families around a nucleus of a church was good politics and made possible the education and proselytizing of the youth.[21]

Acting under Miró's instructions, Grand-Pré had purchased three hundred acres of choice, improved land on the Natchez bluffs from Stephen Minor for $2,000. The purchase price was to be repaid the crown by subdividing the land into "islands," each of which contained twelve lots, and selling these for twenty dollars and up.[22] During the summer of 1788, Grand-Pré located the lots, each of which had 60 feet frontage by 120 feet of depth. Provisions were made for a church and *presbytere* in the center of town to be located on two lots, each 60 by 150 feet. A large plaza, which seemed out of proportion in the small nucleus, would, said Grand-Pré, seem more suitable as the town grew in size.[23]

When Gayoso took charge at Natchez, he continued to build the town along the same lines, but with some modern features such as zoning. The crown had made it plain in granting approval to Miró's request that the town of Natchez would be set aside for merchants, officials, and those who supplied goods and services to the surrounding farmers. The country folk were not expected to live in the town of Natchez.[24] A portion of the tract originally belonging to Minor was reserved by Gayoso until the demand for additional lots necessitated their utilization in expanding the town. The governor also drew a line at Front Street, facing the bluffs, and forbade the granting of lots west of it. He created a public green or

[21]Miró to Marqués de Sonora, No. 182, New Orleans, February 1, 1787; Miró to Valdés, No. 21, January 8, 1788; Miró to Navarro, New Orleans, January 7, 1788, AHN, ESTADO, leg. 3888 *bis*.

[22]Morales to Ulloa, No. 174, New Orleans, October 16, 1797, in *Documents relative to Louisiana*, 12–17, and in manuscript in National Archives, General Records of the Department of State, Record Group 59.

[23]Grand-Pré to Miró, No. 655, Natchez, July 5, 1788, AGI, PC, leg. 14, transcript in Mississippi Archives, III, 265–67. The crown approved Miró's request for the organization of the Natchez District into suitable parishes on May 14, 1789, AHN, ESTADO, leg. 3888 *bis*.

[24]Royal Order, Aranjuez, May 14, 1789.

park which remained undivided into residential lots. When individuals applied for land there, Gayoso always refused, giving as his reason that "health being of the greatest importance to them, he conceived it absolutely necessary that a certain space should be left open, between the Town and the River, in order to contribute to the health of the Settlers."

Trees were planted on this Natchez commons, and by special permission on a public market house was later constructed with funds contributed by interested residents.[25]

This early zoning of Gayoso's was misunderstood by several writers, one of whom wrote, "The residence lots of the various classes and that portion near the bluffs on the river was known to the settlers as 'Spanish Town,' while that portion east of the present Commerce street was designated 'Irish Town.' It is related that a rather well-to-do man, not of Spanish origin, approached the Governor with a request for a building lot near the bluffs. 'No, sir,' was the Governor's reply; 'no, sir. This part of the city is reserved for the residence of Spanish Grandees.'"[26]

Actually, there were two sections of town—the part laid out atop the bluff by Grand-Pré and Gayoso and the now famous (or infamous) Natchez-under-the-Hill. The former was known as Spanish Town and the latter, near the ferry landing which probably witnessed more murders, brawls, and bawds than any other place on the Mississippi, Irish Town. George Willey, who visited Natchez with his father in 1788, said that then there were but two or three houses on the hill. The whole town was then under the hill.[27]

When Samuel Forman visited Natchez in 1791, the town atop the

[25]The town commons was a subject of much later litigation. See Memorial to Congress by the Trustees of Jefferson College, October 5, 1804; deposition of Ebenezer Rees, Adams County, October 11, 1804; deposition of Anthony Hutchins, Adams County, October 13, 1804; and deposition of Polser Shilling, Adams County, October 18, 1804; in Carter (ed.), *Territorial Papers of the United States, V: Mississippi,* 333–38.

[26]"Natchez of Long Ago and the Pilgrimage," Natchez *Democrat,* Pilgrimages Edition, (March, 1942); Major Thomas Grafton, "Natchez: its Past, Present and Future," in Major Steve Power (ed.), *The Memento Old and New Natchez 1700 to 1897* (Natchez, 1897), 29–33; Joseph Dunbar Shields, *Natchez, its Early History* (Louisville, 1930), 44.

[27]Willey, "Natchez in the Olden Times," in Claiborne, *Mississippi,* 527.

bluff was already bustling with building activity though the houses were "generally of a mean structure." [28] When Francis Baily came down the river in 1797, he wrote. "It is situated upon a high hill, which terminates in a bluff at the river, and consists of about eighty or ninety houses scattered over a great space of land. The streets are laid out upon a regular plan; but there is so much ground between most of the houses, that it appears as if each dwelling was furnished with a plantation." [29]

Shortly after the turn of the century, when Spanish government was only a memory, the city planning of Gayoso remained as a living monument to his memory. One visitor wrote:

> The city proper consists of six streets, at right angles with the river, intersected by seven others of the same length, parallel with the stream. The front, or first parallel street, is laid out about 100 yards back from the verge of the bluff, leaving a noble green esplanade along the front of the city, which not only adds to its beauty, but is highly useful as a promenade and parade ground. Shade trees are planted along the border, near the verge of the precipice, beneath which are placed benches, for the comfort of the lounger. From this place the eye commands one of the most extensive prospects to be found on the Mississippi.[30]

By 1832 the city of Natchez was the most important in the state of Mississippi. A writer described its city plan with apparent admiration: "The principal part of the city is near one hundred feet above the Mississippi, and an extensive region spreads out on the east, north and south. The streets are wide, and adorned with the China tree. The houses of the wealthier inhabitants are widely separated, each seeming to occupy a square, surrounded with orange trees, palmetto, and other beautiful shrubbery." [31]

Grand-Pré had also undertaken the ground plan for the town planned for Cole's Creek. He had purchased three hundred arpents from Thomas Calvet in 1787. Unfortunately, Grand-Pré had not taken the time to examine the lands thoroughly during the season

[28]Forman, *Narrative*, 53.
[29]Baily, *Journal*, 279.
[30]Ingraham, *The South-west by a Yankee*, II, 22–23.
[31]R. Baird, *View of the Valley of the Mississippi* (Philadelphia, 1832), 252.

of high water; the man became one of the early purchasers of submarine Florida real estate. Grand-Pré suggested that the crown buy instead three hundred and fifty arpents belonging to James Elliot, located about two miles from the site of the projected town for Cole's Creek. "The plain on which the City might be planted," Grand-Pré wrote, "is located between two other small bayous and is found surrounded by fountains of excellent water. The launches," he continued, "ascended to within a half mile of it when the waters of the Mississippi River reach the middle of their rise." Elliot's house, which could be used for the priest, was new, pretty, and comfortable and included a number of outbuildings. The price was two thousand *pesos fuertes.*[32]

The inhabitants of Cole's Creek declined to move to the site selected by Grand-Pré, however; and when Gayoso inspected the area, he understood why. It was located in a swamp, and there was no good drinking water available. Accordingly, Gayoso selected land belonging to Colonel Thomas Green, located less than a mile from the Mississippi and about three miles from Calvet's land. The rich cypress groves leading to Gayoso's proposed town site surrounded a high, flat plateau with a good view of the river. Two springs nearby provided fresh, healthy water. "This new place," Gayoso wrote, "is so beautiful, that perhaps there is no equal to it in all the province." [33]

The settlers along Cole's Creek agreed with Gayoso. Although they found it impossible to build homes on the inundated site selected by Grand-Pré, they moved with alacrity to establish themselves on the salubrious land chosen by Gayoso. Thomas Green, from whom the land had been obtained, joined fourteen other leading inhabitants of the area in petitioning the governor-general to change the name of Cole's Creek to Villa Gayoso in honor

[32]Grand-Pré to Miró, Fort Panmure de Natchez, No. 408, September 13, 1787, AGI, PC, leg. 13; Grand-Pré to Miró, Natchez, July 14, 1788, transcript in Mississippi Archives, III, 265–74. The *peso fuerte* was a silver coin, minted in Mexico, and used as standard currency in Spanish Louisiana. It was equal in exchange to the French *piastre* and the American dollar. By 1936 American standards, the peso was equivalent to $1.7151: J. Villasana Haggard, *Handbook for Translators of Spanish Historical Documents* (Austin, 1941), 106.
[33]Gayoso to Miró, No. 132, Natchez, June 16, 1791, AGI, PC, leg. 2352.

of their governor. Approval was granted, and Gayoso wrote the settlers, "I cannot but feel a sensible gratification in the wish you have expressed, that the Town now erecting in your vicinity shou'd be known to posterity by my Name." [34] The governor-general was particularly pleased by "an incontestable proof of the satisfaction with which you live under the Spanish Government, & of the affection that you all profess to your Gouvernor. . . . " [35]

While attending to the development of new towns for the inhabitants of his district, Gayoso did not lose sight of the need for better means of communication between the various settlements. When Forman visited Natchez in 1790, he made a wry observation on the condition of the roads: "Ours was the first four-wheeled carriage that ever passed over those grounds—I can't say roads, for the highway was only what was called a bridle-path—all traveling at that day was on horseback." It was customary, Forman added, for his friends on the day set for a visit to have the canebrakes along the trail cleared for his passage, though it was once more obscured with the next small gust of wind. [36]

In 1785 a number of Natchez inhabitants had petitioned the governor-general for permission to open a road from Natchez to

[34]Petition signed by Thomas Green, Sr., Thomas M. Green, Henry Green, Cato West, Filmer W. Green, John Smith, Robert Stark, N. Hunter, Thomas Calvet, and James Truly, Cole's Creek, January 26, 1792, AGI, PC, leg. 41; petition of Thomas Green, et al., Cole's Creek, March 24, 1792, in Kinnaird (ed.), *Spain in the Mississippi Valley*, Part III, 19–20; Gayoso to People of Cole's Creek, (Natchez, 1792), *ibid.*, 20.

[35]Carondelet's draft, one in Spanish, one in English, New Orleans, April 4, 1792, AGI, PC, leg. 41. Villa Gayoso grew rapidly, and by June, 1792, when a census was taken, it showed 909 people—the second most heavily populated in the Natchez District. Census of 1792, AGS, Guerra Moderna, leg. 6928. It is unfortunate that the gratitude of Green and others did not extend beyond five years, and in 1798 when the Spaniards planned to evacuate Natchez, Edward Green threatened to sue for damages if any buildings on the Green lands formerly belonging to the king were destroyed during the evacuation. "I claim the land on which the buildings in question stand with all its appurtinances and shoud they be destroyed I shall expect your property to answer it—those buildings are all the compensation I expect to be able to recover for lying out of the use of my plantation many years. . . . I never will pay one sou for the buildings which the Kings officers have thought proper to place on my land." Evd. Green to Major Stephen Minor, Villa Gayoso, February 4, 1798, AGI, PC, leg. 215-A.

[36]Forman, *Narrative*, 57–58.

Thompson's Creek by taking up a subscription. Miró approved the project and ordered the commandants of Natchez, Punta Cortada, Baton Rouge, and Manchak to contribute to the project. Doctor Benjamin Farrar of Natchez was placed in charge of building the road, and Miró contributed fifty pesos from his own pocket. Farrar wrote about the difficulties of opening roads through the thick, swampy undergrowth of the Mississippi bottom lands:

> The first part from Manchack to Batten Rouge is about three Leagues being a Swamp and has a marked Path already, but would perhaps require some mending, from Batton-Rouge to the Natchez is computed fifty Leagues by Water, and nearly as much by Land; if the Road is carried out thro' the Pine Woods which is further round, but it is certain at all Times of the year, which I understand the other is not; There will be some Bayos to cross which must be made passable by cutting down the Banks and in some Places making a small Bridge; at those Bayos, the cane are thick and must be cut; there will then be nothing impassable to the River *Homochitta* within about six or seven Leagues of the Natchez Fort, which at low Water may be crossed by the assistance of a Tree, but in high Water by a Raft, unless a small Boat is kept there. . . .
> This Sir, is to be understood as a Path for a Horse-Man only; which may I think be done for two hundred & fifty Dollars, or three hundred Dollars Expence; But a good Wagon Road would cost one thousand Dollars or more—[37]

Torrential Mississippi rains often rendered travel, even on these primitive horse trails, difficult if not impossible. The lack of bridges over the numerous streams and bayous endangered the lives of many horses and riders, who were forced to swim them during the season of high water. Gayoso was delayed several days in February, 1792, by such high water.[38] In August of that year, Juan de la Villebeuvre wrote Carondelet about the extremely bad condition of roads leading from Natchez to the posts west of the Mississippi, and

---

[37]Decree of Miró, New Orleans, February 4, 1785, draft; and B. Farar to Miró, New Orleans, August 19, 1785, AGI, PC, leg. 2360.

[38]Gayoso to Carondelet, No. 1, Natchez, March 5, 1792, AGI, PC, leg. 41.

in 1794 the Baton Rouge–Homochitto road was closed by a storm.[39]

A regulation for "making and keeping in repair the Roads and highways throughout the Government" was Gayoso's attempt to solve this problem as far as Natchez was concerned. He divided his district into six subdistricts: Big Black and Bayou Pierre, Villa Gayoso, St. Catherine Creek, Second and Sandy creeks, Homochitto, and the combined settlements of Buffalo Creek, Bayou Sara, and Viejo Tunicas. Fifteen supervisors of the roads were to be appointed by Gayoso for one-year terms. They exercised jurisdiction over the roads in their particular subdistrict. This included the appointment by the supervisors of overseers for specific road projects. The supervisors met as often as necessary to revise the current road regulations and to propose new measures for the improvement of Natchez arteries of transportation.

The overseers were required to notify the inhabitants of the necessary repairs on their roads. Overseers declining to serve on such public business were fined twenty-five dollars and exempt from service for that year only. "Inhabitants who own land shall be obliged to send upon the Roads when called upon by the overseer, a Number of hands in proportion to the Lands he holds in the district where the work is to be done, the ratio to be struck by the Supervisors and not left to the overseer." Tracts of land through which public and private roads led to church and to market, but on which the owners did not reside, were ordered maintained and kept in repair by the owners at their own expense. If the owners refused, they were liable to prosecution, including the confiscation and sale of their land to pay the cost of such repairs.

The four public roads—two leading from the fort to Cole's Creek and two leading from the fort to the Homochitto—were cleared for a width of twenty feet and good bridges made where necessary. Trees which had fallen onto the road were to be cleared immediately, but no one was allowed to cut down trees or fence in the land for a distance of ninety feet from the center of public roads. Persons refusing to meet their obligations under this ordinance were fined, but any individual feeling himself wronged could appeal

[39]Joseph Vazquez Vahamonde to Gayoso, No. 62, Baton Rouge, September 11, 1794, AGI, PC, leg. 47.

to a board of supervisors meeting as a court of inquiry. Further appeal to the governor himself was guaranteed.[40]

Natchez residents who felt the road ordinance interfered with their other duties signed an agreement with Ebenezer Dayton to keep the public roads, particularly the new one from the Catholic Church of San Salvador in Natchez to the boat landing area under the hill, in a good state of repair for twelve months. Dayton posted a bond of $200 and received in return an annual fee from the Natchez inhabitants of $130.[41]

Maintaining the roads between Natchez and other posts in Upper Louisiana, as well as with the capital at New Orleans, was essential to insure rapid communication. Postal couriers were paid to carry dispatches between the Spanish officials, but they were often delayed by the torrential storms which tossed trees on the roads blocking their way.[42] Gayoso proposed the government subsidy of a permanent mail system between the capital and Natchez, but little was done to carry out his suggestion. When Vicente Folch assumed command of the post at San Fernando de las Barrancas in 1795, one of his chief proposals was for the establishment of a permanent courier system of mail delivery which could operate so efficiently that dispatches from New Orleans could reach the most distant posts in Louisiana in a matter of twenty days.[43]

In the matter of the road ordinance and numerous others, Gayoso eschewed arbitrary action in favor of frank discussion with the

[40]Gayoso's ordinance, Natchez, November 6, 1792, AGI, PC, legs. 195, 206. Another copy is in the Natchez Chancery Clerk's Office, MS. Vol. XXXIV, 403–11. There are minor variations between these three copies which do not affect the basic provisions of the regulation.

[41]McBee (ed.), *Natchez Court Records*, 280–81, concerns a lawsuit brought by the inhabitants against Dayton when he failed to fulfill his obligations.

[42]Vahamonde to Gayoso, No. 62, September 11, 1794.

[43]Gayoso to Carondelet, No. 561, Natchez, September 23, 1794, AGI, PC, leg. 30. Folch's ideas on establishing a postal system in Spanish Louisiana are discussed in Jack D.L. Holmes, "Three Early Memphis Commandants: Beauregard, Folch, and Deville Degoutin," a paper read to the West Tennessee Historical Society, Memphis, October 21, 1963, and published in their *Papers* XVIII (1964), 21.

The role of a swift, efficient postal system in the development of the United States, by way of comparison, is mentioned in several informative articles appearing in the *American Pioneer*, I (March, 1842), 106–13; (May, 1842), 190–93; and (December, 1842), 415–20.

leading inhabitants. He left no doubt in anyone's mind that he *was* the governor but that anyone with serious ideas on the improvement of any facet of Natchez administration would be heard. Those appointed to exercise the duties of road supervisor were leading inhabitants of their respective subdistricts. They were not elected but were chosen by Gayoso on the basis of their position in the community. It was not democracy, but it was responsible government.

Even more political power was placed in the hands of local settlements in 1795 when Carondelet set up regulations for the policing of the different posts. Syndics were appointed to represent the people and to supervise local affairs. Although their jurisdiction was narrow and explicit, they formed an important link between the government and the people. Any complaints which the inhabitants presented found rapid disposition by syndics who represented them.[44]

In accordance with the new regulations regarding syndics, acting commandant Grand-Pré selected eighteen leading inhabitants of the Natchez District to exercise the functions during 1795 and 1796.[45] Although Natchez did not have a city council or cabildo as did New Orleans, there was an attempt to institute one during Gayoso's governorship. Gayoso issued a proclamation which stated the following:

[44]Carondelet's Regulation concerning the general police, the repair of bridges, roads, and mounds, and the police of slaves, for the use of the Commanders of Posts and of Coasts and the Syndics of the Province of Louisiana, New Orleans, June 1, 1795, may be found in *Appendix to an Account of Louisiana*, lxvii–lxxxiii; in James A. Padgett (ed.), "A Decree for Louisiana, Issued by the Baron of Carondelet, June 1, 1795," *Louisiana Historical Quarterly*, XX, (July, 1937), 590–605; and in Carondelet to Grand-Pré, New Orleans, June 4, 1795, July 1, 1795, AGI, PC, leg. 22.

[45]Grand-Pré to Carondelet, No. 47, Natchez, August 4, 1795, with enclosure, AGI, PC, leg. 32. Those "elected" for Natchez for the year 1795–96 were Antonio Gras and Juan Murdock (Natchez), Gabriel Benoist (Pine Ridge), Juan Smith and Guillermo Murray (Villa Gayoso), Pedro Bruin and Samuel Gibson (Bayou Pierre), Tobias Brashears (Big Black), Sutton Banks, William Vousdan, and Joseph Calvet (St. Catherine Creek), William Dunbar and Isaac Johnson (Second Creek), Isaac Gaillard and Caleb King (Homochitto), William Cooper (Sandy Creek), Daniel Clark (Buffalo Creek), and Francisco Pousset (Bayou Sara).

Whereas the business of this Country has increased in
proportion to its population, and to the industry of it's inhabitants, & desirous, by every possible means, to facilitate
the most equitable administration of Justice, I have re-
solved to establish a Cabildo or Council, composed of the
Commanding officer, in my absence who shall be President
of the Council and chief Magistrate, of Bernard Lintot,
William Dunbar, Captain Joseph Vidal, and Joseph Bernard, Esquires: who shall sit at Government-House, twice
every week, on the usual days of Audience, and administer
justice under the same Regulations that have hitherto obtained. Each of the Regidores, or Members of the Council,
shall, out of Council, enjoy the same authority as the Al-
caldes of Districts.—Applications for Grants, Permissions,
Passports, or any thing else that does not concern the
regular course of Justice, shall appertain to the Commanding officer that may be for the time being, during my
absence.—⁴⁶

In addition to the syndics and local constables *(alguaciles)*, Gayoso
was surrounded by various officials who attempted with varying
success to lighten his load as governor. Two of the most helpful
were Joseph Vidal, his secretary, and Stephen Minor, his post
adjutant. Born in Galicia—the province Gayoso frequently claimed
as his home—Vidal served in the department of pilots during the
American Revolution. He rose in the accounting and treasury departments after the war and on October 28, 1787, was named
storehouse keeper (*guarda-almacén*) at San Marcos de Apalache.
Appointed interim secretary of Natchez in 1789, at an annual salary
of $840, he served in that post until the end of Spanish rule in
Natchez, after which Vidal remained as "consul" of Spain. He is
noted as the founder of the Spanish post of Concordia, opposite
Natchez on the Louisiana side of the Mississippi (present-day
Vidalia). Vidal served on many special commissions entrusted to
him by Gayoso, including the important Indian negotiations in
1792 and 1793.⁴⁷

⁴⁶Gayoso's undated proclamation, AGI, PC, leg. 195.
⁴⁷A brief sketch of Vidal is in Holmes (ed.), *Documentos de la Luisiana*, 114.
A more extended treatment is in Holmes, "Algunos gallegos notables en la
Luisiana española," *Cuadernos de Estudios Gallegos* (Santiago de Compostela,
Spain), Tomo XIX (1964), 119–20.

Stephen Minor, on whose land the town of Natchez had been laid out, was another administrator of great stature. Born in Virginia (present-day Pennsylvania) in 1760, Minor had descended the Mississippi with Captain Pickles during the American Revolution, and, after a series of hair-raising adventures in the service of Spain and Bernardo de Gálvez, he was named adjutant of the Natchez post in 1781. His knowledge of many languages, including the Indian tongues, his amiability, his wealth and position in Natchez among Americans and Spaniards alike, and his unwavering loyalty to Gayoso were rare qualities which enabled him to perform outstanding services for the Spanish government.[48]

The office of royal inspector or superintendent *(interventor)* in Natchez was held by Francisco Gutiérrez de Arroyo. Born about 1760, Gutiérrez had served in the treasury and comptroller departments of New Orleans and Pensacola since 1783. He was appointed at Natchez in 1792 and remained at his post until June 30, 1795.[49]

In military matters Gayoso depended on Lieutenant Colonel Carlos de Grand-Pré, who remained at Natchez in that capacity and as interim commandant when Gayoso found it necessary to attend to business outside the district.[50]

Three men held the important office of storehouse keeper during Gayoso's Natchez administration—Juan Josef Rodríguez (whose accounts were kept badly), Juan de Castanedo, and Francisco Candel. Typical duties of that position included supervision of supplies, ammunition and artillery, Indian gifts and expenses, and the hospital. Accounts for the office were extremely complex and had to include every nail or penny sent to or from Natchez. Candel, a Spaniard from Alicante, did such a notable job for Gayoso that he was later transferred to New Orleans in 1799 to be with the governor-general.[51]

[48]A brief account of Minor is in Holmes (ed.), *Documentos de la Luisiana,* 186 n.
[49]*Ibid.,* 187–88 n.
[50]Gayoso to Beauregard, Natchez, October 4, 1791, AGI, PC, leg. 41; Grand-Pré to Carondelet, No. 1, Natchez, February 19, 1795; No. 1, Natchez, April 22, 1795, AGI, PC, leg. 31. A biographical sketch of Grand-Pré is in Holmes (ed.), *Documentos de la Luisiana,* 185–86 n.
[51]Holmes (ed.), *Documentos de la Luisiana,* 190 n; Gayoso to Miró, No. 165, Natchez, August 4, 1791; No. 22, April 24, 1790; Gayoso to Carondelet, No. 149,

This office had in its jurisdiction over finances the seeds of jurisdictional conflict with the governor. Where did political and military duties end and financial ones begin? The failure to define the precise duties of each officer caused Gayoso no end of trouble, particularly with Vicente Folch at San Fernando de las Barrancas.[52] When the *guarda-almacén* at the post of Nogales, commanded by Elías Beauregard, challenged the attempt to make him subordinate to the military command, Gayoso wrote that Beauregard was superior to *all* individuals at his post in matters of jurisdiction. "The independence evidenced by that *guarda almacén*," Gayoso added, "is very reprehensible."[53]

When the welfare and security of the Natchez inhabitants were endangered by regulations passed by the commandant of the neighboring *partido* of Punta Cortada, Valentin LeBlanc, Gayoso protested vehemently to the governor-general and asked that the jurisdiction of Natchez extend over lands in dispute between the two.[54] In order to insure that the vague boundaries between the two districts were carefully defined, Gayoso sent surveyor William Dunbar to draw a boundary line from the Tunica stream.[55] When the governor-general ordered Gayoso not to issue passports to Natchez settlers for travel west of the Mississippi, the Natchez governor again protested that such actions would restrict the commercial activities of his people.[56]

Whether his activities included administering the Natchez District or extending Spanish laws and customs to the far corners of the province by the promulgation of decrees for the guidance of different post commanders,[57] Gayoso considered the wishes of the people

---

Natchez, September 7, 1792, AGI, PC, leg. 41; Gayoso to Carondelet, No. 322, Natchez, July 1, 1793, AGI, PC, leg. 42. Candel's reports at Natchez are in AGI, PC, leg. 581.

[52]The quarrels between Folch and Gayoso at San Fernando are discussed in Jack D.L. Holmes, "Fort Ferdinand of the Bluffs: Life on the Spanish-American Frontier, 1795–1797," WTHS *Papers*, XIII (1959), 44–45; and Holmes, "Three Early Memphis Commandants," 16–19.

[53]Gayoso to Beauregard, Natchez, December 4, 1796, AGI, PC, leg. 43.

[54]Gayoso to Carondelet, No. 117, Natchez, June 30, 1792, AGI, PC, leg. 41.

[55]Gayoso to Dunbar, New Orleans, June 7, 1790, *ibid.*

[56]Gayoso to Carondelet, No. 152, Natchez, September 7, 1792, *ibid.*

[57]Gayoso drafted instructions for Elías Beauregard, first commandant of the Nogales post, Nogales, April 1, 1791; secret instructions from Gayoso to

together with the needs of State. It is difficult to state categorically where Gayoso's jurisdiction ended. In Natchez he was almost independent, though he submitted his proposals for new rules and regulations dutifully to the governor-general *after* they were a *fait accompli*. As the duties of the governor-general increased in scope and more attention was devoted to matters of defense, the powers of the Natchez governor also expanded. The Spanish archives are filled with correspondence relating to military matters, over which Gayoso seems to have exercised unusual powers; and he was moreover a liaison between the upper Louisiana commandants and the governor-general in political affairs.

Gayoso was a good administrator in every sense of the word. He was able to act independently, swiftly, and with common sense in carrying out the duties of his office; but he also knew how to delegate responsibility to his subordinates. He expected the same devotion to duty from them as he himself showed. Those who exercised varying degrees of administration themselves earned valuable experience in self-government, and one can see a remarkably high correlation between those who performed political chores under Gayoso's administration and those who were prominent in the American government after 1798.

While practicing the principles of representative government, however, Gayoso had little sympathy with democratic government as it was understood during the closing years of the eighteenth century. He was close in his political philosophy to the contemporary Hamiltonians, as indicated in one of his letters to Minor: "In society every one acts for himself, but in comunion the people never know what they are doing nor which is the object; in spite of the pretended equality that infatuates the mind of the weak, tho' expressed by violence, there is always some insinuating character

---

Beauregard, Nogales, April 2, 1791, AGI, PC, leg. 2352. The secret instructions, bearing the date of April 1, 1791, are also printed in Manuel Serrano y Sanz, *España y los indios Cherokis y Chactas en la segunda mitad del siglo xviii* (Sevilla, Spain, 1916), 85–89. Gayoso also gave Beauregard an elaborate set of instructions when the latter took command of the new post of San Fernando de las Barrancas, San Fernando, July 25, 1795, AGI, PC, leg. 52, and printed in translation by Jack D. L. Holmes (ed. & trans.), "The First Laws of Memphis: Instructions for the Commandant of San Fernando de las Barrancas, 1795," WTHS *Papers*, XV (1961), 93–104.

that influences and at last domineers the passions of the people &
made [sic] them do just what is convenient to some private view." [58]

Gayoso's contribution toward the firm establishment of principles of law and order on a frontier among people of rambunctious
tendencies was little short of miraculous. That he did so without
trampling the personal dignity and rights of the people is equally
true. One writer wrote, "The yoke of their government always sat
easy on the neck of the Anglo-Americans, who lived under it, and
they still speak of Spanish times, as the golden age." [59] Some inhabitants, as is true in any government, resented the power and privileges
of the governor and claimed they were ruled with an iron hand. [60]
But, with the establishment of American rule, many had an opportunity to compare United States territorial government with that
of Spain. "Governor Gayoso has been the Father and Protector of
this District," they later wailed. "He was our true friend but we
failed to appreciate him then." [61] By serving both his king and the
people of Natchez to the best of his ability, Gayoso made the final
phase of Spanish administration in Mississippi renowned for its
liberality, honesty, and progress.

[58]Gayoso to Minor, New Orleans, September 6, 1798, Gayoso MSS., Louisiana State University Archives.
[59]Ingraham, *The South-west by a Yankee*, II, 263–64.
[60]Daniel Clark, Sr. to the Hon. W.C.C. Claiborne, Clarksville (Mississippi),
June 18, 1800, printed in *Papers in Relation to the Official Conduct of Governour Sargent* (Boston, 1801), 20–22.
[61]Vidal to Gayoso, Natchez, September 15, 1798, AGI, PC, leg. 2365.

CHAPTER III

Law and Justice in the Natchez District

FEW ASPECTS of Gayoso's administration in Natchez occupied more time than the administration of justice. In some ways, the Natchez District was governed like other Spanish possessions in the New World. The laws of the Indies, the various edicts and decrees of the king and Council of the Indies, the special orders and regulations promulgated in Louisiana since the time of Governor O'Reilly—these were the codes of law with which Gayoso became thoroughly familiar during his years as governor of the Natchez District.

The general legal procedures first outlined by O'Reilly in 1769 provided for original jurisdiction by Louisiana's commandants in civil cases where the amount in litigation was less than twenty-five dollars. In criminal cases and in civil cases where the amount exceeded twenty-five dollars, commandants examined witnesses, took depositions, collected evidence, and forwarded the case to New Orleans for decision by the governor-general in conjunction with the *auditor de guerra*, an office similar to that of the attorney general.

The rights of appeal were guaranteed, providing the parties at law posted an amount equal to the fines should the appeal go against them. The direction of appeal from the commandants' decisions was to New Orleans, thence to Havana, subsequently to the Audiencia of Santo Domingo, and finally to the Council of the Indies in Spain itself.[1]

One historian commented on this legal procedure: "No code of procedure was ever devised more carefully safeguarding the rights of the individual in theory than the Spanish colonial code. It was merely a matter of money to secure all these rights practically, but the same observation may be applied to every other system of jurisprudence." [2]

Lawlessness in Natchez was rather common prior to the administration of Gayoso. Following the abortive Natchez revolt of 1780, many of the rebels fled to refuge with the Indian nations or to the Chickasaw Bluffs. Operating from these bases, they preyed on Spanish shipping on the Mississippi or raided isolated plantations in the Natchez District.

One of the earliest crimes which disturbed the entire economic well-being of Louisiana was counterfeiting. In 1783 the intendant, Martín Navarro, wrote Governor Gálvez that their paper currency had been counterfeited so successfully that "even after we have examined them we weren't too sure that the signatures and stamps were not our own." Three Americans from the Natchez District were the counterfeiters. Commandant Pedro Piernas caught them red-handed with their press, plates, and counterfeit currency in the woods. Although they were sent to New Orleans and their equipment confiscated, the false currency continued to circulate side by side with the genuine, causing the treasury officials no end of headaches.[3] In 1785, as a result, it was planned to recall all currency

[1] Alejandro O'Reilly, *Instructions sur la maniere de former & de dresser les Procés Civils & Criminels, & de rendre les Jugemens ordinaires* (Nouvelle Orléans, 1769), AGI, PC, leg. 2357. A copy in English is in *Appendix to an Account of Louisiana,* xxviii–lxii. Except where noted, the information in this chapter is based on Jack D. L. Holmes, "Law and Order in Spanish Natchez, 1781–1798," *Journal of Mississippi History,* XXV (July, 1963), 186–201.
[2] Houck, *History of Missouri,* II, 198.
[3] Navarro to Gálvez, No. 148, New Orleans, January 13, 1783, AGI, SD, leg. 2543.

in notes of 50, 30, 25, 20, 10, 5, 2½, and 1 peso and issue new notes of a type much more difficult to copy.[4]

In 1792 Gayoso found several counterfeiters operating in his own district. Buckman Pitman, a close friend of a man wanted for murder, was a known counterfeiter; and Luis Wetsell was captured and imprisoned for this same crime.[5] When a fugitive counterfeiter from the United States named William Dickins crossed into Spanish territory, he was swiftly captured and sent to New Orleans for disposition by the governor-general.[6]

But counterfeiting was only one of many crimes which plagued the Natchez District. In 1785 the commandant at Natchez, Francisco Bouligny, wrote an extensive report describing the lawless conditions of the district. Because the vagabonds and criminals usually rode horses and escaped after their crimes into the wilderness or some nearby Choctaw camp, the inadequate Spanish military forces without horses were virtually impotent. Bouligny recommended the creation of a vigilante force of leading citizens, but no action was taken on the proposal until Gayoso assumed command.

One hair-raising episode seems fictional in its audacity. Near Bayou Pierre lived a wild-eyed bandit named Benjamin Payatt. He had killed an Indian with whose daughter he had lived as man and wife. Gayoso sent his constable, Adam Ware, to capture the outlaw. Ware took Payatt into custody but, believing him ill, failed to tie him and watch him as Gayoso had instructed. Finding his opportunity, Payatt suddenly struck. He stabbed Ware twice, killed him, and stole his weapons. Then the bandit fled to safety with his friends at Bayou Pierre.[7]

Gayoso acted at once to remedy what was becoming a serious threat to the security of the inhabitants of his district. Acting under his extraordinary powers, which he felt could be stretched

[4]Morales to Phelipe Treviño, New Orleans, March 16, 1785, draft, AGI, PC, leg. 590.
[5]Gayoso to Carondelet, Natchez, July 9, 1792; No. 130, July 20, 1792, AGI, PC, leg. 41.
[6]Josef Deville Degoutin to Carondelet, San Fernando de las Barrancas, October 21, 1796, AGI, PC, leg. 34.
[7]Gayoso to Carondelet, Natchez, July 9, 1792.

to meet virtually every emergency, he called together thirty of
the young men and organized a mounted police force. He had no
authority or means to pay them, but he promised each of them a
land grant of two hundred arpents for each six months of service
in the constabulary force. To its commander, Richard King, he
promised five hundred arpents plus a daily salary of one dollar
while on the prowl. The Natchez vigilantes immediately set out for
Bayou Pierre. They tracked Payatt down, arrested him, and sent
him to New Orleans for trial.[8] After several months of action,
Gayoso reported that his vigilante force had restored complete
tranquility to the district. Just a word mentioning the force was
enough to throw the fear of the law into wrongdoers on the one
hand, and instill confidence and security in the hearts of the peaceable inhabitants on the other.[9]

Because so many Kentuckians and other Westerners descended
the rivers in their flatboats, sold their merchandise in Natchez or
New Orleans, and returned home by land via the Natchez Trace,
horse stealing was a common crime in Natchez. It was even prevalent
among the residents of the Natchez District. When John Pitman
needed spare cash for gambling or drinking, he would repeatedly
steal his wife's bald-faced roan gelding, sell it in the Opelousas post
west of the Mississippi, or gamble it away.

In order to stop these abuses and form a regular set of rules and
regulations for the cattle, horse, and indigo industries, Gayoso
called the principal stockmen of the district together in 1793 and
asked them for suggestions to remedy the bad situation. They
came up with regulations governing the branding, fencing, and disposition of stock and the proper way to dispose of "industrial
waste" from the indigo process without polluting the streams. The
following year, the stockmen met with Gayoso once more and

[8]Gayoso to Carondelet, No. 172, Natchez, September 15, 1792, AGI, PC, leg.
41. Additional information on the Payatt case may be found in Gayoso to
Carondelet, No. 130, July 20, 1792; Gayoso to Carondelet, No. 148, Natchez,
September 6, 1792; No. 159, September 13, 1792, all in AGI, PC, leg. 41;
Gayoso to Carondelet, No. 555, Natchez, September 10, 1794, AGI, PC, leg. 30;
Carondelet to Grand-Pré, New Orleans, June 12, 1795, AGI, PC, leg. 22.
[9]Gayoso to Carondelet, No. 172, September 15, 1792.

suggested a few modifications of his earlier decree, which were promptly approved.

Negro slaves, considered as chattels in Natchez, were often the object of would-be thieves. A common practice of the unscrupulous was to mortgage a slave in Natchez and then, surreptitiously, sneak him across the Mississippi to sell at Opelousas, Natchitoches, or another remote post. In order to prevent the practice, Gayoso urged commandants of other Louisiana posts to examine carefully the documents concerning any slave put up for sale.

Even Gayoso was affected by these men who stole Negroes. He offered the hospitality of his home to an American named Edward McCordy. When the visitor complained of the climate and asked permission to return to the United States, Gayoso granted it, not knowing his guest would steal two Negroes, a shotgun, carbine, bridles, and two saddles. When the Indians reported to Gayoso that they had seen a white man and two Negroes mounted and armed on the road to the Choctaw villages, Gayoso sent his two constables, Jeremias Brayn and John Foster, with two deputies to follow and capture them. When they returned with the culprit, he was sent to New Orleans for trial.[10]

Murder and crimes of violence occurred often on the frontier; therefore, their frequency at Natchez was not really unusual. Notwithstanding, Gayoso did all he could to prevent such crimes of violence. When a man named Condy suspected his wife of some intimacy with a Spanish officer, he proved he was "of that wild and roving disposition so common among frontier people" by cutting his wife's throat, murdering his three children, and, after laying the bodies in a neat row on his St. Catherine Creek cabin, stretching out beside them and shooting himself. In 1797 a man named Cobb shot his son-in-law in an argument over a Negro slave.

Governor Gayoso sought to lower the high rate of homicide by banning knives and "other dangerous iron and steel weapons," but eager assassins circumvented the law by fashioning effective stilettos of hardened wood which served the murderers as well. Pistols were also prohibited in Natchez; and when John Fusen fired his pistol

[10]Gayoso to Carondelet, No. 20, Natchez, March 27, 1792, AGI, PC, leg. 41.

near the dock while he was cleaning it, Gayoso arrested him and sent him to New Orleans for trial.[11]

As in other Spanish possessions, the right of sanctuary existed in Natchez; and one resident remembered passing by the Church of San Salvador one early morning and observing a fugitive with his finger in the keyhole who thus saved himself from immediate arrest.

Gayoso felt that effective justice in Natchez was impossible so long as the town had no jail. O'Reilly had ordered the commandants of Louisiana to build suitable jails, but Natchez had only a small room within the fort. Gayoso preferred to incarcerate "vicious civilians" away from the troops, so he proposed the construction of a jail in 1791. Gayoso drew up the plans for a well-ventilated building near the hospital so that one guard could look after both buildings.[12]

At first Miró favored the project, but he hoped that a jailer would forego a regular salary in favor of the emoluments to be derived from his position. Unfortunately, the people of Natchez were not accustomed to the Spanish practice, whereby the local populace cared for the inmates of prisons. Moreover, the Royal Treasury disapproved the project, considering such an expense unnecessary.[13]

In 1792 Gayoso again requested permission to build a jail. He told Carondelet its cost would not exceed five thousand pesos, but that if a piece-on-piece construction were utilized on the first floor alone, the cost could be lowered. For the jailer, Gayoso figured on Jacques Robert, an old Frenchman who was staying at Gayoso's home. This old soldier, with thirty years service in the French army, was a man of good conduct, and Gayoso recom-

[11]Gayoso to Carondelet, No. 304, Natchez, June 11, 1793, AGI, PC, leg. 42.
[12]Gayoso to Miró, No. 73, Natchez, May 6, 1791, AGS, Guerra Moderna, leg. 6928, and also in AGI, PC, leg. 41. The plan, drawn by William Dunbar under Gayoso's directions, is in AGS, Mapas, XIX–131.
[13]Miró to Las Casas, No. 184, New Orleans, May 24, 1791, AGI, PC, leg. 1440; Gayoso to Carondelet, No. 107, Natchez, June 14, 1792, enclosed in Las Casas to Conde del Campo de Alange, No. 232, Havana, November 8, 1792, AGS, Guerra Moderna, leg. 6928.

mended him for a twenty peso monthly salary.[14] The jail was never built, however, and one of the first major expenses for the American government when it took charge of Natchez was the construction of a jail costing $3,300.[15]

Although there was no extradition treaty between Spain and the United States regarding escaped fugitives, there was an unofficial understanding. When John Ahern, an Irishman who had left Natchez with his companion on the road to Kentucky, killed him near Cumberland, he was apprehended, tried, and sentenced to hang in Tennessee. He escaped from jail and fled to Natchez. Gayoso, fearing such a murderer would cause untold troubles in the district, took Ahern into custody and sent him to New Orleans for expulsion from the province. Shortly thereafter, a local settler complained to Gayoso that Ahern had robbed him of his horse. Ahern's brother, a law-abiding, peaceable citizen of Natchez, offered to pay for the stolen animal and pleaded with Gayoso not to press charges against the errant brother. Gayoso attempted to intercede and wrote to Carondelet recommending that the criminal be removed from the province but that his brother not be shamed by the bringing of charges. Carondelet agreed but warned Gayoso that in the future he should start proceedings.[16]

When Elijah Robertson pursued a fugitive debtor from Tennessee into West Florida, he was furnished with a letter of introduction to Gayoso so that the Natchez governor could help him recover his money.[17] The system worked in the other direction, too. James Robertson, the founder of Nashville, wrote Gayoso that he had captured a slave named "Tom or Peter, who is a runaway, but who passed himself off as free." Formerly belonging to Joseph Petit of New Orleans, the slave was returned to Gayoso under guard with

[14]Gayoso to Carondelet, No. 107, June 14, 1792. Another copy of this letter is in AGI, PC, leg. 1441.

[15]*Papers in Relation to the Official Conduct of Governour Sargent*, 9; Dunbar Rowland (ed.), *The Mississippi Territorial Archives, 1798–1803* (Nashville, 1903), 89–92.

[16]Gayoso to Carondelet, No. 29, Natchez, April 3, 1792, AGI, PC, leg. 41.

[17]William Blount to Gayoso, March 8, 1791, AGI, PC, leg. 204, and cited in William H. Masterson, "William Blount and the Establishment of the Southwest Territory, 1790–1791," ETHS *Publications* (1951), 23 n.

a request from Robertson that "the Property of the Citizens of the United States" be equally protected in the dominions of Spain. Robertson said he was sending a Mr. Andrew Jackson with the slave. Jackson, no stranger to Natchez, would soon be married there. Robertson expressed the hope that the mutual return of stolen property between Spanish Louisiana and Tennessee would be desirable.[18] In 1792 the United States proposed an official agreement with Spain regarding the extradition of escaped fugitives.[19]

Escaped fugitives or ordinarily peaceful Natchez settlers had one thing in common—they all liked to visit the twelve Natchez taverns, particularly on Saturdays or court days. Bouligny had observed in 1785, "Every time that an inhabitant comes to present his complaint to the commandant he passes the entire day in the town of Natchez where it is the custom, particularly of the common people, to deliver themselves up to drink with the greatest excess. This gives rise to disputes and fights, which occasion great injuries and inspire in the vicious ones a greater desire to come to the town in order to become intoxicated than does the importance of the complaint that they have to present." [20]

It was not possible to close the taverns permanently, nor was it politic; but Gayoso did the next best thing by regulating their hours of opening and closing and the type of behavior permitted therein, forbidding certain card games, and attempting to hold the tavern keepers personally liable for damages done in their establishments. Those who allowed unruly behavior, who sold liquor to slaves, or who violated other provisions of Gayoso's regulation could be fined a maximum of seventy-five dollars and banished from the district permanently.[21]

In general, litigation in Natchez was no different from that of other areas in Spanish Louisiana, with the possible exception of the

[18]James Robertson to Gayoso, Nashville, May 17, 1790, AGI, PC, leg. 203, in Corbitt, "Papers from the Spanish Archives," No. 23 (1951), 86.
[19]Projected Return of Prisoners Convention with Spanish Government, March, 1792, in *American State Papers, Foreign Relations,* I, 257–58.
[20]Bouligny to Miró, August 22, 1785, in Kinnaird (ed.), *Spain in the Mississippi Valley,* Part II, 138.
[21]Juan Cali *et al.* to Gayoso, Natchez, June 26, 1792, Natchez Chancery Court Records, Vol. D, 108–109.

fact that many cases were held in English, particularly after Gayoso arrived. "The processes were simple, but rigorous, and summary; and many of their maxims of law seem to have been founded in the highest wisdom and equity," related one observer of Spanish jurisprudence.[22] William Dunbar added in his journal, "British property is in perfect security, and an Englishman may come here and recover his debts, and obtain justice as soon as in Westminister [sic] Hall." [23]

As governor, Gayoso was the chief magistrate and possessed the power to adjudicate disputes and arrange settlements. In Natchez Saturday was court day, and Gayoso spent virtually the entire day hearing complaints of various types and rendering his decisions.[24] The most common cases were those involving debts, created through either violation of contract or simple refusal to pay. Claiborne described the procedure generally followed:

> Debts were promptly collected. The initial process was by petition, setting forth the amount of the claim and the consideration, and all the circumstances, whereupon an order issued to the party to appear on a certain day, and arbitrators, usually the best men in the community, were designated by the commandant to decide the matter, a tribunal preferable to the jury system as it is now conducted, when the highest rights of property, depending on intricate questions of law, are submitted to men, often notoriously ignorant and corrupt, picked up in the grog-shops around the court-house.[25]

The right of a trial by jury and the procedural safeguards developed over centuries in Anglo-Saxon jurisprudence were not established in Natchez, but it is doubtful if the settlers concerned themselves over their absence.[26] Property owners were most con-

[22]Ingraham, *The South-west by a Yankee*, II, 263–64.

[23]Quoted in Claiborne, *Mississippi*, 137.

[24]Gayoso to Andrew Ellicott, Natchez, March 25, 1797, copy, Southern Boundary MSS., U.S. and Spain, Andrew Ellicott, National Archives, Record Group 76.

[25]Claiborne, *Mississippi*, 136–37.

[26]The best information on the legal system in Spanish Louisiana is from Daniel Clark, in Carter (ed.), *The Territorial Papers of the United States, IX: Orleans*, 36–39. The lack of a jury system was condemned by H. A. Bullard, "Louisiana Historical Researches," *DeBow's Review*, III (January, 1847), 33.

cerned with the government's protection of their property rights, and in this Gayoso was an impartial judge.

In a typical case between Benjamin Farrar and Isaac Gaillard, Gayoso drew up a list of sixteen leading citizens of the district. Each litigant was to examine the list and choose two arbitrators. No one who was related to either litigant was included on the list; and if either party preferred someone not on the list, they could make the choice. Every effort was made to deal honestly and impartially. In 1794 Stephen Minor brought suit to recover a long over due bill owed him by Anthony Hutchins. Notwithstanding the close friendship between Minor and Gayoso, or Minor's official position as adjutant of the Natchez post, Gayoso allowed Hutchins his day in court and made every attempt to hear his side of the story before decreeing that Minor should pay Hutchins for some cheeses delivered to the government in 1786 and that Hutchins should pay Minor for the past-due note.

Samuel Forman, who had been granted land under generous conditions by Gayoso, was called into court and forced to honor his contract with David Ferguson. Forman had promised to deliver 2,500 pounds of tobacco to Ferguson, and Gayoso decreed that in default Forman was liable for the value of the produce.

Women and mulattoes were afforded the protection of the laws; and when a slave belonging to Grand-Pré stole some merchandise, he was brought to trial on the same basis as if he had been a free man.[27] Not included within the scope of the Natchez civil courts, however, were members of the armed forces or of the Roman Catholic Church. They enjoyed the prevalent system of *fueros*, which meant being tried in special courts composed of their own personnel.[28]

An interesting case involving the reputation of a young girl

---

[27]Gayoso to Miró, No. 99, Natchez, May 14, 1791, AGI, PC, leg. 41; Elas du Bouchet to Gayoso, Natchez, February 22, 1793, AGI, PC, leg. 47.

[28]Clark's statement in Carter (ed.), *Territorial Papers of the United States, IX: Orleans*, 36. Those who fled to refuge in the church were entitled to the *fuero de guerra*. Bernardo de Gálvez to José de Gálvez, No. 316, New Orleans, October 16, 1779, AGI, PC, leg. 223-B. Cases between a military officer and a civilian were also tried in a military court. See the 1792 case involving Cadet Carlos Daunoy and several New Orleans residents, in AGI, PC, leg. 206.

illustrates Gayoso's techniques in handling difficult decisions. Elizabeth Denham became pregnant by a n'er-do-well named Benjamin Kimball. Kimball helped her abort, and then, adding insult to injury, he spread the rumor that the girl's own father was responsible. When Gayoso heard of the matter he ordered his *alguaciles* (constables) Henry Hunter and Daniel Clark to investigate the story. The governor issued a proclamation forbidding the repetition of the unfounded story. When Reuben Denham, the girl's father, brought a suit against Kimball for "making false statements and debauching Elizabeth," the errant lover was banished from the district.

In his act of taking possession of the Natchez post, Gayoso had sworn to carry out the Spanish laws and not enter civil actions against the poor. In the case of Ahern, mentioned above, it is evident that Gayoso used great leniency in dealing with the less fortunate members of his community who ran afoul of the law.[29] As a matter of fact, Gayoso's legal decisions were often tempered with mercy. When George Elhom, a Dane, arrived in Natchez with the astonishing proposition that the district secede from Spanish rule and form an independent state with Georgia, which was expected to leave the United States, Gayoso acted with great moderation. Only four years had passed since Georgia commissioners had arrived in Natchez with a similar suggestion in the Bourbon County matter, but Gayoso's handling of Elhom was quite different. He invited the visitor to spend several weeks in his own home and found, after sounding out the Dane's ideas, that they were harmless dreams with no backing from the United States. Still, such mutterings could lead to an overt action on the part of Natchez residents if carried to extremes, so Gayoso recommended that Elhom be sent to Cádiz at royal expense and given a post at the Royal Observatory. There his scientific training could be put to good use without endangering the security of Louisiana.[30]

[29]Gayoso's act of taking possession of the governorship of Natchez, New Orleans, May 25, 1789, AGI, PC, leg. 140; Gayoso to Carondelet, No. 20, Natchez, March 27, 1792, AGI, PC, leg. 41.
[30]Las Casas to Miró, Confidential, Havana, February 4, 1791, AGI, PC, leg. 1446; Gayoso to Miró, No. 86, Natchez, May 11, 1791, AGI, PC, leg. 41; Gayoso to Miró, Natchez, May 29, 1791, enclosed in Las Casas to Conde del Campo de Alange, Havana, October 5, 1791, AGS, Guerra Moderna, leg. 6928.

Gayoso's brand of personal justice was often misunderstood by those not acquainted with Spanish customs and procedures. When the young English traveler, Francis Baily came to Natchez in 1797 with a cargo of merchandise, he contracted with the secretary of government, Joseph Vidal, to buy the entire lot for a stipulated price. Vidal tendered paper currency to Baily, which the Englishman declined to accept when he learned the certificates generally bore a 12 per cent discount in New Orleans where they were redeemed.

Baily insisted that Vidal pay hard currency. Gayoso's decision sheds considerable light, not only on legal procedure and philosophy, but on the practical matter of currency in Natchez:

> Certificates on the Royal Treasury at New-Orleans are considered throughout this Province as Cash, and no one can refuse to receive them unless it was expressly covenanted this payment should be made in silver or gold, in which case only the debtor can be compelled to pay in specie; and the contract between the Petitioner and Don Joseph Vidal being only for a certain number of Dollars, without specifying that the payment should be made in silver, Francis Baily must receive the certificate which Don Joseph Vidal tenders him in payment of his Debt; to do otherwise would be overthrowing the practice established not only in this place but in others of greater note, such as Cadiz and other Cities in the Dominions of his Majesty; and in deciding thus the said Bailey receives all the Justice to which he can lay claim; nor is he entitled to demand that Don Joseph Vidal shall give security of any kind after paying the debt which he owes him.[31]

The impetuous Baily stormed into the governor's office and demanded that he indicate the law book which required him to accept such paper currency. This was a mistake. According to Baily's account, Gayoso grew furious, threatened him with the

[31]Gayoso's decision, Natchez, May 25, 1797, and accompanying documents in the Baily Case are in the Natchez Chancery Court Records, Vol. G, folios 258–62; Baily's account of the proceedings, in which he claimed his life was endangered by the governor, is in Baily, *Journal*, 289, 299, 331; *cf.* Ellicott to Timothy Pickering (Secretary of State), Natchez, June 4, 1797, Southern Boundary MSS., U.S. and Spain, I.

horrors of "the Callibouse," and laying his hand on his own chest, declared that *he* was the law, and as *he* decided, the case was thereby determined. Baily demanded complete copies of all papers regarding the case so that he could appeal in New Orleans to the governor-general. Carondelet upheld Gayoso's decision, however; and Baily learned the truth of the statement, "Any opposition to the will of the Governor was generally very promptly got rid of, but the execution of justice was just as prompt." [32]

Gayoso was also guided in his legal decisions by numerous edicts emanating from New Orleans. Miró decreed that lawful interest in Natchez could not exceed 5 per cent per annum, nor could interest be charged on interest as the merchants planned to do. It is noted, however, that in special contracts between individuals in Natchez, stipulations were often made for interest to be charged in excess of this amount, sometimes as much as 15 per cent.[33]

In 1792, when numerous complaints from settlers throughout Louisiana reached the governor-general about the commandants' administration of justice, Carondelet issued an order requiring the commandants to keep complete records of all legal decisions, including the date, names of the parties, depositions of witnesses, and the decisions. Two books were to be maintained—one, a *Livre de Sentences,* and the other, a *Livre des Amendes*—in order to insure full and impartial justice throughout the province.[34]

When anyone died in the Natchez District, it was Gayoso's duty to make a detailed inventory of the party's estate and seal the contents in a trunk or house. If the deceased left no will or provision

[32]Willey, "Natchez in the Olden Times," in Claiborne, *Mississippi,* 529.

[33]"It is declared that what is called lawful interest, in the stipulations between the inhabitants of Natchez and their creditors, is to be understood at the rate of *five per centum only,* and the same, by delay in the payment thereof, shall not be converted into principal, and interest be paid upon interest, because that would be manifest usury. The accounts of the said inhabitants shall be settled upon this principle, *abating* such as have been previously paid at a higher rate than is here prescribed. . . ." Miró's decree, quoted in Robert Lowry and William H. McCardle, *A History of Mississippi* (Jackson, Mississippi, 1891), 133–34. When Pedro Surget charged Edward McCabe 15 per cent interest, the debtor appealed to Gayoso for the over-charge. McBee, *Natchez Court Records,* 276.

[34]Carondelet's proclamation (in French), New Orleans, December 4, 1792, AGI, PC, leg. 206.

for paying his creditors, the goods were sold at public auction. The proceeds were used to pay the creditors and defray the costs of auctioning the goods and preparing the legal paperwork; the remainder was distributed among the heirs. Specific regulations regarding the rights of minors (under the age of 25) were also issued by Carondelet.[35]

The regulations most consistently violated in Natchez pertained to religious matters and, as in the United States, the quest of Protestant sects in the Natchez District for open freedom of worship finally led to nascent stirrings of political democracy. The regulations concerning religious freedom in Louisiana were well-known to the new settlers, many of whom marveled at the radical change in traditional Spanish policy.

Miró's proclamation of April 20, 1789, announced to the western settlers that those immigrants wishing to settle on land in Louisiana "will not be molested on religious matters, although no other public worship will be permitted to be publickly exercised than that of [the] Roman catholic Church. . . ."[36] This change in traditional Spanish policy was dictated by the circumstances in Natchez, populated as it was by Anglo-Saxons from the beginning. A 1792 religious decree pertaining to Louisiana explained that the purpose of the freedom of worship was to permit the settlement of the district first. Then, it was planned, several English-speaking Irish priests, operating from the only churches permitted in Natchez, "should teach and attract the colonists, their children and families to our Religion with the suavity and good method which the Church counselled."[37]

With the exception of this statement on proselytizing, the following observation of Claiborne is reasonably accurate:

> A large majority of the settlers were Protestants, who enjoyed their faith and the right of private worship. No

[35]Carondelet to Martin Duralde (commandant of Opelousas Post), New Orleans, September 14, 1795, AGI, PC, leg. 22.

[36]Miró's concessions to Westerners, New Orleans, April 20, 1789, AGI, PC, leg. 2370, printed in Corbitt, "Papers from the Spanish Archives," XX (1948), 104–105.

[37]A royal decree, San Lorenzo, November 30, 1792, BN, Vol. 19,248, folios 233–36.

attempt was made to proselyte or proscribe them, nor was there any official interference unless the parties in their zeal, or under indiscreet advisers, became offensively demonstrative. There was, in fact, more religious freedom and toleration for Protestants in the Natchez district, than Catholics, and dissenters from the ruling denomination, enjoyed in either Old or New England. . . . It was a community of Protestants under a strictly Catholic dynasty, in an age of intolerance. But here there was little persecution, no proscription, no civil distinctions made, and never any interference except, in one or two instances, when the preservation of public order was imperative.[38]

The genesis of Spain's religious policy for the Natchez District dates to 1785 when Miró advocated the establishment of a parish for Natchez, ministered to by three Irish priests or by any who spoke English, for the purpose of converting through preaching and teaching the non-Catholics there. Viceroy Gálvez approved the request and forwarded it to the Minister of the Indies, his uncle, José de Gálvez.[39] The Council of State in Spain tentatively approved the plan and asked Miró in Louisiana and Zéspedes at St. Augustine to draw up suitable plans for their disposition.[40]

The Bishop of Salamanca reported to the Marqués de Sonora (José de Gálvez) in 1786 that the Royal College of Irishmen of the University of Salamanca had recently been reorganized so that all its students were young aspirants just embarking on a study of philosophy. The only ordained priests were William Savage, described as "a subject of great merit and of complete confidence, of whose zeal, education and conduct and his other qualities I am well informed;" and the rector of the university, Patrick Cortes. The bishop wrote that the present needs of the Irish college precluded the absence of its rector. Although Father Savage was supposed to

[38]Claiborne, *Mississippi*, 136–37.
[39]Miró to Conde de Gálvez, No. 228, New Orleans, September 5, 1785, enclosed with comments in Conde de Gálvez to Josef de Gálvez, No. 56, "de preferencia," Mexico, October 27, 1785, AHN, ESTADO, leg. 3888 *bis;* Friar Angel de Revilla Godos had exercised temporary religious duties in Natchez, 1781–1782, as military chaplain: Revilla Godos to Miró, Natchez, November 3, 1782, AGI, PC, leg. 195.
[40]Junta de Estado to Conde de Gálvez, El Pardo, April 5, 1786, draft, AHN, ESTADO, leg. 3888 *bis.*

return to Ireland in fulfillment of his oath when he entered the college, the bishop, in recognition of the many favors bestowed by the Crown upon the college, promised to persuade Father Savage to accept the Natchez mission. He also suggested writing to a number of priests in Ireland, Seville, Cádiz, and Bilbao, where Irish priests were ministering to the people, in an effort to locate several more who would be willing to come to America.[41]

By the end of the summer the bishop had located five priests for the American mission: Miguel Lamport, a resident of the city of Cádiz; Gregorio White and Constantino MacKenna of Seville; Friar Bernardo Lunney, a Dominican from San Pablo in Seville; and William Savage, vice-rector of the College of Nobles from Ireland at the University of Salamanca. They had agreed to come on the condition that their spiritual mission in "the Floridas" not extend beyond ten years and that all their travel expenses be assumed by the Crown. The Marqués de Sonora approved Savage, Lamport, White, and MacKenna, but he asked if they were willing to travel at royal expense with an advance of three thousand *reales* each, a monthly salary of thirty pesos each, no conditions on the time they would spend in America, and no guarantee of salary should they return to Spain. This type of contract had been signed in 1778 by the priests Michael O'Reilly and Thomas Hasset to take care of the St. Augustine, Florida, mission.[42]

The four priests concerned agreed with the terms as outlined by José de Gálvez, except for the salary which they asked be raised to forty pesos monthly. The contracts were signed in 1786, and royal orders were subsequently issued in 1787.[43] When they arrived in New Orleans in August of that year they were already broke, and Miró advanced them five months salary to cover their

[41]Andrés, Bishop of Salamanca, to Marqués de Sonora, Salamanca, April 29, May 16, 1786, *ibid*.

[42]Andrés, Bishop of Salamanca, to Marqués de Sonora, Villa de Miranda del Castañar, September 28, 1786; Marqués de Sonora to the Bishop, San Lorenzo, October 18, 1786, AHN, ESTADO, leg. 3888 *bis*.; Michael J. Curley, *Church and State in the Spanish Floridas* (Washington, 1940).

[43]Savage signed at Salamanca, October 29, 1786; MacKenna, at Seville, November 11, 1786; White, at Seville on November 14; Michael Lamport evidently signed, but without date or place. See AHN, ESTADO, leg. 3888 *bis*.

expenses and pay for their debts occasioned by a delay of two and one-half months in Cádiz.[44]

Michael (or Miguel as he was known in Spanish records) Lamport took over the religious duties at Mobile where he served the post and the Anglo-American settlers on the Tensaw until his death on August 22, 1789.[45]

Constantino MacKenna arrived in New Orleans with the other three priests and evidently never went to Natchez at all, for on February 3, 1792, he was appointed parish priest of the Spanish post on the Tombigbee River, and later in the year, transferred to Mobile. The closest he came to Natchez was to serve as parish priest of Bayou Sara from May 18, 1801, until his death on May 12, 1802.[46]

William Savage went to Natchez where he served as parish priest until his death on April 18, 1793.[47] Gregorio White took over the duties of priest at Cole's Creek until the death of Savage, when he took over at Natchez. Although he was later recommended for the parish of Ascension de la Fourche, he declined the appointment, retired at half pension, and soon returned to Europe in 1800.[48]

Another Irish priest, Father Francis Lennan, subsequently arrived in the province and was named priest at the newly established post of Nogales (present-day Vicksburg, Mississippi), in 1792. The following year he was appointed first to the parish of Cole's Creek and then to Pensacola. He left Pensacola in 1794 and was established once again in Natchez, where he served as the last priest in the Spanish district. When the Spaniards evacuated the district, Father Lennan was charged with caring for the sacred vessels and church

[44]Priests to (Marqués de Sonora), New Orleans, October 15, 1787; Miró to Antonio Porlier, No. 4, New Orleans, October 25, 1787; and approval by Marqués de Sonora to the intendant and governor of Louisiana (Miró), Madrid, March 23, 1789; all in AHN, ESTADO, leg. 3888 *bis*.

[45]Service and payroll records of Lamport, AGI, PC, leg. 538-B; Rev. B. J. Bekkers, "The Catholic Church in Mississippi during Colonial Times," *Publications* of the Mississippi Historical Society, VI (1902), 357; Caroline Maude Burson, *The Stewardship of Don Esteban Miró, 1782-1792* (New Orleans, 1940), 213.

[46]Payroll records of MacKenna, AGI, PC, leg. 538-B.

[47]Payroll records of Savage, *ibid.*; Gayoso to Carondelet, No. 262, Natchez, April 18, 1793, AGI, PC, leg. 42.

[48]Payroll records of White, AGI, PC, leg. 538-B; Gayoso to Carondelet, No. 548, Natchez, September 2, 1794, AGI, PC, leg. 30.

records. He moved to Punta Cortada first, and finally to the St. Francis Parish at New Feliciana, later known as St. Francisville, Louisiana.[49]

Father John Brady, a Carmelite friar, was appointed in 1795 to assist Lennan with the Natchez post's spiritual duties. He shared the duties with Father Lennan until the evacuation in 1798, when he moved to the Parish of Carmen on the Red River. In 1801 he was made priest of the Baton Rouge parish, where he remained until after 1805.[50] Willey remembers Friar Brady as "the best shot, the best rider, and the best judge of horses in the district." [51]

Another Irish priest seems to have occupied the spiritual duties of Natchez, although he is not listed among the regularly appointed priests of Louisiana. Father Malone was described by Willey as an amiable fellow, "with a wink and a joke, and a blessing and an *almo* for every one," always welcome at weddings and dinners. Willey said Father Malone had only one weakness: on St. Patrick's Day his Irish patriotism exceeded his capacity to indulge and he inevitably became inebriated.[52]

In addition to the regular priests, three men served at different times as sacristans at Natchez. The first, Juan Bautista Riao, served from 1788 until 1791.[53] Conrad Heroldy, an ex-sergeant in the Louisiana Infantry Regiment, was appointed by Gayoso as sacristan replacing Riao, an appointment approved by Miró, who was in Louisiana the guardian of the Church. It was a formality to have the bishop of Louisiana ratify the selection made by the governors.[54] Josef Solibellas occupied the post of sacristan at the same low salary of fifteen pesos monthly, but remained only from March

[49]*Ibid.*; payroll records of Lennan, AGI, PC, leg. 538-A.

[50]Payroll records of Brady, AGI, PC, leg. 538-B; Carondelet to Grand-Pré, New Orleans, September 17, 1795, AGI, PC, leg. 22; Grand-Pré's Census of Baton Rouge, June 30, 1805, AGI, PC, leg. 142-A; Grand-Pré to Carondelet, No. 72, Natchez, October 10, 1795, AGI, PC, leg. 32.

[51]Willey, "Natchez in the Olden Times," in Claiborne, *Mississippi*, 527.

[52]*Ibid.*

[53]Payroll records of Riao, AGI, PC, leg. 538-B; Gayoso to Miró, No. 91, Natchez, May 12, 1791, AGI, PC, leg. 41.

[54]*Ibid.*; payroll records of Heroldy [also Herol], AGI, PC, leg. 538-B; Luis, Bishop of Louisiana, to Gayoso, Natchez, May 19, 1796, AGI, PC, leg. 47.

through December of 1795, when once again Heroldy took over the duties.[55]

Gayoso's religious duties were fairly well-defined by law and custom. In America, the governors, governors-general, viceroys, and other royal officials represented the Spanish king. Since the Papal See had conferred upon the Spanish monarchs during the Middle Ages the *Patronato Real*, whereby responsibility for church affairs other than dogma was granted to their royal persons, the Catholic monarchs had seen fit to extend this privilege to the Americas following the sixteenth-century conquests. Thus, the governors had exclusive power over creating new bishoprics, dioceses, parishes, and other church posts. The men they selected to fill important church jobs were always ratified by the appropriate church official, but in practice royal prerogatives were never seriously challenged.

Since one of the duties of the vice-patron of the church in Natchez was to superivse the construction of new churches when approved by the Royal Treasury and governors, Gayoso spent considerable time and energy on the two parishes within his district. The first church at Natchez was actually begun by Grand-Pré, acting under the orders of Miró.[56] It was not until 1790, however, that actual construction of a church was approved by Miró after Gayoso sent him plans of the proposed building, drawn by Gilberto Guillemard, famed New Orleans architect and a longtime military engineer in the service of Spain. Guillemard estimated the church would cost $3,748.50 to build; and Miró approved the costs by signing a contract with Francisco Langlois, a militia officer with a distinguished record.[57] Evidently Langlois did not construct the church, for in June, 1791, Gayoso wrote that John Mills, who was

[55]Payroll records of Solibellas, AGI, PC, leg. 538-B.

[56]Miró to Navarro, New Orleans, January 7, 1788, copy in AGI, PC, transcript in Mississippi Provincial Archives, III, 217–21. This, of course, refers to the Spanish period. The Capuchins maintained a religious community at Natchez from 1726 until the massacre. Claude L. Vogel, *The Capuchins in French Louisiana, 1722–1766,* Vol. VII, Catholic University of America *Studies in American Church History* (Washington, 1928), 43–46; Power, *Memento of Old and New Natchez,* 78.

[57]Gayoso to Miró, New Orleans, March 29, 1790, AGI, PC, leg. 41.

building the Natchez church, had turned over the finishing touches
to a subordinate while Mills went to Cole's Creek to build another
church.[58]

On Sunday, June 12, 1791, Father William Savage called his
flock to a special benediction service for the new church. A large
number of prominent citizens of both sexes attended the ceremony,
after which they attended a party given by Gayoso at his home.
Following the services Gayoso noted the great pleasure the people
obviously felt about having a church and an opportunity to hear
a weekly sermon. Gayoso predicted that the majority of the people
would allow their children to follow Roman Catholicism as they
grew up.

The church was complete except for the windows. Noting the
absence of a baptismal font, Gayoso sketched a four-foot square
enclosure at one corner and provided for another at one side. The
two additions added $20.50 to the cost of the church.[59]

It was not until the middle of January, 1792, that the finishing
touches were placed on the Natchez parish church. Even then,
there was no church bell, and Gayoso asked the governor-general
to order two (one for Cole's Creek) from Havana or to buy one
which belonged to Captain Luis Bertucat of the Louisiana Infantry
Regiment from Charles Norwood.[60]

Father Savage called the church the Iglesia Parroquial del
Salvador del Mundo de Natchez (Parish Church of Our Savior of
the World in Natchez). Because it lacked candles and because the
people of Natchez were not expected to tithe, all expenses had to
be assumed by the Spanish government. Gayoso asked approval for
supplying fifty pounds of wax candles for the year and expressed
his opinion that when the population increased and the church took

[58]Gayoso to Miró, Natchez, June 16, 1791, AGI, PC, transcript in Mississippi
Archives, Spanish Dominion, III, 611–16.

[59]Gayoso to Miró, No. 124, Natchez, June 15, 1791, AGI, PC, leg. 41.
According to one historian, the church erected in the center of town was a
two-story frame structure. Rowland (ed.), *Encyclopedia of Mississippi History*,
I, 378–79.

[60]Gayoso to Miró, New Orleans, December 19, 1791; Gayoso to Carondelet,
New Orleans, February 13, 1792, AGI, PC, leg. 41.

on more members, the people could support the church as was customary in other areas of Spanish America.[61]

Gayoso also approved the repair of the priest's house in 1792 and in 1796 authorized John Scott to spend $67.50 to build an additional room for the assistant pastor, Friar John Brady. As in all cases involving expenditures for the church, the governor approved initial expenses subject to the ratification and payment by the intendant in New Orleans. In this case, the intendant approved of Gayoso's expenses.[62]

The church at Cole's Creek was built on land which Gayoso purchased for $2,000 from James Elliot in 1789. The following year Gayoso had Guillemard draw up plans and make the required estimates, as was customary for anything the Spanish government proposed to build. The cost of the church at Cole's Creek was estimated at $5,658.12½.[63] By December, 1791, Gayoso wrote that it was almost finished; and he asked for a priest, a bell, and the necessary religious materials. By July, 1792, the church was complete, but it consisted only of four bare walls. Gayoso reiterated his request for furnishings, a bell, and a sacristan.[64] When it came time to appoint a priest, Gayoso recommended Father Gregory White.[65]

Gayoso was also responsible for suggesting someone to take charge of the spiritual duties at the post of Nogales. In most cases the governor-general approved the initial suggestion and forwarded the official appointments.[66] It was a difficult duty for two reasons: there were never enough priests in Louisiana to take care of

[61]Gayoso to Miró, New Orleans, December 19, 1791, AGI, PC, leg. 41.

[62]Gayoso to Carondelet, No. 164, Natchez, September 13, 1792, ibid.; Morales to Gayoso, New Orleans, August 17, 1796, AGI, PC, leg. 23.

[63]Gayoso to Miró, No. 15, Natchez, September 15, 1789; Gayoso to Miró, New Orleans, March 29, 1790; Gayoso to Miró, No. 160, Natchez, July 27, 1791; all in AGI, PC, leg. 41.

[64]Gayoso to Miró, New Orleans, December 19, 1791; Gayoso to Carondelet, New Orleans, February 13, 1792; No. 134, Natchez, July 23, 1792, all ibid.

[65]Gayoso to Miró, December 19, 1791. Carondelet appointed Father White parish priest of Villa Gayoso on July 21, 1794: Gayoso to Carondelet, No. 548, Natchez, September 2, 1794, AGI, PC, leg. 30.

[66]Gayoso to Beauregard, Natchez, June 6, 1797, AGI, PC, leg. 43.

the province's needs and there was never enough money, with the possible exception of the Cathedral of St. Louis in New Orleans.[67]

Gayoso was jealous of any infringement of his powers as vice-patron of the church, as indicated by his quarrel with Father Savage. Without seeking permission from Gayoso, who held the keys to the church prior to its dedication, Father Savage announced to the people that he would dedicate the church on May 29. Gayoso called on the priest to remonstrate with him for his public thought-lessness. The governor did not object to the date set for the cere-mony, but only the manner in which it was announced without his prior approval.[68]

Gayoso changed the date of dedication, and this action evidently picqued the priest. He set his watch an hour behind and caused the governor to wait in church for some time in full view of the people of Natchez. When Gayoso warned the priest that this behavior was unbecoming and that he should show more respect to the governor, the priest became surly. He offered many excuses for his conduct, all of which boiled down to one as far as Gayoso was concerned: lack of regard for the political head of the church in Natchez. The priest promised to present the sermon at a prearranged hour the following week, but he began the services an hour early. Gayoso took Grand-Pré, several officers, his secretary, and the surgeon with him as witnesses to call on Father Savage. Gayoso warned Father Savage that in America the priests were subordinate to the king's representatives. The priest claimed he would write directly to the Bishop of Havana, whereupon Gayoso reported the entire matter to the governor-general with the recommendation that the

[67]A contrary view is expressed in Major Amos Stoddard, *Sketches Historical and Descriptive of Louisiana* (Philadelphia, 1812), 316: "Burial and marriage fees were considerable; and these, added to their salaries, afforded the clergy a decent support." Although the bishop of Louisiana received annually $15,000 (compared to only $6,000 for the governor-general), the priests' annual salary ranged between $240 and $480. Payroll records of the Louisiana priests, AGI, PC, leg. 538-A and B; Berquin-Duvallon, *Vue de la colonie espagnole du Mississipi, ou des Provinces de Louisiane et Floride Occidentale, en l'année 1802* (Paris, 1803), 172–75, is highly critical of the Church in Louisiana. Fray Revilla Godos wrote that the fees he collected for services in Natchez were insufficient to make ends meet. Revilla Godos to Miró, November 3, 1782.

[68]Gayoso to Miró, No. 112, Natchez, May 30, 1791, AGI, PC, leg. 41.

vicar general of Louisiana, Father Patrick Walsh, reprimand the errant priest.[69]

If Gayoso was intolerant of any infringement of his gubernatorial prerogatives, he was more than tolerant of the various sects which seemed to flourish under his benign rule. Gayoso's religious policy aimed at persuasion through tact and diplomacy rather than at blunt proscription. The most important means of achieving the desired ends—the development of a Roman Catholic population in Natchez—was the preaching of fine sermons by a capable priest. Although Gayoso found fault with Father Savage's lack of respect, he was fair enough to praise the priest's remarkable preaching abilities. After Father Savage died, Gayoso knew well that the Natchez District had no suitable priest who could preach.[70] The inability of Spain to send a sufficient number of capable preachers to Natchez was the primary reason why her policy of evangelizing the Protestants there failed. Gayoso felt that the anti-Protestant hostility of Father Lennan, who took over the parish in 1794, seemed aimed at driving them out of the district. Yet, it was the Protestants, for the most part, who composed the wealthy, substantial, and reliable portion of the population. The few Catholics, "who are mainly Irish and not the best people of their nation," Gayoso wrote, "are of turbulent and intriguing spirits." Gayoso intended a policy of moderation and tacit approval of Protestant activities, provided they did not exceed the limits imposed by the Spanish laws.[71]

It was decreed that Protestants who wished to be married should be joined together by a Catholic priest, and under no circumstances could a Protestant minister perform the ceremony either in or outside the Natchez District if the couple intended to live in Natchez.[72] There is a legend, unsupported by documentary evidence, that in 1791 Mrs. Rachel Donaldson Robards was married to Andrew Jackson in a civil ceremony, performed by Colonel Thomas Green, Sr.,

[69]Gayoso to Carondelet, No. 26, Natchez, April 2, 1792, *ibid.*

[70]Gayoso to Duque de Alcudia (Manuel Godoy, Minister of State), Natchez, March 31, 1795, AGI, PC, leg. 2354.

[71]*Ibid.*

[72]Religious decree, November 30, 1792.

in his capacity as a justice for the Georgia-created Bourbon County.[73] Regardless of whether the ceremony was actually performed, the fact remains that they were not married by a Catholic priest as decreed by Spanish law for Natchez.

Until 1795 the religious activities of non-Catholic sects in Natchez were quiescent. Tolerance of Jews and Protestants was rather widespread. Benjamin Monsanto was the Jewish merchant, planter, and lumber dealer of Natchez. The Monsantos had been in Louisiana since the time of O'Reilly, and there is some question about whether that governor expelled a Monsanto in 1769 on religious grounds or whether the expulsion was caused by Monsanto's contraband and smuggling activities.[74]

The Jews caused no trouble in Natchez, but the situation with the Protestants differed. Although the law forbade Protestant pastors to practice in Louisiana,[75] it was not always obeyed. Gayoso had permitted a Baptist minister to preach a sermon in Natchez in 1791.[76] According to one reliable history of Protestantism in Mississippi, the first minister who came to Natchez was the

[73]There is no documentary evidence available to prove that Andrew Jackson was married in this fashion, but most accounts of this period in Jackson's life mention similar events as probable. Eron Rowland, *Andrew Jackson's Campaign against the British* (New York, 1926), 17–22; Edith Wyatt Moore, "The Marriage of General Andrew Jackson and Mrs. Robards," Natchez *Democrat*, Pilgrimages Edition (March, 1942), 11; Pauline Wilcox Burke, *Emily Donelson of Tennessee* (2 vols.; Richmond, 1941), I, 17–18.

[74]Forman, *Narrative*, 56, describes the Monsantos as "the most kind and hospitable of people." Documents on the Monsanto family in Natchez and Louisiana include his last will and testament (Benjamin Monsanto), in McBee (ed.), *Natchez Court Records*, 116–17; inventory and succession of Isaac Monsanto, May 7, 1778, Pointe Coupée Parish records, New Roads, Louisiana [furnished transcript through the kindness of Winston DeVille]; and a list of references to the Monsanto family from Dr. Bertram W. Korn to Jack D. L. Holmes, Wynecote, Pennsylvania, November 15, 1963. The expulsion of Monsanto by O'Reilly in 1769 is explained by David K. Bjork as "on account of their industries, and not for the religion which they professed" in "The Establishment of Spanish Rule in the Province of Louisiana, 1762–1770," (Ph.D. dissertation, University of California, 1923), 144; and by Kinnaird "for the reason that all three are undesirable on account of their businesses and the religion they profess" in *Spain in the Mississippi Valley*, Part I, 103; both translate the same document: O'Reilly to Arriaga, No. 3, October 17, 1769, AGI, SD, 80–1–7. This writer has not seen a copy of the original document.

[75]Houck, *History of Missouri*, III, 202.

[76]Forman, *Narrative*, 57.

Reverend Samuel Swayze, a Congregationalist who arrived in 1773 and proceeded to establish the "Jersey Settlement" on the Homochitto River. Following this establishment of the "first Protestant Church ever organized in this country," Swayze began a vigorous ministry that lasted until the Spaniards took control of the Natchez District. Swayze's religious activities were then confined to a private reading of his Holy Bible in the canebrake while seated in a hollow of a large sycamore tree. Public worship was forbidden, but it was secretly continued. If the coast was clear, a cow's horn was blown on Sunday morning to assemble the believers for service. When Swayze died, his son, although not ordained, took his place. When the younger Swayze died, the church declined also.[77]

The climate of religious toleration, the live-and-let-live attitude of Gayoso, received a rude jolt in 1795. The arrival of Father Lennan the previous year had precipitated the change. Father White had had a seizure, perhaps caused by epilepsy, while attempting to perform marriage ceremonies for a large number of Natchez residents. When the secretary, Joseph Vidal, persuaded the people to return to their homes in an effort to prevent their discovering White's condition, they misunderstood and thought this represented a change in Spanish policy toward the Natchez Protestants. Father Lennan did nothing to dissuade them of this notion; rather, he added fuel to the fire of their doubts.[78]

Several days later a number of prominent Natchez planters, including Ezekiel Forman, Ebenezer Rees, and Joseph Bernard, visited Gayoso and asked for an official explanation of Spain's attitude toward the Protestants in Natchez. Gayoso promised to give them a complete and unequivocal statement the following week. When they returned, Gayoso suggested that they all reaffirm their loyalty to the Spanish government, and the king would at the same

[77]Rev. John G. Jones, *A Concise History of the Introduction of Protestantism into Mississippi and the Southwest* (St. Louis, 1866), 12–17. This narrative, while not objective, is interesting because of the personal acquaintance which the author had with various people who remembered how it was in Spanish Natchez. The Rev. Jedediah Smith, a Connecticut, Yale-trained Presbyterian, arrived and died at Natchez in 1776. McBee (ed.), *Natchez Court Records*, 600.

[78]Gayoso to Lennan, Natchez, March 21, 1795, copy enclosed with comments of Gayoso to Carondelet, No. 61, Confidential, Natchez, March 21, 1795, AGI, PC, leg. 43.

time reaffirm his pledges of religious toleration toward the private worship by Protestants. Gayoso was able to prevent their forming an official petition to the king, on the assumption that conditions would calm down during his absence of eight to ten months from the district.[79]

Once, under pressure from the parish priest, Gayoso ordered the arrest of John Bolls, a ruling elder in the Presbyterian Church, who had violated the ban against public preaching.[80] But the governor was not so intolerant of other religions as this action might indicate. At another time he attended a sermon delivered by the Episcopalian, Adam Cloud, and on leaving, expressed his private belief in religious freedom to a friend, but added significantly, "You know I have a master." [81]

Adam Cloud had lived for many years in the Natchez District, and Gayoso had no desire to see him expelled, as William Vousdan wanted. During the crisis of 1793–1795, when it was believed that Kentuckians were launching an expedition against Louisiana, Cloud had made a trip to the United States and returned with a detailed report of their activities, composition of the expedition, plans, and other information of a highly important nature, which he revealed to Gayoso. Vousdan, a prominent planter known for his quarrelsome spirit (he was Anthony Hutchins' son-in-law as well), attempted to have Cloud ejected from Natchez, primarily because he coveted Cloud's property which lay adjacent to his. Vousdan reported that Cloud had instilled the spirit of rebellion in Vousdan's slaves, but an investigation by Gayoso revealed the opposite: Vousdan had on occasion persuaded Cloud's slaves to escape. Gayoso spoke with Vousdan and advised him to be quiet; but this only

[79]Gayoso to Carondelet, No. 617, Natchez, March 24, 1795, AGI, PC, leg. 41; Gayoso to Carondelet, No. 2, Confidential, Nogales, April 26, 1795, AGI, PC, leg. 43.

[80]Rev. T. L. Haman, "Beginnings of Presbyterianism in Mississippi," *Publications* of the Mississippi Historical Society, X (1909), 205. An interesting story of a Presbyterian is recounted in Pope, *A Tour*, 38: "I observed a young Kentuckean who had been educated in all the Strictness of Presbyterianism, from which he had apostatized, and embraced Anabaptism and Methodism, which he highly honoured, by using each Profession alternately, as Hypocrisy might suggest. . . ."

[81]Willey, "Natchez in the Olden Times," in Claiborne, *Mississippi*, 528.

angered him further, and he plotted to get his revenge on Cloud.[82]

Carondelet chose to believe the reports he had received that Cloud had not only preached in public, but had even shown the audacity to suggest a change in the loyalty of the people. Because he had violated the regulations on public preaching by non-Catholic ministers, Cloud was ordered out of the province without the benefit of a trial, which Carondelet was afraid might incite the people even more. Gayoso's intercession on Cloud's behalf availed little; the man was given a few days to settle his affairs, and then he and his family were forced to leave Natchez for New Orleans and subsequent expulsion from the province of Louisiana.[83]

Of all the Protestant sects in Natchez, none was more active than the Baptists in violation of the known restrictions on public ceremonies of a religious nature. The Baptists were not famed for their self-control nor for unwavering loyalty toward the Spanish government. A Connecticut Presbyterian named Ebenezer Dayton, whose own religious beliefs and his close connection with the Spanish government do not proclaim him as an unbiased observer, wrote that the Baptist preachers were "weak men, of weak minds, and illiterate, and too ignorant to know how inconsistent they act and talk . . . too weak and undesigning to lay any treasonable plans . . . but . . . they would call any chastisements from Government for their disobedience, persecution, and suffering for Christ. . . ."[84]

If this was the aim of the Baptists in Natchez, they went about it in the right way. Richard Curtis, Sr., who married Phoebe Jones,

[82]Gayoso to Carondelet, No. 59, Confidential, Natchez, February 12, 1795, AGI, PC, leg. 43. Adam Cloud lived at Villa Gayoso with his wife and three children in 1792. He owned three horses, fifteen cattle, ten pigs, and his land produced seventy minots of corn. Census of Natchez, 1792, AGI, PC, leg. 2353.
[83]Carondelet to Gayoso, New Orleans, March 7, 1795, AGI, PC, leg. 22; Gayoso to Carondelet, No. 623, Natchez, April 2, 1795, AGI, PC, leg. 43. His controversial sermon was discussed in Joseph Harrison to Francisco Lennan, November 24, 1794, AGI, PC, leg. 102: Patricio Walsh to Carondelet, New Orleans, February 28, 1795, *ibid.*
[84]Dayton to Gayoso, August 3, 1795, AGI, PC, leg. 202, quoted in Arthur P. Whitaker, *The Mississippi Question, 1795–1803, a Study in Trade, Politics, and Diplomacy* (New York, 1934), 63; a contrary view is in Z. T. Leavell, "Early Beginnings of Baptists in Mississippi," *Publications* of the Mississippi Historical Society, IV (1901), 245–53.

and brought his family from Virginia and Charleston to Natchez after 1780, was the first Baptist to operate in the district. They settled on Cole's Creek, hacked their homes out of the wilderness, and spent most of their Sundays praying and reading scriptures in the privacy of their own homes. Curtis died in 1784, and his son, Richard Curtis, Jr., assumed the preaching duties, ably assisted by John and Jacob Stampley, gifted "natural" preachers. The young Curtis had none of the reserve or respect for the law that his father had shown, and he soon embroiled his sect in an argument with the Catholic priests and the Spanish government.[85]

In the Spring of 1795, as the religious situation grew more tense in Natchez, Gayoso called Curtis to government house and asked him to swear that he would not preach in public again, under pain of confiscation of his goods and expulsion from the province.[86]

Curtis signed the agreement, but as soon as Gayoso left the province for top secret business up the Mississippi River, the Baptists operated openly. The crisis developed when David Green-leaf, a noted Natchez mechanic who built the first cotton gins in Natchez, decided to marry Phoebe Jones, the daughter of John Jones, who wanted the ceremony performed by her uncle, Richard Curtis, Jr. The couple arranged for an elaborate meeting in the woods. Greenleaf and his companions would ride south from Villa Gayoso, while Miss Jones and her entourage rode north. With a sign and countersign, they would meet and be married. Practical jokers in Greenleaf's party persuaded him to ride past the meeting without acknowledging the sign (or did he have cold feet?), but they returned within minutes and the couple laughingly rode to William Stampley's plantation and were married by torchlight.

The ceremony was secret, but what married couple are able to

---

[85]Jones, *History of Protestantism,* 19–32.

[86]*Ibid.,* 34; the document signed by Curtis on April 6, 1795, is in AGI, PC, leg. 22. It says nothing about confinement in the "Mexican silver mines" as Jones reports. It was a common myth, which seldom became reality, that all felons convicted by the Spaniards for crimes were automatically sent to the Mexican mines. If this were true, the labor supply in Mexico must have been plentiful indeed. Actually, the common penalty for those Americans in Natchez who violated a serious law was banishment from the district, usually to the United States. An analysis of the legal files in the Spanish archives supports this statement.

live together clandestinely? Greenleaf's fame as a mechanic and his numerous contacts with the Spanish government made him anything but inconspicuous. The secret was uncovered, and the Spanish priest demanded to know who had performed the illegal ceremony.

When it was discovered that not only had Curtis done the honors in the Greenleaf-Jones nuptials, but, in addition, had baptized William Hamberlin and Stephen deAlvo, acting commandant Grand-Pré issued orders for their arrest. But sentries posted on the roads leading to Curtis' home warned the trio, and they escaped through the wilderness to South Carolina, not to return during the Spanish rule.[87]

Having observed the repercussions possible in allowing the Protestants to worship openly, Carondelet wrote Grand-Pré that the Curtis case proved that "if disputes and quarrels over religious matters are not cut off at their roots or checked, they will have the most perverse and evil results." [88] The relationship between freedom of religion and political democracy was drawn by one severe critic of the Spanish action: "The name of Gayozo [sic] stood for that nonentity, the divine right of kings; Curtis for a government of the people and by the people. Gayozo enforced bondage; Curtis, glorified freedom." [89] It might be argued with equal logic that Gayoso stood for law and order and obedience to government, while Curtis represented rebellion, lawlessness, and irresponsibility.

The experience of Natchez with modified religious toleration had mixed results. As will be seen below, in studying the Natchez revolt of 1797, religious overtones were very important. On the other hand, the Natchez experiment was hailed as a success by such officers as Luis de Vilemont, who proposed that new Dutch settlers emigrating to Louisiana be given the same privileges in

[87]Grand-Pré to Carondelet, No. 1, Confidential, Natchez, July 9, 1795, AGI, PC, leg. 32; Jones, *History of Protestantism*, 35–49. Curtis set up a church called Salem when he returned in 1798. He died in Amite County on October 28, 1811, of cancer.
[88]Carondelet to Grand-Pré, New Orleans, July 26, 1795, AGI, PC, leg. 22.
[89]Charles H. Otken, "Richard Curtis in the Country of Natchez," *Publications* of the Mississippi Historical Society, III (1900), 152.

matters of religion as those successfully enjoyed in Natchez.[90]

It is difficult to discover just how widespread crime and lawlessness really were in Natchez during Gayoso's administration. Ingraham wrote that crimes were rare because the people of Louisiana
attached more importance to a criminal prosecution than inhabitants of the same area in later days.[91] When Governor Winthrop
Sargent took charge of the Mississippi Territory in 1798, however,
he felt that lawlessness was widespread.[92] Of course, Governor
Sargent had arrived at a difficult time of transition between two
governments when neither Spanish law nor yet American law prevailed, and the lawless elements took full advantage of the situation.

Gayoso's administration of justice was, for the most part, fair, impartial, and in keeping with Spanish legal traditions. When the case
seemed to require it, Gayoso was not above modifying written
laws, including his instructions, so long as justice was served. His
primary concern was to protect the rights of the Natchez inhabitants and create a law-abiding population, loyal to the Spanish
Crown. If this meant bending the laws, Gayoso did just that. If

[90]Petition of Luis de Vilemont, enclosed in Carondelet to Alcudia, New
Orleans, July 30, 1795, AHN, ESTADO, leg. 3890; another example is in
the petition of James Mackay asking for religious toleration for the settlers at
St. Andrew in Missouri: Mackay to Gayoso, St. Andrew on the Missouri,
November 28, 1798, AGI, PC, leg. 215-B.

[91]Ingraham, *The South-west by a Yankee*, II, 263–64, based on Timothy
Flint, *A Condensed Geography and History of the Western States or the
Mississippi Valley* (2 vols.; 3rd ed.; Cincinnati, 1833), I, 273–74.

[92]Sargent wrote, "Diffused over *our* Country, are Aliens of Various Characters and amongst them the most Abandoned of *Vilains* who have escaped from
the Chains and Prisons of Spain, and been Convicted of the Blackest of
Crimes. . . .We have no Prisons, no sufficient places of Confinement, and
the Vilest offenders therefore Calculate with some Certainty upon im-
punity. . . ." Sargent to Timothy Pickering, Natchez, December 20, 1798, in
Dunbar Rowland (ed.), *The Mississippi Territorial Archives, 1798-1803,
Executive Journals of Governor Winthrop Sargent and Governor William
Charles Cole Claiborne* (Nashville, 1905), 89; Andrew Ellicott had divided the
people of Natchez into three classes: 1) ambitious men seeking wealth and
fame, 2) fléeing debtors, and 3) fleeing criminals. From an early expression
of belief in representative government, Ellicott was persuaded that it should
not be practiced in Natchez. Ellicott to Secretary of State (Pickering), Camp,
7 miles from Natchez, September 24, 1797, Southern Boundary, U.S. and Spain,
I. William Dunbar said Natchez was a "country without Government or law."
Dunbar to Gayoso, (Natchez), April 15, 1798, AGI, PC, leg., 215-b.

stiff penalties and stern justice were required, Gayoso employed them because he believed his people should have respect for the majesty of the law. A few inhabitants complained about "arbitrary" administration of justice, but the vast majority approved of Gayoso's procedures and, in the final analysis, considered their governor a just and wise judge.

CHAPTER IV

The Natchez Economy

V ITAL to an understanding of the political and military aspects of Gayoso's administration of the Natchez District is an analysis of the economic fortunes of the settlers there. In 1789 Spain greatly modified its traditional restrictive mercantilistic policy toward her American colonies by allowing Louisiana to enjoy unusual economic freedom. The aim was not to promote free trade nor to extend these benefits to Louisiana and Natchez particularly on a permanent basis. Spain's goal was to attract American settlers into Spanish Louisiana.

Following the American Revolution the dammed-up population of the Atlantic seaboard burst through the mountain barriers of the Appalachians and Alleghanies seeking land and economic opportunity. Not for several decades did the United States government attempt to give these frontiersmen the liberal homesteads they demanded. By contrast the Spanish government at New Orleans beckoned them toward free lands in Natchez.

Representative Thomas Scott of Pennsylvania warned his fellow Congressmen in a debate over land policy: "There are seven thousand souls waiting for lands; they will have them here or else-where; but there is some danger, if they cannot be accomodated within the boundaries of the United States, they will do one of two things: either move into the Spanish territory, where they are not al-together uninvited, and become an accession of power to a foreign nation, forming to us a dangerous frontier; or they will take this course, move on the United States territory, and take possession without your leave . . . ." [1] The frontiersmen did both.[2]

The lists of immigrants arriving in 1789 and 1790 show that many Americans were attracted to Natchez by the new policies of Miró and Gayoso.[3] The immigrants brought with them those goods which were most wanted at Natchez—tools, farming equipment, iron, and hardware. Gayoso proposed to the governor-general that wealthy Americans be allowed to bring desirable goods to New Orleans, even if they intended to return to the United States; Carondelet, constantly faced with a shortage of goods needed in Louisiana but virtually unobtainable through legal commerce, fre-quently consented in special cases.[4]

Prices at Natchez were excessive; they were even higher than in New Orleans.[5] There was a great demand for manufactured goods which could never be met under the restrictive Spanish mercantilis-

[1]Speech of Rep. Scott, May 28, 1789, in *Abridgment of the Debates of Con-gress, from 1789 to 1856* (New York, 1857), I, 100.
[2]The most interesting account of westward expansion, albeit superseded by more objective and intensive studies, is Roosevelt, *The Winning of the West.* Cf. Thomas P. Abernethy, *The South in the New Nation, 1789–1819* (Baton Rouge, 1961); John Anthony Caruso, *The Southern Frontier* (Indianapolis, 1963); and Dale Van Every, *Ark of Empire: the American Frontier, 1784–1803* (New York, 1963).
[3]Regular reports were filed by Grand-Pré and Gayoso. Many have been published in Kinnaird (ed.), *Spain in the Mississippi Valley*, Part II, *passim.*
[4]Patrick Sharky, from Virginia, arrived in Natchez in 1790 with a load of 8,600 pounds of pots, pans, chimney and wagon irons. Gayoso to Carondelet, No. 39, Natchez, April 17, 1792, translated in Corbitt (ed.), "Papers from the Spanish Archives," XXVIII (1955), 82–83. James Hoggett, on the personal recommendation of James Robertson of Nashville, was allowed to dispose of his goods in New Orleans, and Carondelet approved of allowing other influential Americans to sell their merchandise in the capital without paying duties. Robertson to Gayoso, Nashville, July 1, 1796, AGI, PC, leg. 212; Gayoso to Carondelet, Natchez, August 4, 1796, AGI, PC, leg. 43.
[5]Gayoso to Miró, No. 24, Natchez, March 12, 1791, AGI, PC, leg. 41.

tic policy which was characteristic of her other American possessions. The history of Spanish economic policy in Louisiana from
1786 to 1800 was, in Professor Whitaker's phrase, "evolving from
monopoly through contraband to partial freedom, then greater
freedom, and finally separation from Spain . . . ." ⁶ An elaborate
tariff for Louisiana was established in 1796 in an effort to control
the import of so-called "luxury goods." ⁷ It is impossible, however,
to understand Spanish economic policy by reading the various decrees passed on the subject, for there were more exceptions to the
rule than might be imagined.

Gayoso exercised considerable common sense in his application
of these economic restrictions to Natchez. When a boatload of
merchandise belonging to a Natchez physician, Dr. Samuel Flowers,
arrived in 1791, Gayoso allowed the iron, tobacco, soap, lead, medicines, wool carding machine, and thread making machine to enter
duty-free.⁸ Because good American milled flour was always scarce
in Natchez, Gayoso evaded the laws and admonitions from both
Miró and Carondelet in buying flour for the account of the Royal
Treasury without charging a cent of duty.⁹ Duties on American produce sent down the river to New Orleans were finally reduced
from 15 per cent to 6 per cent in 1796, but only after considerable
pressure by Carondelet on various Spanish ministers. Even this
tariff was resented by the merchants of New Orleans who clamored
for 4 per cent or nothing.¹⁰ Luxury goods came into Natchez

⁶Arthur P. Whitaker, "The Commerce of Louisiana and the Floridas at the
End of the Eighteenth Century," *HAHR*, VIII (May, 1928), 203. An analysis
of Spanish economic policy in Louisiana is in Jack D. L. Holmes, "Some
Economic Problems of Spanish Governors of Louisiana," *ibid.*, XLII (November, 1962), 521–43.

⁷Morales, Tariff, New Orleans, August 24, 1796, AGI, PC, leg. 184-A.

⁸Gayoso to Miró, No. 11, Natchez, February 12, 1791, AGI, PC, leg. 41.

⁹Gayoso to Carondelet, No. 320, Natchez, June 28, 1793, AGI, PC, leg. 42.
Flour was important in opening a wedge in Spanish restrictions on trade,
for Philadelphia merchants sold their cargoes in New Orleans and thereby
obtained specie illegally. C. Richard Arena, "Philadelphia–Spanish New Orleans
Trade in the 1790's," *Louisiana History*, II (Fall, 1961), 429–45.

¹⁰Carondelet to Gayoso, New Orleans, September 16, 1796, AGI, PC, leg.
23. On Carondelet's support for free trade, see Holmes, "Some Economic
Problems of Spanish Governors of Louisiana," 535–39.

before Gayoso's administration and continued to find a ready market after the American occupation.[11]

Of course, the ability to pay for any merchandise, whether flour or luxuries, depended on the settlers' ability to raise a cash crop which would find a ready market and produce a balance of payments in their favor. The success of the immigration movement to Natchez would depend on the solution to the problem of finding this cash crop. Fortunately, the land and climate favored a number of possibilities. Surrounding the well-wooded bottoms of the bayous, lakes, and rivers were extensive natural meadows of "the most luxuriant soil," composed of a black mold about one and one-half feet deep, very loose and rich, occasioned by the frequent burning of the savannas.[12] Andrew Ellicott described eloquently the region's latent possibilities in 1797: "The soil of the District of Natchez is of an excellent quality, and produces exclusive of the necessaries of life, cotton & indigo in abundance . . . . I can assure you, that I know of no place where life can be supported, & enjoyed with more ease & less labour, by the poorer class of our citizens, than in this district. . . ." [13]

Indigo was one of the earliest export crops produced in Louisiana, and it is probable that Natchez produced its share. At first, its quality was equal to the best produced by Santo Domingo, and it sold from $1.50 to $2.50 per pound. The depredations caused by an insect and the exhaustion of the land lowered the indigo's quality, however; by 1795 its price had dropped, and many planters in Natchez and elsewhere were searching for another crop.[14]

[11]John Perry's five boatloads of merchandise, valued at $3,925.56, arrived at Natchez in 1786 with such items as shoe buckles, hats, spurs, ink stands, cupboard locks, corduroy, stockings, and thimbles. Grand-Pré's statement, Natchez, July 7, 1786, AGI, PC, leg. 12. Men's white silk stockings, playing cards, soap, and blue stationery made up a cargo in 1800. Mack Swearingen, "Luxury in Natchez in 1801, A Ship's Manifest from the McDonogh Papers," *Journal of Southern History*, III (May, 1937), 188–90.
[12]Imlay, *Topographical Description*, 422–23; Pope, *A Tour*, 33–34.
[13]Ellicott to Secretary of State (Pickering), Natchez, April 13, 1797, Southern Boundary MSS, U.S. and Spain, I.
[14]E. Wilson Lyon (ed.), "Moustier's Memoir on Louisiana," *MVHR*, XXII (September, 1935), 257, 261; Imlay, *Topographical Description*, 414–15; Clai-

The planters next turned their attention to tobacco. Although tobacco had been planted in Louisiana since the French dominion, it was not given much encouragement.[15] The English settlement at Natchez produced its first crop of tobacco for export in 1779 amounting to 550 hogsheads, and when the Spanish government occupied the Natchez District, it devoted immediate encouragement to tobacco production.[16] During Gayoso's administration tobacco became the most important cash crop of the area, and many fortunes were made—and lost—in its production. The rich soil yielded from 1,500 to 2,000 pounds per acre. Cured tobacco was transported on flatboats to New Orleans for grading and selling. It was sent either in hogsheads or packed in ten-pound "carrots." In New Orleans the practice of selling required an experienced hand because the Spanish inspector, Mathias de Alpuente, rigorously inspected all tobacco and frequently threw out more than half the crop of disappointed planters who had not yet learned the power of a bribe.[17]

---

borne, *Mississippi*, 140; Holmes (ed.), *Documentos de la Luisiana*, 155 n. Many of the Natchez artisans were employed during 1792 in making vats and other accoutrements for the indigo industry. Gayoso to Carondelet, No. 16, Natchez, March 24, 1792, AGI, PC, leg. 41. An excellent description of the indigo process is by William Dunbar, published in Ingraham, *The South-west by a Yankee*, 273–74.

[15]N. M. Miller Surrey, *The Commerce of Louisiana during the French Regime, 1699–1763* (New York, 1916), 174, says that the French government urged settlers in Louisiana to grow tobacco. Many of the early records state that tobacco was grown but not how important it was. In 1722 a marvelous future was predicted for tobacco in Louisiana. See William Beer (ed.), "Early Census Tables of Louisiana," *Publications* of the Louisiana Historical Society, V (1911), 98. *Noticia general de lo que produce la Provincia de la Luisiana*, New Orleans, October 26, 1771, AGI, PC, leg. 110, indicates tobacco was one of the products produced in Natchitoches. According to Charles Gayarré, "Historical Notes on the Commerce and Agriculture of Louisiana, 1720–1766," *Louisiana Historical Quarterly*, II (July, 1919), 286, the French India Company agreed to buy first-rate tobacco at 25 *livres* per hundred pounds in 1720. Tobacco could also be used as payment for imported Negro slaves. Lyon (ed.), "Moustier's Memoir," 256–57, says tobacco was a thriving crop by 1789.

[16]Robert Ross to Earl of Dunmore (John Murray), Charleston, South Carolina, Chalmer Papers, New York Public Library Manuscript Section; Jack D. L. Holmes, "Robert Ross' Plan for an English Invasion of Louisiana in 1782," *Louisiana History*, V (Spring, 1964), 166.

[17]Sydnor, *A Gentleman of the Old Natchez Region*, 10–11; Claiborne, *Mississippi*, 140. Mathias de Alpuente was employed as inspector of tobacco

Tobacco offers a good illustration of Spanish mercantilistic policy toward Natchez. On June 15, 1777, Governor Gálvez issued a regulation governing the price to be paid for tobacco from the Louisiana settlements.[18] Although Natchez was not included in the early regulations, after Spain occupied the Natchez District, it was included in the generous provisions. Natchez tobacco was needed in its raw material state for the world-famed tobacco factory at Seville.[19] In order to favor the home industry, Spain offered generous subsidies for raw tobacco and, at the same time, prohibited the manufacture of tobacco products in Louisiana. The first and second grades of tobacco belonged exclusively to the king; but third grade and "culls" could be sold to inhabitants, Indians, and slaves. Stern prohibitions against exporting tobacco to any country but Spain were provided.[20] Most Louisiana tobacco was forwarded to Veracruz for transhipment to Cádiz and Seville, but occasionally merchants would send tobacco directly to Europe from New Orleans.[21]

For the Natchez planters, the royal grace in offering ten silver dollars per hundred pounds for tobacco in unlimited quantities seemed munificent. Many of them went deeply into debt buying

until August 31, 1794, and "performed his job well," according to Carondelet's certification, New Orleans, February 10, 1796, AGI, PC, leg. 23. An example of his zeal is furnished in his destruction of almost one-sixth of the total crop from Francisco Rouquier's Natchitoches plantation in 1792. Statement by Mathias de Alpuente, New Orleans, June 4, 1792, AGI, PC, leg. 206. In Miró's *residencia* (official examination of his conduct of office), it was charged that the governor-general had profited from the sale of tobacco in New Orleans. *Residencia* of Miró, and Pesquiza (complaint examination) (1802), AHN, Consejo de Indias, legs. 20927, 21055; *cf*. Burson, *The Stewardship of Miró*, 289.

[18]Gálvez, printed regulation, New Orleans, June 15, 1777, AGI, PC, leg. 190.

[19]Gardoqui to Intendant of Louisiana (Rendón), San Ildefonso, August 22, 1795, AGI, PC, leg. 32.

[20]Gálvez' regulation, June 15, 1777.

[21]After the royal monopoly on tobacco terminated in 1790, Santiago Fortier sent his brother Honorato on the frigate *Victoria* to Nantes with a large shipment of tobacco. When he was detained in port for four months, causing the tobacco to spoil, Fortier claimed and collected damages from the Spanish crown. The case is dated Council of the Indies, March 23, 1795, AGI, SD, leg. 1145. In 1795, the brigantine *El Malabar* carried 129,534 pounds of Louisiana tobacco to Hamburg. Rendón to Carondelet, New Orleans, April 9, 1795, AGI, PC, leg. 31.

land, tools, slaves, and seed. Their confidence in prosperity received additional support when the rich Natchez land produced abundant quantities, and the early planters reaped great rewards from their toil.[22]

The tobacco crop of the Natchez District for 1786 amounted to 589,920 pounds.[23] Unfortunately for the Natchez planters, the following year General Wilkinson visited New Orleans with a load of top grade Kentucky tobacco and a proposition for Miró to buy more of the same at prices lower than those offered to the Natchez inhabitants.[24] When Gayoso arrived in New Orleans, a number of planters from his district were there to meet with the governor-general in an effort to have the Spanish government continue the lucrative subsidies. In their pleas, the Natchez planters said that, acting on the promise of the king to buy all their tobacco at ten dollars per hundredweight, they had mortgaged their homes and farms. Should the king now decide otherwise, they would be ruined and along with them, the merchants of Natchez who had extended them credit. Faced with a lack of ready money to buy food crops (neglected because of the rush to plant and harvest tobacco), the Natchez planters were in dire straits indeed.

Miró heard their complaints, discussed the matter with them,

[22]Thomas Green sent a shipment of tobacco to New Orleans early in 1784, representing the 1783 crop. McBee (ed.), *Natchez Court Records*, 22. According to the census of 1784, AGI, PC, leg. 116, Natchez produced 63,749 carrots of tobacco in 1783. On their indebtedness, see Petition of Natchez District Inhabitants, Natchez, December 21, 1792, printed in Claiborne, *Mississippi*, 139; Petition of Inhabitants of District of Natchez, Mississippi Territory, December 6, 1800, in *Papers in relation to the Official Conduct of Governour Sargent*, 54. Pope, *A Tour*, 34, remarks on the price in 1790 as being $8 per cwt.

[23]Grand-Pré's return, Natchez, January 18, 1787, AGI, PC, leg. 200, cited in Whitaker, *Mississippi Question*, 281 n.

[24]Wilkinson proposed that Miró buy Kentucky tobacco at $2 per cwt. and sell it at New Orleans for $9 per cwt. Jacobs, *Tarnished Warrior*, 81. Gardoqui wrote that a hundredweight of good tobacco in Kentucky was worth $2 cash or $3 in goods, which was the usual means of payment in specie-scarce America. Transportation to New Orleans cost planters a maximum of 50¢ per cwt. If Kentucky tobacco was purchased there for $6, the planters would enjoy a 100% profit which, said Gardoqui, "is a profit that the most favored nation does not gain on a voyage to China in which capital is employed for more than two years." Gardoqui to Conde de Floridablanca, No. 21, Confidential, New York, October 24, 1788, AHN, ESTADO, leg. 3893; and also printed in Corbitt, "Papers from the Spanish Archives," XVIII (1946), 135.

and finally suggested that the king buy the 1789 crop, estimated at two million pounds, at the present rate and then purchase eight million pounds of Louisiana tobacco the following year at the same price. The planters agreed to accept bills of credit to be redeemed in December, 1789, for their current crop rather than face the disaster of not selling their tobacco at all.[25]

When Gayoso arrived in Natchez he was surrounded by problems connected with the tobacco industry. Miró had ordered him to sound out the inhabitants but to allow no tobacco to be shipped to New Orleans without prior authorization from the governor-general.[26] On August 12, 1789, Gayoso called a meeting of the leading tobacco planters at his home to discuss the problem. They approved the suggestion of Sebastián de Arrieta that the tobacco should be sent in leaf, packed in casks, rather than twisted together into carrots, which damaged the tobacco and placed immature tobacco with the better quality.[27]

The planters agreed to take a cut in the government subsidy of slightly more than two cents a pound. Since the burning of tobacco not considered of sufficient quality for the royal requirements had antagonized many of the Natchez planters, Gayoso had several pertinent suggestions. He called for men of training and intelligence in the inspection of tobacco for members of the Inspection Commission at New Orleans; the destruction of bad quality tobacco by the planters themselves in advance, as was customary in Virginia; inspection of tobacco after it had aged sufficiently and not during its maturing process when it gave the appearance of rotting leaf; the inclusion on the Inspection Commission of several Natchez settlers, demonstrating thereby Spanish confidence in the integrity of the planters; and the increase in tobacco sales under these new conditions.[28]

In 1789 the total tobacco crop amounted to 1,402,725 pounds.[29] Most was grown in the fertile lands around St. Catherine Creek,

[25]Petition of tobacco growers to intendant of New Orleans; Minutes of the Council meeting, New Orleans, April 1, 1789, AGI, SD, leg. 2553.
[26]Miró to Gayoso, "Mr. Conway's House," July 14, 1789, AGI, PC, leg. 6.
[27]Gayoso to Miró, No. 13, Natchez, August 12, 1789, AGI, PC, leg. 41.
[28]Ibid.
[29]Grand-Pré to Miró, Natchez, February 23, 1790, AGI, PC, leg. 16.

but a large amount was also produced along the Homochitto and Cole's Creek.[30] Although Miró had received no official word from the court, he issued instructions announcing his determination to buy the 1789 crop at the price of eight pesos per *quintal*, as he had informed the king, payable in certificates of credit, which were redeemable upon the sale of the 1788 crop in Mexico. Miró had taken this extraordinary action on his own, and it turned out to be an error.[31] It did instill in the Natchez planters, however, confidence in the government's guarantees of a secure market.

The decision of the Supreme Council of the Indies on Natchez tobacco purchases was finally reached on December 20, 1790. Disregarding Miró's suggestion that surplus tobacco be disposed of through sale to Portugal or France,[32] the Crown decreed that Miró's precipitate action in buying 2,500,000 pounds of the 1789 tobacco crop would be approved for the use of the Peninsula and Mexico. Henceforth, beginning with the 1791 purchases of the 1790 crop, the king would buy no more than 40,000 pounds.[33]

Hardly able to believe this terrible news, Gayoso must have wondered at the wisdom of Charles IV's advisors. The Natchez governor clearly recognized the relationship between tobacco and the desired goal of Spanish policy in Natchez: creating a wealthy, responsible, and loyal population determined to prevent any invasion of their domains. In 1790 Gayoso had written:

> These people having been accustomed to the cultivation of tobacco, and the Territory of Natchez being noted for the production of this crop, have dedicated themselves completely to this labor. In order to stimulate production, we

[30]A statement by Grand-Pré, enclosed in Grand-Pré to Miró, Natchez, March 2, 1790, shows the names of the 263 tobacco producers in Natchez as well as the production by districts. It is in AGI, PC, leg. 16, and has been printed in Kinnaird (ed.), *Spain in the Mississippi Valley*, Part II, 305–11.

[31]Circular order of Miró, New Orleans, February 3, 1790, draft, AGI, PC, leg. 41.

[32]Miró to Luis de Las Casas, New Orleans, September 10, 1790, copy enclosed in Gayoso to Conde de Floridablanca, New Orleans, September 10, 1790, AHN, ESTADO, leg. 3902.

[33]Minutes of Royal Order, Madrid, December 25, 1790, forwarded to Gayoso, AHN, ESTADO, leg. 3902; Floridablanca to Gayoso, Confidential, Madrid, December 25, 1790, AGI, PC, leg. 176-b.

have until now bought their crops on the account of the Royal Treasury. This procedure not only has satisfied them, but has served as a stimulus for innumerable people up North to come as vassals of His Majesty. Many will arrive during the closing months of this year, and many more are disposing of their possessions to come after them . . . in the belief of a sure sale for their tobacco to the king. . . . These matters are urgently in need of solution for they endanger this land that had already begun to flourish. . . . Should his Majesty not wish to continue buying the tobacco crops, let us ship it to any foreign European port, thus extending the privilege which only the French now enjoy. . . .[34]

Unfortunately, Gayoso's ability to predict future events and see through shortsighted measures was not shared by the ministers in Spain who advised Charles IV. For the people of Natchez, the Christmas message of 1790 from Floridablanca brought utter discouragement, although they produced their tobacco and hoped for a last-minute reprieve from what seemed to be certain bankruptcy. During 1790, there were 1,443 *toneles* and 9,667 *andullos* (rolled leaf packages), amounting to slightly more than a million pounds produced in the Natchez District. When Minister of Finance Diego de Gardoqui raised the amount of tobacco to be purchased on the royal account to 120,000 pounds in 1794, it hardly helped. The tobacco crop of 1791 was much smaller than that of 1790.[35] In 1796 Gayoso wrote that his district no longer exported tobacco and produced barely enough for its own needs.[36]

Having stimulated overproduction, deficit spending, and excessive credit buying, the Spanish government changed its agricultural policies and, in so doing, lost the loyalty of its subjects, at least in Natchez. Of course, there was always the possibility of

[34]Gayoso to Floridablanca, September 10, 1790.
[35]Grand-Pré to Miró, Natchez, January 30, 1792, AGI, PC, leg. 17; Gardoqui to the Governor-Intendant of Louisiana, No. 1, Aranjuez, February 14, 1794, AGI, PC, leg. 21; Gayoso to Miró, No. 16, Natchez, February 15, 1791, with enclosure, AGI, PC, leg. 41.
[36]Gayoso to Morales, (Natchez), December 29, 1796, copy enclosed in Morales to Gardoqui, No. 81, New Orleans, January 21, 1797, AGI, SD, leg. 2614.

further government intervention, in the form of a moratorium on debts. Gayoso had recognized the necessity of protecting both debtor and creditor from ruin following the tobacco disaster. On November 20, 1791, he wrote Miró that it was absolutely essential to provide a moratorium, and the following spring Miró's successor called a meeting with his auditor of war, Nicolás María Vidal, to discuss the question. Gayoso's request for a three-year period of grace in which the planters would attempt to find another crop to bring in the necessary funds was approved.[37]

Indebtedness was not new to the Natchez District. In 1790, eleven merchants had drawn up a list of their outstanding accounts, showing $146,000 owed. In addition, there were sixteen mercantile firms in New Orleans which had extended credit to Natchez planters. The planters offered to mortgage their property and their present and future crops to pay off the debts if the creditors would not press charges for immediate payment.[38] Unfortunately, the difficulty in obtaining a cash crop prevented the planters from making any payments to the merchants at all. In 1792 the debtors again appealed to Gayoso for relief from their distress, claiming that the merchants charged high prices, and that the cost of living had risen 100 per cent in four years.[39]

The merchants replied to these charges with cogent arguments on their side. They had extended loans to some of the planters since 1771 on the basis that the notes be gradually retired by regular annual payments. Some planters had never made a payment on account. "It is not the design of the creditors to distress or ruin any honest, industrious debtor," they said. However, they insisted on a prompt reckoning of their accounts and agreed to publish the current prices for commodities based on the highest prices charged for those items in New Orleans.[40]

[37]Gayoso to Miró, New Orleans, November 20, 1791; opinion of Nicolás María Vidal, New Orleans, February 13, 1792; Decree of Carondelet, New Orleans, March 15, 1792; all in BN, Vol. 19,248, folios 253–68.

[38]Gayoso to Miró, New Orleans, December 13, 1790, with enclosed lists, AGI, PC, leg. 2362.

[39]Memorial of Natchez planters to Gayoso, Natchez, December 31, 1792, printed in Claiborne, *Mississippi*, 139–40.

[40]Circular of Natchez merchants, *ibid.*, 140.

As the first five-year moratorium granted by Gayoso in 1790 came to a close, many planters had still not made any payments, although some had recovered from the initial set-back in tobacco and were producing cash crops in other produce. It was the turn of the Natchez creditors to appeal, and a number of them signed a petition asking that the three-year grace period granted in 1792 not be extended. Their petition breathed a warning to an over-indulgent government:

> A very large majority of the Debtors, so far from exerting their endeavours, to extricate themselves from their difficulties; having no longer the dread of the Law before their Eyes; have become indolent, Dissipated, and Deaf to the calls of their Creditors. . . . A large proportion of the Creditors are Industrious young Merchants whose Capitals [sic] are inconsiderable; but supported by the aid of foreign Merchants, who have entrusted them with their Properties, they have aspired by honest Industry to acquire a Subsistance, and by regularity in their transactions, to secure the favourable opinion, and future aid of their foreign creditors. . . .[41]

Of course, the Natchez debtors had their memorial to the government, too. They claimed they had been charged 10 per cent interest in violation of Miró's regulation. The merchants bled the poor debtors, they charged, and were opulent.[42]

The crux of the dispute between the Natchez planters and debtors originated in Gayoso's well-meaning attempt to prevent economic ruin by suggesting the renewal of the three-year moratorium for a period of five years, running from 1795 to 1800. It was granted, and then the petitions followed close behind—the merchants complaining, "Had the new Indulgence been granted with the express condition of an Annual punctual payment of one fifth, with Interest of the whole Debt; in this case, a faint hope would have remained to the distressed Creditor of retreiving [sic] a certain part at least of his shattered fortune, but it is by no means known to the

[41]Memorial to Gayoso, Natchez, November 9, 1795, AGI, PC, leg. 23.
[42]Petition of Natchez debtors to king, Natchez, December 21, 1795; petition of debtors to Carondelet, same date; Gayoso to Carondelet, New Orleans, March 14, 1796, AGI, PC, leg. 43. Cf. draft of same in AGI, PC, leg. 23.

Creditors, that they have a right to exact one farthing from their Debtors, until the expiration of the term of the Indulgence."

The creditors also had a word for the success of government intervention in private debts which is deserving of repetition:

> The Industrious and upright Debtor has never been distressed by his Creditor, neither does he seek to take advantage from the Indulgence. But the profligate, idle, and dishonest, eagerly shelter themselves under your Majesty's Indulgence: contrary to the benevolent intentions of your Majesty, this indulgence becomes a cloak for their fraud, they now boldly stand forth and laugh at the just claims of their distressed Creditors.
>
> From woefull experience, it is well known to the Creditors that if payments are to depend upon the Justice, Discretion & promises of these men, the whole of the Debt may be considered as a total loss.
>
> It is a certain but lamentable truth, which the past and present ages evince beyond a doubt; that if the coercive power of the Law is for a moment suspended; Justice and virtue are no longer to be found among men.[43]

These were words to be remembered as Natchez approached the fateful year, 1797. It is ironic to note the phrases used by the Natchez debtors—who were the ringleaders in the revolt *against* Spanish rule in 1797—in "grateful appreciation": ". . . We resolve that they shall not have cause to blush before the Throne; for allegiance is our ambition, we pride in acts of duty and firmness. . . ." [44]

Gayoso firmly believed in paternal government, however; and he felt for the good of the Natchez District, the five-year extension of the moratorium should be granted. He wrote Carondelet that the majority of the Natchez debts would have been paid already had it not been for the obstinate attitude of the merchants. On the other hand, Gayoso felt that many of the debtors deliberately shirked their responsibilities. Both petitions, in Gayoso's opinion, evinced animosity and opposition toward the other. Both operated in bad faith, and this was the cause of the troubles. Another cause was Carondelet's failure to tell the people of Natchez that their

[43]Memorial to Gayoso, November 9, 1795.
[44]Petition of Natchez debtors to king, December 21, 1795.

complaints must be given first to Gayoso in the chain of command. Like Miró, Gayoso was jealous of his position and privileges.[45]

Fortunately the furor soon dissolved as the Natchez planters turned their attention toward cotton. The first seed was procured from Georgia and Jamaica. Planting seasons for cotton began in early April, and the harvests were large. Following the invention of the cotton gin and the numerous imitations or adaptations built in Natchez after 1795, the export of cotton assumed a major role in the economy.[46]

Like many Natchez planters, John Barcley was in debt in 1793. When the governor-general ordered his goods attached for payment of a debt to the mercantile firm of Espíritu Liotau and Fabre, Gayoso wrote that Barcley had left in April for North Carolina with his passport but that he promised to return in the spring of 1794.[47]

In 1795 Barcley returned to the Natchez District, where he soon turned his attention to the construction of a cotton gin. Perhaps while he was in the United States, settling his business affairs, he had visited Whitney and observed the almost childlike simplicity with which the crank-turned cylinder's teeth pulled the seeds from the cotton. Barcley's completed gin was inspected by a committee of Natchez planters at Daniel Clark's plantation. Despite the early morning fog which dampened the cotton and made it difficult to handle, in forty-five minutes the machine removed the seeds and cleaned expertly eighteen and three-quarters pounds of cotton. None of the cotton was damaged.

During Gayoso's absence, Grand-Pré forwarded Barcley's petition to the governor-general asking for some recompense for inventing such a useful machine. Carondelet recommended the granting of an exclusive franchise for five years. Anyone wishing to use a ma-

---

[45]Gayoso to Carondelet, March 14, 1796. The moratorium's conditions were explained in Carondelet to Gayoso, New Orleans, April 27, 1795, AGI, PC, leg. 22. It is interesting to compare the effect of boom-and-bust in the tobacco industry of Natchez with that of Cuba as described in Fernando Ortiz y Fernández, *Cuban Counterpoint: Tobacco and Sugar,* trans. Harriet de Onís (New York, 1947).

[46]Claiborne, *Mississippi,* 140; Ingraham, *The South-west by a Yankee,* II, 281–91.

[47]Gayoso to Carondelet, No. 307, Natchez, June 15, 1793, AGI, PC, leg. 42.

chine of like nature would be required to pay Barcley the sum of ten dollars.[48]

Soon Barcley was followed by other imitators. David Greenleaf, the mechanic whose marriage by Reverend Richard Curtis caused considerable stir in 1795, made a living manufacturing Whitney gins in 1796 and built a public or toll gin on Curtis' land.[49] Thomas Wilkins built a gin on Pine Ridge.[50] Richard Harrison built a gin in 1795 for his first cotton crop.[51] James McIntyre agreed to build a gin for George Cochran in 1795, and the finished price was $150.[52] Benito Truly's gin was defective and ruined twenty-two out of thirty-seven sacks of cotton he processed. Richard Harrison also damaged some cotton, but unintentionally. Truly had allegedly intended fraud; but he escaped an order to arrest him and fled the district, leaving his ill-constructed gin and other property behind to be confiscated.[53]

Cotton production grew rapidly. In the 1792 census, there were only 75,227 pounds of cotton shown as having been produced in Natchez the preceding year.[54] Eight years later, conservative estimates of the cotton crop were for 1,200,000 pounds, and some guesses ran as high as 3,000,000 pounds![55] William Dunbar, whose

[48]Col. Daniel Clark, Sr. to Col. Anthony Hutchins, August 21, 1795, in Claiborne, *Mississippi*, 143: "Barclay will soon have his gin sufficiently forward to essay how it will work. I have done a great deal to bring this brat into the world, and if it succeeds shall put in a claim for my share of the honor." Inspection of Barcley's gin, fragment of MS, AGI, PC, leg. 23; Grand-Pré to Carondelet, No. 68, Natchez, September 21, 1795, with enclosures, AGI, PC, leg. 32; Carondelet to Grand-Pré, New Orleans, October 3, December 12, 1795, AGI, PC, leg. 22.

[49]Claiborne, *Mississippi*, 143.

[50]Rowland (ed.), *Encyclopedia of Mississippi History*, I, 572.

[51]Petition of Richard Harrison, Natchez, May 28, 1796, in McBee (ed.), *Natchez Court Records*, 286.

[52]Cochran v. McIntyre, 1796, *ibid.*

[53]George Cochran et al. v. Bennet Truly; William Foster v. Bennet Truly; David Ferguson and John Murdoch v. Truly, 1796, all *ibid.*; Gayoso to Carondelet, No. 642, Natchez, June 6, 1796, AGI, PC, leg. 43.

[54]Census of 1792, AGI, PC, leg. 2353. The census of 1784 shows no cotton as being produced, in AGI, PC, leg. 116. According to the census of 1795, cotton production in 1794 was only 36,351 pounds of cotton. AGI, PC, leg. 31.

[55]N. Hunter to the editor of the *Impartial Observer*, Philadelphia, February 4, 1800; Col. Daniel Clark, Sr. to W.C.C. Claiborne, Clarksville, June 18, 1800; both in *Papers in Relation to the Official Conduct of Governour Sargent*, 8, 26.

scientific ideas were soon put to use for the benefit of the cotton industry, ordered a screw press from Philadelphia, made from his own designs, and was one of the pioneer developers of a use for cotton seed oil.[56]

Further diversification of Natchez agriculture was encouraged by the Spanish government in other ways. For instance, a royal decree of 1789 created the Royal Maritime Company, which offered exemptions to fishermen from paying certain taxes and duties and from serving in the militia. This was one of the earliest efforts to build up the Louisiana fishing industry.[57] By 1798, William Dunbar reported the following products being raised in Natchez: sugar cane, indigo, cotton, tobacco, corn, rice, okra, squash, sweet potatoes, Irish potatoes, millet, pumpkins, musk and watermelons, tomatoes, eggplants, quinces, almonds, plums, peaches, pears, and apricots.[58]

Governor Gayoso stimulated the nascent cattle industry by calling the stock growers together and jointly promulgating laws to foster and protect their stock from each other and from the pollution often attendant upon the processing of indigo. New strains were brought from Texas and the other north Mexican provinces, while a regular trade developed between Natchez and the Opelousas and Attakapas settlements of Louisiana. Fences protected farmers from the ravages usually committed by loose running stock in homesteading territory. Bounties were placed on the "tyger" and wolves taken within five miles of any inhabited plantation in the Natchez District. Brands were registered and an annual round-

---

According to Andrew Ellicott's letter to Secretary of State Pickering, New Orleans, January 10, 1799, Southern Boundary, III, in 1798 the Mississippi Territory produced four thousand bales of cotton which sold in New Orleans for $40 per bale.

[56]Claiborne, *Mississippi*, 144. Within two decades there were two steam-driven oil mills in Natchez which produced an oil "said to be superior to sperm oil, and the finest paint oil." Ingraham, *The South-west by a Yankee*, 160.

[57]Royal Decree of Charles IV, Madrid, September 19, 1789, enclosed in Valdés to Miró, San Lorenzo, October 23, 1789, AGI, PC, leg. 176-b.

[58]Dunbar's report to the Spanish Government, in Rowland (ed.), *Life and Letters of Dunbar*, 98–99. Cf. list of seeds, trees, etc., at Natchez, (1797), AGI, PC, leg. 2371.

up was provided to protect ownership rights in the stock.[59] Gayoso often permitted the stock growers of Natchez to graze their cattle west of the Mississippi on the rich bottom lands around present-day Vidalia.[60]

In 1784 there were approximately 3,000 steers in Natchez. Other stock included 1,153 horses, 7,111 pigs, and 117 sheep.[61] By 1792 and 1794, livestock had increased as shown in the following charts. Undoubtedly the encouragement given the cattle and livestock industry in Natchez by Gayoso was a major factor in the increase during these years. In addition to the regulations for the industry, Gayoso fought for the right of the Bayou Sara cattlemen to permit their stock to graze on unoccupied lands in dispute with the district of Punta Cortada.[62] Gayoso argued against the order of Carondelet forbidding residents to go west of the Mississippi by remarking that it was essential that cattle business between Natchez and Opelousas be continued for the welfare of both settlements.[63] He encouraged cattle drives between Natchez and Nogales and stimulated the growth of cattle herds, particularly in the districts of Bayou Pierre and Big Black.[64] In an effort to stop rustling by dishonest Americans who returned to their Kentucky homes via the Natchez District, Gayoso ordered Richard King's volunteer company to patrol the roads leading from Bayou Pierre and ordered all stock sold publicly with announcements on the public bulletin

[59]Gayoso's proclamations, Natchez, February 28, 1793, Hicky Papers, Louisiana State University Archives, September 19, 1794, AGI, PC, leg. 210. Both have been translated and printed with a survey of livestock in Spanish Natchez in Jack D.L. Holmes, "Livestock in Spanish Natchez," *Journal of Mississippi History,* XXIII (January, 1961), 15–37.

[60]This privilege was revoked by Gayoso following the American occupation of Natchez in 1798, although the governor-general suggested the possible renting of pasture lands across the Mississippi to Natchez cattlemen at a price. Gayoso to Minor, New Orleans, January 10, 1798, Gayoso MSS., Louisiana State University Archives; Minor to Gayoso, Natchez, January 20, 1798, AGI, PC, leg. 215-B; Gayoso to Joseph Vidal, New Orleans, January 19, 1798, AGI, PC, leg. 154-A.

[61]Census of Natchez, 1784, AGI, PC, leg. 116.

[62]Gayoso to Carondelet, No. 117, Natchez, June 30, 1792, AGI, PC, leg. 41.

[63]Gayoso to Carondelet, No. 152, Natchez, September 7, 1792, *ibid.*

[64]Gayoso to Carondelet, No. 670, Natchez, July 18, 1796, AGI, PC, leg. 2364.

TABLE 1

LIVESTOCK IN THE NATCHEZ DISTRICT, 1792*

District	Horses	Cattle	Sheep	Pigs
Homochitto........................	282	1,492	127	1,208
Bayou Sara........................	49	130	No Entry	187
Buffalo Creek......................	181	1,003	115	1,150
Big Black..........................	12	50	No Entry	238
Bayou Pierre......................	248	920	2	938
Santa Catalina....................	1,258	4,583	626	4,007
Second and Sandy creeks............	726	4,028	112	3,641
Villa Gayoso......................	750	2,975	149	2,584
Totals....................	3,506	15,181	1,131	13,953

*Compiled from information in the Census of 1792, AGI, PC. leg. 2353.

TABLE 2

LIVESTOCK IN THE NATCHEZ DISTRICT, 1794*

District	Horses	Cattle	Sheep	Pigs
Homochitto........................	270	1,959	130	2,057
Bayou Sara........................	154	1,107	204	1,299
Buffalo Creek......................	97	822	158	916
Bayou Pierre and Pos Black...........	6	254	1,297	4
Santa Catalina....................	1,099	4,881	677	5,273
Sandy Creek......................	255	1,175	13	1,472
Second Creek......................	521	2,690	201	2,950
Villa Gayoso......................	2,727	140	2,778	3,970
Pine Ridge........................	412	1,644	80	2,165
Totals....................	5,541	14,672	5,538	20,106
Spanish totals..............	3,944	18,302	1,607	18,302

*Compiled from information in the Census of 1794, AGI, PC. leg. 31. For some reason not apparent to the author, Spanish totals in their census reports do not match the sums of their individual figures. For this reason, both totals have been indicated in Table 2.

boards throughout the district.[65] Gayoso also attempted to eliminate the abuse in supplying meat rations to the troops and to the hospital by ordering the quartermaster to distribute rations bought by the government to the troops every three days and to end private purchases of meat.[66]

The difficulty in obtaining nails, hardware, tools, and machinery at Natchez led to experiments in home industry. The production of lumber, staves, and naval stores had existed in Louisiana since its first settlements in the eighteenth century. The pine forests of Natchez were rich in resources for many of the settlers who processed the turpentine and tar.[67] Natchez supplied New Orleans with ready-cut staves,[68] and several planters mortgaged their property in order to build sawmills.[69]

As early as 1720 Natchez boasted a grist mill, a forge, and a machine shop; by 1812 it had more than seventeen factories of varying types and sizes.[70] There was a great demand for Missouri lead and American iron, and nails at Natchez sold for twenty-five cents a pound.[71] Antonio Monge, an iron monger in Natchez, drew an official salary of $45 per month plus two daily rations; but when

[65]Gayoso to Carondelet, No. 159, Natchez, September 13, 1792, AGI, PC, leg. 41; Holmes, "Livestock in Spanish Natchez," 22.

[66]Proclamation of Gayoso, Natchez, July 21, 1791, enclosed in Gayoso to Miró, No. 149, Natchez, July 22, 1791, AGI, PC, leg. 41. Sutton Banks got the contract to supply meat. Gayoso to Miró, No. 161, Natchez, July 28, 1791, *ibid.*

[67]Baily, *Journal*, 346, contains an interesting description of the manufacture of pitch, turpentine, and other naval stores in Natchez.

[68]Gayoso to Carondelet, No. 181, Natchez, October 17, 1792, AGI, PC, leg. 41.

[69]Pedro Bryan Bruin mortgaged his plantation to build a sawmill on December 4, 1794; and the following year Juan Bautista Macarty presented a petition to obtain a Natchez cypress grove to supply his sawmill. McBee (ed.), *Natchez Court Records*, 106; Carondelet to Grand-Pré, New Orleans, October 29, 1795, AGI, PC, leg. 22. Early pioneers in the sawmill business were David Smith, John Burnet, and Philip Alston, who operated them beginning in 1780. Alston to Elihu Hall Bay, Natchez, September 27, 1780, AGI, PC, leg. 113; McBee (ed.), *Natchez Court Records*, 23. On the lumber industry in Louisiana, see Holmes (ed.), *Documentos de la Luisiana*, 161 n.

[70]Rowland (ed.), *Encyclopedia of Mississippi History*, II, 25–26.

[71]Gayoso to Miró, No. 187, Natchez, September 7, 1791, and Gayoso to Carondelet, No. 16, Natchez, March 24, 1792, AGI, PC, leg. 41. About the supply of lead and iron in Upper Louisiana, see Holmes (ed.), *Documentos de la Luisiana*, 267–68.

he left for New Orleans in 1792, Gayoso replaced him with two
Negro iron mongers at equal salary. The Negroes, Gayoso wrote,
were competent in their trade and, moreover, "it is always pre-
ferable to choose the labor of a robust Negro to that of a white
man, because their strong constitution resists fatigue better and
they are more constant in their work." [72]

Evidently their work was satisfactory. Although Gayoso had
been forced to import 150 shovels and twenty adzes in 1792,
Natchez soon began to manufacture its own; by 1798 Gayoso
could write, "With regard to tools, I am of the opinion that axes
made at Natchez would answer better, the spades I'll get here. . . ." [73]
Natchez had its share of carpenters and construction contractors,
such as William McFarland and "big-nosed" John Teer, John
Scott and John Smith of Villa Gayoso, and John Girault of Bayou
Pierre.[74] There were David Greenleaf, Henry Hunter, and John
Barcley famed as mechanics. In order to aid the construction of
new buildings, Gayoso proposed the construction of a brick kiln;
adobe bricks were useless in the rainy Mississippi climate.[75]

In 1791 Gayoso had complained to Miró that the poor quality of
bread produced at Natchez was a result not of the flour but of the
ignorance and carelessness of the baker. He suggested a civilian
baker be appointed to provide good bread, thus saving the king
from waste and furnishing better rations for the people of Natchez.[76] Almost a year had passed without relief for the Natchez post

[72]Gayoso to Carondelet, No. 154, Natchez, September 7, 1792; and Gayoso
to Carondelet, No. 213, Natchez, December 6, 1792, AGI, PC, leg. 41. In 1794,
James McIntyre, a Natchez resident with some experience in working metals,
offered to cast light bronze cannon for Gayoso to use in the difficult canebrakes of the Natchez District, and the governor approved the request. Petition
of McIntyre, Natchez, November 3, 1794, enclosed with comments in Gayoso
to Carondelet, No. 616, Natchez, March 24, 1795, AGI, PC, leg. 43.
[73]Gayoso to Minor, New Orleans, February 5, 1798, Gayoso MSS., Louisiana
State University Archives. On the shortage of tools in Natchez, see Gayoso
to Carondelet, No. 16, Natchez, March 24, 1792, and No. 41, Natchez, April
18, 1792, AGI, PC, leg. 41.
[74]Minor to Gayoso, Natchez, October 8, 1797, AGI, PC, leg. 2371; Gayoso
to Beauregard, Natchez, September 24, 1792, AGI, PC, leg. 41; Gayoso to Miró
No. 160, July 27, 1791, *ibid.*
[75]Gayoso to Beauregard, Natchez, May 17, 1791; Gayoso to Miró, No. 155,
Natchez, July 26, 1791, AGI, PC, leg. 41.
[76]Gayoso to Miró, No. 90, Natchez, May 12, 1791, *ibid.*

when Gayoso renewed his request. Enrique Vidal, a soldier in the regiment, acted as temporary baker at $15 per month until his discharge in April, 1792.[77]

Hemp production and factories for making rope were encouraged throughout Louisiana; and in 1789 Robert Cochran arrived at Natchez with two boatloads of flour, pelts, and various tools which he was allowed to sell duty-free in the hope that he would establish his planned cordage factory.[78] James Elliot, another Natchez settler, had come in 1786 for a similar purpose.[79] Elisha Winters, a Kentucky settler, offered a like proposal in 1790 which was approved.[80] In each of these cases, the Spanish government allowed special privileges and exemptions in an effort to foster the creation of industry in the Natchez District.

√ As in many of the settlements along the Mississippi frontier, Natchez was always short of ready cash. Most contracts specified payment in hard money, the *peso fuerte* of Mexican mints, which found its way to Louisiana via Veracruz and Havana during the annual shipments of Louisiana's subsidy.[81] For most government expenditures Gayoso relied on certificates of credit drawn on the New Orleans treasury. Because subsidies were invariably delayed, these certificates were not always honored upon presentation, and as a result they frequently bore a 12 per cent discount.[82] The word spread swiftly along the frontier, unfortunately causing prices on goods sold to Spanish commandants to be raised to meet the rise in expenses in connection with the collection of debts. Gayoso pleaded with the governor-general to send him cash for

[77]Gayoso to Carondelet, No. 18, Natchez, March 24, 1792; No. 37, April 12, 1792, AGI, PC, leg. 41.

[78]Gayoso to Miró, No. 10, Natchez, August 6, 1789, *ibid.*

[79]Navarro to the Administrador General de Reales Rentas, New Orleans, November 3, 1786, AGI, PC, leg. 12.

[80]Lerena to Intendant of Louisiana, Madrid, March 23, 1791, AGI, PC, leg. 184-A. On the importance of hemp and its early production in Louisiana, see Holmes (ed.), *Documentos de la Luisiana*, 154 n.

[81]Holmes, "Some Economic Problems of Spanish Governors of Louisiana," 522–43.

[82]Gayoso to Miró, No. 187, Natchez, September 7, 1791, AGI, PC, leg. 41; Sydnor, *A Gentleman of the Old Natchez Region*, 10–11. As mentioned in Chapter III, this was the reason for Baily's reluctance to accept certificates of credit for goods he sold to Vidal at Natchez.

payment of essential materials in order to save the Royal Treasury at least 15 per cent.[83]

Those living in Natchez failed to appreciate Spanish taxation until they found themselves living under American laws and customs. "No direct Taxes of any kind are imposed in Louisiana," said Governor William C. C. Claiborne, referring to the Spanish domination.[84] Daniel Clark reported, "There are no local taxes whatever, each land holder is obliged to keep up the Road on his own land . . . . The Established duties are 6 P C^t, on Imports, & as much on exports. . . ." [85] It must have pleased inhabitants of the Natchez District no end when Adams County placed taxes on tavern licenses and highways and levied a general head tax, all of which amounted to $6,040![86] Under the Spanish government there was considerable paternal interest in economic affairs, but it was often arbitrary. Although Gayoso attempted to intercede on behalf of the Natchez debtors, he only succeeded in aggravating an already impossible situation, created in part by government intervention into the economy.

Transportation was always difficult in colonial Louisiana, and river transport usually replaced all other forms. Roads were few, in poor condition, and, except for the Natchez District, seldom kept in repair despite regulations to the contrary. Sudden flash floods during the rainy season often made the roads impassable. So it was to the vast Mississippi and those rivers which flowed into it that the Natchez settlers turned. Of course, it was no problem to

[83]Gayoso to Miró, No. 157, Natchez, July 26, 1791, AGI, PC, leg. 41. Gayoso asked Carondelet for a revolving account of $500–2,000 for the use of the Natchez quartermaster (*guarda-almacén*). Gayoso to Carondelet, No. 30, Natchez, April 3, 1792, AGI, PC, leg. 41.

[84]Claiborne to the President (Jefferson), near Natchez, August 24, 1803, in Carter (ed.), *Territorial Papers of the United States, IX: Orleans*, 22.

[85]Clark to Secretary of State, New Orleans, September 8, 1803, with enclosure, *ibid.*, 41.

[86]Clark to Claiborne, Clarksville, June 18, 1800, in *Papers in Relation to Conduct of Governour Sargent*, 26–27. An ordinance setting a land tax for Orleans Territory was similarly adopted in 1805, *Moniteur de la Louisiane* (New Orleans), December 11, 1805. For the reaction of residents of Louisiana to American government, taxation, and ideas of representation, see *Mémoire presenté au congres des etats-unis d'Amérique par les habitans de la Louisiane* (New Orleans, 1804), a printed copy of which is in AGI, PC, leg. 2368.

carry goods from Natchez to New Orleans; the trick was getting
back up the stream. By tacking with sails, rowing, and pulling the
boats, the three hundred miles between Natchez and New Orleans
up the Mississippi could take several weeks.

One Dutchman with an ingenious flare for invention, came up
with a boat, "the propelling force of which consisted of two large
wheels on each side, which were partly immersed in water and
formed somewhat like the waterwheel of a mill . . . [and] turned
by eight horses." He claimed he could make the trip from New
Orleans to Natchez in only six days, but he was unable to persuade
anyone to sponsor his idea. In disgust, he sold both boat and horses
and went home along the Natchez Trace.[87]

[87]Bailey, *Journal*, 327–28. An equally imaginative idea was conceived by a
New Orleans resident named Angel Babini, who proposed that the Spanish
government support his invention in 1790. Although Charles IV and his ministers
sponsored a host of equally peculiar projects, experts considered Babini's
project visionary and unnecessary. *Expediente* of Babini in the Archivo and
Museo Álvaro de Bazán, Marina de Guerra (El Viso del Marqués, Spain),
Indiferente. For a sketch of the ubiquitous keelboat so popular along the
Mississippi and Ohio Rivers, see Victor Collot, *A Journey in North America*,
Atlas, plate 7. On land travel via the Natchez Trace, see Jonathan Daniels,
The Devil's Backbone, the Story of the Natchez Trace (New York, 1962);
U.S. 76th Congress, 3d Session, Senate Document No. 148, *Natchez Trace
Parkway Survey* (Washington, 1941).

CHAPTER V

Social Life in Natchez

ANDREW ELLICOTT, who first visited Natchez in 1797, left the following description of its people:

> The natives of the southern part of the Mississippi are generally a sprightly people, and appear to have a natural turn for mechanics, painting, music, and the polite accomplishments, but their system of education is so extremely defective, that little real science is to be met with among them. Many of the planters are industrious, and enjoy life not only in plenty but affluence, and generally possess the virtue of hospitality, which never fails to impress the stranger and traveller with a favourable opinion of the country, and its inhabitants.[1]

Natchez was not during the Spanish period a "closed society"; yet Governor Gayoso believed in protecting the inhabitants of his district from the Kentucky frontiersmen who ran their cargoes

---

[1]*Journal of Andrew Ellicott*, 135.

down the river, returned via the Natchez District, and frequently committed crimes of various sorts. "The Spaniards," according to one report, "were very strict in their police, forbidding any strangers or boatmen to go up into the town, seated on a high bluff, without a written permission from the commandant or governor of the place." This prohibition did not extend to substantial, respectable, and desirable visitors, such as young Philip Dodridge, a well-educated son of an early Virginia settler, who visited Natchez in 1796 and walked up the road toward the town, despite the prohibition circulated in Natchez-under-the-Hill. When he had reached the halfway point to the bluff, he was met by a well-dressed gentleman who spoke to him in Spanish. Dodridge did not understand all of what was said, but finding Spanish similar to Latin, which he knew well, he replied in that tongue. To his surprise, the Spaniard answered in perfect Latin and introduced himself as the governor, Manuel Gayoso de Lemos.

The governor was pleased with Dodridge's manners and his ready wit and humor. He escorted the young visitor around town, invited him to dine at Government House, and requested his presence during the ensuing week, during which Dodridge had free use of the governor's carriage to visit nearby points of interest. When he left, Gayoso gave him letters of introduction to leading residents of New Orleans, which gained for Dodridge entrée into the wealthy and prominent homes of the capital. The visitor's companions looked "with wonder and astonishment at the gracious reception and attention paid to their cousin by the governor, while they were barely allowed to step on shore and not suffered to leave the vicinity of the landing." [2]

Not all visitors to Natchez praised the hospitality. Francis Baily tells of arriving at a poor plantation in Natchez: "When we did arrive there, a poor hut was our only shelter, and we were obliged to unpack our horses ourselves, and turn them into the pasture; and if we could get a mess of *mush* and milk, some fried

[2]Dr. S.P. Hildreth, "History of an Early Voyage on the Ohio and Mississippi Rivers, with Historical Sketches of the Different Points along them," *The American Pioneer,* I (March, 1842), 134–35.

bacon, or some fresh meat of any kind, it was as much as we expected, and for this we were charged enormously high." One understands, perhaps, the cause. When Baily obtained food from a generous settler, he went outside to eat alone on the grass, "in cleanliness and comfort, rather than be surrounded with such a nest of filth and dirt." Exorbitant prices? Baily objected to a charge of twenty-five cents for lodging in the garden and mush cooked with milk.[3]

In contrast to Baily's experience, Colonel John Pope had occasion in 1791 to enjoy typical Natchez hospitality. Below the Walnut Hills Pope encountered Gayoso's barge and "was regaled with declicious Nuts and excellent Wines." Pope wrote of Gayoso, "This Gentleman has a majestic Deportment, softened by Manners the most engaging and polite. Having been brought up at the Court of *London*, he is well acquainted with the Etiquette of Mortals who move in the more exalted and splendid Scenes of Life." [4] At Natchez, Pope was entertained by the military commander of the Natchez District's troops, Colonel Carlos de Grand-Pré: "Here I was regaled with different Kinds of Fruits, Wines and Parmesan Cheese, which were succeedent to a very good substantial Dinner. Hospitality and Urbanity presided at his Board. . . . We carried on a brisk and cheerful Conversation. The *Spanish* Gentlemen and Ladies with whom I had an Opportunity of conversing, do not possess that Austerity and Reserve, which are so generally ascribed to their Nation." [5]

In addition to the prevalent private hospitality of Natchez, weary travelers often visited the inns and taverns of the district. Francis Baily, in his usual critical vein, wrote, "There are two or three places here which go under the denomination of Taverns, and where you may get accomodated with board and lodging. I put up at one of them (at which there was a billiard table kept) and

---

[3]Baily, *Journal*, 351–52. Baily also wrote, "As there are no publichouses, a spirit of hospitality is kept up between all neighbours. This hospitality. . . is only shown amongst neighbours, or the friends of neighbours. . . ." *Ibid.*, 284–85.
[4]Pope, *Tour*, 29.
[5]*Ibid.*, 31.

paid my landlord a dollar per day, which was enormous, considering the fare. . . ." [6]

There were at least twelve taverns in Natchez in 1792 because that many tavern keepers signed a pledge to abide by Gayoso's regulations.[7] James Ross and John Olaverry both operated taverns in which stolen goods frequently changed hands for the price of a few drinks.[8] Benjamin Belk operated a tavern in St. Catherine Creek District.[9] Baily mentioned Seltzer's Tavern, located twelve miles from Natchez on the Natchez Trace.[10] Madame Chabot maintained an inn in Natchez where rates were as low as thirty dollars a month for lodging and food.[11] Patrick Connelly purchased a large brick and wood structure located on a hill about one thousand yards from the Spanish fort with a delightful view of the bluffs and the river. He converted this building into a tavern catering to the Natchez elite in 1798.[12] By 1800, Natchez tavern keepers contributed $965 annually to the support of the Mississippi Territory in the form of a tax which represented almost one-fifth of the total tax revenues of the territory.[13]

Food supplies were not always abundant in Natchez, but the inhabitants used ingenuity from the earliest settlements. Turkey baked dry served as bread, while venison was often boiled to serve as meat. A "mess of fish fried in bear's oil" was an early staple food.[14] Private contractors later supplied fresh beef to the Spanish garrisons at Natchez and Nogales, and smoked meat was a common

[6]Baily, *Journal*, 285.

[7]Statement, Natchez, June 26, 1792, Natchez Chancery Court Records, Vol. D, 108–109. Those signing were Juan Cali, Manuel López, Simón de Arze, Pedro Camus, Manuel García de Fernández, Edward McCabe, James Willey, Juan Carreras, Pedro Hunsir, David Ferguson, Joseph Murray, and George Overaker.

[8]Gayoso to Miró, No. 21, Natchez, March 12, 1791, AGI, PC, leg. 41.

[9]Ellicott to Pickering, Natchez, June 27, 1797, Southern Boundary MSS, U.S. & Spain, I.

[10]Baily, *Journal*, 347.

[11]Carondelet to Grand-Pré, New Orleans, September 4, 1795, AGI, PC, leg. 22.

[12]Harnett T. Kane, *Natchez on the Mississippi* (New York, 1947), 90; Natchez *Democrat*, Pilgrimages Edition, 1939.

[13]Statement of expenses for Adams County, 1800, in *Papers in Relation to the Official Conduct of Governour Sargent*, 35.

[14]Jones, *History of Protestantism*, 28.

commodity on the frontier.[15] Almost constant shortages of good Philadelphia flour induced many entrepreneurs to establish flour mills, but the majority of flour supplies for Natchez were obtained from American settlements along the upper rivers which floated their merchandise down to the Spanish markets. Good quality flour was frequently mixed with lesser grades, and rigid regulations governing the sale and distribution of flour helped prevent speculation. Mixtures of rice and flour were not uncommon, and rice was a regular component of army rations along with the proverbial *chícharos*.[16]

To supplement this diet, most settlers maintained their own vegetable gardens and fruit orchards. The wealthy contractor and

[15]Sutton Banks had such a meat-supplying contract in 1791, by which he sold meat obtained from Natchez cattlemen at 6.25 cents per pound. Gayoso to Miró, No. 125, Natchez, June 15, 1791, and No. 161, July 28, 1791, AGI, PC, leg. 41. Garet Rapalye supplied meat for Nogales, but smoked meat was also laid in against a possible shortage and because of the difficulty in keeping fresh meat in summertime. Gayoso to Beauregard, Natchez, May 17, 1791, *ibid.*

[16]Flour sold for $3 a barrel delivered at Natchez in 1786. List of John Perry's merchandise, Natchez, July 7, 1786, AGI, PC, leg. 12. In 1789 Gayoso paid $10 a barrel for 18,000 pounds (Spanish weight) of flour in 100 barrels of 180 pounds each. Gayoso to Miró, No. 9, Natchez, August 6, 1789, AGI, PC, leg. 41. In 1791 and thereafter, except for periods of famine, flour generally sold for $7 a barrel, payment extended in certificates of credit. Gayoso to Miró, No. 116, Natchez, May 31, 1791, No. 64, April 28, 1791, *ibid.* On shortages of flour and the use of rice to make an *ersatz* bread, see Carondelet's Proclamation, New Orleans, April 23, 1796, AGI, PC, leg. 34; Pontalba to (Jeanne Françoise LeBretton des Charmeaux) his wife, New Orleans, April 28, 1796 (W.P.A. translation of copies made by J. W. Cruzat of Pontalba's journal, Louisiana State University Archives), 71; hereinafter cited as *Pontalba's Journal.* Two ounces of rice daily were provided in rations to sailors, the troops, workers on fortifications, Indians, hospital patients, and indigent settlers of Natchez, which amounted to a total of 12,265 pounds, ten ounces, of rice yearly. Gayoso to Carondelet, No. 219, Natchez, December 14, 1792, AGI, PC, leg. 41. A proposed warehouse for rice was designed by Carondelet to meet the needs of New Orleans in 1796. Carondelet to Las Casas, New Orleans, May 31, 1796, AGI, SD, leg. 2643, and plan in Planos, Louisiana y Floridas, No. 175. Mills in Missouri attempted to meet the needs of Lower Louisiana with varying degrees of success. Trudeau to Carondelet, St. Louis, November 14, 1795, in Nasatir (ed.), *Before Lewis and Clark,* 370; Bartolomé Tardiveau to Carondelet, New Orleans, January 30, 1796, and Carondelet to Alcudia, New Orleans, March 1, 1796, AGI, PC, leg. 178, and AHN, ESTADO, leg. 3900.

militia commander, the Baron Joseph X. Pontalba, proudly wrote about his cabbages, broccoli, lettuce, and spinach.[17] Gayoso also loved to putter about his own garden; and when he left Natchez for New Orleans, he had a large variety of vegetable seeds and fruit tree cuttings forwarded to him by Stephen Minor.[18]

By Baily's standards, however, the people of Natchez were anything but "forward either in the luxuries or even the conveniences of life," and the English critic described the people of Natchez as similar to the second-class settlers in America.[19] It was an undeniable fact that Natchez was a frontier district composed of rustic settlers whose primary concern was in making a living from the soil. As such, it possessed all the characteristic features of a typically American frontier society.

The population, broken down into its various components by age, sex, and race, as was customary in Spanish census tables, shows that young people predominated in the district. The first census was apparently taken in 1784 when the population was 1,619. This included 616 white men, 505 white women, 275 male Negro slaves, and 223 female Negro slaves. Sixty-seven children were born during the year preceding the census, thus representing a birth rate of 41.3 per thousand. The twenty-four persons who died illustrate a death rate of 14.2 per thousand.[20]

Apparently another census was taken in 1791 by Gayoso, but it has not been located in the archives. Gayoso wrote that he did not make an earlier census because of misleading instructions, poor weather, and a desire to be accurate for the purposes of determining how many men could perform militia duty.[21]

An initial census taken in 1792 by Grand-Pré was replaced by another, presumably more accurate, count under the direction of

[17]Pontalba to his wife, New Orleans, March 24, 1796, in *Pontalba's Journal*, 47; April 20, 1796, *ibid.*, 60. Pontalba's gardening activities were so successful that he often sent his household slaves out with baskets of rich, red strawberries and other produce to sell in New Orleans.

[18]Fragment [without signature, place or date, Minor to Gayoso, 1797], AGI, PC, leg. 2371.

[19]Baily, *Journal*, 351.

[20]Census of 1784, AGI, PC, leg. 116.

[21]Gayoso to Miró, No. 27, Natchez, March 12, 1791, AGI, PC, leg. 41, mentions enclosing the census; but it is not in this legajo.

TABLE 3

CENSUS OF THE POPULATION OF NATCHEZ
JUNE 14, 1792*

	White Men			White Women			Male Negro Slaves			Female Negro Slaves			Totals
	1st Age	2nd Age	3rd Age	1st Age	2nd Age	3rd Age	1st Age	2nd Age	3rd Age	1st Age	2nd Age	3rd Age	
Santa Catalina...............	218	308	10	183	174	8	99	283	2	85	143	3	1,516
Villa Gayoso................	175	173	13	150	112	14	47	96	4	57	68	0	909
Sandy Creek and Second Creek.	81	104	20	98	66	9	81	166	8	85	97	3	818
Homochitto.................	30	43	2	22	30	2	55	83	3	64	60	7	401
Buffalo Creek..............	14	47	2	13	17	1	24	77	9	12	26	3	245
Old Tunica.................	6	38	0	6	8	0	8	15	0	1	15	4	101
Bayou Pierre...............	53	66	8	48	56	2	42	16	2	16	11	3	323
Big Black..................	3	9	0	3	8	0	5	1	2	0	2	0	33
Totals................	580	788	55	523	471	36	361	737	30	320	422	23	4,346

*Manuel Gayoso de Lemos, "Census of the Population of Natchez," Natchez, June 14, 1792, enclosed in Luis de las Casas to Conde del Campo de Alange (Havana), November 8, 1792, AGS, Guerra, leg. 6928 (Library of Congress transcript); also in AGI, PC, leg. 1441.

Gayoso in June. The results are indicated in Table 3.[22] The complete census roster which lists the heads of households offers some interesting information.[23] The population increase from 1,619 in 1784 to an estimated 4,691 in 1792 represents a 289 per cent rise in eight years. By way of comparison, Kentucky's population jump from 73,677 in 1790 to 220,955 in 1800, represents an increase of 299 per cent over a ten-year period. Tennessee, with a population of 35,691 in 1790 and 105,602 in 1800 illustrates a 295 per cent climb over the decade.[24]

Gayoso sent in his census report for 1793,[25] and the following year another census revealed the Natchez population was only 4,446.[26] The effects of the termination in royal subsidies to the tobacco planters explain the low figures. It is possible that Gayoso took no more census counts of the district; but in 1796 he estimated his population at 5,318 for the entire district, including white and colored individuals.[27] Victor Collot, who visited the Natchez

[22]Gayoso to Carondelet, No. 5, Natchez, March 10, 1792, in *ibid.;* census of June 14, 1792, AGI, PC, leg. 1441; Las Casas to Conde del Campo de Alange, Havana, November 8, 1792, AGS, Guerra Moderna, leg. 6928.

[23]Census of Natchez, 1792, AGI, PC, leg. 2353. An incomplete part of this census was published without editing by Mrs. Dunbar Rowland in "Mississippi's Colonial Population and Land Grants," *Publications* of the Mississippi Historical Society, Centenary Series, I (1916), 418–28; and by Dunbar Rowland, *History of Mississippi* (Jackson, Mississippi, 1925), 326–34. My figures were taken from the original documents but may be no more accurate because of the conflicting totals in almost all Natchez counts. By Gayoso's breakdown, the population was only 4,346 in eight counties. By adding the population by counties in the complete census, however, the total is 4,691. This was also true for the 1795 census.

[24]Statistics on the 1790–1800 population from the Census Bureau, are printed in the *World Almanac, 1960* (New York, 1960), 262. Some interesting observations on the character of frontier populations in 1790 are in Marcus L. Hansen, "The Population of the American Outlying Regions in 1790," American Historical Association *Annual Report, 1931* (3 vols.; Washington, 1932), I, appendix C, 398–408. On Louisiana's population, see *ibid.*, 404–406.

[25]It had originally been sent in Gayoso to Carondelet, No. 270, Natchez, April 27, 1793, AGI, PC, leg. 42.

[26]Gayoso's "Resumen general del padrón del Districto de Natchez," as of the end of 1794, Natchez, April 14, 1795, AGI, PC, leg. 31. Gayoso gets a total of 4,446; by adding each category I obtain 4,888.

[27]Gayoso to Carondelet (Natchez, June, 1796), draft, AGI, PC, leg. 33. Luis de Vilemont believed there were 4,000 white people in Natchez in 1795. Petition of Vilemont, undated, enclosed in Carondelet to Alcudia, New Orleans, July 30, 1795, AHN, ESTADO, leg. 3890.

District in 1796, exaggerated the population at 10,000.[28] Bishop Luis de Peñalver y Cárdenas, following his inspection in 1796 and 1797, stated that Natchez had a population of 4,556, but he probably omitted the Negro slaves.[29]

Francis Baily visited Natchez in 1797 and thought its population was about 5,000.[30] Narsworthy Hunter felt the 1800 population included 6,000 free inhabitants,[31] but Daniel Clark, Sr., wrote in the same year that there were only 4,500 whites and 2,400 Negroes.[32] According to Jedediah Morse's gazeteer, the three counties of the Mississippi Territory—Washington, Pickering, and Adams—had a population respectively of 1,250, 2,940, and 4,660. The total of 8,850 represented a slave population of 3,489.[33]

The increase of Negro slaves owes much to the successful development of the cotton industry, but slavery itself dates back to the British occupation. When the Spaniards gained control of Louisiana in 1766, a number of British subjects were anxious to open up the slave trade between Jamaica and New Orleans. Robert Ross, a Scot who lived in Natchez and was connected with the British firm of David Ross & Co., suggested in 1767 to Antonio de Ulloa, the ill-fated first governor, that an *asiento,* or slave trade franchise be granted to a number of British merchants in Jamaica to supply slaves at Pensacola, at prices equal to or better than those charged by the slave traders in the American colonies.[34]

Bernardo de Gálvez opposed the granting of private contracts on the ground that slaves thus purchased would sell at higher costs. Francisco Bouligny, later colonel of the Louisiana regular regiment, proposed that his family connections in Alicante, Spain, be granted a private contract, which Gálvez opposed, although he recognized the merits of Bouligny's own contacts and ownership of eighty slaves

[28]Collot, *A Journey in North America,* II, 62.

[29]Luis, Bishop of Louisiana, to Llaguno, New Orleans, February 16, 1797, cited in Whitaker, *Mississippi Question,* 276 n.

[30]Baily, *Journal,* 283.

[31]Hunter to editor of *Impartial Observer,* Philadelphia, February 4, 1800, in *Papers in Relation to the Official Conduct of Governour Sargent,* 8.

[32]Daniel Clark, Sr., to Claiborne, Clarksville, June 18, 1800, *ibid.,* 26.

[33]Jedediah Morse (comp.), *The American Gazetteer . . . with a Particular Description of Louisiana* (2nd ed.; Boston, 1804).

[34]Robert Ross to Antonio de Ulloa, Pensacola, April 29, 1767, AGI, PC, leg. 187-A.

on a fine Louisiana plantation. Louisiana needed an estimated 1,500 slaves annually, according to Gálvez, but the royal decree of May 10, 1777, allowing Louisiana to exchange its products for Negroes brought from the French islands evidently met the needs of the province.[35]

By 1794 there were about 25,000 Negro and mulatto slaves in Louisiana, representing more than half the total population.[36] Following an abortive revolt of the Negro slaves at Punta Cortada in 1795 and threatened outbreaks near Opelousas, Carondelet issued an order banning the further introduction of Negro or mulatto slaves.[37]

Throughout the 1790's, the prices of Negro slaves varied, but a sound average was $300 for females and $400 for males.[38] When Gayoso arrived in Natchez, he found there were approximately 1,200 slaves, 800 of whom were owned by forty wealthy families.[39] By 1800—ten years later—the number of Negroes in the Mississippi Territory was estimated at between 2,400 and 3,500.[40] In 1791 Gayoso himself purchased four slaves from Daniel Clark, who acted as the agent of Pensacola merchant, Enrique O'Neill, in disposing of a total shipment of eighty-three slaves valued at $34,511. Gayoso's four slaves cost him $1,800.[41] The governor bought a Negro named August whose age was listed as 22, from David Williams on April 16, 1792. Two years later he sold the same Negro to Elías Beauregard.[42] When Gayoso's estate was appraised in 1799, he owned fifteen slaves valued at $5,700.[43]

---

[35]Bernardo de Gálvez to Joseph de Gálvez, No. 172, Confidential, New Orleans, July 10, 1778, AGI, PC, leg. 223-B.

[36]Carondelet to Las Casas, No. 104, Confidential, New Orleans, February 9, 1794, AGI, PC, leg. 1447.

[37]Carondelet's order of New Orleans, February 19, 1796, copy enclosed in Carondelet to Antonio de St. Maxent, draft, New Orleans, February 20, 1796, AGI, PC, leg. 23. On the Negro revolt, see Carondelet to Las Casas, New Orleans, August 22, 1795, with enclosures, AGI, PC, leg. 1443-B.

[38]Bernard Marigny, *Thoughts upon the Foreign Policy of the United States* (New Orleans, 1854), 17, says females sold for $180, males for $250.

[39]Gayoso to Miró, Natchez, December 13, 1790, AGI, PC, leg. 2362.

[40]See *supra*, notes 32, 33.

[41]McBee (ed.), *Natchez Court Records*, 83. Gayoso also presided over numerous slave sales as the Natchez Chancery records show.

[42]*Ibid.*, 91.

[43]Inventory sale of Gayoso's estate, in his *causa mortuoria*, 1799, AGI, PC,

So permanently had the institution of slavery become entrenched by 1797, that Andrew Ellicott, a Quaker who personally disliked it, was forced to write, "Although domestic slavery is extremely disagreeable to the inhabitants of the eastern states, it will nevertheless be expedient to tolerate it in the district of Natchez, where that species of property is very common, and let it remain on the same footing as in the southern states, otherwise emigrants possessed of that kind of property, would be induced to settle in the Spanish territory." [44]

As the population of Natchez grew, the standard of living improved. A shortage of board lumber at first limited the size and complexity of the houses. Ezekial Forman first rented a house in 1790 as a temporary abode, which his nephew described: "The place had a small clearing and a log house on it, and he put up another log house to correspond with it, about fourteen feet apart, connected them with board, with a pizza [piazza] in front of the whole. The usual term applied to such a structure was that it was 'two pens and a passage.' This connecting passage made a fine hall, and altogether gave it a good and comfortable appearance. . . . Natchez was then a small place, with houses generally of a mean structure. . . ." [45]

Gayoso wrote that before he laid out the town plan for Natchez there were only twenty houses in the area below the hill. By 1791, however, following the construction of a church and hospital, the number of houses in Natchez had increased to thirty.[46] On the banks of Bayou Pierre stood three small houses, but further up the stream were other cabins.[47] Francis Baily, that roving critic, had a few choice words to say about housing in the Natchez District:

> The houses are chiefly framed buildings; but, though this country has been settled so long, there is all that inattention to neatness, cleanliness, and the comforts attending thereon, that there is in a country just cleared. I have seen

leg. 169. The purchase of these slaves cost the governor $5,435, showing that slaves had increased in value from 1790 to 1799.
[44]*Journal of Andrew Ellicott*, 153.
[45]Forman, *Narrative of a Journey*, 53.
[46]Gayoso to Carondelet, New Orleans, January 6, 1792, AGI, PC, leg. 2353.
[47]Pope, *Tour*, 33.

houses in this place (and those possessed by persons assuming a degree of consequence in the country) scarcely
furnished beyond the first stage of civilization, when a
few boards nailed together have served for a bedstead, and
a mattress covered with a few blankets for a bed, when
there has been scarcely a chair to sit down upon, or a
table to place anything on, but everything is in the greatest
confusion and disorder about the room. This, to be sure,
is not universally so: on the contrary, I have seen others
fitted up in the neatest manner possible; but then in the
greatest plainness, without any of those luxuries which
decorate even the cottages of our English farmers.[48]

Later, Baily added that the houses were built after "the Chinese
style—seldom more than a ground floor, and the doors of most
of the apartments opening from the street. . . . My bedroom
opened immediately on the road. . . ." [49] In one house, Baily saw the
one room filled with all manner of goods, including lumber.[50]

This rustic description did not extend to Gayoso's mansion,
which soon became the social and political center of Natchez.
When Grand-Pré complained that there was no suitable residence
for the commandant of Natchez in 1788, the governor-general
recommended renting a house from Juan Vaucheret until a new
structure, not to exceed $8,000, could be built. It was this house
that Gayoso occupied when he first arrived in Natchez.[51] By 1794
Gayoso had received land grants totaling 1,242 acres, the largest of
which included the mansion known as Concord. The house and its
thousand acres of excellent land, outbuildings, and improvements
were transferred to Margaret Cyrilla Watts in 1796, at which time
Concord was valued at $11,500.[52]

[48]Baily, *Journal*, 283.
[49]*Ibid.*, 289.
[50]*Ibid.*, 352.
[51]Pay sheet for Vaucheret and Minor for rental of government house
from 1789 to 1797, AGI, PC, leg. 538-B. The annual rental was $360. A royal
decree of July 1, 1789, gave the Natchez commandant $365 annually for
renting the house. The background of this provision is in Grand-Pré to Miró,
No. 730, Natchez, October 25, 1788, copy enclosed with comments of Miró
to Valdés, No. 134, New Orleans, November 12, 1788, AHN, ESTADO, leg.
3888 *bis*.
[52]McBee (ed.), *Natchez Court Records*, 405; *American State Papers*,
Class VIII: *Public Lands* (Washington, 1834), I, 875-76; Statement of
Stephen Watts, Natchez, March 4, 1796, in Gayoso's matrimonial *expediente*,

An interesting description of Concord was rendered by a lady who remembered the mansion as a young girl:

> The very first sight of the house, seen through a long vista of noble trees, as you enter the gate, forms a splendid picture. About half way from the gate is a large pond surrounded by gnarled old cedars, after which the road branches into two, on each side of an extensive sloping lawn, and the end of the delightful drive brings us to the house itself.
>
> Built of brick with walls fully two feet thick, there is an air of massiveness and solidity about this grand old house that gives promise of centuries of useful existance before it shall succumb to the leveling hand of time.
>
> On the ground floor a broad gallery paved with brick completely circles the house, and lofty pillars reaching to the roof support another broad gallery upon which all the second story rooms open. These pillars are about four feet in diameter, made of brick covered with mortar, which gives them the appearance of stone. Two winding flights of stairs, one on each side of the entrance, made of the purest white marble, lead from the ground to the upper gallery, where they meet in a solid slab of snow white marble about six feet wide by ten feet long. . . . A vestibule paved with alternate squares of black and white marble, after the houses of Pompeii, leads through the richly carved front door into a broad hall extending the full length of the house. . . .[53]

Gayoso filled his mansion with ornate furniture imported from Spain and Santo Domingo.[54] Bernard Marigny, who knew Gayoso,

---

AGMS; Marriage contract, Gayoso and Margaret Cyrilla Watts, Natchez, January 14, 1796, Cole Papers. In 1799 Daniel Clark, Jr., bought Concord from Gayoso's widow for $5,000. Clark sold it to William Lintot in 1800 and later that year Stephen Minor bought it for $10,000. McBee (ed.), *Natchez Court Records*, 405; *American State Papers*, Class VIII: *Public Lands*, III, 466.

[53]"Concord, a Relic of Spanish Rule—Gubernatorial Mansion of Governor Gayoso," undated clipping from the *Times-Democrat* (New Orleans), in Cole Papers. Another description of Concord, which was destroyed by fire in 1900, is in Mrs. N. D. Deupree, "Some Historic Homes of Mississippi," *Publications* of the Mississippi Historical Society, VI (1902), 255–56.

[54]Grace King, "The Real Philip Nolan," *Publications* of the Louisiana Historical Society, X (1917), 91; inventory of Gayoso's property in *causa mortuoria*, 1799, AGI, PC, leg. 169. Mrs. C. Grenes Cole of New Orleans, a lineal descendant of Gayoso, still owns Gayoso's mahogany bed.

wrote that Gayoso was "of high stature, and stoutly built." He spoke English fluently and was quite American in his manners. "He was fond of horses, of good cheer and madeira," added Marigny.[55] To this beautiful home, Gayoso brought his second wife, Elizabeth Watts, daughter of Stephen and Frances Assheton Watts.[56] Gayoso's first wife, Theresa Hopman y Gayoso, had died in Natchez on September 3, 1790.[57] Less than two years after her death, it was rumored in New Orleans that Gayoso was paying court to the young Watts girl. However, according to the Baron de Pontalba, "no one believes in that marriage." [58] Yet on April 23, 1792, eleven days after Pontalba stated this opinion, Gayoso and Elizabeth Watts were married.[59]

It was an unusual ceremony because Gayoso failed to request permission from the Secretary of War in Spain for the nuptials, as was customary for those wishing their widows to be elegible for the military pension. No military records have been located which mention the fact that Gayoso was married to Elizabeth Watts, nor does he mention her in requesting official permission to marry again in 1796.[60] Unfortunately, Gayoso's second wife also contracted a fever. Within three months after the marriage, Elizabeth Watts died, and Gayoso was once again a widower. A curious legend concerning Gayoso's second wife relates that the grief-stricken governor kept his dead wife in a tub filled with embalming fluid on the second story of Concord.[61]

Several years passed before Gayoso began courting the younger sister of his deceased wife, Elizabeth. Margaret Cyrilla Watts was born on Belmont Plantation March 23, 1775, and baptized by

[55]Marigny, *Thoughts upon the Foreign Policy of the United States,* 16.
[56]Elizabeth Watts was born in Philadelphia on May 4, 1773. Stanley Clisby Arthur and George Campbell Huchet de Kernion (eds.), *Old Families of Louisiana* (New Orleans, 1931), 311.
[57]Certificate of burial by Gregorio White, Natchez, September 3, 1790, copy in Gayoso's matrimonial *expediente,* 1797, AGMS.
[58]Pontalba to Miró, New Orleans, April 12, 1792, in Cruzat (trans.), "Letters written to Miró by Pontalba," 399.
[59]Family records, Cole Papers.
[60]Matrimonial *expediente* of Gayoso, AGMS.
[61]Typed MS, anonymous and without date, in Cole Papers. Mrs. Cole, the owner of the document, states there is no truth to the legend.

the bishop, Fray Cyrillo de Barcelona at La Fourche in October, 1785.[62] The road to matrimony was not completely smooth, however, and several curious incidents illustrate the problems encountered by military officers in Louisiana. When Gayoso sailed north to New Madrid in 1795, ugly rumors circulated to the effect that he was keeping a mistress there, had built a house for her, and intended to marry her. Carondelet, the governor-general heard these rumors and reminded Gayoso that it was already common knowledge that he had lived as a husband to Margaret Watts in Natchez; he warned him that the Natchez governor should not make a habit of such practices because of the opposition of the Bishop to irregularities in moral standards.[63]

It is highly possible that the rumor was unfounded and originated in the quarrel between Gayoso and the commandant of San Fernando de las Barrancas, Captain Vicente Folch. Someone had written to the intendant with the story, and the pernicious character of the story fits Folch's mood at that time. In any event, Gayoso was still in the good graces of the bishop in 1796.[64] It is highly doubtful that Gayoso requested permission to marry Margaret Cyrilla Watts before April 10, 1796.[65] On January 14, 1796, Gayoso and Margaret signed a marriage intention contract in Natchez in which they promised "to celebrate their Nuptials according to the Rites of the Church as soon as the Royal license is obtained and by promise they now constitute the same as legitimate and true Matrimony. . . ."[66]

Carondelet forwarded Gayoso's request to marry through the captain-general of Cuba to the secretary of war, but these official

[62]Arthur and Kernion (eds.), *Old Families of Louisiana*, 311; baptismal statement of Cyrillo Barcelona, Havana, March 4, 1793, copy in Gayoso's matrimonial *expediente*. The original baptismal statement of Margaret was stolen along with other family papers in Willing's 1778 raid on Tory plantations along the lower Mississippi. Statement of Stephen Watts, Natchez, March 5, 1796, and baptism *ibid*.

[63]Carondelet to Gayoso, New Orleans, December 16, 1795, Bancroft Library, translation furnished through the courtesy of Professor A. P. Nasatir of San Diego State College.

[64]Carondelet to Gayoso, New Orleans, May 30, 1796, AGI, PC, leg. 23.

[65]Gayoso's petition to marry, New Orleans, April 10, 1796, in his matrimonial *expediente*.

[66]Contract in Cole papers. Arthur and Kernion (eds.), *Old Families of Louisiana*, 311, gives the date as July 14, 1796.

channels took considerable time. Official permission was not forth-coming from the Council of War until March 11, 1797, and not forwarded to Gayoso until March 13,[67] As Margaret grew heavy with child, Gayoso grew concerned over their official status and wrote Carondelet asking the governor-general to grant interim permission, which Carondelet declined to do in the circumstances.[68]

On Friday, July 14, 1797, at seven minutes to one in the morning, Margaret Watts de Gayoso gave birth to "a strong, healthy son" whom Gayoso named Fernando. When the Gayosos went to New Orleans later that year, an interesting religious ceremony took place when the bishop, Luis Peñalver y Cárdenas, baptized young Fernando and married his parents on the same Sunday, December 10, 1797.[69]

Gayoso's marriage to an American should not be considered unusual. Gayarré calls attention to the fact that the lack of Spanish women frequently influenced Spanish governors, military officers, and Louisiana residents to marry into American families of French or American descent.[70] Gayoso recognized that his American wife was a valuable asset. Their home in Natchez became a social center; and Gayoso once wrote the Indian leader, Piomingo, who was pro-American, "If I am anything else than a Spaniard, I am an American as I have married one." [71]

Gayoso and his lady entertained in the grand continental man-ner, thus bringing a touch of European manners and customs to the rustic Spanish-American frontier. The governor made extensive use of "banquet diplomacy," and on more than one occasion a potential enemy was disarmed by a charming dinner followed by a glass of mellow Madeira wine or a fine Havana cigar. Gayoso

[67]*Expediente* of Gayoso, 1797, AGMS.

[68]Carondelet to Las Casas, No. 926, New Orleans, August 8, 1796, AGI, PC, leg. 1444; Carondelet to Gayoso, New Orleans, December 29, 30, 1796, AGI, PC, leg. 23.

[69]Certificate of Gayoso, Natchez, July 14, 1797, Cole Papers; Baptismal certificate, St. Louis Cathedral Archives, folio 50; Marriage certificate, *ibid.*, folio 115.

[70]Gayarré, *History of Louisiana, The Spanish Dominion*, 311.

[71]Gayoso to Piomingo, St. Ferdinand of the Bluffs, June 23, 1795, AGI, PC, leg. 211.

himself enjoyed cigars and took snuff on occasion.[72] He maintained an excellent wine cellar, much of which he took to New Orleans with him.[73]

With only $500 extra from his pay for the payment of "table expenses," it was obvious that Gayoso's free-spending manner of winning friends for the king of Spain was going to cost more than his meager salary would cover. After several years, Gayoso wrote directly to the Spanish ministers and to his superior in Louisiana explaining his destitute situation. When the Duke of Kent proposed a trip to Louisiana in 1794, Gayoso intended to borrow money to present a fancy front for the visiting royalty.[74] From John McDonough of New Orleans Gayoso had borrowed more than $3,200 at 10 per cent interest; when Gayoso was unable to repay the note despite repeated dunning requests, McDonough instituted legal action against the governor.[75]

The Natchez governor was undoubtedly careless with money and the records of his expenditures. When he handled millions of pesos

[72]Gayoso to Peggy [Watts Gayoso], Natchez, June, 1797, Cole Papers; Gayoso to Minor, New Orleans, December 20, 1797, Gayoso MSS., Louisiana State University Archives.

[73]Gayoso wrote to his wife from New Orleans, "There is not a bottle to be had for love or money, therefore leaving in the house as many as three or four hundred you would do well to send down all the rest." Gayoso to Peggy, New Orleans, August 22, 1797, Cole Papers. An inventory of Gayoso's wines was taken at his death, showing the large variety. *Causa mortuoria,* 1799, AGI, PC, leg. 169.

[74]"I have earned the affection of these people, using all my power having entertained and dined them all of which I do to the sacrifice of my own interests to the point of going into debt." Gayoso to Miró, No. 4, Natchez, January 17, 1791, AGI, PC, leg. 152, and leg. 1446. "I find myself completely destitute of all means having already borrowed considerably, in consequence of His Majesty's order when I came to this province to invite, dine and do whatever necessary to carry out my commission." Gayoso to Floridablanca, New Orleans, January 26, 1792, AHN, ESTADO, leg. 3902. "I propose to borrow some money in order to receive His Highness with proper attention. . . ." Gayoso to Alcudia, Confidential, Natchez, February 18, 1794, in "Selections from the Draper Collection in the Possession of the State Historical Society of Wisconsin, to Elucidate the Proposed French Expedition under George Rogers Clark," American Historical Association *Annual Report, 1896* (2 vols.; Washington, 1897), I, 1044.

[75]James Carrick [power of attorney for Juan McDonough] *v.* Gayoso, AGI, PC, leg. 169; Case tried in New Orleans, December 14, 1795, AGI, PC, leg. 22.

salvaged from the wreck of the *San Pedro de Alcántara* off Peniche, Portugal, in 1786, Gayoso misplaced a receipt for $16,000. Ten years later, after he had already paid the sum from his own pockets, he discovered the receipt.[76] Again, on March 17, 1797, when Gayoso received 16,000 *reales* for the purpose of supplying the boundary commission, he failed to keep accurate records of his expenses. The officer who had taken charge of the money subsequently left for Ecuador with Carondelet, and Gayoso's estate was held liable for the 16,000 *reales*.[77]

When the governor died, his father-in-law wrote, "Mr. Gayoso died considerably in debt so that the widow's income is but small." [78] The total indebtedness, according to the records, exceeded $16,500, while the total income from sales of his property was only $11,700.69.[79]

In addition to entertaining the people of Natchez and worthy transients, Gayoso spent considerable time and money in promoting the sport of kings—horse racing. Most of the prominent men in the Natchez District were connected with the sport. Andrew Jackson owned a quarter horse track near Bayou Pierre.[80] In 1795 Richard King received a franchise to supply refreshments to the gentlemen of the "Turff" attending the annual course events at his track in Natchez. King was one of the pioneers of Natchez racing, having created a subscription organization in 1794 for stake races. Gayoso had contributed ten dollars for the prizes, and the list of fellow contributors reads like a who's who in colonial Natchez: Francisco Lennan, William Dunbar, Ezekiel Forman, Robert Scott, James McIntosh, William Vousdan, Stephen Minor, Joseph Vidal, Luis Faure, Abner Green, Stephen Watts, and Parker Carradine to name a few of the thirty-nine subscribers. The track was called Fleetfield, and races were initiated on October 29, 1795. Regulations carrying weights for horses of various ages were set forth;

[76]Gayoso to Carondelet, New Madrid, December 3, 1795, AGI, PC, leg. 43.

[77]*Causa mortuoria* of Gayoso, AGI, PC, leg. 169; Holmes (ed.), *Documentos de la Luisiana*, 70.

[78]Stephen Watts to [addressee unknown], New Orleans, October 28, 1799, Cole Papers.

[79]*Causa mortuoria,* AGI, PC, leg. 169.

[80]Moore, "Marriage of General Andrew Jackson and Mrs. Robards," 11.

entrance fees of fifteen dollars were to be paid three days before the day of running and horses were to be entered by name, age, and color with Captain King. Ezekiel Forman and Stephen Minor were named managers of the races. Two sweepstakes were also included during each racing day.[81]

Gayoso owned matched bay horses and a black and a roan. His correspondence with Stephen Minor, another admirer of good horseflesh, was filled with references to their mutual interest in horses.[82] Early in 1799 Gayoso ordered from John Forbes of William Panton's firm "an elastic jacket, which is a very convenient apparell [sic] for a corpolent [sic] person to ride on horse back." [83]

Other amusements in Natchez included gambling and strawberrying on the nearby prairies.[84] While the agricultural duties were often monotonous and time-consuming, as the Natchez planters grew more prosperous there was additional time to enjoy life; and many seem to have lived well and employed leisure time to their advantage.

Educational opportunities were often indifferent in Louisiana and West Florida, offering little contrast with those enjoyed in southern areas of the United States. The harshest critic of Spanish Louisiana, Berquin-Duvallon, wrote in 1803: "There is in that land no public institution suitable for the education of the youth other than one simple school maintained by the Government, and composed of some fifty children, almost all from poor families, where they learn to read, write, and count in both the French and Spanish tongues; and the home of French Nuns where a few young girls board and where is also a class for day students. There is also a boarding school started about fifteen months ago for young

[81]Grand-Pré to Carondelet, No. 136, Natchez, February 29, 1796, with various enclosures, AGI, PC, leg. 33.

[82]Gayoso to Minor, New Orleans, August 8, September 5, December 20, 23, 1797, February 5, 1798, in Gayoso MSS., Louisiana State University Archives; Minor to Gayoso, Natchez, October 1, 11, 21, November 19, 23, 1797, AGI, PC, leg. 2371; Minor to Gayoso, Natchez, January 15, 1798, AGI, PC, leg. 215-A.

[83]Gayoso to John Forbes, New Orleans, March 18, 1799, Cole Papers. Gayoso's estate shows he had borrowed a coach from the bishop and owned six horses valued at $335. *Causa mortuoria,* 1799, AGI, PC, leg. 169.

[84]Forman, *Narrative,* 57.

creoles, which is directed by a man not lacking in talent for that vocation." [85]

Because the creoles objected to paying for education, schools in New Orleans were poorly attended, according to Berquin-Duvallon; and the newest one was about to fold for want of support. Many children were sent to private schools at two dollars a month; but in the rural areas planters frequently picked up a "poor wretch" from along the highway and gave him room, board, and a small fee in exchange for his teaching their children all he knew—which was seldom much. Berquin-Duvallon suggested using the prospect of good salaries to attract good teachers and insure proper education of the youth. [86] A contemporary American officer estimated that illiteracy exceeded 50 per cent, and even those who were taught reading and writing did not excel in it. [87]

If the quality of education in more cosmopolitan New Orleans was as low as stated by Berquin-Duvallon, what must it have been in Natchez when Gayoso once wrote his friend Minor to send his daughter to New Orleans where educational opportunities were better? [88] As early as 1785, governor-general Miró suggested the establishment of a public school in Natchez, staffed by English-speaking Irish priests who would teach the children of Anglo-Americans there not only the Spanish language but also the Roman Catholic religion. [89]

When Gayoso arrived and expressed his feelings about the district under his command, he included some remarks on education:

> The defects noted in the present generation cannot be completely remedied but those in the next generation can be by means of a public education which will instill in the hearts of the youth a sincere appreciation toward whomever has given instruction to him. This country lacks

[85]Berquin-Duvallon, *Vue de la colonie*, 293. J. M. Bart planned to open a school in New Orleans in 1803. *Moniteur de la Louisiane*, No. 345 (May 28, 1803).

[86]Berquin-Duvallon, *Vue de la colonie*, 294-95.

[87]Stoddard, *Sketches, Historical and Descriptive of Louisiana*, 320.

[88]Gayoso to Minor, New Orleans, November 29, 1798, Gayoso MSS., Louisiana State University Archives.

[89]Bernardo de Gálvez to José de Gálvez, No. 56, by preference, Mexico, October 27, 1785, AHN, ESTADO, leg. 3888 *bis*.

this support; there is only one Spanish public school in New Orleans; if His Majesty would see fit to order several more established in this large province, especially three in the jurisdiction of my Government, they would have most advantageous results, for not only will they form the tender hearts, but they will also fill those of their parents with gratitude.[90]

Although there were no regularly established schools in Natchez during the Spanish period, there were schoolmasters. Gayoso suggested that surveyors' fees, doctors' bills, and wages of daily workers and schoolmasters be privileged debts under the moratorium.[91] Patrick Taggert was a Natchez schoolmaster whose theoretical training was supplemented by a good deal of natural mechanical skill. He was suggested by William Dunbar for the post of deputy surveyor of the Spanish boundary commission in 1798, and Ellicott has described his invention of a wooden sight for the old surveying compass then in use.[92]

In 1792 Valentine Thomas Dalton contracted to dwell in Carlos de Grand-Pré's home for three years and teach all his children to speak and write the English language in exchange for board and lodging plus $100 per annum and 250 arpents of land on Cole's Creek. But three years later Dalton admitted that he had not lived up to his part of the bargain and that the contract was therefore null and void.[93]

Berquin-Duvallon was also critical of the lack of interest in New Orleans in the printed word. "A book-seller," he wrote, "would die of hunger in the middle of his books unless he sold a book of interest to his readers on how to double your money in one year." [94] The first newspaper of the lower Mississippi Valley, *Moniteur de la Louisiane*, began publication in New Orleans under Louis Duclot's

[90]Gayoso's State of the Province of Louisiana, Natchez, July 5, 1792, forwarded to Alcudia, AGI, PC, leg. 2353. *Cf.* the translation in Robertson (ed.), *Louisiana*, I, 288–89.
[91]Gayoso to Carondelet, No. 221, Natchez, December 14, 1792, AGI, PC, leg. 41.
[92]Dunbar to Gayoso, Natchez, March 29, 1798, AGI, PC, leg. 215-A; *Journal of Andrew Ellicott*, appendix, 48.
[93]McBee (ed.), *Natchez Court Records*, 93.
[94]Berquin-Duvallon, *Vue de la colonie*, 295–96.

direction in 1794. In 1797, the *Moniteur* changed hands and began a new series under Jean Baptiste LeSieur Fontaine.[95] Printing in Spanish New Orleans dated back to O'Reilly's arrival when the former French official printer, Antoine Boudousquier, accepted a contract with the Spanish government to publish their official decrees.[96] It was the *Moniteur*, however, that circulated throughout the province, though it was difficult to find subscribers in the Natchez District because of a lack of rapid communication and transportation.[97] There was no press in Natchez until the arrival of Andrew Marschalk with the American troops in 1798. He brought a small mahogany press to the Walnut Hills and thirty pounds of type with which he printed the first territorial laws of Mississippi.[98]

With no newspapers and few books available for most of the population, it was little wonder that the most antiquated ideas regarding medicine should prevail. Natchez was not particularly unhealthy; and Andrew Ellicott wrote, "Notwithstanding the heat of the climate the inhabitants enjoy a good state of health. The bad effects of the heat are in some manner counteracted by high winds & constant breezes." [99] Nevertheless, hot weather played havoc with horses from San Antonio to Opelousas, and a strange distemper called "Yellow Water" attacked horses throughout the South in the 1790's.[100] Natchez had other extremes of weather which the residents had to endure. In 1792 there was record flooding following heavy rains which damaged the fortifications from

[95]Jack D. L. Holmes, "The Two Series of the *Moniteur de la Louisiane*," *Bulletin* of the New York Public Library, LXIV (June, 1960), 323–28; Jack D. L. Holmes (ed. & trans.), "The *Moniteur de la Louisiane* in 1798," *Louisiana History*, II (Spring, 1961), 230–53.

[96]Denis Braud was another early printer who printed one of O'Reilly's regulations governing cabarets in New Orleans, October 8, 1769. Bernardo de Gálvez to José de Gálvez, No. 231, New Orleans, January 15, 1779, AGI, PC, leg. 223-B; Acts of the New Orleans Cabildo (5 vols.; New Orleans Public Library), January 31, 1777, I, 220.

[97]Minor to Gayoso, Natchez, December 14, 1797, AGI, PC, leg. 2371.

[98]John Hebron Moore (ed.), "Claiborne's Journal in 'Mississippi' a Fragment from the Unpublished Second Volume of the History of Mississippi," *Journal of Mississippi History*, XXII (April, 1960), 88–89.

[99]Ellicott to Secretary of State, Natchez, April 13, 1797, Southern Boundary MSS, U.S. and Spain, I.

[100]*Letters of Benjamin Hawkins, 1796–1806*, Vol. IX, *Collections* of the Georgia Historical Society (Savannah, 1916), 46.

Natchez to Nogales.[101] On Sunday, December 3, 1797, there was a record snowfall in Natchez with attendant cold and hardship.[102]

There were numerous cases of illness at Natchez of interest to medical historians. In the summer of 1796 and 1797 many of the inhabitants fled the town of Natchez for the more healthy highlands when a "fever" struck down people by the hundreds. Andrew Ellicott was forced to move his camp seven miles from town to a shady grove.[103] A list of ailments encountered at Natchez includes venereal disease,[104] apoplexy,[105] sore eyes,[106] pleurisy,[107] "remitting and intermitting billious fevers," inflammation of the liver, cholera, dysentery, milk sickness, goiter, typhus, dyspepsia, measles, smallpox, and scarlet fever.[108] Among the slaves, common ailments included worm fever, leprosy, elephantiasis, and body yaws. One writer reported, "You will scarcely find among ten persons under thirty, one whose teeth are entirely sound." [109] Poison ivy plagued Andrew Ellicott and Francis Baily.[110]

Various folk remedies were employed along the Spanish-American frontier with varying degrees of success. Against a poisonous honey made from the white wolf's tongue flower, milk was the most effi-

[101]Gayoso to Carondelet, No. 199, Natchez, November 26; No. 196, November 19, 1792, AGI, PC, leg. 41.

[102]Minor to Gayoso, Natchez, December 3, 1797, AGI, PC, leg. 2371.

[103]Ellicott to Secretary of State, Camp, Seven Miles from Natchez, September 12, 1797, Southern Boundary MSS, U.S. and Spain, I; Jack D. L. Holmes, "Medical Practice in the Lower Mississippi Valley during the Spanish Period, 1769–1803," *Alabama Journal of Medical Sciences*, I (July, 1964), 332–38.

[104]William Collins *v*. Ebenezer Rees, in McBee (ed.), *Natchez Court Records*, 181.

[105]Minor to Gayoso, Natchez, October 1, 1797, AGI, PC, leg. 2371.

[106]Gayoso to Peggy, New Orleans, October 18, 1797, Cole Papers; Gayoso to Minor, New Orleans, October 23, 1797, Gayoso MSS., Louisiana State University Archives.

[107]Minor to Gayoso, Natchez, January 15, 1797, AGI, PC, leg. 215-A.

[108]R. Baird, *View of the Valley of the Mississippi* (Philadelphia, 1832), 74–75; Gayoso to Minor, New Orleans, November 29, 1798, Gayoso MSS., Louisiana State University Archives; Forman, *Narrative*, 57.

[109]Constantin François Chasseboeuf, Comte de Volney, *Tableau du Climat et du Sol des Etats-Unis d'Amerique* (2 vols.; Paris, 1803; English translation, Philadelphia, 1804), 226.

[110]Baily, *Journal*, 383.

cacious antidote.[111] To get rid of a four-day fever, Henry Owen tanned himself.[112] William Dunbar tried the ubiquitous cure-all, bleeding, to cure a violent fever and headache,[113] while Gayoso did the same to cure lameness and a touch of scurvey.[114] Ellicott employed a pill made by Dr. Rush in Philadelphia consisting of two grains of calomel and one-half grain of gamboge, combined by means of a little soap, to avoid the fever. It worked until he ran out of pills.[115]

Herbe à Béquet was said to cure venereal disease.[116] William Panton of the famous mercantile firm wrote for a steel truss to keep his "guts together." [117] Spain, during the closing decade of the eighteenth century, was more than a little interested in improving medical knowledge, as the number of medical books translated into Spanish, schools of veterinarian science, and medical schools established indicates.[118] It was no surprise, therefore, that the Ministry of War forwarded new recommended prescriptions for curing rheumatism and yellow fever. Both remedies were employed in Natchez and Louisiana.[119]

Shortly after his arrival at Natchez, Gayoso inspected the hospital facilities and was appalled at his discovery. The sick could find no shelter from the rain because the sides and roof leaked. When the river rose, the hospital was flooded. Repairs to the building, which was almost destroyed during a hurricane, would cost more than the complete reconstruction of a new hospital on a better location.

---

[111]*Letters of Hawkins*, 46–47. Carondelet also took milk to cure himself of illness. Carondelet to Gayoso, New Orleans, October 12, 1796, AGI, PC, leg. 23.

[112]Owen to Joseph Vidal, New Madrid, October 19, 1794, AGI, PC, leg. 2371.

[113]Dunbar to Gayoso, Natchez, November 7, 1798, AGI, PC, leg. 215-B.

[114]Gayoso to Carondelet, New Madrid, September 27, 1795, AGI, PC, leg. 43.

[115]*Journal of Andrew Ellicott*, 292; Catharine Van Cortlandt Mathews, *Andrew Ellicott, His Life and Letters* (New York, 1908), 177.

[116]Pierre Lyonnet, Observations on Louisiana (November, 1794), Archive Etrangere (Paris), Etats-Unis, VII, 18.

[117]Panton to unknown addressee, Pensacola, July 19, 1794, Forbes Collection, Mobile Public Library Archives.

[118]Serrano (ed.), *Príncipe de la Paz, Memorias*, I, 198–202.

[119]Carondelet to Gayoso, New Orleans, December 12, 1793, AGI, PC, leg. 2363; Morales to Gardoqui, New Orleans, October 31, 1796, Spanish MSS., Mississippi Valley (New Orleans Public Library), IV, 266–68.

Gayoso handled the groundwork, drew a sketch of what he wanted, and went to New Orleans where he found support for the project from Miró.[120] Miró testified that he had built the original Natchez hospital as a campaign building in 1782. In 1784 the orderly who exercised the functions of surgeon was dismissed from the service for some unknown crime.[121]

Gayoso liberally interpreted the functions for which royal hospitals were created in Spanish America.[122] Sometimes this meant trouble with the army accountant Josef de Orué. Gayoso had ordered ill transients admitted on the same basis as properly qualified military personnel. When the accountant challenged this "breach of established procedure," Gayoso argued that the lack of a charity hospital and the demands of humanity dictated his actions, and he refused to change without express orders from the king.[123] On another occasion, when one of his men injured the son of the great Choctaw chief, Zapatos Colorados, Gayoso ordered him admitted to the hospital and cured.

Another duty which Gayoso performed in the face of innumerable difficulties was securing sufficient medicines of adequate quality. Glover's salt, quinine powder, and cream of tartar were among the most useful pharmaceuticals; but it was often difficult to obtain enough fresh stock.[124] In order to provide sufficient water for baths and other needs of the ill, Gayoso proposed the construction of a new well or a road to connect with the river and

[120]Gayoso to Miró, No. 11, Natchez, August 8, 1789, New Orleans, August 27, 1790, March 29, 1790, AGI, PC, leg. 41; *expediente* on the Natchez Royal Hospital, 1790, AGI, PC, leg. 481; Planos, Luisiana y Floridas, No. 136 (AGI).

[121]Phelipe Treviño to Navarro, Natchez, August 28, 1784, AGI, PC, leg. 590.

[122]For the regulations on royal hospitals, Madrid, 1776, AGI, PC, leg. 569, see A. P. Nasatir (trans.), "Royal Hospitals in Colonial Spanish America," *Annals of Medical History*, Third Series, IV (1942), 481–503.

[123]Gayoso to Miró, No. 147, Natchez, July 19, 1791; Gayoso to Carondelet, New Orleans, February 11, 1792, AGI, PC, leg. 41.

[124]Inventory of Natchez hospital by Juan Joseph Rodríguez, Natchez, January 2, 1790, enclosed in Grand-Pré to Miró, Natchez, June 14, 1790, AGI, PC, leg. 16. Other lists of medicines and their quality are in Gayoso to Miró, No. 81, Natchez, May 9, 1791; Gayoso to Carondelet, No. 112, Natchez, June 18, 1792, AGI, PC, leg. 41; Gayoso to Carondelet, No. 557, Natchez, September 19, 1794, AGI, PC, leg. 30; Gayoso to Carondelet, Natchez, August 31, 1796, AGI, PC, leg. 1447.

received authorization from the Spanish government to carry out both plans.[125]

Medical ethics and rigid licensing were carefully supervised by the Spanish government in New Orleans. Even pharmacists were expected to undergo a thorough examination of their medical skill.[126] When Paul Alliot, a French physician, attempted to practice without first securing official permission and licensing, he was arrested and deported from Louisiana.[127] Dr. John Sappington of the Opelousas Post was called to task for over-charging the priest, Father Pedro de Zamora, and the government cut the cost from $58.50 to $16.[128] Perhaps the most curious example of medical professional ethics occurred in Natchez in 1794 when Doctor of Physic Benjamin Adams signed a contract with Polser Shilling, by which Shilling, who was "deprived of the use of one of his thighs," promised to pay Adams $100 for attention and medical ability if, within three months, Adams' cure enabled the man to walk without the help of a staff.[129]

Natchez never had enough surgeons or physicians to meet the medical needs of its growing population. Dr. Abner West died shortly after Gayoso arrived in 1789.[130] Other physicians practicing or residing in Natchez included Dr. John Brady, Dr. Thomas Wood, Dr. Charles West, and Juan Monge.[131] The most outstanding surgeon in Natchez was Louis Faure, who arrived from France in 1784 as a surgeon on a merchant vessel. He joined the Spanish medical service and was sent to Natchez at an annual salary of $360. He also served as chief pharmacist of Natchez, but the accountant declined to allow him financial responsibility for the purchase of the medicines.[132]

[125]Gayoso to Miró, New Orleans, August 27, 1790, AGI, PC, leg. 41.

[126]Peyroux de Rochemolive's examination, New Orleans, 1770, in *Actas*, New Orleans Cabildo, I, 9–11.

[127]Robertson (ed.), *Louisiana*, I, 145–46.

[128]Zamora to Carondelet, Opelousas, September 5, 1796, AGI, PC, leg. 34; Carondelet to Duralde, New Orleans, September 26, 1796, AGI, PC, leg. 23.

[129]Dated Natchez, June 9, 1794, in McBee (ed.), *Natchez Court Records*, 152.
[130]*Ibid.*, 71.
[131]*Ibid.*, 94, 118, 120, 124, 136.
[132]Petition of Luis Faure, Natchez, September 5, 1792, enclosed with Gayoso's recommendations to Carondelet, No. 151, Natchez, September 7, 1792, and accountant Orue's replies, November 14, 1792, in AGI, PC, leg. 41; Holmes (ed.), *Documentos de la Luisiana*, 209 n.

Dr. Charles Todd was little help because he contracted the fever when he was most needed at Nogales.[133] Dr. Samuel Flowers took Faure's job at the Natchez hospital when Faure was needed at Nogales.[134] A Dr. Charles Watrous accompanied Francis Baily on his trip to Natchez and bought land near Natchez. He died prior to 1805.[135] A surgeon of the second battalion in the Louisiana Infantry Regiment, José Fernández, had served in the Mississippi Squadron; but fever ended his usefulness at Natchez.[136] Dr. Samuel W. Dorsey, a planter at Tensaw, served as surgeon at Nogales in 1797 and 1798.[137]

In addition to the surgeons and physicians, a number of lesser medical men worked in the Natchez Royal Hospital. The majordomo from 1782 to 1783 was Manuel García de Texada.[138] Andrés Gil, the intern from 1792 to 1796, was a former bleeder on a troop transport.[139] For six years, from 1792 to 1798, Juan Pérez served as orderly or *cavo de sala*, at an annual salary of $180.[140]

By 1797 Natchez was no second New Orleans, but it did enjoy some of the amenities of more established communities on the frontier. Gayoso watched the town grow and experienced considerable pleasure in the prosperity and happiness of those over whom he had been chosen to rule. In a measure, the social and economic facets of Gayoso's administration help to explain the success and failure of other aspects of his task, particularly the defenses of the Natchez District.

[133]Gayoso to Beauregard, Natchez, July 24, 1792, and Gayoso to Carondelet, No. 135, Natchez, July 24, 1792, AGI, PC, leg. 41.
[134]*Ibid.* Flowers lived twenty-one leagues from Natchez and was the only other qualified surgeon in Natchez in 1796. Gayoso to Carondelet, No. 676, Natchez, July 27, 1796, AGI, PC, leg. 43.
[135]Baily, *Journal*, 286; McBee (ed.), *Natchez Court Records*, 131, 571.
[136]Petition of José Fernández, enclosed in Grand-Pré to Carondelet, No. 79, Natchez, October 23, 1795, AGI, PC, leg. 32.
[137]Rowland (ed.), *Encyclopedia of Mississippi History*, I, 653; Gayoso to Minor, New Orleans, December 5, 1797, Gayoso MSS., Louisiana State University Archives; Gayoso to Beauregard, New Orleans, January 10, 1798, AGI, PC, leg. 2354.
[138]Pay sheet of García, AGI, PC, leg. 538-A.
[139]Pay sheet of Gil, *ibid.*; Gayoso to Beauregard, Natchez, May 23, 1797, AGI, PC, leg. 43; Carondelet to Gayoso, New Orleans, August 2, 1796, AGI, PC, leg. 23.
[140]Gayoso to Miró, No. 22, New Orleans, April 24, 1790, AGI, PC, leg. 41; pay sheet of Pérez, AGI, PC, leg. 538-A.

CHAPTER VI

Frontier Defense, 1789-1797

THE REORGANIZATION of the Natchez District into a government and the appointment of Gayoso armed with extraordinary powers were dictated by Spain's precarious defensive position in the Mississippi Valley after the American Revolution. Although Spain had fought against England in that war, she did not consider the American colonists her allies; many Spanish ministers predicted dire results for Spanish-American colonies should the North American colonies succeed in winning their independence from England.[1] Most quoted, perhaps, was the following prescient prediction of the Conde de Aranda:

This federal republic is born a pigmy, if I may be allowed

[1]Manuel Conrotte, *La intervención de España en la independencia de los Estados Unidos de la América del Norte* (Madrid, 1920); Juan F. Yela Utrilla, *España ante la independencia de los Estados Unidos* (2nd ed.; 2 vols.; Lérida, 1925); Samuel Flagg Bemis, *Pinckney's Treaty, America's Advantage from Europe's Distress, 1783–1800* (2nd. ed.; New Haven, 1960).

so to express myself. It has required the support of two
such powerful States as France and Spain to obtain its
independence. The day will come when she will be a
giant, a colossus formidable even to these countries. She
will forget the services she has received from the two
powers, and will think only of her own aggrandize-
ment. . . .

The first step of this nation, after it has become powerful, will be to take possession of the Floridas in order
to have the command of the Gulf of Mexico, and, after
having rendered difficult our commerce with New Spain,
she will aspire to the conquest of that vast empire, which it
will be impossible for us to defend against a formidable
power established on the same continent, and in its immediate neighborhood. These fears are well founded; they
must be realized in a few years, if some greater revolution,
even more fatal, does not sooner take place in our Americas.[2]

Westward expansion by the American colonists had continued
in the face of mounting opposition from Parliament after 1763. The
acid test of Spain's attempt to hold the Mississippi Valley in the
face of the now independent American frontiersmen's advance lay
in the overall defensive program adopted and supported by the ministers and American governors of Charles IV. This policy was not
consistently supported, but several salient features emerge to char-
acterize the basic ideas behind Spain's defenses in the Mississippi
Valley.

First, it was necessary to create a barrier against American expansion. Already American fur traders had pushed into Texas and
the Great Plains despite Spanish prohibitions.[3] Spain planned two
ways of stopping this westward expansion from the United States:
first, an offensive-defensive alliance with the Indian nations whose
settlements already formed a barrier to the Americans; and second,
the population of unsettled and strategic areas along the Spanish-
American frontier by Americans somehow miraculously transformed
into loyal Spanish vassals.

[2]Quoted in Gayarré, *History of Louisiana, the Spanish Domination*, 393–94.
[3]Herbert E. Bolton, *Athanse de Mézières and the Louisiana-Texas Frontier,
1768–1780* (2 vols.; Cleveland, 1914), I, 76–79.

Second, Spain had to control navigation of the Mississippi to prevent a possible invasion of Louisiana by "an army of boatmen." [4] This was the key to the so-called "Mississippi Question," for the western settlers coveted the access to the Gulf of Mexico which the Mississippi and Ohio and Tennessee rivers provided for their produce—*if those courses were free.* When Spain announced that the United States no longer had free and unauthorized right to descend the Mississippi, Westerners threatened to take matters into their own hands to right what they considered a moral wrong. Take the following representative article from the Knoxville *Gazette:* "The western people consider the navigation of the Mississippi as the light of the sun, a birth right that cannot be alienated. . . . Are the inhabitants of such a country to be restrained from going to sea by means of a river that washes their land? Is the little colony of New Orleans, by the help of a few soldiers, to sustain the weight of such a people; and prevent them from descending? . . . Spain . . . may consider the free navigation of the Mississippi as a certain event." [5]

Third, there was the possibility that by offering the prospect of using the Mississippi River to those western settlements which would declare their independence of the United States, Spain could buy and intrigue for protection of Lower Louisiana. This idea was not as farfetched as it might appear, for the Westerners expressed their dissatisfaction with the federal government over the Jay-Gardoqui negotiations of 1785 and over the whiskey excise tax in 1794.

Fourth, the construction of nonpermanent "campaign" forts at strategic points along the Mississippi and other vital arteries of commerce was essential.

Fifth, the always undermanned Regular Louisiana Infantry Regiment was supplemented with troops from Mexico and Cuba, and the militia forces in Louisiana were organized on a minute-man basis.

Although additional plans developed from these basic points, Gayoso's overall defensive plans were generally followed by Miró

[4] Stoddard, *Sketches, Historical and Descriptive of Louisiana,* 81.
[5] "A Short Description of the Territory of the United States South of the River Ohio," pamphlet dated 1793, excerpted in the Knoxville *Gazette,* February 17, 1796.

and Carondelet. In many instances Gayoso initiated reforms on the local level to a degree far above his military rank or political position. Because he carried imagination and fresh ideas to the defensive problems of Louisiana, Gayoso was the key figure in the province whenever reforms came up for discussion. By employing his military skill to supplement his diplomacy, Gayoso was able to check American expansion from the time he arrived in Natchez.

The so-called "Spanish Conspiracy" was an example of diplomacy, cunning, and maneuvering for the purpose of defense. James Wilkinson argued to Miró that Spanish-supported Kentucky would be a barrier to American expansion, and James White suggested the same to Gayoso. Gayoso, who had seen diplomatic maneuvering at the courts of Europe, quickly grasped the significance of Wilkinson's proposals. The new governor wrote an extensive report to the influential Spanish minister, the Conde de Floridablanca, in which he traced the history of the western policy and particularly the role of Wilkinson. Miró and Gayoso were both favorably impressed by Wilkinson at first. Gayoso wrote, "The circumstances of this individual," referring to Wilkinson, "recommend him, particularly his natural frankness, which characterizes and gives weight to his ingenuity." [6]

During the balance of his American career Gayoso learned considerably more about this "tarnished warrior" because Gayoso became the principal go-between in the conspiracy. Wilkinson visited Gayoso at Natchez in the fall of 1789. Correspondence between the two illustrates the extent to which Wilkinson was willing to sell out the interests of the United States, Kentucky, his friends, and anything that stood between him and his ambitious goal—to be the "George Washington of the West." [7] Gayoso soon recognized Wilkinson for what he was, and he wrote "that the conduct of Wilkinson is purely based on personal interest"; but since Spanish goals and those of the "artful dodger" were often similar, Gayoso observed, "I consider his ambition as a favorable

[6]Gayoso to Floridablanca, New Orleans, May 8, 1789, AHN, ESTADO, leg. 3902.
[7]Jacobs, *Tarnished Warrior*, 98–101 ff.

circumstance which we may make use of for our own part." [8]

On frequent occasions Wilkinson betrayed Americans who revealed similar ambitions in the West which might endanger Spanish security and disrupt Wilkinson's plans for the future. In this sense Gayoso was right in assessing the general's value to the Spanish crown. On the other hand, it is difficult to find out whether Wilkinson was using Gayoso more than the Natchez governor was making use of the American officer. Wilkinson was able to supply the names of persons of importance in Kentucky and Tennessee who might and should be corrupted by Spanish gold: Harry Innes, Benjamin Sebastian, John Brown, Benjamin Logan, Isaac Shelby, George Nicolas, and Thomas, and Humphrey Marshal.[9] Wilkinson himself enjoyed a pension of $2,000 yearly beginning on January 1, 1789, though payments were frequently disguised as profits on tobacco sales at New Orleans.[10]

Wilkinson's plans for the future received a rude jolt when the Council of the Indies authorized the opening of the Mississippi in 1789 to those Westerners willing to pay 15 per cent duties on the merchandise they brought to New Orleans. Moreover, the decision of the king to end tobacco purchases by the State dashed the hopes of many Kentuckians who had planned to emigrate to Natchez. Wilkinson urged the end of all commerce between Kentucky and New Orleans so that the Mississippi would be closed. This, he hoped, would force the Westerners to secede from the United States and form independent states allied with Spain. All hope of such separation depended on Spain's careful use of the navigation privilege as a carrot before the donkey.[11]

When Wilkinson realized that Spain had no intention of yielding to his proposals, his interest in the conspiracy lagged but never

[8]Gayoso to Carondelet, No. 45, Confidential, Natchez, May 23, 1794, AGI, PC, leg. 2354.

[9]Wilkinson to Miró, New Orleans, September 18, 1789, AHN, ESTADO, leg. 3886, translated in William R. Shepherd (ed.), "Papers Bearing on James Wilkinson's Relations with Spain, 1787–1789," *American Historical Review*, IX (July, 1904), 764–66.

[10]Wilkinson thus "explains" the money carried to him, sometimes secreted in sugar barrels. Wilkinson, *Memoirs of my Own Times*, II, *passim*. See also Thomas Robson Hay and M. R. Werner, *The Admirable Trumpeter, a Biography of General James Wilkinson* (New York, 1941), 137.

[11]Miró to Campo de Alange, Madrid, August 11, 1792, in Holmes (ed.), *Documentos de la Luisiana*, 22–26.

stopped completely. He continued to draw his Spanish pension while returning to active military service with the United States Army. On several occasions Wilkinson was able to betray those who had placed their confidence in him, sometimes to the advantage of Spanish defenses in Louisiana.

Before Gayoso arrived at Natchez in 1789 he had studied the Indian problem in the West and had come to the conclusion that Spanish defenses in the Mississippi Valley required the support and cooperation of the various Indian nations. "The means by which we may gain the Indians' confidence and keep them off the warpath is to make sure they never lack suitable goods at favorable prices and of a quality to which they are accustomed." [12] However, the necessity of supplying English goods to the Indians presented a rather thorny problem to Spanish-American traditions of closed ports and mercantilistic restrictions.

To meet the needs of the Indians temporarily, the British mercantile firms of Mather and Panton at Mobile and Pensacola were allowed to introduce British goods into Spanish Florida by paying 6 per cent duties. Mather's firm quit the business in the face of imminent economic ruin, and Panton also considered withdrawal from the difficult business. At Miró's urging, supported by Gayoso's cogent arguments, royal policy bent enough to exempt the firm of Panton, Leslie, and Company from duties. From 1790, when Miró granted Panton his liberal license, until 1797 when it was finally renewed, Panton extended his operations to posts as far north as the Chickasaw Bluffs (present-day Memphis) and east to St. Augustine, Florida. Virtually the entire load of Indian goods was supplied by this enterprising Scot. [13]

Gayoso wrote that it was necessary to put into practice what-

[12]Gayoso to Floridablanca, May 8, 1789.
[13]*Ibid.;* on Panton, see biography and bibliography in Holmes (ed.), *Documentos de la Luisiana,* 236 n. A large number of documents relating to Panton's operations are in the Panton-Forbes Papers, Mobile Public Library. Benjamin Hawkins, American commissioner to the Creeks, wrote, "Mr. William Panton has engrossed the greatest part of the trade of this nation, his establishment is at Pensacola; he supplies not only the white traders, but he has set up a number of Indian factors. They are both behind-hand with him, and the Indians are indebted to them to a considerable amount. . . ." Benjamin Hawkins to Secretary of War (James McHenry), No. 2, Coweta, January 6, 1797, in *Letters of Hawkins,* 57.

ever seemed necessary to win and preserve the friendship of the Indians,[14] and throughout his Louisiana career he did his best to implement this plan. Numbering about 15,000 warriors, the great southern Indian nations included the Choctaws, Chickasaws, Cherokees, Creeks, Talapoosa Creeks, and Alibamons. "Facing the Americans on the north and east they were at the same time a threat to the southern frontier and a barrier to southern expansion." [15] It was Gayoso's intention to see that the situation remained as it was and to counter any and all attempts by the United States to change it.

Following the American Revolution, Spain took the initiative by holding Indian congresses at Pensacola and Mobile in 1784. By the provisions of treaties signed there, those Chickasaws, Creeks, Alibamons, and Choctaws residing below the line in territory claimed by Spain were guaranteed protection and suitable trade goods at equitable prices. The Indians agreed to oppose any American invasion of their or Spanish territory. As one historian wrote, "By the treaties of Pensacola and Mobile Spain made herself the protector of the southern Indian tribes and thus strengthened her position in the disputed area." [16]

Alexander McGillivray, that noble Indian characterized by Pickett as the "Talleyrand of Alabama," had taken the lead in proposing to the Spaniards that the firm of William Panton be granted the necessary license to provide the southern nations with desirable English trading goods; and his remarks that the "Indians will attach themselves to & Serve them best who Supply their Necessities," bore

[14]Gayoso's State of the Province of Louisiana, Natchez, July 5, 1792, AGI, PC, leg. 2353.

[15]R. S. Cotterill, "Federal Indian Management in the South, 1789–1825," *MVHR*, XX (December, 1933), 333. Carondelet estimated it would cost the Spaniards $50,000 to train and maintain 15,000 warriors in peace and $150,000 in time of war. Carondelet to Alcudia, No. 18, Confidential, New Orleans, September 27, 1793, AHN, ESTADO, leg. 3898.

[16]Kinnaird (ed.), *Spain in the Mississippi Valley*, part II, xvi. Copies of the Treaties of Pensacola and Mobile dated May 31, June 1, and June 23, are in AGI, PC, leg. 2360. A portion of the Pensacola Treaty of June 1st relating to the Creeks is in John W. Caughey, *McGillivray of the Creeks* (Norman, Oklahoma, 1938), 75–76. On the effects of these treaties on the Choctaws and Chickasaws, see Serrano y Sanz, *España y los indios*, 24–25, 82–85; Rowland (ed.), *Encyclopedia of Mississippi History*, II, 812–14.

considerable weight with Miró and the commandant of Pensacola, Arturo O'Neill.[17] Spain had clearly won the first round in the fight to win the friendship of the Indians so recently devoted to the British cause.

The Americans, in this case the United States government and that of Georgia, attempted to undo the Spanish advantage by proposing various temporary measures, often reinforced by the promise of bountiful gifts or by veiled threats. Two results were the Treaty of Hopewell of 1785, by which the Chickasaws became attached to the American cause, and the Treaty of New York of 1790, in which McGillivray drew the Creeks into an alliance with the United States.[18] Unfortunately for the United States, official policy was often frustrated by the demands of frontiersmen for lands which, more often than not, were located on Indian hunting grounds. This precipitated new conflicts and enabled Spain to take advantage of the Indians' disgust.

American historians have generally followed Theodore Roosevelt's interpretation of Spanish Indian policy during the Miró and Carondelet administrations. Roosevelt was not kind in promoting a neoblack legend against the "treacherous" Spaniards who, he claimed, "incited the Indians to war against the Americans, while protesting to the latter that they were striving to keep the savages at peace. . . . Throughout these years the Spaniards thus secretly supplied the Creeks with the means of waging war on the Americans, claiming all the time that the Creeks were their vassals and that the land occupied by the southern Indians generally belonged to Spain and not to the United States." [19]

[17]The phrase is quoted in Albert James Pickett, *History of Alabama* (2nd. ed.; Birmingham, 1962), 432, and repeated in Caughey, *McGillivray of the Creeks*, 34. McGillivray to O'Neill, Little Tallassie, January 1, 1784, AGI, PC, leg. 36, quoted *ibid.*, 65.

[18]Treaty of Hopewell, November 28, 1785, copy translated by Gayoso, AHN, ESTADO, leg. 3888 *bis*. A copy dated January 3, 1786, appears in AGI, PC, leg. 12. The New York Treaty, August 14, 1790, is printed in the *City Gazette or the Daily Advertiser* (Charleston), August 28, 1790, copy in AGS, GM, leg. 7245; and in the *Pennsylvania Packet and Daily Advertiser*, August 18, 1790, copy in AGI, PC, leg. 2362. The latter is discussed in Caughey, *McGillivray of the Creeks*, 40–46.

[19]Roosevelt, *Winning of the West*, (1894), III, 133–34. As recently as 1959 a historian specializing in frontier history wrote, "This well-conceived plot

The Indians were by no means steadfast in their loyalties, however; and it was one of the chief functions of Spanish governors in Louisiana to cajole, bribe, wine and dine, and, where necessary, browbeat those chiefs and warriors of influence in their tribes. Many governors were successful in this type of frontier diplomacy, but Gayoso was one of the best. He was no idealist in dealing with the Indians, but he insisted on justice and fair play at all times, and the southern nations came to rely upon his word. Unlike many frontier governors, Gayoso did not speak with a forked tongue.

As Gayoso arrived in Natchez he found the outlying settlements in danger of constant attack and massacre from marauding bands of overzealous Talapoosas who made no distinction between American farmers living on Spanish lands with royal permission and those land-hungry Americans who penetrated traditional Creek hunting grounds. Gayoso found militia colonel Pedro Bryan Bruin, a recent arrival to the Bayou Pierre settlement, leading a type of minute-man frontier ranger force.[20] In 1790 a band of Choctaws threatened a large group of planters, notably the Rapalye family on the Big Black, warning them to leave the Natchez District or face destruction. It seems they had settled on lands the Choctaws claimed. Since the English had never paid them for the cession of that part of the Natchez District, the Choctaws demanded its return.[21] In 1792 six renegade Talapoosa braves massacred the MacFarland family on the Big Black; Gayoso ordered blockhouses constructed on the remote frontiers for protection against subsequent raids and at the same time appealed to the tribal chiefs to prevent similar horrors.[22]

---

was launched in 1784 when the Mississippi was closed to American flatboats and a leading Creek Indian chief, Alexander McGillivray, encouraged to take the warpath against the backcountry settlements." Ray Allen Billington, *The Westward Movement in the United States* (Princeton, 1959), 32. From a careful examination of records in the Spanish archives it appears that the initiative was taken by the Creeks themselves in opposition to continued American expansion onto their lands. Miró secretly supported them with private shipments of arms and powder for a short period only, after which he attempted to bring peace to the frontiers. A similar conclusion was reached by Burson in *The Stewardship of Miró*, 48–70.

[20]Grand-Pré to Miró, Natchez, May 15, 1789, AGI, PC, leg. 41.

[21]Grand-Pré to Miró, Natchez, October 2, 1790, AGI, PC, leg. 16; Gayoso to Miró, No. 15, Natchez, February 15, 1791, AGI, PC, leg. 41.

[22]Gayoso to Carondelet, General garrison of the Bayou Pierre Mill post,

By careful handling of the Indian problem in the Natchez District, Gayoso was able to reduce the depredations to the point of virtual nonexistence. In 1791, however, Spanish relations with the Choctaws underwent a serious turn for the worse when Gayoso began construction of a military post at the Walnut Hills, near the confluence of the Yazoo and the Mississippi. The background of this fort may be traced to 1789 when three land speculation companies were formed in the United States—the Tennessee Company under the leadership of Zachariah Cox, the Virginia Company, which numbered Patrick Henry among its members, and the one which threatened Gayoso's position the most, the South Carolina Yazoo Company under the direction of Alexander Moultrie, William Clay Snipes, and Isaac Huger.

The South Carolina Yazoo Company, undaunted at the failure of the Georgia-sponsored Bourbon Company of 1785 to establish and maintain a beachhead in the Natchez District, hoped to use almost ten million acres of land bounded by the Mississippi River, the thirty-first parallel, and the Tombigbee River in Alabama to induce settlers to come to the Yazoo. Dr. James O'Fallon, general agent for the company, sought to persuade Miró and General Wilkinson of the desirability of the project. Both opposed it, however, and soon the United States President, George Washington himself, expressed opposition to the company's plans.[23]

In order to forestall these and further ambitious plans of the Americans, Gayoso won consent from Miró to establish a military post at the Walnut Hills. Gayoso kept a diary at the settlement he called Nogales of his operations there from March 23, 1791, until May 10, during which time the fort's foundations were laid and the surrounding cane and brush cleared. Gayoso designed the fortifications himself, with Miró's approval, although the commandant of en-

---

October 31, 1792; No. 189, Natchez, November 10, 1792, AGI, PC, leg. 2353; Gayoso to Carondelet, No. 197, No. 203, Natchez, November 26, 27, 1792, AGI, PC, leg. 41. The danger of these attacks on the frontier seemed to disappear in 1793. Gayoso to Beauregard, Natchez, June 12, 1793, AGI, PC, leg. 47.

[23] John Carl Parish, "The Intrigues of Doctor James O'Fallon," *MVHR*, XVII (September, 1930), 230–63; Jack D. L. Holmes, "The Spanish-American Struggle over the Yazoo, 1789–1798," paper read at the Southern Historical Association, Tulsa, Oklahoma, November 12, 1960.

gineers and captain-general of Havana suggested entirely different plans.[24] The fort was built with some semblance of permanence. Governor-General Carondelet later approved highly of the fort's position by characterizing it as one of "the keys to the Mississippi." [25] Several years after its construction, when fears of American invasion were temporarily quieted, Carondelet and the captain-general, Luis de las Casas, ordered Gayoso to stop work on the fort. Acting on prior orders direct from the Crown, Gayoso refused and continued to build the necessary protective batteries on Mount Vigia and on another rise called Gayoso Battery.[26]

However successful the fort may have been in dissuading the South Carolina Yazoo Company from challenging Spanish hegemony in the Natchez District, it provoked the Choctaw nation. The fort was located near their hunting lands on territory which the Choctaws alleged had never been paid for by the English and, therefore, could not belong to the Spaniards. War councils were held, and Gayoso faced his first major challenge as a frontier military governor.

The manner in which Gayoso handled this delicate problem was indicative of his diplomatic skill. First, he calmed the fears of the Natchez settlers who expected to be massacred momentarily. Then he turned to his troubleshooting aide, Stephen Minor, and sent him to the Choctaw nation with personal letters for the major

[24]Gayoso to Beauregard, Natchez, March 23, 1791, AGI, PC, leg. 41. Gayoso's plan of the fort dated Natchez, March 12, 1791, is in AGI, Planos, Luisiana y Floridas, No. 140. Cayetano Paveto's plan for Nogales is dated Havana, June 11, 1791, in AGS, Planos, XIX–69. A plan showing the fort and its environs is in ASHM, K–b–4–63, and published in Holmes (ed.), *Documentos de la Luisiana.*

[25]Gayoso to Miró, Nos. 22, 23, Natchez, March 12, 1791, copies enclosed in Las Casas to Conde del Campo de Alange, No. 76, Havana, June 4, 1791, AGI, SD, leg. 2556; Gayoso to Miró, Natchez, May 10, 1791, copy enclosed in Las Casas to Campo de Alange, No. 125, Havana, November 5, 1791, *ibid.; expediente* on Nogales, AGS, Guerra Moderna, leg. 7245.

[26]Gayoso to Carondelet, New Orleans, January 17, 1792; January 2, March 16, 1792, AGI, PC, leg. 18; Gayoso to Carondelet, No. 32, Natchez, April 3, 1792, AGI, PC, leg. 177; Gayoso to Carondelet, No. 253, Natchez, April 5, 1793, enclosing copy of Floridablanca to Gayoso, Madrid, December 25, 1790, AGI, PC, leg. 178; Carondelet's report on Louisiana fortifications, New Orleans, April 18, 1793, AGI, PC, leg. 2353; and February 24, 1794, in Spanish MSS., Mississippi Valley, New Orleans Cabildo Museum Library, IV.

chiefs, particularly the grand chief, Franchimastabé.[27] Gayoso told the Choctaws that Spain had absolutely no territorial ambitions as far as the Indians' lands were concerned; the King already had more land than he could populate. The small cession of territory required for the fort was, explained Gayoso, for the purpose of protecting the Indians and their lands from rapacious American frontiersmen. The Spanish claim to the territory, based on conquest from the British, should be recognized; but Gayoso cleverly hinted that a conference might be desirable for the purpose of granting the Indians gifts, not as payment for the cession, but in recognition of the mutual friendship between the Choctaws and their governor-general in New Orleans.[28] In all, Minor made two journeys to the Choctaw villages and succeeded admirably in preparing the climate for the subsequent favorable negotiations at Natchez.[29]

[27]Stephen Minor was born on February 8, 1760, in what is Mapletown, Pennsylvania today; then it was Virginia. During the American Revolution he descended the Mississippi to New Orleans with a load of merchandise and attempted to return with war material for the Western patriots. His party was ambushed, however, and only illness prevented Minor from being with them. Minor returned to New Orleans and joined the Spanish army and fought gallantly in the Pensacola campaign. Gálvez recognized his merit and appointed him adjutant of the Natchez post. A wealthy landowner, upon whose property the town of Natchez was built, Minor became acting governor in 1797 when Gayoso became governor-general. Holding a captain's commission in the Spanish army and a major's rank in the militia, Minor served as commissioner for Spain in drawing the thirty-first parallel with Andrew Ellicott from 1798 to 1800. He subsequently spied on American filibuster movements, such as the Burr party, and made reports to the Spanish authorities. An organizer and first president of the Bank of Mississippi, he finally died on Gayoso's old plantation, Concord, November 29, 1815. Papers in collection of Mr. Lloyd Robertson (a descendant), New Hyde Park, New York, who also owns two oil paintings of Minor; obituary, *Mississippi Republican* (Natchez), December 6, 1815.

[28]Franchimastabé and Taboca to Gayoso, May 14, 1791; Gayoso to Franchimastabé, Natchez, May 28, 1791, AGI, PC, leg. 41; Miró to Las Casas, New Orleans, June 28, 1791, AGI, SD, leg. 2556; Gayoso's instructions to Minor, Natchez, January 13, 1792, in Gayoso Papers, Louisiana State University Archives; and a portion printed in Serrano y Sanz (ed.), *Documentos de la Luisiana*, 407–14.

[29]Minor's diary, March 13, 1792 to April 3, 1792, enclosed in Gayoso to Carondelet, Natchez, April 20, 1792, AHN, ESTADO, leg. 3898; AGI, PC, legs., 1446, 2353, printed in Serrano y Sanz (ed.), *Documentos de la Luisiana*, 418–

Over the objections of many chiefs in the Choctaw nation, Franchimastabé continued to oppose the Spanish settlement at the Walnut Hills. In a poignant letter to Gayoso the aging chief wrote, "I am old, tired, and destitute." He accused the Spaniards of attempting to rob the Indians as they had always done.[30] Gayoso had read the documents in the New Orleans archives and discovered that Franchimastabé was a past master at the fine art of blackmail. In 1787 he had threatened to join forces with the Americans if the Spaniards failed to raise their tariff on animal pelts. But Gayoso was not easily pressured. He worked carefully and diplomatically behind the scenes to engage the cooperation of the Chickasaws.

Piomingo, or Mountain Leader, was one of the most redoubtable Chickasaw chiefs in the brilliant history of that proud tribe. Long a foe to the Spaniards, he was not easily persuaded to embrace the Natchez governor with friendship. Gayoso invited him to Natchez and provided hospitality for the chief and his son in the governor's own home. During their discussions, Piomingo grew to respect the Spanish governor who "spoke with a straight tongue" about the problems facing the Indians and the Spaniards in the West. Gayoso was careful not to attack the American government directly. Rather, he pointed to President Washington's avowed declarations in favor of preserving the Indians' lands, but suggested that the American government was powerless to prevent frontiersmen from spreading in the direction of the Red Man's hunting lands. Gayoso won grudging support from Piomingo for the fort at the Walnut Hills by expressing his desire to supply both the Chickasaws and Choctaws with trading goods from the post.[31]

36, and translated with editing by Edward Hunter Ross and Dawson A. Phelps, "A Journey over the Natchez Trace in 1792: a Document from the Archives of Spain," *Journal of Mississippi History*, XV (October, 1953), 252–73. Gayoso's reports on his negotiations with the Choctaws are told in Gayoso to Miró, No. 15, Natchez, February 15, 1791, AGI, PC, leg. 41; Gayoso to Miró, No. 144, Natchez, July 15, 1791, in Mississippi Archives, Spanish Dominion, Jackson, III, 606–11; Las Casas to Campo de Alange, Havana, October 31, 1791, AGS, Guerra Moderna, leg. 6928.

[30]Franchimastabé to Gayoso, Choctaw Nation, March 28, 1792, AGI, PC, leg. 1446, and printed in Serrano y Sanz, *España y los indios*, 35–42.

[31]Piomingo or Payemingo was known to the English as "Captain Snagle or Snagbe." He is sometimes confused with the Choctaw chief Taboca. He told Gayoso that his real name was Payo-Mataha and that Piomingo was

Leaving no stone unturned, Gayoso also turned to other chiefs of the Choctaws and, by promising them rich rewards should they back Spain in its differences with Franchimastabé, won the majority of important chiefs to his way of thinking. Great Medal Chief Italaghana expressed such confidence in Gayoso that he left his thirteen-year-old son with Gayoso for his education, and Sulumastabé (Zapatos Colorados) intended the same for his son.[32] Gayoso also won the confidence of the Chickasaw chief, Ugulayacabé, known by the Americans as Ugly Cub or Wolf's Friend, and the king of all the Chickasaws, Tascahetuca (Tascaotuca).[33] By May 14, 1792, Gayoso had virtually a united front to present against the feeble arguments of Franchimastabé.

On May 10 the Choctaw and Chickasaw delegations arrived at Cole's Creek with two hundred warriors and the leading chiefs. Gayoso was on hand to greet the Indians. Following the preliminary discussions, the conference adjourned to Concord where, on the marble steps of Gayoso's mansion, the peace pipe was passed. In the shade of the nearby fruit trees Spanish officers and Indian warriors chatted and achieved the necessary basis of understanding. With the permission of Father Gregorio White, the delegations repaired to the Church of San Salvador de Natchez for the signing of the treaty.

A last-minute protest by Franchimastabé was dramatically forestalled by a decisive and bold move on the part of Gayoso. Confident of his own military force, and having previously ordered the artillery loaded and trained on the Indians, Gayoso grabbed

---

merely a tribal designation meaning leader. Gayoso to Carondelet, No. 133, Natchez, July 21, 1792, ANC, Floridas, leg. 2, printed in Corbitt (ed.), *Publications* of the East Tennessee Historical Society, XXVII (1955), 90; *cf.* James H. Malone, *The Chickasaw Nation, a Short Sketch of a Noble People* (Louisville, 1922), 333; Harry Warren, "Some Chickasaw Chiefs and Prominent Men," *Publications* of the Mississippi Historical Society, VIII (1904), 555-70. Gayoso's experience with Piomingo is described in Gayoso to Carondelet, No. 2, Confidential, Natchez, April 14, 1792, AGI, PC, leg. 2353.

[32]Gayoso to Carondelet, Natchez, Nos. 14, 21, March 24, 31, 1792, AGI, PC, leg. 41; Gayoso to Carondelet, Natchez, September 12, 1793, copy enclosed in Carondelet to Alcudia, No. 18, Confidential, New Orleans, September 27, 1793, AHN, ESTADO, leg. 3898.

[33]Gayoso to Tascahetuca, Natchez, March 21, 1792, AGI, PC, leg. 2353, and printed in Serrano y Sanz (ed.), *Documentos de la Luisiana*, 414-15.

Franchimastabé by the hand and commanded him to look into his eyes. "Do you see any evidence of falsehood there?" Gayoso demanded. The old chief, visibly moved, hesitated, then shook his head. Amid the approving murmurs of the chiefs who were impressed by the mailed fist beneath the velvet glove of the Spaniard, Gayoso suddenly turned to the king of the Chickasaws and gave him the keys to the royal storehouse and virtually invited the Indians to help themselves. The ice was broken; agreement followed.

The Treaty of Natchez, signed on May 14, 1792, was a complete diplomatic triumph for Gayoso. The land on which Fort Nogales had been erected was ceded to the Spaniards, and mutual protection clauses of the Mobile conference were renewed. For some $2,000 in gifts and $500 for banquet expenses, Gayoso had obtained one of the most strategic points on the Mississippi River and had won the admiration and respect of the Indians in so doing.[34] Moreover, the newly appointed Spanish Minister of State, Manuel de Godoy, wrote the Natchez governor that the king was suitably impressed by Gayoso's consummate skill and diplomacy. Stephen Minor and Gayoso's secretary, Joseph Vidal, were rewarded for their participation in the conference, and Gayoso was recommended for military promotion.[35]

During his negotiations with the Chickasaws and Choctaws, Gayoso also worked for the overall, long-range goal of the Spaniards—an offensive-defensive alliance of all the southern Indian nations to protect both Indian lands and Spanish territory against

---

[34]Carondelet's instructions to Gayoso are dated March 29, 1792, copy enclosed in Carondelet to Floridablanca, No. 17, Confidential, New Orleans March 29, 1792, AHN, ESTADO, leg. 3898. Gayoso's account of the conference is in Gayoso to Carondelet, Natchez, May 29, 1792, copy enclosed in Carondelet to Aranda, No. 3, Confidential, New Orleans, June 11, 1792, *ibid.* The treaty is also *ibid.*, and a copy is enclosed in Gayoso to Carondelet, No. 30, Natchez, May 14, 1792, AGI, PC, legs. 1446, 2353. It is printed in Serrano y Sanz (ed.), *Documentos de la Luisiana*, 436–39; and translated in *American State Papers, Foreign Relations*, I, 280. The approval of expenses is in Campo de Alange to Las Casas, Madrid, December 22, 1792, AGS, Guerra Moderna, leg. 6928. As usual, Gayoso's liberality confused accounts: Gutiérrez de Arroyo to Gayoso, Natchez, November 22, 1793, AGI, PC, leg. 47.

[35]Duque de Alcudia to Gayoso, Madrid, December 26, 1792, AGI, PC, leg 176; Alcudia to Carondelet, Madrid, December 26, 1792, AGI, PC, leg 2317-b.

any and all aggressors. It is difficult to trace the origin of the idea of confederation among the southern nations, but it is possible to trace Spanish support for the notion. Stephen Minor returned from the Choctaw camp with information concerning a looseknit confederation of the four nations—Creeks, Choctaws, Chickasaws, and Cherokees—under the ostensible leadership of King Tascahetuca of the Chickasaws, acknowledged as "the elder brother of all the Indian nations." [36]

The redoubtable William Augustus Bowles also had dreams of confederation, with himself as director of a vast empire of Indians in the lower Mississippi Valley. Carondelet's predecessor, Esteban Miró also suggested a defensive confederation of the southern nations under Spanish protection. Carondelet modified the idea to include offensive, as well as defensive, elements. [37] The successful conclusion of the famous Treaty of Nogales, which consolidated Spanish influence with the southern nations while confederating them, owes much to the two leading negotiators—Juan de la Villebeuvre and Manuel Gayoso de Lemos.

Juan de la Villebeuvre had been working silently and effectively to win the unqualified support of the Chickasaws and Choctaws since 1787. In 1792 Gayoso recommended him as special commissioner to the Choctaw nation with an annual salary of $850 in addition to his pay as captain in the Regular Louisiana Infantry Regiment. His 1792 mission to the Choctaws resulted in a treaty the following year for the cession of additional strategic points along the Tombigbee River in Alabama, which were utilized for Spanish military posts in the same way as Nogales. [38]

[36] Mary A.M. O'Callaghan, "The Indian Policy of Carondelet in Spanish Louisiana, 1792-1797" (Ph.D. dissertation, University of California, 1942), 47-48. ·

[37] Bowles to Floridablanca, London, March 25, 1791, Mississippi Archives, Spanish Dominion, III, 493-502; Arthur P. Whitaker, "Spain and the Cherokee Indians, 1783-1798," *North Carolina Historical Review*, IV (July, 1927), 254-56; Jane M. Berry, "Indian Policy of Spain in the Southwest, 1783-1795," *MVHR*, III (March, 1917), 469-72, contrasts Miró's and Carondelet's theories and practices; Serrano y Sanz, *España y los indios*, 70-73.

[38] Juan de la Villebeuvre was born in Brittany, France, in 1738 and died in New Orleans in September, 1797. He was married to Juana Darby y Corbin and had a son, also named Juan, who served with his father in the

Carondelet's instructions to Gayoso on the nature of the proposed alliance were modified by the Natchez governor, especially on those points which seemed to Gayoso unnecessarily belligerent. Point eight suggested, for example, that "in the event that the United States refuses these peaceful propositions (regarding the boundaries between the Indian territory and the United States), the four nations will join in support of the Cherokees and Creeks, combined with those of the North, if necessary, to make common war until they secure those concessions so indispensable for their existence and tranquility." [39] In the finished treaty Gayoso simply omitted this clause and referred all disputes to the ministerial level, which is where they should have been settled anyway.[40]

The Treaty of Nogales was signed at the Walnut Hills post on October 28, 1793. It was called a "treaty of friendship and guarantee." Signing for the Spaniards were Gayoso, Villebeuvre, Beauregard, John Turnbull, John Girault, Benjamin Fooy, Simon Favre, Antonio Marmillón, and Juan Barnó y Ferrusola. Signing for the Chickasaws was Ugulayacabé; for the Creeks, Tallapoosa, and Alibamon was Sulumastabé (Zapatos Colorados); and for the Choctaws, Franchimastabé, Mingo Pincus, and Mistechico. The treaty contained nineteen clauses which guaranteed the treaties and conventions entered into between the Indians and the Spaniards at Mobile and Pensacola in 1784. Although the Cherokees did not attend the original conference, they sent representatives who asked that they be included in the terms of the conference. The most

---

Louisiana Infantry Regiment. Service sheets, AGI, PC, leg. 161-a; pay sheet for widow's pension, AGI, PC, leg. 538-b; documents on retirement and widow's pension, AGI, PC, leg. 1501-b. On his mission to the Choctaws in 1792, see Gayoso to Carondelet, No. 141, Natchez, August 6, 1792, AGI, PC, leg. 41; Gayoso to Carondelet, Natchez, April 14, 1792, enclosed in Carondelet to Floridablanca, No. 24, Confidential, New Orleans, April 21, 1792, AHN, ESTADO, leg. 3898. The treaty signed with the Choctaws by de la Villebeuvre is dated May 10, 1793, and is in AGI, PC, leg. 2353.

[39]Carondelet to Gayoso, New Orleans, January 28, 1793, AGI, PC, leg. 178; Berry, "Indian Policy of Spain in the Southwest, 1783–1795," 476.

[40]Berry, "Indian Policy of Spain in the Southwest, 1783–1795," 476; Carondelet to Gayoso, New Orleans, February 26, 1793, quoted in Serrano y Sanz, *España y los indios*, 73–75; Gayoso to Carondelet, No. 12, 13, Natchez, December 6, 1793, AGI, PC, leg. 2353, 42; Gayoso's account of the negotiations are in Mississippi Archives, Spanish Dominion, V, 23–92.

important clause was number four, which stated, "The Chickasaw, Creek, Tallapoosa, Alibamon, Cherokee and Choctaw nations make an offensive and defensive alliance, so that generally and particularly each nation promises to consider the other as part of his own nation, to help one another reciprocally and to determine nothing unilaterally which will affect the security and safety of the others."

For its part, Spain guaranteed the boundaries of the various signatory Indian nations and promised to protect them against all incursions in Louisiana and the Floridas. Spain promised to deal with the United States diplomatically to assure the Indian boundaries. Each of the Nations was to receive annual gifts according to the proximity of their villages to the distribution centers. Thus, the Chickasaws were given to understand that their goods would be distributed "where His Catholic Majesty determines on the banks of the Mississippi River." This clause was to have far-reaching effects on the hegemony of Spain in the Mississippi Valley. The Creek, Tallapoosa, and Cherokees were to receive their goods at Pensacola, while the Alibamon tribe were to pick theirs up at Mobile. No exact point was determined for distribution of the Choctaw goods.[41]

A highly important point of the treaty, one for which Gayoso and Villebeuvre had both worked for years, was that which allowed the sending of Spanish commissioners into the Indian villages. Both Spaniards realized that without the steady support and continual presence of Indian agents devoted to the Spanish cause, the entire goal of support from the Indians might be frustrated by the presence of commissioners appointed from the United States. Miró had suggested sending trained commissioners to the Indians back in 1787; but little was done in this direction until 1792, when Gayoso's

[41]Gayoso to Carondelet, No. 367, Natchez, November 1, 1793, AGI, PC, leg. 42; copy of treaty enclosed in Gayoso to Carondelet, No. 389, Natchez, December 7, 1793, AGI, PC, leg. 42. Expenses for the treaty were $2,000: Gardoqui to Carondelet, Madrid, July 9, 1794, *ibid*. Carondelet described the negotiations in Carondelet to Alcudia, No. 26, Confidential, New Orleans, January 24, 1794, AHN, ESTADO, leg. 3899. Several copies of the treaty are in AGI, PC, leg. 2353. It is printed in Serrano y Sanz, *España y los indios*, 91–92. A summary is in Gayarré, *History of Louisiana, The Spanish Dominion*, 328–29; and Thomas R. Hay, "Treaty of Nogales," in *Dictionary of American History*, ed. James Truslow Adams (5 vols.; New York, 1940), III, 136.

firm recommendations were followed. Turner Brashears, a Maryland native who had lived for years in the Indian camp and was married to a squaw, joined Villebeuvre among the Choctaws and Chickasaws. Pedro Olivier was sent to the Talapoosa. Money was found to hire capable interpreters of the Indian tongues such as Ebenezer Fulson, Benjamin Fooy, Simon Favre, Thomas Price, William McFarland, and St. Germain.[42]

Spain had clearly scored a notable triumph in signing the various southern Indian nations to the mutual defense treaty, but the victory was not without cost. Although Alejandro O'Reilly had provided for annual gifts to Indian tribes in 1769, the amount was only $4,000. After the Mobile and Pensacola conferences, annual gifts increased in proportion to the additional costs of defending the provinces. Yet, after the Nogales conference of 1793, the annual presents for the Indians and the salaries for interpreters, commissioners, and other employees of that branch of government amounted to $55,209—roughly 10 per cent of the total money spent by Spain to support the two provinces of Louisiana and West Florida.[43] Moreover, Spain soon realized that the friendship of the Indians was elusive. Unless the gifts continued and the work of the commissioners expanded, Spain could not be sure of continued support from the savages. Gayoso recommended furnishing the Indians a few goods of high quality rather than large amounts of merchandise they neither wanted nor valued.[44]

Yet, the alliance of the Indians undoubtedly provided a strong, if temporary, deterrent to American expansion; and Gayoso felt the

[42]Gayoso to Aranda, July 5, 1792; Serrano y Sanz, *España y los indios*, 37–42; Campo de Alange to Las Casas, December 22, 1792, AGS, Guerra Moderna, leg. 6928; Villebeuvre to Gayoso, Boucfouca, September 10, 1792, in Serrano y Sanz, *España y los indios*, 89–90; Carondelet to Gayoso, New Orleans, July 11, 1793, August 31, 1793, Mississippi Archives, Spanish Dominion, V, 4–7, 18–23; Gayoso to Carondelet, Natchez, July 18, 1792, AGI, PC, leg. 41; Gayoso to Carondelet, No. 133, Natchez, July 21, 1792, printed in Corbitt (ed.), *Publications* of the ETHS (1955), 90.

[43]Holmes, "Some Economic Problems of Spanish Governors of Louisiana," 524–37; Carondelet to Gardoqui, New Orleans, February 24, 1794, Spanish MSS., Mississippi Valley, New Orleans, IV, 213–17.

[44]Gayoso to Carondelet, No. 9, New Madrid, September 22, 1795, AGI, PC, leg. 34; Gayoso learned from his own sad experience with the Indians. Villebeuvre to Carondelet, Boucfouca, January 25, 1793, AGI, PC, leg. 147-a.

money spent was worth it. At least it was less costly than the maintenance of vast numbers of regular and militia forces along the frontiers. To this end, Gayoso worked continually to keep peace among the various allies. Unfortunately, in 1793 a band of Creeks hunting in Chickasaw territory killed one of Piomingo's warriors and that Chickasaw chief led a punitive party against the Creeks in which three of the latter were killed, including the nephew and son of Chief Fahakio or Mad Dog. War broke out almost immediately. The Chickasaws sent deputies to enlist Choctaw aid and the Americans promised to support Piomingo.[45]

This war represented a clear and present danger to Spanish authority in the Mississippi Valley. In the first place, Spain as signatory to the Nogales treaty, found herself obligated to support both the Creeks and the Chickasaws in their dispute or, what was worse, watch the Americans gain an advantage by offering to support the Chickasaws. Already Governor William Blount and James Robertson had persuaded the Chickasaws to permit the establishment of a blockhouse and defensive post on the Muscle Shoals. It was well known that the Americans also had designs on the Chickasaw Bluffs. Should they succeed in establishing a post on that strategic Mississippi River location, Spain's communications between Upper Louisiana and New Orleans could be easily cut.

Acting under orders of Carondelet, and ably supported by Captain de la Villebeuvre, Gayoso arranged for a truce and was responsible for the ultimate peace established between the warring nations.[46]

Gayoso also acted as peacemaker in the traditional rivalry between the Choctaws and Chickasaws on one hand, and the vastly scattered Caddoan tribes from Natchitoches to Arkansas. Long accustomed to hunting west of the Mississippi, the Choctaws saw nothing amiss in picking up a few Caddo scalps now and then. When the western tribes threatened an offensive alliance against the Choctaws, Gayoso spearheaded the attempt to make peace and, with the grudging support of Natchitoches' commandant, Louis de Blanc, succeeded in curtailing the Choctaws' incursions, if not

[45]Jack D. L. Holmes, "Spanish-American Rivalry over the Chickasaw Bluffs, 1780–1795," *Publications* of the ETHS (1962), 38–39.
[46]*Ibid.*, 39–41.

in stopping them altogether.[47] Carondelet told Pedro Olivier, the Spanish commissioner among the Choctaws, that if they continued their forays against the Caddos, the Spaniards would stop their annual presents; but this threat failed to stop the raids completely.[48] In 1798 the Choctaws asked Governor Winthrop Sargent of the Mississippi Territory to supply them with arms and powder for a campaign against the Caddos; the request was vehemently denied.[49]

Isolated Indian attacks against white settlers and travelers continued in spite of Gayoso's attempts to maintain peace on the frontiers, but the Natchez governor zealously tried to prevent them whenever possible. With the omnipresent threat of ending Indian gifts, Gayoso was able to make the chiefs responsible for the bad conduct of their warriors. On the other hand Gayoso was just as concerned over white men's attacks on the Indians. When a royal official wounded the son of Zapatos Colorados (or Sulumastabé) near Natchez, the governor ordered the Indian cared for in the Royal Hospital and promised justice to the Indians. When Americans fired on several peaceable Choctaws in 1789, Gayoso attempted to arrest the white men and restore tranquility.[50]

The Baron de Carondelet, who became governor-general replacing Esteban Miró in December, 1791, had his own ideas about Indian policy. As former governor of the Province of San Salvador in the captaincy-general of Guatemala, Carondelet had been instrumental in winning the friendship of numerous Indian tribes and of settling them in the traditional Spanish-supported Indian towns

[47]Gayoso to Carondelet, Natchez, September 27, 1792, quoted in Carondelet to deBlanc, New Orleans, October 18, 1792, in Kinnaird (ed.), *Spain in the Mississippi Valley*, Pt. III, 92–93; O'Callaghan, "Carondelet's Indian Policy," 65–66.

[48]Carondelet to Olivier, New Orleans, April 19, 1797, AGI, PC, leg. 2365; Grand-Pré to Carondelet, No. 37, Avoyelles, November 21, 1796, AGI, PC, leg. 34; Manuel de Lanzós' diary of the Natchez revolt, enclosed in Gayoso to Carondelet, No. 820, Natchez, July 7, 1797, AGI, PC, leg. 2354, and printed in Holmes (ed.), *Documentos de la Luisiana*, 346.

[49]Minor to Gayoso, Boundary Line, Thompson's Creek, October 24, 1798, AGI, PC, leg. 215-a.

[50]Gayoso to Miró, No. 101, Natchez, May 14, 1791; No. 151, July 22, 1791, AGI, PC, leg. 41; Miró to Gayoso, New Orleans, August 10, 1789, in Houck (ed.), *Spanish Régime in Missouri*, I, 316.

where they were no threat to neighboring white villages.[51] Unfortunately, this mode of dealing with the Indians was not suited to the relatively underdeveloped tribes in Louisiana. On numerous occasions Gayoso and Carondelet differed over Indian policy.

On one occasion, when Carondelet had inadvisedly given liquor to a group of Choctaws and Cherokees, two opposing chiefs became intoxicated and fought with each other over some trifle. The bested Indian, sporting a chewed nose, secretly slipped to the nearby cypress grove where the Cherokee kept his horse, killed the animal, and stole his eyes. Gayoso brought peace between the two tribes over the incident.[52]

Gayoso was not opposed to giving the Indians liquor, but he felt that the time and place were important. A drunken tribe in its own village was less apt to provoke trouble than the same inebriated band of Indians near some Spanish posts or in proximity with other Indians.

Unaware of the realities of Indian policy on the Spanish-American frontier, Carondelet pursued a bellicose plan which had repercussions from Philadelphia to Madrid. When Carondelet sought to nullify the treaties signed by the Indians with the United States government, Gayoso pointed out that this attitude was impractical and even dangerous. "I have always operated under the assumption," Gayoso wrote, "that the Creeks or Tallapoosas, Choctaws, and Chickasaws are free and independent nations; although they are under His Majesty's protection, we cannot forcibly prevent them from signing a treaty with the United States. . . ." [53]

In 1792 Carondelet reversed Miró's policy of preventing the Indians from needless and wanton attacks on the Cumberland settlements. With the assurance of Spanish support for whatever incursions they might make on the American frontier settlements, the Creeks stepped up their attacks on settlers and virtually ruined any long-range Spanish plans of consolidating the support of the

[51]Within two years, Carondelet formed sixty Indian towns in the three provinces of San Salvador, San Vicente, and San Miguel. Carondelet to Alcudia, New Orleans, April 29, 1793, AHN, ESTADO, leg. 3898; biographical note on Carondelet in Holmes (ed.), *Documentos de la Luisiana*, 144–45.
[52]Gayoso to Carondelet, No. 13, Natchez, March 24, 1792, AGI, PC, leg. 41.
[53]Gayoso to Alcudia, No. 2, Natchez, May 14, 1793, AGI, PC, leg. 177.

disgruntled Westerners in favor of Spain. Professor Whitaker writes, "As Gayoso pointed out, Carondelet was pursuing mutually contradictory policies. . . . The frontiersmen rightly attributed this change to Carondelet's advent; and the intrigue with the frontiersmen suffered in consequence. . . . Gayoso freely criticized Carondelet for stirring up the Indians against the Americans." [54] Gayoso wrote Carondelet that if the Americans didn't complain to the Spanish Court, they would do even worse—possibly attack and capture Spanish Louisiana in retaliation for the increased Indian attacks. [55]

President Washington addressed the Congress in December, 1793, with these words: "I had the best reason to believe that the hostilities threatened and exercised by the Southern Indians on our border, were excited by the agents of that Government [Spain]. . . . In the mean time, corresponding suspicions were entertained, or pretended to be entertained, on their part, of like hostile excitements, by our agents, to disturb their peace with the same nations. . . ." [56] The United States expressed through its ministers in Madrid, William Carmichael and W. Short, its complaint against Carondelet's warlike policy of using the Indians against the United States. [57]

An example of Carondelet's rash policy is his orders to Gayoso and Lieutenant Colonel Carlos Howard in 1794 to incite the Chickasaws against the American post at Fort Massac, on the Ohio River below the confluence of the Cumberland and Tennessee rivers. Carondelet explained that the American settlement was too close to the Chickasaw Bluffs and Muscle Shoals. Gayoso fully realized the serious nature of Carondelet's decision. He once wrote, "The service of the Indians is very partial and precarious; I consider them only useful with a corps of troops or fortifications superior to them,

[54]Whitaker, *The Spanish-American Frontier*, 169, citing Gayoso to Alcudia, No. 1, Confidential, Natchez, September 19, 1794, AHN, ESTADO, leg. 3902.

[55]Berry, "Indian Policy of Spain in The Southwest, 1783–1795," 472–73.

[56]Message of Washington to Senate and House, December 16, 1793, in *American State Papers, Foreign Relations*, I, 247; Jaúdenes and Viar to Jefferson, Philadelphia, June 18, 1793, *ibid.*, I, 265.

[57]Carmichael and Short to Diego de Gardoqui, Madrid, August 11, 1792, *ibid.*, I, 276–77.

and which they respect. . . . The expense they would cause is greater than their usefulness." [58]

Even more to the point, however, was the fact that the American government had authorized the construction of Fort Massac to protect Spanish Louisiana from unauthorized bands of filibusters, allied with French agents. Such a fort would be difficult to capture and, moreover, any Spanish attempt to incite the Indians against the Americans would meet with disaster. Gayoso appealed over Carondelet's head to Madrid and, fortunately for peace on the frontier, Godoy supported Gayoso's stand in the matter.[59]

When Carondelet expected firm devotion and unwavering loyalty from the allied Indian nations, Gayoso warned him to be realistic. "Whilst you bestow on Indians," he wrote, "they are devoted to you, but as soon as their avarice leads them to think that they will do better elsewhere, they forget your bounties without the least return of gratitude." [60] For this reason Gayoso preferred to employ more than tangible gifts in dealing with the Indians. With a sparkling sense of humor and an uncanny appreciation of the Red Man's own level of understanding, Gayoso was able to accomplish more on occasion than he could have with material gifts. During the Nogales conference of 1793 Gayoso was given the name "Chactimataha" or "The King of the Choctaws" by the assembled tribe members. After smoking the peace pipe Gayoso stood and delivered a burlesque harangue with humorous allusions to the Choctaws. The Indians burst into laughter and stood up in appreciation. Taboca then turned to them and said that Gayoso was a friend of the Red Men and

[58]Gayoso to Carondelet, No. 34, Confidential, Natchez, February 20, 1794, AGI, PC, leg. 2354.

[59]Carondelet to Gayoso, Confidential, New Orleans, September 28, 1794; Gayoso to Carondelet, No. 52, Confidential, Natchez, September 9, 1794, AGI, PC, leg. 42; Carondelet to Gayoso, New Orleans, August 20, 1794, printed in "Selections from the Draper Collection in the Possession of the State Historical Society of Wisconsin to Elucidate the Proposed French Expedition under George Rogers Clark," American Historical Association *Annual Report, 1896* (2 vols.; Washington, 1897), I, 1081–84; Gayoso to Alcudia, No. 1, Confidential, Natchez, September 19, 1794, AHN, ESTADO, leg. 3902; Alcudia to (Carondelet), Aranjuez, January 24, 1795, AGI, PC, leg. 176.

[60]Gayoso to William Blount, Nogales, July 24, 1793, AGI, PC, leg. 208.

had an Indian name by which he might be known to all.[61]

Despite their differences, Gayoso and Carondelet often worked together in close cooperation to achieve some definite goal in Indian policy. During the outbreak of hostilities between the Creeks and the Chickasaws in 1795, the governors worked as a team and secured a measure of peace on the frontier.[62] Gayoso was one of the few Spanish governors who took an active role in seeking cooperation with the American frontier governors for a unified Indian policy. In 1793 he had written Blount assuring him that it was not Spanish policy to incite the Indians against any whites.[63] Gayoso attempted to meet with Governor Arthur St. Clair in 1795 to discuss Indian policy along the Upper Louisiana frontier.[64]

Gayoso's relations with the Indians did not always lead to unqualified success, but his few failures were not caused by lack of effort. Rather, they were inevitable, given the circumstances of the frontier, the character of the Indians, and the often frustrating and vacillating policy of the Spanish crown toward the Indians. In bringing relative tranquility and order to the Natchez District, Gayoso exercised restraint and a keen understanding of human nature which resulted in his being considered trustworthy by both Indians and whites alike. It was a difficult role, but Gayoso played the part well.

Moreover, as his success in Natchez spread over the vast frontier, Gayoso's Indian policy set a pattern for other frontier governors and commandants. Soon after the signing of the Treaty of Natchez,

[61]Gayoso to Carondelet, No. 12, Natchez, December 6, 1793, AGI, PC, leg. 2353.

[62]Gayoso to William Glover, to Ugulayacabé, Natchez, March 14, 1795, AGI, PC, leg. 211. The Creeks signed a peace treaty in 1796. Albert V. Goodpasture, "Indian Wars and Warriors of the Old Southwest, 1730–1807," *Tennessee Historical Magazine*, IV (December, 1918), 285–89.

[63]Blount to Secretary of War (Knox), Knoxville, May 23, 1793, in Carter (ed.), *Territorial Papers of the United States*, IV: *Southwest*, 260; Gayoso to Blount, Nogales, July 24, 1793, AGI, PC, leg. 208; Gayoso to Blount, on board the *Vigilante*, before the Ohio, November 22, 1795, AGI, PC, leg. 211; Gayoso to Blount, fragment, Natchez, (1791–1792), AGI, PC, leg. 47.

[64]Gayoso to St. Clair, New Madrid, September 26, 1795, printed in William Henry Smith (ed.), *The St. Clair Papers* (2 vols.; Cincinnati, 1882), II, 389–90; Gayoso to Carondelet, New Madrid, October 6, 1795, AGI, PC, leg. 32.

Juan de la Villebeuvre was able to negotiate a treaty with the Choctaws by the terms of which other choice strategic points in Alabama on the Tombigbee River were ceded to Spain for the construction of Forts San Esteban de Tombecbee and Confederación.[65] By insisting on a commonsense approach to Indian affairs in the Old Southwest, Gayoso was best able to counter the precipitate and often dangerous moves of Carondelet. Furthermore, Gayoso attempted to maintain contact with the American frontier governors for the long-range purpose of promoting a unified policy with regard to the Indians. If one of the goals of the Spanish government was to win the support of the southern Indians against a possible American invasion of Louisiana, by 1796 it was apparent that Gayoso had accomplished much in that direction. But Gayoso was the first to admit that the friendship of the Indians was illusory; that it could be made and broken by a careless or thoughtless act on the part of one of the American or Spanish soldiers. For the time being, however, the friendship of the Indians towards the Spaniards did effectively slow down the pace of American expansion westward.

A firm and constructive Indian policy was only one of Gayoso's proposals to the Baron de Carondelet regarding defenses of Louisiana. Absolutely essential to Spain's control of the Mississippi River was a fleet of galleys, galiots, and gunboats. As early as 1777 Governor Bernardo de Gálvez had suggested the construction of three or four cannon launches (*cañoneras*), each supplied with a 24- or 18-pounder cannon in the prow. He considered these more useful than the larger, unwieldy frigates and much cheaper.[66] In one of his many letters to Esteban Miró, General Wilkinson had written, "The more compleat, the more effectual & the more economical plan of defence would be by Armed Galleys & gun boats stationed as high up the Mississippi as Margot. The number & force of these should be proportional to the strength & equipment of the Enemy, for so long

---

[65]Treaty signed at Boucfouca, May 10, 1793, AGI, PC, leg. 2353; Gayoso to Carondelet, No. 12, Natchez, December 6, 1793, *ibid.*

[66]Bernardo de Gálvez to Joseph de Gálvez, New Orleans, June 2, 1777, copy in AGI, PC, leg. 223-b.

as you command the passage of the Mississippy above, the Settlements below will rest in peace & safety. . . ."[67] Miró did little to carry out Wilkinson's suggestion, however, and it remained to Carondelet to create the Squadron of the Mississippi.[68] What influenced Carondelet in favor of naval power? Undoubtedly it was Gayoso's dispatch of January 6, 1792, which outlined the Natchez governor's suggestions on defending the Province of Louisiana. Gayoso had written, "Floating forces are indispensable on this river, for without them the fortifications we have or may build will be far less useful." [69] Gayoso estimated that each galley constructed for the squadron would cost about fifteen hundred pesos; a gunboat or galiot only a thousand. Artillery should consist of at least one 12-pounder cannon for each galley and one 8-pounder for every gunboat.[70]

Ultimately, the Spanish Light Naval Squadron of the Mississippi came to include six galleys, four galiots, one bombardier *(bomba-*

---

[67]Wilkinson to Miró, Lexington, April 29, 1790, AGI, PC, leg. 2374, and printed in Corbitt (ed.), *Publications* of the ETHS 1951, 81.

[68]In 1788 a small naval force at New Orleans consisted of two galleys and three gunboats *(lanchas cañoneras)*. They were then employed in defending the river from Natchez south; instructions to Alejandro de Bouilliers (by Miró), New Orleans, February 24, 1788, AGI, PC, in Mississippi Archives, Spanish Dominion, III, 257–64. By 1792 Miró had only two gunboats described as virtually useless; therefore, he approved of Carondelet's decision to build two galleys in 1792. Miró to Campo de Alange, August 11, 1792, in Holmes (ed.), *Documentos de la Luisiana*, 50.

[69]Gayoso to Carondelet, New Orleans, January 6, 1792, AGI, PC, leg. 2353. The following day Gayoso prepared a statement of the naval forces he thought were necessary to defend the Natchez District: two galleys manned by twenty-four rowers and garrisoned by twenty soldiers with a 12-pounder cannon and twelve swivel guns; three cannon launches, each with an 8-pounder gun in the prow and two swivel guns in the stern, manned by twelve rowers and eight soldiers; and a galiot or *falua* with a permanent stateroom for the governor's use on the rivers. Gayoso's note, New Orleans, January 7, 1792, AGI, PC, leg. 206. Professor A. P. Nasatir, whose student, Frances Coughlin, wrote her M.A. thesis, "Spanish Galleys on the Mississippi River, 1792–1796," (Claremont College, 1946), does not believe Gayoso suggested the Mississippi Squadron to Carondelet. Upon available documentation, however, this writer has so far accepted Gayoso's own statements that he was the "father" of the fleet: Gayoso's political state of Louisiana, July 5, 1792, AGI, PC, leg. 2353; Carondelet to Floridablanca, No. 1, Confidential, New Orleans, January 13, 1792, *ibid.*, leg. 18.

[70]Gayoso to Carondelet, January 6, 1792.

dera), and six cannon launches.[71] In 1795 the crew members numbered more than 300.[72] The Spanish government built most of the crafts in New Orleans at official treasury expense; but the galley *La Leal* was built in 1793 with contributions from the officers in the Spanish Regular Infantry Regiment of Louisiana.[73]

The larger galleys boasted an 18-pounder cannon in the prow and eight to ten swivel guns along the port and starboard flanks.[74] They were used for reconnaissance, as in the case of Pedro Rousseau's 1793 and 1794 expeditions on the Mississippi, or Juan Barnó y Ferrusola's inspection trip up the river in 1794.[75] Gayoso was supported by a majority of the ships in the squadron when he established a new military post at the Chickasaw Bluffs in 1795.[76] Carondelet employed the galleys to keep the Negro slaves and pro-French dissidents in Louisiana under control.[77] On occasion they were sent to the mouth of the Mississippi to prevent raiding corsairs from ravaging Lower Louisiana plantations.[78] As for their primary function, to insure Spanish control of the Mississippi, their success exceeded even the sanguine expectations of Gayoso and Carondelet.

Gayoso also recommended to Carondelet construction of additional forts in the Mississippi Valley. Nogales, which Gayoso had

[71]An interesting account of the squadron in 1799 is Gayoso to Francisco Saavedra, No. 19, New Orleans, June 9, 1799, AHN, ESTADO, leg. 3901.

[72]Accounts of José Zamora, accountant of Squadron, San Fernando de las Barrancas, July 31, 1795, AGI, PC, leg. 533-b; Manuel García to Carondelet, No. 67, Galera *Venganza* en el Puerto de San Fernando de las Barrancas, August 24, 1796, AGI, PC, leg. 33.

[73]Joseph Xavier de Pontalba to Miró, New Orleans, May 7, 1792, in Cruzat (trans.), "Letters Written to Miró by Pontalba," 409, tells about the launching of the *Phelipa*, named for Carondelet's daughter. Carondelet to Alcudia, No. 15, Confidential, New Orleans, August 27, 1793, AHN, ESTADO, leg. 3898, tells of the *Leal*.

[74]Zamora's artillery inventory, January 4, 1794–March 11, 1796, AGI, PC, leg. 533-b.

[75]Rousseau's 1793 log is in Kinnaird (ed.), *Spain in the Mississippi*, Pt. III, 111–33. Barnó's diary covers 1793–1794 in the same vessel, *La Flecha;* see Holmes (ed.), *Documentos de la Luisiana*, 75–130. On Rousseau's 1794 voyage, see Holmes, "Spanish-American Rivalry over the Chickasaw Bluffs," 53–54.

[76]Holmes, "Spanish-American Rivalry over the Chickasaw Bluffs," 55–57; Holmes (ed.), *Documentos de la Luisiana*, 173–302.

[77]Carondelet to Grand-Pré, Very Confidential, New Orleans, May 5, 1795, AGI, PC, leg. 22.

[78]Carondelet to Gayoso, New Orleans, October 29, 1795, *ibid.*

begun under Miró's administration, was continued, amplified, and improved under Carondelet's suggestions. Ultimately, Carondelet came to depend more on Nogales than any other post in the Mississippi Valley. In addition to directing the various fortifications at the Nogales post, Gayoso prepared instructions for the commandant, Captain Elías Beauregard, governing the fort, defenses, settlers, control of navigation, Indian relations, and supplies and gave him secret instructions about what to do if any Americans came into his jurisdiction.[79] When Beauregard's work on Nogales fortifications fell below the standards established by Gayoso, the commandant was replaced by Captain Ignacio de Lino Chalmette.[80]

Gayoso had praised the natural situation of Nogales so highly to Carondelet in January, 1792,[81] that the governor-general soon came to regard Nogales as more important to the defenses of Lower Louisiana than Natchez. Located on the site of the ancient French fort called Rosalie and changed but little during the British occupation as Fort Panmure, the little Natchez stockade was imperfectly constructed of pounded dirt and faced with rotting planks. The site was militarily defenseless, being dominated by a nearby plateau. Moreover, it was too far from the river to check the passage of enemy craft descending the rapid current. With only one cannon, the loyalist settlers of Natchez had retaken the fort in 1781 from the Spanish defenders, and the following year Miró came to Natchez to build a stouter fort. The greatest defect to the economizing governor-general was its constant expense. Between 1784 and 1792, Spain had poured more than $32,415 into repairs on the fort. Every time it rained, which was often in the Mississippi Valley, portions of the fort caved in and necessitated repairs. Between January and July of 1792 alone, Carondelet spent $15,000 on the Natchez fort.[82]

[79]Gayoso to Carondelet, New Orleans, January 17, 1792, AGI, PC, leg. 18; Gayoso's instructions to the commandant of Nogales, Nogales, April 1, 1791; secret instructions, Gayoso to Beauregard, Nogales, April 1, 1791; Gayoso to Beauregard, Nogales, April 22, 1791, AGI, PC, leg. 2352.
[80]Holmes (ed.), *Documentos de la Luisiana*, 191–92, n.
[81]Gayoso to Carondelet, New Orleans, January 6, 1792, AGI, PC, leg. 2353.
[82]Carondelet to Las Casas, No. 136, Confidential, New Orleans, July 20, 1792, AGI, PC. leg. 1441; Carondelet to Floridablanca, No. 8, Confidential, New Orleans, February 25, 1792, AHN, ESTADO, leg. 3898, and also in

When Carondelet arrived at his new post in New Orleans he was appalled at the defenses he found there. The lack of troops and the poor state of the Natchez fort—"only defense of New Orleans up the river"—caused him to take decisive measures. In the deliberations at New Orleans, Gayoso figured prominently. The Natchez governor suggested spending at least $60,000 on the fort at Natchez to pay for mounting artillery at two advanced batteries, one near the landing and another at the cemetery. These suggestions were at first followed by Carondelet, and within six months, Gayoso had made remarkable progress in the works, all of which were directed by Lieutenant Antonio Soler of the Royal Artillery Corps.[83]

Gayoso used troops from his garrison and volunteers from among the inhabitants of the district who supplied Negroes and gladly participated in the works. Unfortunately, as the advanced batteries were almost completed, a strong storm hit the Natchez and virtually demolished the works and reduced their platforms to a sea of mud. It was not difficult to understand Carondelet's orders that all work on Natchez, except those repairs absolutely essential to keep the fort from disintegrating, be stopped, while at the same time, Nogales was made the point of defense in Lower Louisiana.[84]

Gayoso insisted, over his immediate superiors' heads to the Minister of State, Godoy, that Natchez be maintained. Even such an expense as the worn-out fort would require would be essential,

---

Serrano y Sanz (ed.), *Documentos de la Luisiana*, 403; memorial of Carondelet on fortifications (1793), Spanish MSS., Mississippi Valley, III; Gayoso to Miró, New Orleans, December 19, 1791, AGI, PC, leg. 41; Miró to Bernardo de Gálvez, New Orleans, November 7, 1782, copy in BN, vol. 19,247, folios 121-26; Collot, *Journey in North America*, II, 59-61; Pope, *A Tour*, 31.

[83]Carondelet to Floridablanca, No. 8, Confidential, February 25, 1792; pay sheet of Soler, AGI, PC, leg. 538-a; Gayoso to Miró, New Orleans, December 19, 1791, AGI, PC, leg. 41; Gayoso to Carondelet, Nos. 15, 21, 28, 29, Natchez, March 24, 31, April 3, 1792, AGI, PC, leg. 41; Miró to Campo de Alange, August 11, 1792, in Holmes (ed.), *Documentos de la Luisiana*, 49; Gayoso's note of artillery needed for advanced batteries, New Orleans, January 7, 1792, AGI, PC, leg. 206.

[84]Gayoso to Carondelet, No. 199, Natchez, November 26, 1792, AGI, PC, leg. 41; Gayoso to Carondelet, No. 21, March 31, 1792; Carondelet to Gayoso, Confidential, New Orleans, April 18, 1793, AGI, PC, leg. 47.

in Gayoso's opinion, for Natchez was the center of a populous district. Unless the settlers had confidence in the Spanish government's ability to protect them during time of invasion, Gayoso felt that no fort, not even Nogales, could hold against an armed attack supported by artillery. On the other hand, granted the loyalty of the Natchez inhabitants, they could unite with Gayoso at the small Natchez fort and repel any large force for sufficient time to enable those in Lower Louisiana to come to the rescue of their province.[85] Carondelet sent his engineer, Juan María Perchet, to inspect Natchez fortifications in 1795; and the engineer agreed with Gayoso and acting commandant Carlos de Grand-Pré that some expenses were essential to keep the fort from falling to the ground. Some money was allotted for this purpose, but it was obvious that Carondelet had no intention of maintaining Natchez as a strong post. By 1798 the oldest fort in the Mississippi Valley was virtually a refuse pile of rotting lumber and mud.[86]

Gayoso also supervised the construction of other batteries, blockhouses, and forts in the Mississippi Valley. In the Natchez District he urged the continuing use of the blockhouse and the advanced battery at Bayou Pierre near the Grand Gulf of the Mississippi.[87] Although, technically speaking, Gayoso had no supervision over the posts of Arkansas and Baton Rouge, frequently Carondelet placed the responsibility for their works on Gayoso's shoulders. As he accepted these added burdens, Gayoso soon came to exercise, perhaps, the major role in establishing and maintaining Spanish hegemony in the valley.

His most spectacular success in this direction occurred in 1795 when a race for the Chickasaw Bluffs between Spanish and American forces was won by the former. Long a point of contention between the opposing sides in the struggle for control of the

[85]Gayoso to Alcudia, Natchez, March 31, 1795, AGI, PC, leg. 2354; Gayoso's account of Louisiana, July 5, 1792.

[86]Perchet to Carondelet, Natchez, March 11, 1795; Grand-Pré to Carondelet, No. 18, Natchez, May 23, 1795, AGI, PC, leg. 31; Grand-Pré to Carondelet, No. 39, Natchez, July 9, 1795, AGI, PC, leg. 32; Gayoso to Carondelet, New Madrid, October 6, 1795, *ibid.*; Carondelet to Gayoso, New Orleans, February 18, 1796, and to Grand-Pré, New Orleans, February 22, 1796, AGI, PC, leg. 34; Minor to Gayoso, Natchez, January 12–15, 1798, AGI, PC, leg. 215-a.

[87]Gayoso to Carondelet, January 6, 1792; state of Louisiana, July 5, 1792.

Mississippi, the *Ecores á Margot* dominated the Upper Mississippi at the present site of Memphis. Gayoso capped a three-year program of negotiation with the Chickasaws, who technically owned the Bluffs, and won the consent of a majority of the nation to permit the establishment of a small military post on terms similar to those won at the Treaty of Natchez in 1792.

In the spring of 1795, supported by a number of galleys and lesser craft of the Mississippi Squadron under the command of Pedro Rousseau, Gayoso succeeded in establishing a post which he named San Fernando de las Barrancas. He supervised the clearing of the brush and trees, selected the site (which was militarily very poor), and advised the engineer on its proper construction. By the end of the summer of 1795, Fort San Fernando de las Barrancas was in a state of preparation for any attack from above. For two years it held the key to the Mississippi River by dominating the passage as the current swept boats close to the eastern shore in range of the heavy artillery mounted at several batteries.[88]

Gayoso recommended that Elías Beauregard, the commandant at Nogales, take over the reins of government, and he prepared an elaborate set of instructions for governing the new post. Beauregard, unable to maintain proper discipline among the troops and mariners and faced with an alarming increase of serious illness and fever among troops and workers alike, was soon relieved by the irascible, proud, and arrogant Catalán, Vicente Folch. Folch and Gayoso had more than one argument over jurisdiction, and both were probably relieved when Folch was appointed commandant at Pensacola in 1796. The last commandant of San Fernando, Josef Deville Degoutin Bellechasse, worked harmoniously with Gayoso and the restless Indians to insure security for the far distant Spanish post.[89]

As Gayoso had written to Godoy, the primary defense of Louisiana lay not in expensive permanent forts, but in the willingness of

[88]On the founding of San Fernando, see Holmes, "Spanish-American Rivalry over the Chickasaw Bluffs," 26–57; Holmes (ed.), *Documentos de la Luisiana,* 173–240.

[89]Holmes, "Fort Ferdinand of the Bluffs," 38–54; Holmes (ed.), "The First Laws of Memphis," 93–104; Holmes, "Three Early Memphis Commandants," 5–38; Jack D. L. Holmes, "The Ebb-Tide of Spanish Military Power on the Mississippi: Fort San Fernando de las Barrancas, 1795–1798," *Publications* of the ETHS (1964), 23–44.

the Natchez settlers to fight to protect their homes and plantations.[90] Louisiana had a regular battalion of infantry for duty at the numerous military posts scattered throughout the territory; another battalion was stationed at Pensacola; and a third was supposed to defend New Orleans. First organized in 1765, the Louisiana troops were never able to furnish the type of defense that the vast province required. In 1791 the effective force was only 1,345; it was 511 men short. Despite recruiting efforts in Mexico and the emptying of jails throughout the Spanish empire, the *Regimiento Fijo de Infantería de Luisiana* was never able to meet its ideal paper strength. Moreover, the quality of the troops was the worst in the Spanish Empire. Desertion, murder, and lesser crimes were too numerous to mention. Few capable Spaniards composed its ranks. Of the approximately 257 officers and sergeants in 1793, 85 were born in New Orleans and 3 others in other areas of Louisiana. Andalucía in Spain furnished 26; Castilla la Vieja, 21; Cataluña, 15; Galicia, 12; Castilla la Nueva, 8; and the rest of Spain only 31. There were 15 who were born in France, 4 in Germany, 2 in Ireland, 5 in Italy or Sardinia, and 2 in Portugal. It was a heterogenous organization with all the privileges and defects of Spanish military organization during the eighteenth century. After the glorious campaigns against the British in West Florida from 1779 to 1781, the morale, subordination, and efficiency of the battalion had declined until they reached a nadir.[91]

To supplement this declining force Gayoso and Carondelet both used extraordinary powers to organize militia. Carondelet proposed in 1792 an elaborate list of militia for Lower Louisiana which in-

[90]Gayoso to Alcudia, March 31, 1795.
[91]Marqués de Croix to Antonio Ulloa, Coruña, July 7, 1765, AGI, PC, leg. 2357; Bucareli to Grimaldi, Havana, May 12, 1769, AHN, ESTADO, leg. 3883; statement of regimental strength by Phelipe Treviño and Francisco Bouligny, New Orleans, September 21, 1791, AHN, ESTADO, leg. 3898; Grand-Pré's statement of regiment, New Orleans, June 30, 1793, AGI, PC, leg. 161-a; service sheets of officers compiled from AGI, PC, legs. 161-a, 161-b; and AGS, Guerra Moderna, leg. 7292; Las Casas to Floridablanca, Havana, December 3, 1791, in Mississippi Archives, Spanish Dominion, III, 795–800; Bouligny to Carondelet, No. 526, New Orleans, March 22, 1796, AGI, PC, leg. 33; Carondelet to Alcudia, No. 129, New Orleans, November 24, 1794, AHN, ESTADO, leg. 3899.

cluded two battalions, one regiment, and a legion. Unfortunately, Carondelet never really trusted the settlers of Lower Louisiana, and accordingly he did not extend any more power to them than was absolutely necessary.[92] Of a different nature, however, was the population of Natchez, composed almost entirely of persons of American or British extraction who felt little sympathy for the French in Louisiana.

Francisco Bouligny first recommended the organization of a quasi-military mounted police force in Natchez during his inspection of 1785.[93] In 1788 Miró asked commandant Grand-Pré to form a paper force of four companies of Natchez militia without letting the inhabitants know about it, and the Natchez commandant furnished his lists.[94] Nothing concrete was done about a militia force until Gayoso arrived in Natchez.

Finding there were no organized militia in the district, despite the obligation of all settlers in Spanish Louisiana and West Florida to take arms in defense of king and home, Gayoso suggested the establishment of free companies of volunteers with locally selected officers in each of the sections of the Natchez District, all under the general command of the governor.[95] Carondelet distrusted Natchez settlers, however, and it was not until 1792 that Gayoso acted to form a mounted company of "police" to keep peace on the frontiers.[96]

While Gayoso was forming his police force, his adjutant, Stephen Minor, was trying to persuade him to create a company of cavalry militia to be called the "Monteros de Natchez" (Natchez Mounties). Minor, an experienced officer who had been in the Spanish army

[92]Carondelet to Las Casas, No. 100, New Orleans, May 16, 1792, and plan of organization, May 31, 1792, enclosed in Las Casas to Conde del Campo de Alange, No. 281, Havana, April 5, 1793, a large *expediente* on the militia with names of officers recommended, in AGS, Guerra Moderna, leg. 6925.

[93]Bouligny to Miró, Natchez, August 22, 1785, in Kinnaird (ed.), *Spain in the Mississippi Valley*, Part II, 139–42.

[94]Grand-Pré's list, enclosed in Grand-Pré to Miró, No. 582, Natchez, April 5, 1788, AGI, PC, leg. 14.

[95]Gayoso to Carondelet, January 6, 1792.

[96]Gayoso to Carondelet, No. 172, Natchez, September 15, 1792, AGI, PC, leg. 41. This mounted force's police work is discussed *supra*, Chapter III.

since the days of the American Revolution, offered to provide at his own cost sixty horses for the use of the troops and suggested a uniform with a jaunty round cap.[97]

Gayoso estimated his district could furnish at least 800 militiamen, and he examined the various census reports carefully to determine the number of men capable of bearing arms in defense of the district. To ensure their loyalty and cooperation, Gayoso recommended that the Natchez militia be organized on a local basis in keeping with American traditions of minute-man defense and that officers chosen by the men be appointed.[98]

By the fall of 1793, Gayoso had organized two companies of infantry, two of cavalry, and one of artillery militia for Natchez.[99] When the Jacobin menace seemed to spread into Lower Louisiana in 1793, Carondelet desperately wrote Gayoso for several hundred Natchez militiamen to come immediately to New Orleans. Over 300 served in New Orleans for several months, during which they calmed the rebellious spirits and eased the worries of Carondelet.[100] In 1795 Carondelet wrote that the patriotism of the Natchez militia

[97]Petition of Stephen Minor, Natchez, September 14, 1792, enclosed in Gayoso to Carondelet, No. 187, Natchez, November 9, 1792, AGI, PC, leg. 41; Gayoso to Carondelet, No. 171, Natchez, September 14, 1792, *ibid.*

[98]Gayoso to Miró, No. 27, Natchez, March 12, 1791; proposal of militia, Natchez, September 16, 1792, enclosed in Gayoso to Carondelet, Natchez, September 16, 1792, AGI, PC, leg. 41; Gayoso to Carondelet, No. 6, Natchez, March 10, 1792, *ibid;* Gayoso to Carondelet, January 6, 1792; Gayoso's political state of Louisiana, July 5, 1792.

[99]*Ibid.;* roster of Real Carlos unit, no date [1793], AGI, PC, leg. 41; roster of Natchez militia officers, November 18, 1793, AGI, PC, legs, 131-a, 161-a; account of officers and volunteers for Natchez, October 16, 1792, AGI, PC, leg. 41; Gayoso to Carondelet, No. 631, Natchez, April 14, 1795, AGI, PC, leg. 31.

[100]Muster rolls of Natchez militia, New Orleans, November 18, 1793, AGI, PC, leg. 161-a; Carondelet to Gayoso, New Orleans, October 29, 1793, copy enclosed in Carondelet to Alcudia, No. 21, Confidential, New Orleans, November 6, 1793, AHN, ESTADO, leg. 3898; Gayoso to Alcudia, Natchez, February 18, 1794, AHN, ESTADO, leg. 3902, in AHA *Annual Report,* 1896, I, 1042–45; Gayoso to Carondelet, No. 402, Natchez, January 25, 1794, AGI, PC, leg. 42; Gayoso to Daniel Clark, Natchez, January 31, 1794, Cole Papers; Gayoso to Alcudia, Natchez, March 31, 1795, AGI, PC, leg. 2354; Gayoso to Carondelet, Nogales, October 18, 1792 (1793?), and Vidal to Gayoso, New Orleans, September 14, 1793, cited in Ernest R. Liljegren, "Jacobism in Spanish Louisiana, 1792–1797," *Louisiana Historical Quarterly,* XXII (January, 1939), 80–82.

had endeared the members of those units to him and to the king.[101] The militia was also ready to take up arms when a Negro revolt threatened at Punta Cortada and Baton Rouge; and in 1796, when the fear of an English attack on virtually defenseless Pensacola seemed imminent, Gayoso wrote that the Natchez militia was ready and willing to go into action. As a police force and effective military arm of the Spanish government, the militia backed up the glowing predictions of Gayoso himself.[102]

The major challenges to Spanish defenses in the Mississippi Valley occurred after the demise of the South Carolina Yazoo Company. There were no battles or campaigns, but the movements of the United States troops to the frontier in 1794 to counter the growing attacks of the northern Indians caused considerable speculation in Lower Louisiana. Could not these same troops be used to force the opening of the Mississippi as the Westerners continually demanded? Accordingly, Gayoso and Carondelet organized their troops at key points along the frontier, especially at Nogales and San Fernando de las Barrancas.[103]

The Jacobin scare of 1793 and 1794 enabled Carondelet to ask and receive additional funds for placing the provinces in a state

[101]Carondelet to Grand-Pré, New Orleans, June 4, 1795, AGI, PC, leg. 22; Carondelet to Gardoqui, New Orleans, February 24, 1794; Gayoso to Carondelet, Very Confidential, Natchez, June 2, 1796, AGI, PC, leg. 2354.

[102]Beauregard to Gayoso, No. 229, Nogales, February 4, 1793, AGI, PC, leg. 47; Carondelet to Gayoso, New Orleans, September 16, December 29, 30, 1796, AGI, PC, leg. 23; Carondelet to Grand-Pré, New Orleans, May 26, 1795, AGI, PC, leg. 22; Grand-Pré to Carondelet, Nos. 3, 4, Confidential, Natchez, October 10, 17, 1795, AGI, PC, leg. 32; Carondelet to Grand-Pré, New Orleans, November 28, 1795, AGI, PC, leg. 22. General Collot estimated the Natchez militia in 1796 at 2,000 with 200 dragoons; see his *Journey in North America*, II, 62. Governor Winthrop Sargent, notoriously ignorant of Spanish rule in the Natchez District, claimed there never was a militia in the area under the Spaniards. Sargent to Timothy Pickering, Natchez, March 21, 1799, in Rowland (ed.), *Mississippi Territorial Archives*, I, 116.

[103]Carondelet to Aranda, No. 19, Confidential, New Orleans, October 20, 1792; Carondelet to Aranda, No. 1, New Orleans, November 6, 1792; and Carondelet to Alcudia, No. 3, Confidential, March 11, 1793, in AHN, ESTADO, leg. 3898; Gayoso to Carondelet, No. 139, Natchez, August 5, 1792; No. 195, November 17, 1792, in AGI, PC, leg. 41; Proclamation of John Breckinridge, Democratic Society of Kentucky, December 13, 1793, AGI, PC, leg. 2354; *Gazette of the United States*, September 1, 1792.

of defense.[104] Although the governor-general spent nothing near the estimated $4,000,000 which General George Rogers Clark boasted he had forced the Spaniards to do, Carondelet did spend almost $300,000 in excess of the funds granted for defenses. When the Council of War in New Spain considered the needs, the viceroy was able to make up the extra expenditures, an action which was approved in Spain.[105]

When Citizen Edmond Genêt attempted to enlist disgruntled Westerners such as Clark in the French cause, Carondelet issued numerous proclamations warning inhabitants of Lower Louisiana to avoid any contact with the French agents of discontent.[106] From Natchez, Gayoso issued a similar warning and made special attempts to improve the defenses of the river, including those at Nogales, by deploying the galleys in the squadron to patrol the approaches to Louisiana.[107]

[104]On the Jacobins, see Liljegren, "Jacobism in Spanish Louisiana; Frederick Jackson Turner, "The Origin of Genêt's Projected Attack on Louisiana and the Floridas," *American Historical Review*, III (1898), 650–71; Marigny, *Thoughts upon the Foreign Policy of the United States*, 18–19; AHA *Annual Report, 1896*, I, 930–1107; Richard Lowitt, "Activities of Citizen Genêt in Kentucky, 1793–1794," *Filson Club Historical Quarterly*, XXII (October, 1948), 252–67; Archibald Henderson, "Isaac Shelby and the Genêt Mission," *MVHR*, VI, (March, 1920), 451–69; F. R. Hall, "Genêt's Western Intrigue, 1793–1794," *Journal of the Illinois State Historical Society*, XXI (October, 1928), 359–81; Abernethy, *The South in the New Nation*, 123–28.
[105]Clark to Genêt, Louisville, April 28, 1794, *American Historical Review*, XVIII (July, 1913), 782; Carondelet to Las Casas, No. 128, New Orleans, November 22, 1794, copy enclosed in Las Casas to Branciforte, Confidential, Havana, January 7, 1795; Minutes of the Junta Superior Extraordinaria de Real Hacienda, Mexico, February 11, 1795, enclosed in Branciforte to Las Casas, Mexico, February 28, 1795; Alcudia to Branciforte, Confidential, San Ildefonso, July 17, 1795, AGN, Historia, Tomo 430, folios 69–76.
[106]Carondelet to Alcudia, No. 20, Confidential, New Orleans, October 25, 1793, AHN, ESTADO, leg. 3898; No. 21, Confidential, November 6, 1793, *ibid;* proclamation of Carondelet, New Orleans, February 12, 1794, Kuntz Collection, Tulane University; Carondelet's proclamation, February 15, 1793, in Kinnaird (ed.), *Spain in the Mississippi Valley*, III, 139–40.
[107]Gayoso to Carondelet, No. 34, Confidential, Natchez, February 20, 1794, AGI, PC, leg. 2354. Gayoso issued his proclamation in 1793 or 1794, in AGI, PC, leg. 193-A. Oaths of loyalty were also taken from the sailors on the galleys suspected of Jacobin sympathies. Gayoso to Carondelet, No. 339, Natchez, August 7, 1793, AGI, PC, leg. 42. Gayoso also supervised the detection and apprehension of two French agents in Upper Louisiana, Jean Pierre Pisgignoux and Pogniat de Bonnevie. Holmes (ed.), *Documentos de la*

Ultimately, because of the firm defenses of the Spaniards and the hands-off neutrality of the United States, the Jacobin scare subsided; but as late as 1798 Gayoso was still unsure of the loyalty of the French descent population in Louisiana.[108]

By the close of 1795, thanks to the efforts of Gayoso and Carondelet, the Louisiana defenses in the Mississippi Valley were stronger than they had been at any time since the American Revolution. With a chain of forts stretching from the Missouri settlements to Balize near the mouth of the Mississippi and from St. Marks, Florida, to Natchitoches on the Texas frontier, Spain was reasonably secure. Staffed by troops from the thinly filled Louisiana Regiment and the burgeoning regiments of militia from throughout the provinces, the manpower shortage was less evident. The ultimate weapon—the Mississippi Squadron—still dominated the waterways and made secure the communications between Upper and Lower Louisiana. The friendship and alliance of the southern Indian nations merely tipped the balance of power further in Spain's favor.

With such a powerful array of forces and defensive potential, it is difficult to understand why Spain should have feared a war with the United States in 1795. Yet, according to most historians, this is exactly what caused Spain to make the most serious blunder in her American colonial policy: she decided to surrender control over the military posts north of the thirty-first parallel to the United States. With the signing of the Treaty of San Lorenzo at the Spanish Court on October 27, 1795, all the sacrifice, patient manipulation of forces, money and time, and the efforts of Spanish governors from Gálvez to Gayoso were undone. Spain's defense of Louisiana required the possession of the Mississippi River and the Natchez District. Once lost, they were never to be regained; the cardhouse of Spanish power in America soon collapsed, albeit over the constant protests of such frontier governors as Gayoso.

Luisiana, 124-26; Gayoso to Carondelet, No. 19, Confidential, New Madrid, September 26, 1795, AGI, PC, leg. 2364. Additional data on the French agents is found in A. P. Nasatir and Ernest R. Liljegren, "Materials Relating to the History of the Mississippi Valley," *Louisiana Historical Quarterly*, XXI (January, 1938), 35-36.

[108]Gayoso to Santa Clara, No. 17, Confidential, New Orleans, July 30, 1798, AGI, PC, leg. 1502-b.

CHAPTER VII

Aftermath of San Lorenzo

UNMINDFUL or neglectful of the success with which Caron-delet and Gayoso had endeavored to protect Spanish hegemony in the Mississippi Valley, the Spanish Council of State in August, 1795, prepared to follow the direction indicated by Manuel de Godoy. Scarcely pausing to rest on his newly won laurels as "Prince of Peace" for his work in signing the secret Treaty of Basel, which ended the war between France and Spain and took Spain out of the "strange-bedfellow' alliance with England, Godoy attempted to in-sure Spanish possessions in America by appeasement. Suspicious of John Jay's Treaty, news of which had arrived during negotiations with the American minister to Spain, Thomas Pinckney, Godoy sought to prevent a possible *rapprochement* between England and the United States. He felt that by sacrificing control over the Mis-sissippi River and by yielding the disputed territory north of the thirty-first parallel, Spain would ensure the security of her other North American possessions.[1]

[1]The major studies of the Treaty of San Lorenzo (Pinckney's Treaty) are Bemis, *Pinckney's Treaty;* Whitaker, *Spanish-American Frontier,* 201–02;

Even as the diplomats met and discussed the provisions of the vital treaty in Spain, Gayoso and Carondelet continued their efforts toward separating the western states from the United States in a revival of the "Spanish Conspiracy." Following his establishment of Fort San Fernando de las Barrancas, Gayoso sailed up the Mississippi River to the Spanish settlements in Missouri. Ostensibly his mission was to inspect Spanish defenses there and describe conditions for the benefit of the governor-general's policies. In fact, however, Gayoso had highly secret instructions and a rendezvous with certain prominent men in Kentucky who were known to favor the cause of separation. They included Judge Benjamin Sebastian, John Brown, Harry Innes, Benjamin Logan, George Nicholas, and William Murray.[2]

Wilkinson received additional money from Carondelet and a promise to increase expenditures should the intrigue develop along lines favorable to Spanish interests. Clearly, Carondelet was influenced by the Whiskey Rebellion in western Pennsylvania and believed the opposition to the federal government was so strong in the West as to tear asunder the bonds that tied these states to the Union.[3] Gayoso found little support in Kentucky, however, and only Sebastian met with him. After relaying Carondelet's terms for an independent Kentucky to Sebastian in exchange for broad commercial advantages at New Orleans, Gayoso and the would-be conspirator sailed down river to New Orleans for further discussions

---

Arthur P. Whitaker, "New Light on the Treaty of San Lorenzo: an Essay in Historical Criticism," *MVHR*, XV (March, 1929), 435–54; Raymond A. Young, "Pinckney's Treaty—a New Perspective," *HAHR*, XLIII (November, 1963), 526–35.

[2]Humphrey Marshall to George Mutter and Benjamin Sebastian, October 2, 1795, and Mutter and Sebastian to Marshall, October 13, 1795, printed in the *Aurora and General Advertiser* (Philadelphia), February 9, 1796; Gayoso to Conde de Santa Clara, No. 11, Very Confidential, New Orleans, June 5, 1798, and Gayoso to Carondelet, No. 5, Very Confidential, New Madrid, December 2, 1795, AGI, PC, leg. 2354; Carondelet to Gayoso, New Orleans, Very Confidential, July 18, 1795, AGI, PC, leg. 48; Carondelet to Gayoso, New Orleans, October 31, 1795, AGI, PC, leg. 22. Gayoso's voyage to New Madrid, St. Louis, Ste. Geneviève, and other Missouri posts is described in Holmes (ed.), *Documentos de la Luisiana*, 253–302.

[3]Carondelet to Las Casas, No. 128, New Orleans, November 22, 1794, copy in AGN, Historia, tomo 430, folios 69–70; Gayoso to Carondelet, No. 45 Confidential, Natchez, May 23, 1794, AGI, PC, leg. 2354; Gayoso to Carondelet, No. 5, Very Confidential, December 2, 1795.

with Carondelet. Unfortunately, news of the Treaty of San Lorenzo dashed Sebastian's hopes, and he sailed for the east coast without much interest in continuing the conspiracy. Although Carondelet and Gayoso both continued to support the movement with Wilkinson, that American officer's attitude grew increasingly cautious as Federalist agents heard rumors of his activities with the Spaniards. For all practical purposes, the Treaty of San Lorenzo ended Wilkinson's interest in pursuing his goal to be "Washington of the West," but he was not opposed to accepting secretly additional funds from the Spaniards.[4]

By the terms of the Treaty of San Lorenzo, one commissioner and one surveyor were to be appointed each by Spain and the United States and ordered to meet in Natchez within six months following the exchange of ratifications. They were then directed to draw the initial point marking the thirty-first parallel of latitude North and continue the line from the Mississippi to the Atlantic, as provided in the terms of the treaty. Copies of the treaty finally arrived in New Orleans in August, 1796. Because of pressing business in connection with his closing months as governor-general of Louisiana, the Baron de Carondelet appointed Gayoso as Spanish commissioner in his place. Lieutenant Colonel Gilberto Guillemard, famed New Orleans architect and longtime military engineer in the Spanish army, was chosen as surveyor.[5]

President Washington appointed Andrew Ellicott and Thomas

[4]Gayoso to Santa Clara, No. 11, Very Confidential, June 5, 1798; Thomas Marshall Green, *The Spanish Conspiracy, a Review of Early Spanish Movements in the South-west, containing Proofs of the Intrigues of James Wilkinson and John Brown; of the Complicity therewith of Judges Sebastian, Wallace, and Innes; the Early Struggles of Kentucky for Autonomy; the Intrigues of Sebastian in 1795–7, and the Legislative Investigation of his Corruption* (Cincinnati, 1891); Hay and Werner, *The Admirable Trumpeter,* 134–62; Elizabeth Warren, "Benjamin Sebastian and the Spanish Conspiracy in Kentucky," *Filson Club History Quarterly,* XX (April, 1946), 107–30; A. P. Whitaker (ed.), "Harry Innes and Spanish Intrigues, 1794–1795," *MVHR,* XV (September, 1928), 236–48.

[5]Carondelet to Gayoso, New Orleans, August 22, 1796, AGI, PC, leg. 23; royal orders, No. 6 (1796) and No. 56 (1797), Archivo Nacional de Cuba (Havana), legajos 14, 15, cited in Archivo Nacional de Cuba, *Catálogo de los fondos de las Floridas* (Havana, 1944), 83–84. Ultimately, Gayoso appointed Stephen Minor as deputy commissioner in his stead; William Dunbar replaced Guillemard. See *infra,* Chapter IX.

Freeman to the posts of commissioner and surveyor, respectively; and on May 24, 1796, their appointments were confirmed by the Senate.[6] Ellicott was an experienced surveyor whose early training in medicine was supplemented by a lifetime devoted to mathematics. His previous work at Niagara Falls, on the boundary line between Pennsylvania and Virginia, and on the surveys of the new cities of Washington, D.C., Buffalo, and Presqu' Isle had caught the attention of his superiors who found him ideal for the post of American boundary commissioner at Natchez.[7] Ellicott's departure was delayed until September 16, 1796, when he left Pittsburgh for the long trip down the Ohio and Mississippi rivers. By the time he arrived in Natchez on February 24, 1797, his patience had already been stretched to the danger point. He was in an ill humor because of the record cold winter and the low water level of the rivers which prevented his boats from continuing, and because he had been forced to spend more than $12,000 in excess of the $30,000 voted by Congress to pay his boundary commission expenses. Spanish commandants along the river were surprised at the nature of Ellicott's mission, which caused the irascible Quaker to suspect Spain's word about fulfilling the terms of the treaty. Virtually devoid of tact and other qualities demanded in such a difficult diplomatic mission, Ellicott complained loudly to all who would listen that the word of the Spaniards was not to be trusted.[8]

[6]Carlos Martínez de Irujo to Prince of Peace, No. 71, Philadelphia, September 8, 1796, AHN, ESTADO, leg. 3896 *bis.*; Senate Executive Journal, I, 210–11, cited in Carter (ed.), *Territorial Papers of the United States, V: Mississippi,* 3; Isaac Joslin Cox, *The West Florida Controversy, 1798–1813, a Study in American Diplomacy* (Baltimore, 1918), 33.

[7]Most historians confine their examination of the boundary commission to Ellicott's obviously biased *Journal.* Biographical notes on Ellicott are in Mrs. Sally Kennedy Alexander, "A Sketch of the Life of Major Andrew Ellicott," *Records* of the Columbia Historical Society (Washington), II (1899), 158–202; G. Hunter Bartlett, "Andrew and Joseph Ellicott, the Plans of Washington City and the Village of Buffalo and some of the Persons Concerned," *Recalling Pioneer Days,* Vol. XXVI, *Publications* of the Buffalo Historical Society (Buffalo, 1922), 1–48; Harrison Griswold Dwight, "Andrew Ellicott," *Dictionary of American Biography,* ed. Allen Johnson and Dumas Malone (23 vols.; New York, 1928–1958), VI, 89–90; Mathews, *Andrew Ellicott, his Life and Letters.*

[8]Ellicott to Secretary of State, Philadelphia, September 6, 1796, and Major Isaac Craig to Timothy Pickering, Pittsburgh, October 28, 1796, Southern

Actually, Ellicott was partially correct in assuming the Spanish officers opposed the execution of the Treaty of San Lorenzo. Gayoso was a constant foe of the treaty. When he heard of its terms in the summer of 1796, he attempted to do everything in his power to reverse the onward rush of history which he felt threatened not only Louisiana but also Spain's entire American empire. On June 2 he wrote a highly confidential dispatch to Carondelet in which he reiterated the arguments based on seven years' experience as a frontier governor facing the advancing United States frontier. Since Jay's Treaty had influenced the signing of Pinckney's Treaty, the failure of England to fulfill the provisions of the former would allow Spain to escape its obligations under the latter. The animosity of the Indians would increase against Spain should the Americans be allowed to move into the claimed territory. Within five years the West would be so populated that it would seek independence from the United States and thus form a barrier to further expansion. Should the treaty be carried out, Americans would pour into Texas and other domains of New Spain and foment a revolution. Natchez inhabitants would fight rather than submit to domination from the Georgia legislature, which in 1795 had renewed its claims to the Yazoo lands in the notorious grants to speculators.⁹

To his friend, Daniel Clark, Sr., Gayoso wrote, "I have powerful reasons to believe that the part of the treaty concerning limits will never be accomplished." He made several revealing statements concerning the entire basis of Spain's diplomacy during these critical times:

> In the time that the treaty was signed the political affairs of Europe determined our court to do any thing to

Boundary MSS., I; Pickering to Ellicott, Philadelphia, April 26, 1798, *ibid.*, II, and printed in Carter (ed.), *Territorial Papers of the United States, V: Mississippi*, 26; Josef Deville Degoutin to Gayoso, San Fernando de las Barrancas, December 27, 1796, AGI, PC, leg. 48; C. F. Volney, *A View of the Soil and Climate of the U.S.A.*, 123–24; Ellicott's *Journal*, 1–40.
⁹Gayoso to Carondelet, No. 1, Very Confidential, Natchez, June 2, 1796, AGI, PC, leg. 2354; Gayoso to Carondelet, No. 2, Confidential, Natchez, June 7, 1796, AGI, PC, leg. 2364; Carondelet to Alcudia, No. 70, Confidential, New Orleans, June 12, 1796, AGI, PC, leg. 178-b; Gayoso to Prince of Peace, Natchez, June 6, 1797, AHN, ESTADO, leg. 3902. Carondelet agreed to delay execution of the treaty only a few months. Carondelet to Gayoso, New Orleans, August 22, 1796, AGI, PC, leg. 23.

keep the U.S. in a perfect neutrality, and thereby destroy a new plan that was forming to renew and continue a destructive war. The treaty with England had a different object; it was to attract the Americans to their interest in such a manner as to have still in her power to keep them dependant; the plan has fallen through, and the British will no longer deliver the posts; our treaty, that was made to counter-balance that, will suffer equal difficulties; for the circumstances being altered will be the conditions on every side. Spain made a treaty with the Union, but if this Union is dissolved, one of the contracting parties exists no longer and the other is absolved from her engagement. It is more than probable that a separation of several states will take place which will alter the political existence of a power that could influence on the ballance of that of others; therefore Spain, being deprived of that assistance which could arise from her connexion with the Union, will alter her views. . . . Therefore even when no change should happen in the U.S. the treaty will be reduced to the navigation of this river. . . . I have already represented in the strongest and most energetic manner on the subject of real property; without a solution from Court, it will be out of our power to fulfill the contents of the treaty.[10]

Despite Gayoso's warning to Carondelet to suspend all plans to carry out the treaty, the governor-general went ahead with his original orders. Carondelet was, after all, responsible for following his instructions from the Court. Unaware that Godoy had decided to follow Gayoso's suggestions and delay the execution of the treaty, Carondelet issued orders to evacuate the posts known to be well above the thirty-first parallel. Lieutenant Colonel Carlos Howard was sent up river with the galleys on a mission so secretive that Gayoso was not told of its nature. On March 16, 1797, the Spanish fort at San Fernando de las Barrancas was evacuated and the blockhouse and artillery transferred to the opposite bank of the Mississippi where the post of Esperanza was established.[11] Similar orders were issued to evacuate Fort Confederación on the Tombig-

---

[10]Gayoso to Daniel Clark, Sr., Natchez, June 17, 1796, Parsons Collection, now in the Humanities Division, Manuscript Collection, University of Texas. The letter is paraphrased in Stoddard, *Sketches, Historical and Descriptive of Louisiana,* 99; it is also found in *American State Papers, Miscellaneous,* I, 707.

[11]Holmes, "The Ebb-Tide of Spanish Military Power."

bee in Alabama. Carondelet urged haste to prevent the Indians from learning that the Spaniards were going to evacuate those posts they had been granted on the condition they never allow the Americans to possess them.[12]

Gayoso announced to the inhabitants of the Natchez District the terms of the Treaty of San Lorenzo on December 3, 1796.[13] He continued to argue against its execution, but apparently Carondelet was going through with the spirit as well as the letter of the treaty. The royal order of October 29, 1796, ordering Carondelet to suspend the evacuation until further orders from the Court, did not arrive in New Orleans until after the evacuation of San Fernando de las Barrancas and Confederación. Then Carondelet attempted to salvage something from his hasty implementation of orders by showing the American commissioner that Spain had acted in good faith, but that further evacuation of posts and the drawing of the boundary line might have to wait until additional clarification arrived from the Court.[14]

If British relations with the United States in 1794 and 1795 had originally been the cause of Spain's precipitate signing of the Treaty of San Lorenzo, British activities in the upper Mississippi and Missouri valleys in 1796 furnished Carondelet with a reasonable pretext for refusing to carry out the terms of the treaty. As early as 1796 Carondelet asked the commander in chief of Upper Canada, Lieutenant Governor J. G. Simcoe, if Canada would come to Spain's aid should St. Louis be attacked by the United States. The reply was cordial, but noncommittal.[15] Carondelet urged that the Company of Explorers of the Missouri River be approved and given

[12]Whitaker, *Mississippi Question*, 56.
[13]Gayoso's proclamation, Natchez, December 3, 1796, is in the Parson's Collection, University of Texas. Washington's annual address to Congress, December 7, 1796, in which he refers to the Treaty of San Lorenzo, was published in the Knoxville *Gazette* of January 23, 1797, and the Indians soon learned of its terms. Holmes, "The Ebb-Tide of Spanish Military Power"; Holmes, "Three Early Memphis Commandants." The first news published in Philadelphia about the treaty was based on an account brought on the *Ruby*, seven days out of Spain. *Aurora and General Advertiser* (Philadelphia), February 26, 1796.
[14]Whitaker, *Mississippi Question*, 215–16.
[15]Simcoe to Carondelet, at the Rapids of the Miami River and Lake Erie, April 11, 1794, AGI, PC, leg. 2371.

permission to maintain militiamen along the upper frontiers near Canada to prevent the continual advance of British fur traders into Spanish territory. Long neglected in the overall fortification plans of Louisiana, St. Louis soon became the focal point of Carondelet's attention; and he issued orders to attack any English traders found in Spanish territory.[16]

That England and the United States might join forces in an assault on Louisiana in 1796–1797 was not without foundation, especially after Carondelet heard from the French general, George Henri Victor Collot. This former governor of the French island of Guadaloupe found himself a prisoner in Philadelphia awaiting trial for seizing an American's ship prior to the French governor's capture by the English. He eagerly accepted the suggestion of French minister to the United States Adet that he undertake a reconnaissance of the Ohio and Mississippi rivers. Armed with a Spanish passport, he left Philadelphia on March 21, 1796, and arrived in Natchez that October. To Gayoso he revealed news of an imminent invasion of Louisiana by a strong British force from Canada as soon as the spring thaws raised the level in the rivers. Amid talk of a possible retrocession of Louisiana to France, yet cognizant of the suspicious fact that Collot and his adjutant had mapped and sketched Spanish fortifications throughout the valley, Carondelet did not lose sight of the information that the Frenchman had given him on the British plans.[17]

The story had its incredible features. Involved were Senator William Blount, former governor of the Southwest Territory, and

[16]Carondelet to Prince of Peace, No. 8, Confidential, New Orleans, June 3, 1796, AGI, PC, leg. 2364. Spain's policy in the Upper Mississippi and Missouri valleys is best covered in the articles of A. P. Nasatir, "The Anglo-Spanish Frontier on the Upper Mississippi, 1786–1796," *Iowa Journal of History and Politics*, XXIX (April, 1931), 155–232; "The Formation of the Missouri Company," *Missouri Historical Review*, XXV (October, 1930), 3–15; and "Anglo-Spanish Rivalry on the Upper Missouri," *MVHR*, XVI (December, 1929–March, 1930), 359–82, 507–28, which is also in his edited *Before Lewis and Clark*, I, 75–115.

[17]Collot's journey is adequately described in his own *Journey in North America*. A brief sketch of his trip and its significance to Louisiana defenses based on additional, unpublished sources, is included in Jack D. L. Holmes, "Some French Engineers in Spanish Louisiana," in John Francis McDermott (ed.), *The French in The Mississippi Valley* (Urbana, Ill., 1965).

Robert Liston, British minister to the United States. British aid had been sought for a plan of attack against Spanish Louisiana, and the British minister had encouraged the conspirators to believe that Louisiana might be retroceded to France or that the war against the Family Pact signatories might continue. The various letters exchanged by Blount's fellow conspirators, Captain John Chisholm and James Carey, were intercepted; and when Blount deserted the Federalist party, Secretary of State Timothy Pickering exposed the entire unsavory affair. Blount was almost impeached, and the entire incident afforded the Spaniards a plausible excuse for refusing to evacuate military posts which might be essential to the security of Lower Louisiana.[18]

With the declaration of war between Spain and England, Carondelet had his hands full tending to the many exposed areas of Louisiana, especially St. Louis in the north and Pensacola in the south. English and French corsairs soon ranged between Providence in the Bahamas and New Orleans, taking potshots at each other or capturing Spanish and American ships as the case might warrant.[19] The English Ministry of War considered a proposal for invading Louisiana with between 2,000 and 3,000 men carried in shallow-draft cannon launches to New Orleans by way of the Lakes Maure-

[18]Included among the vast literature on the "Blount Conspiracy" are Abernethy, *The South in the New Nation, 169–91;* William H. Masterson *William Blount* (Baton Rouge, 1954), 286–323; Walter B. Posey, "The Blount Conspiracy," Birmingham-Southern *Bulletin,* XXI (1928), 11–21; Isabel Thompson, "The Blount Conspiracy," *Publications* of the ETHS, II, (1930), 3–21 Contemporary sources include the *Aurora and General Advertiser* (Philadelphia), June 27, July 8, 13, 26, 1797; Frederick Jackson Turner (ed.), "Documents on the Blount Conspiracy, 1795–1797," *American Historical Review* X (April, 1903), 574–606; "Correspondance qui devoile la Trahison du Senateur Américain W. Blount" (printed pamphlet, Philadelphia, 1797), copy enclosed in Irujo to Prince of Peace, No. 66, Philadelphia, July 20, 1797, AHN ESTADO, leg. 3889 *bis.*

[19]Carondelet to Zenon Trudeau, New Orleans, November 22, 1796, and Carondelet to Gayoso, New Orleans, December 16, 1796, AGI, PC, leg. 23 royal instructions for commanders of merchant vessels with letters of marque and reprisal against ships, goods, and subjects of the King of Spain, St James, November 15, 1796; June 26, November 20, 1797; Nassau, April 1 1798; St. James, January 25, April 27, 1798, AGI, PC, leg. 215-a; Gayoso to William Panton, New Orleans, March 10, 1798, Panton-Forbes Papers Mobile Public Library; Carondelet to Prince of Peace, No. 92, Confidential New Orleans, April 19, 1797, AGI, PC, leg. 178.

pas, Pontchartrain, and Borgne. Pensacola was almost defenseless; it was weaker than it had been in 1781 when Bernardo de Gálvez captured it. Accordingly, one of Carondelet's principal concerns was to improve the fortifications of West Florida.[20]

Meanwhile, Ellicott's boundary commission party drifted toward Natchez and a bristling encounter with Gayoso, disputes with its own surveyor, and trouble with the Choctaws. When Ellicott reached Natchez on February 24, 1797, he was already convinced that the Spaniards had no intention of fulfilling their promises made at San Lorenzo. In one sense, the treaty was already a dead letter because the third article provided that the boundary commissioners from both sides were to begin their operations within six months of the exchange of ratifications. Ratifications had been exchanged on April 25, 1796; Ellicott did not arrive at Natchez until ten months later.

Anxious, however, to avoid an open break with the Americans, Gayoso used all his tact and diplomatic guile to persuade the stubborn Quaker that all things would come to whoever was most patient. In February the rivers were so high from the spring floods that much of the land over which the commission had to pass was already inundated. To allay Ellicott's fears that the Spaniards would take the first opportunity to assassinate him, Gayoso allowed the military escort under Lieutenant Piercy Smith Pope to come to Natchez, although the treaty merely allowed for American troops on the boundary line and not in the Spanish capital of the Natchez District. Even this concession was misinterpreted by Ellicott, who suspected another Spanish trap.[21]

[20]The 1796 English plans were obtained by the Spanish ambassador in London during 1803 and forwarded to the Spanish Minister of War. Minutes of the Council of Generals and Fortifications, Madrid, June 25, 1803, ASHM, 5-1-7-10; Francisco de Paula Gelabert to Vicente Folch, Pensacola, December 3, 1796, AGI, PC, leg. 2354; Carondelet to Gayoso, New Orleans, December 29, 1796, AGI, PC, leg. 23; *expediente* on Pensacola fortifications, 1797, AGS, Guerra Moderna, leg. 7245.

[21]Gayoso to Pope, Natchez, March 25, 1797, Pope Papers, Missouri Historical Society, St. Louis; Ellicott to Gayoso, Natchez, March 11, 1797; Gayoso to Ellicott, March 12, 1797; Ellicott to Gayoso, March 13, 1797, Southern Boundary MSS., I; Ellicott's *Journal*, 52. "Crazy Pope", as he was known, had been chosen by "Mad" Anthony Wayne—an interesting combination! When not intoxicated or bereft with fever, Pope ranged over the Natchez

GAYOSO

Ellicott jealously forwarded American rights in Natchez by raising the American flag over his camp directly opposite the Spanish fort. When Gayoso warned him that the flying of the Stars and Stripes would have an adverse effect on those Indians living nearby, Ellicott ignored the request to strike his colors on the grounds that the flag flew over American territory. The arrival of the American troops also enraged the Indians and, following a rather inebriating evening, the Indians insulted Ellicott. The Quaker feared the worst, and he wrote that the Spaniards were deliberately inciting the Indians against him and his party.[22]

Still trying to win the friendship of the difficult commissioner Gayoso wrote, "I pledge you my honor and friendship that every step of my conduct shall be guided by the principle impressed in me by my duty and by the very particular attachment I have for you." [23] But Ellicott refused to believe the governor's words, especially after he witnessed the remounting of cannon at Fort Panmure and the apparent preparation for war. Ellicott wrote that the rearming of the fort and the "insolent treatment which the Citizens of the United States have received at the Walnut Hills, and the delay in the business upon which I came concur in giving me reasons to suppose that the Treaty will not be observed with the same good faith and punctuality by the subjects of his Catholic Majesty as it will by the Citizens of the U.S." Ellicott demanded an explanation.[24]

Gayoso tried his best to oblige. The ammunition at Fort Panmure came from the Walnut Hills, and the governor was preparing for the subsequent evacuation. Would Ellicott prefer that the Indians be allowed to obtain arms and ammunition? he asked. Gayoso added that if the American were really observant, he would notice that

countryside sowing trouble. He was appointed captain on April 24, 1798, and died near Natchez on July 11, 1799—exactly one week before Gayoso. Francis B. Heitman (comp.), *The Historical Register and Dictionary of the U.S. Army* (2 vols.; Washington, 1903), I, 798; T. H. Cushing to Gayoso, Camp Mulberry Vale, near Natchez, July 20, 1799, AGI, PC, leg. 2371; Pope Papers, Missouri Historical Society, St. Louis.

[22]Gayoso to Ellicott, Natchez, February 17, Ellicott to Gayoso, March 11, 12, 1797, Southern Boundary, I; Ellicott's *Journal*, 36–44; Gayoso to Santa Clara, No. 19, New Orleans, September 24, 1797, AGI, PC, leg. 1502-b.

[23]Gayoso to Ellicott, Natchez, March 14, 1797, Southern Boundary MSS., I.

[24]Ellicott to Gayoso, Natchez, March 23, 1797, *ibid.*

the governor also sent arms and reinforcements to the Arkansas Post, which in no way was affected by the treaty. The reason in both cases, he explained, was fear of Indian uprisings. Despite what Ellicott believed and charged, the Spanish government was making every effort to keep the Indians peaceable. Any untoward action at the Walnut Hills was due, he said, to that commandant's personal errors, and not to any orders from Gayoso or Carondelet. The delay of the survey was occasioned by the necessity of obtaining instruments and transporting them with the surveyor, Lieutenant Colonel Guillemard, who was said to be on his way from New Orleans to Natchez. Gayoso's irritation was apparent in his concluding remarks: "I request that you will be so kind as to take such measures as to suppress untimely expressions that can only tend to disturb the tranquility of the public of which I am solely answerable for the present." [25]

Ellicott replied to Gayoso's explanation, "I have & shall continue to discountenance every measure, & the propagation of any opinion which may have a tendency to disturb the good order & harmony of this settlement." [26] Ellicott's actions were not in keeping with his promises, however; and the already tense situation in Natchez worsened.

Meanwhile, Carondelet continued to send Gayoso useless suggestions on how to keep Ellicott happy and in check. Carondelet invited the Quaker to spend some time in New Orleans; Ellicott merely suspected another trick. The governor-general suggested that Gayoso bribe one of the American military officers. To divert attention from Guillemard's tardiness, Carondelet suggested that Gayoso complain about placing a white Spanish officer side by side with the American mulatto.[27] In reality, Carondelet and Gayoso were playing for time; word from the Court was expected momentarily. Carondelet had full authority to act independently in the matter because the captain-general of Cuba, Luis de las Casas, had resigned

[25]Gayoso to Ellicott, Natchez, March 23, 1797, *ibid.*
[26]Ellicott to Gayoso, Natchez, March 24, 1797, *ibid.*
[27]Carondelet to Gayoso, New Orleans, March 4, 1797, AGI, PC, leg. 2354; Carondelet to Gayoso, New Orleans, April 26, 1797, in Mississippi Archives, Spanish Dominion, VI, 425–28; Carondelet to Gayoso, New Orleans, March 24, 1797, *ibid.*, VI, 342–48.

in the fall of 1796. Until the Conde de Santa Clara arrived the following spring, Carondelet communicated directly with the Crown.[28]

By early March, however, Carondelet had received Godoy's orders calling for a suspension of evacuation and boundary line plans.[29] Thereafter, Gayoso was directed to offer plausible excuses for the suspension and at the same time maintain the friendship of Ellicott—a virtually impossible task. Gayoso did the best he could, but he must have been aware that Ellicott was in no mood to suffer further delays and that all the excuses were considered mere pretexts to avoid Spanish obligations under the treaty.[30]

Already cognizant of rumors about the "Blount Conspiracy" from General Collot and others, Carondelet's fears of an imminent attack from Canada were reinforced by a warning from the Spanish minister in Philadelphia, Carlos Martínez de Irujo. Irujo wrote in March, 1797, that a force of 350 men was forming at Montreal Pass with the intention of invading Carondelet's province. Known movements of the Canadian troops and British reluctance to surrender her northern posts to the United States as agreed in Jay's Treaty stirred the restless Spanish commanders in Louisiana even more. Instead of meeting Ellicott to proceed with the boundary work, Lieutenant Colonel Guillemard joined another engineer, Juan María Perchet, at Nogales where the rotting defenses were repaired and readied for the expected attack from the English.[31]

Of course, all these defensive preparations were interpreted by Ellicott as directed against the United States. The American began to stir the thick brew of revolt among dissidents and malcon-

[28]Carondelet to Gayoso, New Orleans, November 22, 1796, AGI, PC, leg. 23.

[29]Whitaker, *Mississippi Question*, 280 n. 10–11; Carondelet to Santa Clara, No. 1, Confidential, New Orleans, April 21, 1797, AHN, ESTADO, leg. 5549; No. 1, Confidential, New Orleans, April 22, 1797, AGI, PC, leg. 1502-a.

[30]A pro-Ellicott, anti-Spanish interpretation of these delays is in Franklin L. Riley's two articles, "Transition from Spanish to American Rule in Mississippi," and "Spanish Policy in Mississippi after the Treaty of San Lorenzo," in *Publications* of the Mississippi Historical Society, III (1900), 261–311; and I (June, 1898), 50–66. A more reasonable and objective treatment is in Cox, *West Florida Controversy*, 34–37.

[31]Irujo to Carondelet, Philadelphia, March 13. 1797, AGI, PC, leg. 2365; Holmes, "French Engineers in Spanish Louisiana,' see *supra*, note 17.

tents in the Natchez District. Ellicott did not have far to look for those who were outspoken in opposition to Spanish rule. Long meek under the benevolent paternalism of Gayoso's rule, they grew brave in sight of the American troops and the all-too-willing American commissioner. An accurate account of the situation is difficult to obtain because of the prejudices of those who wrote; but an impartial observer, Daniel Clark, Sr., who was friend to Gayoso and to the United States alike, wrote that there were two classes of discontented people in Natchez. In one group were "those who complained that Governour Gayoso had, at various times, insulted, wronged, and refused to grant land to them." They included Colonel Anthony Hutchins, the vitriolic Tory whose extensive landholdings and irascible temper tyrannized his acquaintances and family alike; and Colonel Thomas Green, Sr., who had been allowed to return from a banishment decree through the leniency of Gayoso. The other group "was in general composed of *low* characters, inured to the practice of murdering and plundering, during the revolutionary war." According to Clark, "*Their* view was to set the country in a flame, the more readily and successfully to pursue their ancient practices of horrid and barbarous murdering and robbing among us."

These two factions united in common complaint against Gayoso. In addition, many of the planters favored revolt because they were deeply in debt. They had conveniently forgotten that Gayoso had interceded for them and obtained two moratoriums on the payment of these debts. What they did remember and realize was that without the conservative Spanish laws protecting property, there would be no government strong enough to force them to pay their debts.[32]

Even as Gayoso sought Spanish guarantees for the land grants extended to his enemies,[33] they caught the ear of Ellicott with pitiful stories of Spanish cruelty, which the gullible Quaker ac-

[32]Daniel Clark, Sr. to William C. C. Claiborne, Clarksville, June 18, 1800, in *Papers in relation to the Official Conduct of Governour Sargent*, 20–22; Gayoso to Santa Clara, No. 2, Confidential, New Orleans, September 24, 1797, AGI, PC, leg. 1502-a.

[33]Gayoso to Carondelet, No. 1, Very Confidential, June 2, 1796; No. 2, Confidential, June 7, 1796; Carondelet to Gayoso, New Orleans, November 22, 1796, AGI, PC, leg. 23.

cepted as literal truth. A typically prevaricating communication of this type painted dark pictures of Spanish tyranny and atrocities: "Some have been already torn away from the bosom of agricultural life, and conveyed to prison with every indignant epithat [*sic*] that malevolence could invent. Scouts are crossing the Country in various directions, breathing threats of vengeance against those who had unguardedly thrown aside the Mask of Duplicity; and a number are awaiting with solitude the moment of their fate." [34]

Gayoso was astounded when Ellicott confronted him with the malevolent letter. He tried to explain the principles of Spanish government to Ellicott. Any resident had, and had always enjoyed, the privilege of returning to the United States or wherever he came from at any time. Only one person was in the fort stockade at that moment, and he had been judged guilty of a nonpolitical crime. As for vigilante patrols scouring the country and intimidating those friendly to the United States, that was a scurrilous lie. Gayoso added, however, that should it be necessary to maintain peace and suppress disorder in the Natchez District, he would employ "every means." [35] Ellicott, of course, considered Gayoso's answer another prevarication in a growing list which he dutifully sent to Secretary of State Pickering.

Meanwhile, "Crazy Pope" was scouring the streets and hills himself looking for "deserters." Some of the Natchez inhabitants had indeed fled from the distasteful service on the frontier to refuge in Spanish territory; but Pope's impressment not only violated the courtesy extended by Gayoso in allowing him to come into Natchez in the first place, but also transgressed international law and was repugnant to the American government as well as that of Spain. When Gayoso requested that Pope release those inhabitants taken into American service and cease such activities in the future, the American commander ignored him. [36]

Throughout April and May the bitter exchange of letters between Gayoso and Ellicott continued to exacerbate both factions. Ellicott

[34]Two paragraphs of a letter from a number of respectable inhabitants in the country to Andrew Ellicott, Natchez, March 29, 1797, copy enclosed in Ellicott to Pickering, Natchez, April 14, 1797, Southern Boundary, I.
[35]Gayoso to Ellicott, Natchez, March 31, 1797, *ibid.*
[36]Gayoso to Ellicott, Ellicott to Gayoso, Natchez, April 14, 1797, *ibid.*

would demand to know when the Spaniards intended to fulfill their promises; Gayoso would retort with some heat, "Both you and the Commander General of this province will be informed of the time that the boundaries are to be determined," implying that until the Court send additional orders, no positive action was possible.[37]

In an effort to calm the growing restlessness in Natchez, Gayoso called on the people to show their "upright sense of duty" in supporting the Spanish government until such time as a proper transfer of territory to the United States could take place. He explained the basic reasons for delaying the treaty—the need for ministerial agreement on protection for the people's lands, protection against irate Indian tribes, and continuance of the moratorium on debts. Gayoso warned against the "malignant minds" which sought to "disturb the tranquility of its inhabitants." Until they became Americans by evacuation of the district and the official demarcation of the boundary line, all Natchez inhabitants were to remain loyal vassals of the Spanish king.[38]

On May 31, 1797, Carondelet ordered published an ordinance relating to the suspension of evacuation and the reasons for the action. He cited the dangers of British invasion and the apparent contradiction between Jay's Treaty and Pinckney's Treaty. This proclamation, wrote Ellicott, was so transparent that it required no further comment. It did arouse the people of Natchez, however; and continual threats and dark mutterings filled the air.[39]

Ellicott wrote in his journal, "The public mind might be compared to inflammable gas; it wanted but a spark to produce an explosion." [40] Bearing more than mere sparks, several Protestant ministers appeared in Natchez to challenge Gayoso's proclamation against public preaching of any but the Catholic religion. In the American

[37]Ellicott to Gayoso, Gayoso to Ellicott, Natchez, May 11, 1797, *ibid.*

[38]Gayoso's proclamation, Natchez, March 29, 1797, copy enclosed in Ellicott to Secretary of State, Natchez, April 14, 1797, *ibid.*

[39]Carondelet's printed broadside proclamation [in French], New Orleans, May 31, 1797, copies in AGI, PC, leg. 178, and the Bancroft Library, University of California. My copy is based on a photostat copy of the latter, obtained from the New York Public Library. An English copy appears in Ellicott's *Journal,* 101–03, and was sent to Pickering on June 27, 1797; Ellicott's comments are addressed to Pickering, Natchez, June 4, 1797, Southern Boundary, I.

[40]Ellicott's *Journal,* 96.

camp William and Bailey Chaney of South Carolina preached to an "immense congregation . . . under the 'Stars and Stripes.'" One Brother Harigail tried his hand at fire-and-brimstone preaching when he not only attacked the despotism of the Papal hierarchy, but finished his sermon with a quote from Hebrews, "Ye have not resisted unto blood striving against sin." [41]

The Chaney brothers and Harigail were as babes compared to an itinerant Virginia shoemaker named Barton Hannon, who took his Baptist theology seriously enough to engage in violent argument with the Irish Catholics of Natchez.[42] Most writers have based their accounts of the events that followed on Andrew Ellicott's journal. He gives a highly entertaining narrative which agrees but little with the records. According to Ellicott, "Hannah" was an itinerant Baptist preacher who preached a sermon. "The preacher being a weak man, was extremely puffed up with the attention he received on that occasion." In an argument with Catholics in the lower section of the town, Hannon was soundly thrashed. He then sought justice from Gayoso, "threatening at the same time to do it for himself, if his request was not complied with."

Ellicott said that Gayoso, "with more patience and temper than ordinary," requested Hannon to reflect a few minutes and then repeat his request, but the irate Baptist immediately demanded that Gayoso do something or he would. With an obvious threat to the public order on his hands, Gayoso did just that—he ordered Hannon confined in the stocks at the fort.[43]

The interrogation of Hannon brings another side to the story. Stephen Lynch testifed that on June 8 Hannon had come to his house with a petition directed against the Spanish government and signed by fifty-six men. When Lynch refused to sign and announced his loyalty to that government, Hannon cursed the "government, his Excellency and all the Whole fraternity, and said if he was sent to the fort it should be consumed into ashes before Morning." [44]

[41]Jones, *A History of Protestantism*, 50–51.
[42]Interrogation of Barton Hannon by Captain Manuel de Lanzós, Natchez, June 10, 1797, enclosed in the Case against Hannon, AGI, PC, leg. 163-a; Holmes (ed.), *Documentos de la Luisiana*, 318 n.
[43]Ellicott's *Journal*, 97–100.
[44]Testimony of Stephen Lynch to Gayoso, Natchez, June 10, 1797, in the Case against Hannon, AGI, PC, leg. 163-a.

Even less savory was Hannon's own account of events. He claimed he was so drunk on June 9 that he did not recall what had happened. When asked if it were true that he had gone armed to see Lynch in the company of several other armed men, he admitted the story's truth. Hannon vaguely recalled having a quarrel with someone but could not pinpoint the cause. When quizzed about the petition, Hannon claimed it was merely a list of members of the Baptist Society of Natchez. From subsequent testimony from Parker Carradine, Gayoso learned that Hannon had been accompanied by five or six armed men, that he was seeking revenge from those Catholics who had mistreated him, and that fifty other armed men were soon to follow. When Carradine suggested that Hannon seek redress from Gayoso, the drunken shoe-maker agreed, but his seditious conduct was such that the governor decided to incarcerate him to preserve the peace.[45]

Captain Manuel de Lanzós, an eyewitness to most of the events concerning the subsequent uprising, wrote that Lieutenant Domingo Bouligny made the arrest. As he conducted Hannon to the fort, the prisoner attempted to escape, yelling to the nearby Americans who watched the proceedings from their camp, "Help me, fellow-Americans!" He was recaptured swiftly and conducted to the fort where his feet were placed in the stocks as ordered.[46] The reaction throughout the Natchez District was as violent as might have been expected. Stephen Stephenson told the syndic of Second Creek, Isaac Johnson, that a group of men were planning to capture Gayoso and exchange him for Hannon.[47] Colonel Hutchins had his own ideas: he wanted to capture Gayoso and carry him to the Chickasaw nation.[48]

Gayoso soon learned this was the incident Pope and Ellicott were waiting for to incite the revolt. At eleven o'clock on the evening of June 9, Gayoso appeared at the fort to interview the prisoner. Hearing of the threat to storm the Spanish defenses,

[45]*Ibid.*, including testimony of various witnesses; Gayoso to Santa Clara, No. 2, Confidential, September 24, 1797.

[46]Lanzós' diary of the revolt is printed in Holmes (ed.), *Documentos de la Luisiana*, 318–55.

[47]Deposition of Isaac Johnson, June 10, 1797, in Case against Hannon.

[48]Clark to Claiborne, June 18, 1800; Stephen Minor to Gayoso, Natchez, October 21, 1797, AGI, PC, leg. 2371.

eighteen loyal militiamen appeared to take up positions on the rotting ramparts. Wild rumors circulated among the small group of defenders. The entire district was said to be in a state of open revolt. Armed settlers ranged in patrols to block all roads and highways, and the word was they intended to take the fort the very next day and plunge "cold steel" into its defenders.[49]

Pope issued a letter of congratulations and support to the rebels on June 12, and said, "I shall expect your assistance to repel any Troops or Hostile parties that may make an attempt to land for the purpose of reinforcing this Governor or other purposes detrimental to the Interest of this Country." [50] Pope had good reason to worry about reinforcements, for Gayoso had written Carondelet the same day with a plea for troops under Captain Francisco Collell.[51] Moreover, Carondelet soon alerted the militia units of lower Louisiana for possible action should the Natchez revolt attempt to spread.[52]

Gayoso confidently worked on the miserable defenses of the fort, secure in the belief that Carondelet would come to his aid. The governor wrote his wife, who was almost due to give birth to Gayoso's child, to send tallow candles, lanterns, his uniform, his oilcloth raincoat, and a generous supply of snuff. In one letter he wrote, "Since I have been here some people have come again with their new invented stories, therefore to show them that I am ready I ordered all men to keep good watch & it is natural that [I] should remain with them or else they would not remain willingly." [53]

Sentry patrols were stationed outside the fort; they reported much movement but no aggression. Morale was high; those in the fort were pleased by the opportunity to fight for the King. The

[49]Lanzós' diary, in Holmes (ed.), *Documentos de la Luisiana,* 319–26.
[50]Proclamations of Ellicott and Pope, June 12, 1797, in Pope Papers, Missouri Historical Society; AHN, ESTADO, leg. 3900.
[51]Gayoso to Carondelet, No. 811, Natchez, June 12, 1797, AGI, PC, leg. 43.
[52]Pedro de Marigny organized the Mixed Mississippi Coastal Militia and Pablo Luis LeBlanc took provisional command of the Acadian and German Coast militia units. Certificates of Carondelet, New Orleans, August 5, 1797, AGI, PC, leg. 23.
[53]Five letters, Gayoso to Peggy Watts Gayoso, without date [June, 1797], Cole Papers, New Orleans.

American forces were not as confident of taking the fort without a fight as they had been. Even the militia appeared on schedule to take their posts by night and allow the regular troops a chance to catch a few hours' sleep. On June 14, Gayoso sneaked out of the fort for a conference with Ellicott and Pope. This was extremely risky, for there were more than 300 armed men on patrol; but Gayoso left Lanzós in command of the fort with orders not to surrender it even with a written order from Gayoso. Gayoso discovered that bands of rebels were on guard at the landing hoping to intercept Collell before he could come to Gayoso's aid.

Still, no attack came. Unsure of their position and convinced that Gayoso intended to make a gallant defense of the fort, few loud-mouths were willing to translate words into deeds. They met at Belk's Tavern on the Natchez Trace, but no aggression ever came of their deliberations. Various inhabitants visited the fort to tell the governor of threats and plans of attack, but each of them carried away the news that Gayoso was fully prepared for any eventuality. The lack of suitable fortifications was supplemented by stern courage and determination. The palisade was repaired with dirt and the inflammable shingles closely watched. Because the powder magazine could be fired by any enemy and thus cause untold damage, Gayoso ordered the supplies moved to the stockade. In the storehouse he drilled holes and placed thirty quintals of powder in them. Workers who had come from outside were urged not to reveal that the fort was thus mined. Gayoso was confident they would spread the news immediately, and he was not disappointed.

"The rebels, believing we had mined the fort . . . now talked in a different tone," Lanzós wrote. The following evening the Spanish patrol fired on a group of rebels trying to capture the rise of ground which dominated the fort. No one was wounded, but an American patrol of twenty-four men was immediately sent to investigate. Learning that Pope had almost precipitated a war, Ellicott gave orders that no further incidents should take place. With this turn of events, Ellicott was no longer convinced that rebellion was the key to his own frustration. Rather, he came to appreciate Gayoso's position. In this frame of mind he was amenable to compromise.

On June 19, Guillemard and Sub-Lieutenant Juan Ferrusola arrived from Nogales. They conferred with the governor at the fort, but Gayoso was no longer worried about the outcome of the revolt. He told them to leave for New Orleans as planned and that he would take care of Natchez. The following day a band of Choctaws returned from a raiding party in Caddo territory west of the Mississippi. Their arrival convinced the rebels that Gayoso had called on the support of the Indians to break up the revolt. One of the delegates who attended a new meeting of the rebels reported to Gayoso that everyone was more disposed to reach an agreement with the governor. The yells of inebriated Indians pierced the night and punctuated Gayoso's demands that law and order return to the District—or else.

On June 21, Gayoso boldly mounted his horse and left for Government House. He negotiated with the various factions and agreed to generous terms for settling the revolt. When he returned from spending the night in his own home at Concord, he had good news for his small garrison. The revolt was all but finished. The carbine shots that pierced the black night were not intended to frighten the defenders; they were fired to celebrate the end of the revolt.

Gayoso was aided in his peacemaking role by the substantial citizens who condemned further opposition. Should the Coles' Creek rebels refuse to lay down their arms as agreed by the other sections of the district, then they would be forced to do so by their own kith and kin. At this juncture of events, Captain Collell arrived with fifty men bound for the Nogales post. Gayoso met with him and told him to proceed without landing, for negotiations were at the critical stage and an undue show of force from the governor might upset the feelers for peace. Gayoso accepted the petitions presented to him and wrote the governor-general that he had arranged for the settlement of the dispute. Gayoso agreed that the inhabitants who had acted as citizens of the United States were not to be persecuted or prosecuted for their actions. He agreed that none would be called upon to serve in the militia except during an Indian attack or an internal riot. No one would be transported out of the district for trial, and the neutrality of the settlers was guaranteed. Finally, Gayoso persuaded the people of Natchez to obey Spanish law until Spain evacuated the District.[54]

The revolt was finished. Weary defenders opened the fort's gates and strolled past friendly townspeople who had threatened them only days before. For some, the revolt brought them close to their only military action; for others, the peaceful solution was distasteful. For many, peace with honor demonstrated how successfully Gayoso's policies had won the hearts of the people.

How did Gayoso himself feel about the revolt? Did he survey the ruins of his once-powerful domain with regret? Had he learned anything in his eight years' service?

Most writers are convinced that Spain's policy of encouraging immigration to the Natchez District was a failure. Many Spanish governors were convinced that the attempt to make silk purses out of sows' ears was doomed to failure. Pedro Grimaret's report of 1792 warned against permitting Americans of different customs, religion, and language to settle in Spanish territory.[55] Captain General Luis de las Casas concurred: "I fear that by populating these areas adjacent to the territories of the United States with subjects of the same United States it will be dangerous for us when they expand toward the western American settlements; the frequent and inevitable contact with our colonists, their mutually-shared language, religion, customs, and ancestors, and the ties which they maintain, will preserve a spirit of brotherhood, which in the case of some outbreak in our territory, would prevent these colonists

[54]The story of the revolt is told in Gayoso to Prince of Peace, No. 5, Natchez, June 25, 1797, AHN, ESTADO, leg. 3902; Gayoso to Santa Clara, No. 2, Confidential, September 24, 1797; Carondelet to Gayoso, New Orleans, July 1, 1797, AGI, PC, leg. 2354; Ellicott's *Journal*, 105–17; Manuel de Lanzós' diary in Holmes (ed.), *Documentos de la Luisiana*, 318–55; Ellicott to Secretary of State, Natchez, June 27, 1797, Southern Boundary, I; *Aurora and General Advertiser* (Philadelphia), June 27, July 13, September 16, 18, 1797. The correspondence between Gayoso and the "Committee of Correspondence" dated June 20–June 22 is included in Carondelet to Irujo, New Orleans, July 20, 1797, AHN, ESTADO, leg. 3900, and AGI, PC, leg. 1502. A copy of Gayoso's June 22, 1797, proclamation is also in the Gayoso Papers, Louisiana State University, and in Carter (ed.), *Territorial Papers of the United States, V: Mississippi*, 11–12.

[55]Pedro Grimaret's report on Louisiana defenses, Madrid, July 12, 1792, ASHM, 5–1–7–6.

from defending the province against the arms of their friends, in contrast to their oath of loyalty." [56]

Captain Luis de Vilemont referred to the "vandals" who surrounded the Spaniards as did the barbarian hordes who during the sunset of the Roman Empire peacefully penetrated the weakened defenses of Rome's outposts. But Vilemont believed the Natchez experiment was a success.[57] Gayoso was not as confident after the Natchez revolt. He issued orders forbidding Natchez settlers who had taken an active role against him from receiving Spanish land grants in New Feliciana.[58] His subsequent decrees on immigration to Louisiana were unanimously opposed to Americans settling in the province.[59] Yet, Gayoso found many pro-Spanish families in Natchez willing to give up their homes and prospects of American citizenship in order to emigrate into the nearby Spanish territories at Concordia, across the Mississippi, or below the line at Bayou Sara, Thompson's Creek, and New Feliciana. When the novelty of American government wore off, when American taxes replaced Spanish economic paternalism, and when political factionalism grew stale, many yearned to return to the halcyon days of Gayoso's government.[60]

[56]Luis de Las Casas to Campo de Alange, Havana, February 17, 1791, in Mississippi Archives, Spanish Dominion, III, 800–808.

[57]Petition of Vilemont, enclosed in Carondelet to Alcudia, New Orleans, July 30, 1795, AHN, ESTADO, leg. 3890. The term, "like the ancient Goths and Vandals," was also used by James Wilkinson in Vicente Folch's (written by Wilkinson) Reflections on Louisiana, in Robertson (ed.), *Louisiana*, II, 337–38; and Isaac J. Cox, "The New Invasion of the Goths and Vandals," *Proceedings* of the Mississippi Valley Historical Association, VIII (1914–1915), 176–200.

[58]Gayoso's instructions for New Feliciana, New Orleans, June 26, 1798, in Dispatches of the Spanish Governors (10 vols.; W.P.A. translations and typescripts, copy in Tulane University Archives and in Louisiana State University Archives), XI, 146.

[59]Circular to commandants on admission of new settlers, New Orleans, February 20, 1798, AGI, PC, leg. 2365; Gayoso to Zacharias Cox, New Orleans, October 16, 1798, AGI, PC, leg. 2365; decree, New Orleans, January 1, 1798, copy, Territorial Papers, Louisiana, National Archives, Record Group 59; translations are in Gayarré, *History of Louisiana, The Spanish Dominion*, 386–88, and Martin, *Louisiana*, 276–77.

[60]Gayoso to Isaac Johnson, New Orleans, November 30, 1798, AGI, PC, leg. 215-a; Clark to Claiborne, June 18, 1800; Minor to Gayoso, Natchez, October 8, 1797, AGI, PC, leg. 2371; petition of John Tear and Patrick Gurnet, Bayou Boeuf, September 13, 1798, AGI, PC, leg. 215-b.

Stephen Minor wrote, "Generally speaking the People are getting heartily tired of all party business, and American politicks is now becoming an old thing. They would give half what they have if it was possible to place them as they were three years ago even in the uncertain situation of things I can with confidence presume to say that I could raise as great a party at present in favor of Government as cou'd be raised on the opposite side." [61] Joseph Vidal wrote that the people complained of Ellicott and Pope as being the authors of their misfortunes. They yearned to return to the government of Gayoso, later called by them "the Father and Protector of this District. . . . He was our true friend but we lost the opportunity to realize it." [62]

The Spanish government recognized Gayoso's accomplishments by promoting him to brigadier general on September 4, 1795.[63] This promotion came as a result of Gayoso's work in establishing the post at San Fernando de las Barrancas. It was additional satisfaction to Gayoso inasmuch as his earlier request for advancement was denied.[64] He could thank Carondelet for a solid recommendation.[65]

During the years Gayoso governed the Natchez District he grew discouraged on numerous occasions. He requested the post of governor-general to replace Miró, but his plea was denied when Carondelet was appointed.[66] Amid a growing list of his creditors, Gayoso vainly asked for relief from the tasks at Natchez in 1794.[67] On another occasion he requested the government of Trinidad because

[61]Minor to Gayoso, Natchez, November 4, 1797, AGI, PC, leg. 2371.
[62]Vidal to Gayoso, Natchez, September 15, 1798, AGI, PC, leg. 2365.
[63]Copy of royal appointment, San Ildefonso, September 4, 1795, in Gayoso's *expediente matrimonial*, AGMS. Acts of the Supreme Council, November 13, 1795, AHN, ESTADO, leg. 3888; Prince of Peace to Carondelet, San Lorenzo, November 25, 1795, enclosed in Carondelet to Gayoso, New Orleans, February 29, 1796, AGI, PC, leg. 34.
[64]Gayoso to Alcudia, Confidential, New Madrid, September 5, 1795, AHN, ESTADO, leg. 3902.
[65]Gayoso to Carondelet, New Orleans, February 4, 1796, AGI, PC, leg. 43.
[66]Gayoso to Floridablanca, New Orleans, October 12, 1790, AHN, ESTADO, leg. 3902. Miró recommended that Gayoso be charged to conduct the secret negotiations with Wilkinson and other conspirators in Kentucky. Miró to Campo de Alange, August 11, 1792, in Holmes (ed.), *Documentos de la Luisiana*, 38–39.
[67]Nicolás d'Aunoy to the crown, petition, New Orleans, July 10, 1794, AGI, PC, leg. 1443-a. D'Aunoy wanted Gayoso's job; he mentions hearing that Gayoso had requested relief from the command.

of his knowledge of English and French.[68] With so many failures, it must have come as final justice when he received news that he would succeed the Baron de Carondelet at New Orleans.[69]

Gayoso announced his promotion to the "worthy inhabitants" of Natchez in a farewell address. "I have lived with you eight years," he wrote. "I have seen you in difficulties, & have struggled with them to relieve you.—I have, with the anxious solicitude of a Parent, devoted my labors to the Welfare of the Country." Gayoso remarked that his being promoted to New Orleans where he could still "attend to . . . [the] business" of the Natchez inhabitants pleased him. He also had a few words of advice for the people:

> Continue unshaken in your fidelity and adherence to his Majesty, and obedient to the existing regulations. Wait, unconcerned for the political change that is expected, and never let your minds be troubled by insidious and artful suggestions. Look forward; consider from whence you are to derive the profits of your Industry, and let not your titles to Indulgence & Favor be destroyed by the inconsiderate and rash conduct of [a] few.—If there be any ill-disposed & mischievous persons among you, prevent their designs by your admonitions, and, if necessary, defeat their plots by aiding the measures of Government.—Such, I conceive, is the Duty, and such, I flatter myself, is the general temper of the Inhabitants of Natchez—and, under this impression, I shall always respect, and do every thing, within the compass of my power, to serve them.—[70]

On July 29, 1797, Gayoso turned over the reins of government

[68]Las Casas to Campo de Alange, No. 355, Havana, November 15, 1793, draft, AGI, PC, leg. 1484. The author wishes to thank Juan José Andreu of Zaragoza for calling this document to his attention.

[69]Gayoso's official appointment was dated San Lorenzo, December 16, 1796, but it mentions an earlier royal order of October 20 which first named Gayoso governor-general. A copy is in the New Orleans Cabildo records, August 5, 1797, IV, No. 2, 72. In the list of governors of Louisiana, MS, Territorial Papers, Louisiana, National Archives, Record Group 59, the date of appointment is given as October 28, 1796. A certificate in the Cole Papers, New Orleans, gives November 5, 1796, as the date of appointment. According to Gayoso's pay records, the royal title was dated December 16, 1796, and became effective when Gayoso took official charge of his office on August 5, 1797: AGI, PC, leg. 538-a.

[70]Proclamation of Gayoso, Natchez, 1797, AGI, PC, leg. 213.

to his longtime friend and post adjutant, Stephen Minor.[71] His wife and two-week-old son, Fernando, remained in Natchez while Gayoso prepared a home for them in New Orleans.[72] The first phase of his distinguished career drew to a close, and with it, the first phase of a new order began: the United States marked its initial territorial advance. It is doubtful whether any man or group of men could have blocked the seemingly inexorable advance of the American frontiersman. Yet, by pursuing policies of moderation, wisdom, and kindness, Gayoso won more friends to the Spanish monarchy than any other Louisiana governor. Few men were more qualified to handle the difficult task that remained ahead for the governor-general of Louisiana during the closing years of the eighteenth century.

[71]Drafts of Gayoso's proclamation, July 24, 1797, and Gayoso to Minor, Natchez, July 26, 1797, in AGI, PC, leg. 213, indicate that Minor was given the interim command of the Natchez District with the exception of the post of Nogales.

[72]Fernando Gayoso de Lemos y Watts was born on Friday, July 14, 1797, at seven minutes to one in the morning. He was baptized December 10, 1797, by Bishop Luis at New Orleans' St. Louis Cathedral. Baptism certificate, St. Louis Cathedral, folio 50; statement of Gayoso, July 14, 1797, Cole Papers. Fernando died at Natchitoches on January 14, 1837. He had been married first to Julia Anne Wickoff in 1810, but she and their young children died soon after. Fernando's second wife, Victoria Lodoiska Pérez, was the grand-daughter of Elías Beauregard, Gayoso's fellow officer at Nogales and San Fernando de las Barrancas. One of the five children, Felicité Toutant Beaure-gard Gayoso de Lemos, born at Natchitoches, February 1, 1836, was the grandmother of Hallette Mary Tennent Barrow, the present Mrs. C. Grenes Cole of New Orleans, whose family papers include many letters from Gayoso to his wife and the genealogy of the governor's family. The sketch appearing in Arthur and Kernion (eds.), *Old Families of Louisiana*, 279–83, makes use of these papers.

CHAPTER VIII

The Provincial Governor-General

ITS DELICATE and complex situation makes its Government the most difficult, perplexing and assiduous of all His Majesty's Dominions." *Gayoso to the Prince of Peace, Sept. 5, 1797.*

The newly appointed governor-general of Louisiana and West Florida left his former command at Natchez on July 29, 1797, and traveled to New Orleans. Stopping at the home of his friend, Étienne Boré, Louisiana's first successful sugar producer, Gayoso wrote to the municipal council of New Orleans. He advised the cabildo members that he would soon arrive to take his oath of office. On August 5 he appeared in the chambers of that massive cabildo building, delivered his appointment and instructions to the Baron de Carondelet, and then took his oath to protect the Roman Catholic Church, to defend all royal edicts, and to promote justice and wise government in accordance with Spanish laws and customs.[1]

[1]Gayoso to cabildo of New Orleans, House of Mons. Boré, August 4, 1797, Parsons Collection, University of Texas; minutes of New Orleans cabildo, August 5, 1797, IV, 20–24. Gayoso advised the crown he had taken official

In many ways the new post was not altogether strange to Gayoso. Having advised governor-general Miró and Carondelet and participated in their defensive plans for the province during his nine years at Natchez, Gayoso was familiar with most of the features of Louisiana provincial administration. The multiplicity of duties pressed upon him, the host of new officials, both religious and secular, military and civilian, and the pressing problems of defense against potential enemies in the United States, England, and France, offered renewed challenges to a man skilled at solving the tangled puzzles of Louisiana politics. True, the people of Lower Louisiana were of French extraction, with different customs, laws, and language from those Anglo-Americans in Natchez. But Gayoso was as fluent in French as he was in English. His pleasing personality, coupled with a profound sense of the royal dignity incumbant upon the king's messengers, prepared him for another opportunity to serve his master's interests.

For almost two years Gayoso combined the functions of magistrate, municipal council chairman, vice-patron of the church, commander in chief of the regular and militia forces, guardian of the purse strings, and social leader of a growing metropolitan area at the heart of a vitally important province. Although his hands were tied more than at Natchez by the Spanish colonial system of conflicting jurisdiction, Gayoso brought his virtues—as well as his vices—to the office. In comparing the greatest governors-general of the Spanish Dominion of Louisiana, historians usually place Bernardo de Gálvez, Alejandro O'Reilly, or the Baron de Carondelet at the apex of success. Gayoso was given but two years to demonstrate that he belonged in the first rank.

His first duties were naturally confused with the final actions of his predecessor, Carondelet, who had been appointed to the Presidency of Quito.[2] The outgoing governor-general spent many hours

charge of his office as required by law. Gayoso to Pedro Varela y Ulloa, New Orleans, August 9, 1797, and Varela y Ulloa to Gayoso, Madrid, December 19, 1797, AGI, SD, leg. 2546.

[2] Juan Manuel Álvarez to Prince of Peace, San Ildefonso, August 14, 1797, AHN, ESTADO, leg. 3900; Carondelet to Favrot, No. 34, New Orleans, March 12, 1797, in Favrot Papers, V; Marigny, *Thoughts upon Foreign Policy of the United States*, 20, thinks the position to which Carondelet was appointed, was "beneath his talents and the rewards that he deserved." Carondelet did not so express himself.

signing certificates of merit for the military, religious, and political
members of his administration, most of whom remained to assist
the new governor-general. There was considerable packing, and his
wife and two children were ill. Finally, there was the matter of
Carondelet's *residencia*. Unless otherwise exempted, royal governors,
governors-general, viceroys, and other major officials underwent an
examination of their years in power. In some cases the hearings were
conducted secretly by judges appointed for that purpose, as in the
case of Governor-General Esteban Miró.[3] In other cases, as in the
example of Carondelet, the governor-general succeeding to that
office conducted the examination of his predecessor's conduct in
office.[4]

On August 7, Gayoso ordered his proclamation posted at convenient public gathering places throughout New Orleans. Citizens read
that anyone having a complaint against Carondelet would have
thirty days to appear at Government House. At the end of that time
three men and/or their families had filed their protests for being expelled from Louisiana during the 1793 French Jacobin scare, and
Nicolás Forstall protested being relieved from command of the
post of Opelousas. Inasmuch as these complaints were not directed
against the $3,000 Carondelet had deposited in his *residencia* account,
but represented general complaints on which the king had already
acted negatively, Gayoso ruled that the *residencia* was completed.
The cabildo listed the merits of Carondelet's term as governor-general and wished him bon voyage as he left for the Balize in September.[5]

[3]Two *expedientes* dealing with Miró's *residencia* and complaint session
(pesquiza), done between 1793–1805, are in AHN, Consejo de Indias,
Escribanía de Cámara, leg. 21055, No. 5; and 20927, No. 5. See Holmes (ed.),
Documentos de la Luisiana, 8. The only other governor-general besides Miró
and Carondelet to have a *residencia* was Luis de Unzaga y Amezaga, taken
by Miró as judge from 1785–1791, *ibid.*, 20900. A discussion of the *residencia*
is in Charles H. Cunningham, "The Residencia in the Spanish Colonies,"
Southwestern Historical Quarterly, XXI (January, 1918), 253–78.
[4]Carondelet's *residencia* is in AHN, Consejo de Indias, Escribanía de
Cámara, leg. 20925, No. 3.
[5]*Ibid.* There is a story told in Martin, *Louisiana*, 284, accepted by Gayarré,
History of Louisiana, The Spanish Dominion, 404, that Gayoso found Carondelet guilty of condemning a Negro slave to death against the wishes of the
judge advocate merely because Colonel Pedro Marigny, the slave's owner,

Gayoso's behavior toward Carondelet at this point was most generous, considering that the new governor-general felt he had been betrayed during the Natchez revolt because Carondelet failed to send reinforcements. Gayoso had not forgotten what Carondelet had done—or had not done—on that occasion, but his revenge took interesting form. Rather than show his displeasure to Carondelet, Gayoso took every opportunity to show attention and regard toward the Carondelet family and the former governor-general. Gayoso wrote his wife, "I am happy that it has been in my power to revenge myself of him by overcoming him with every attention and regard; I am fully convinced that he is sorry for what he did." [6] Stephen Minor approved of Gayoso's subtle style of revenge, too: "I am doubly happy your Excellency had it in your power to mortify him handsomly—it's at least some satisfaction for us poor devils who suffered so long on his account in ye Fort. . . ." [7]

As Carondelet sailed to his new post, Gayoso turned his full attention to the problems of Louisiana. Social festivities followed his inauguration. There were fancy banquets and numerous toasts given by members of the cabildo, New Orleans merchants, and individuals anxious to make the acquaintance of their new governor-general. When the society matrons proposed a fancy ball, Gayoso suggested they wait until the arrival of Mrs. Gayoso. He wrote her, "The ladies here are very anxious to have you in Town." [8]

From the time of Alejandro O'Reilly, it had been customary for governors-general to issue a *bando de buen gobierno,* which was a proclamation of general laws governing the policing and regulation of public morals in New Orleans. [9] In January, 1798, Gayoso fol-

---

insisted. Allegedly, Gayoso fined Carondelet $500. There is nothing in the official records of the *residencia* to support the tale.

[6] Gayoso to Peggy, New Orleans, September 1, 1797, Cole Papers, New Orleans.

[7] Minor to Gayoso, Natchez, October 6, 1797, AGI, PC, leg. 2371; Gayoso to Minor, New Orleans, January 10, 1798, Gayoso Papers, Louisiana State University Archives.

[8] Gayoso to Peggy, September 1, 1797.

[9] O'Reilly's regulations are sketched in Holmes, "Some Irish Officers in Spanish Louisiana," 236–39. A discussion of Miró's *bando,* June 1, 1786, is in Burson, *The Stewardship of Miró,* 108–09, 205. Carondelet's police ordinance of June 1, 1795, can be found in the Louisiana file, Miscellaneous manuscripts,

lowed the custom and issued a *bando* published by the *Moniteur de la Louisiane* printer. The regulation consisted of eleven pages and twenty-three articles in French and Spanish. Although Gayarré said, "It contained nothing worthy of any special notice," [10] Gayoso's *bando* was one of the most interesting pieces of local legislation in Spanish Louisiana. A cursory examination of its provisions gives one a glimpse of Spanish social and economic practices. Because they believed in keeping the Sabbath, for example, the *bando* provided penalties for working or running carts on that day. The authorities disapproved of such games as monté, roulette, craps, and lansquenet. Firearms, knives of certain types, and bayonets were also forbidden. Persons without jobs or visible means of support were to be sentenced to the public works. All visitors to the city were required to be registered with the ward commissioners or magistrates within twenty-four hours. Billiard parlors and taverns were to keep set hours of opening and closing; but the latter might, according to the regulation, keep their doors slightly open to deliver necessary beverages to "sick persons" at unseasonable hours.

Other local regulations attempted to protect the New Orleanians against fires. The city had been almost totally destroyed in 1788 and again in 1794. When disastrous fires of this nature showed the need for engines, pumps, buckets, and axes to fight fires, they were purchased and placed at convenient locations in the various wards. When another fire broke out on May 26, 1795, two additional policemen were added to the New Orleans force to guard against arson.[11]

Library of Congress; and has been published in *Appendix to an Account of Louisiana* (1804), lxvii–lxxxiii; and edited by Padgett in "A Decree for Louisiana, issued by the Baron de Carondelet," 590–605. Another copy is in BN, tomo 19,509, fol. 1.

[10] Gayarré, *History of Louisiana*, the Spanish Dominion, 386; a copy of the *bando* is in the Bancroft Library, University of California, from which the New York Public Library's copy was made. Another copy is in the Missouri Historical Society, Gayoso de Lemos Papers. It has been translated in Frederic L. Billon (comp.), *Annals of St. Louis in its Early Days under the French and Spanish Dominations* (St. Louis, 1886), 275–83. Newspaper accounts were written by W. D. Hays, Jr., "Tulane Acquires Tome Unseen by Most Historians," and Perry Young, "Crap-shooting, Blasphemy, Liquor, were Banned by Blue Laws of de Lemos," for the *Times-Picayune* (New Orleans), undated clippings in Cole Papers.

[11] Document No. 39, May 31, 1795, Miscellaneous Spanish Records, New

Laissez-faire was virtually unknown in Spanish New Orleans. Most economic activities were regulated by the government. Prices of meat, bread, and rice were rigidly set on a weekly basis; and all sales of merchandise were equally supervised. As in O'Reilly's time, taverns were licensed and regulated. No liquor could be sold to Indians or Negro slaves.[12] The cabildo appointed a commissioner to make monthly inspections of the meat and fish markets near the river to determine the quality, condition, and quantity of cattle butchered, to inspect weights, and to fix prices. Merchants led by Fernando Alzar & Co., protested against allowing Negroes to sell goods on the streets and levees as peddlers, and Gayoso replied by requiring all proper merchants and slaves to be duly licensed by the governor-general.[13]

Because many New Orleanians complained about the pressure from the Charity Hospital to buy their caskets there, the cabildo ruled that the public was free to purchase these terminal resting places from whomever they pleased.[14] In order to prevent crime in the dark shadows of New Orleans' streets, the cabildo created a force of night watchmen (serenos) and constructed the now famous Bourbon Street-style lamps on the principal corners. From special funds in the Lighting Department wicks, sulphur, flint, and broken panes of glass were replaced.[15]

To pay for fire fighting equipment, Gayoso followed the cabildo's 1795 decree and ordered the residents of New Orleans taxed on the number of chimneys they owned in their houses or properties. Thus, the philanthropist Andrés Almonester y Roxas paid an annual tax

---

Orleans Public Library, I, 15–16; Carondelet to Gayoso, New Orleans, December 11, 14, 1794, AGI, PC, leg. 30. Interesting accounts of fire-protection are in Henry P. Dart (ed.), "Fire Protection in New Orleans in Unzaga's Time," *Louisiana Historical Quarterly*, IV, (1921), 201–204; John Bunyan Clark, "Fire Protection in the Old South," (Ph. D. dissertation, University of Kentucky, 1957).

[12]Jack D. L. Holmes, "Spanish Regulations of Taverns and the Liquor Trade in Colonial Louisiana," unpublished paper read at the Louisiana Academy of Sciences, Lafayette, Louisiana, April 15, 1961.

[13]Minutes of the New Orleans cabildo, September 30, 1797, IV, 82–84; October 6, 1797, IV, 85–86.

[14]*Ibid.*, September 7, 1797, IV, 77.

[15]Documents, 1795–1797, in Miscellaneous Spanish Documents, New Orleans Public Library, I, 13–17, 71–76, 90–91; Whitaker, *Mississippi Question*, 39.

of $9.38 for his twenty-five chimneys, and the annual revenue from this source from the four wards often exceeded $4,000. Master bricklayers were paid two dollars each per day spent inspecting the chimneys. Funds from this source also went into the Lighting Department.[16]

When the inhabitants protested against this tax because it hit the lower classes as well as those most able to pay, Gayoso was persuaded to change the form of taxation in 1799. Because the poor presumably ate little bread, their diet consisting primarily of rice and corn, Gayoso persuaded the cabildo to pass a tax of fifty cents a barrel on flour consumed by bakers in the manufacture of bread, less 5 per cent for loss occasioned by rats. The new source of revenue, which was destined to the Lighting Department, amounted to $275 for January and February, 1799; and in March, $222.[17]

In other ways the New Orleans cabildo was successful in obtaining revenues for specific purposes. Taxes on sugar cane rum, or tafia, produced almost $3,000 annually. Rental of the government houses constructed by Bernardo de Gálvez produced enough money to construct a storehouse for rice amounting to almost $5,000. Thirty-six tavern keepers paid an annual license fee of forty dollars each. A tax on each head of beef slaughtered at the market and wharfage duties made up additional sources of revenue.[18]

Gayoso discovered that the low-lying city was constantly inundated during times of the river's rise. Carondelet had asked for $6,000 in 1792 to pave the sidewalks; and Gayoso ordered all inhabitants to keep their sidewalks clean, swept, and sprinkled at least once a day in the summer and as often as possible in winter. By 1803, how-

[16]Statement of Juan de Castanedo, January 30, 1795, and revenues, January 1–December 31, 1797; inspection by Francisco Bernucho and Antonio Dubois, September 23, 30, 1797, in Miscellaneous Spanish Documents, New Orleans Public Library, I, 17–26, 70; Minutes of the New Orleans cabildo, September 30, 1797, IV, 82–84.

[17]Minutes of the New Orleans cabildo, April 19, 1799, IV, 14–16, 25; Whitaker, *Mississippi Question*, 277 n. 32.

[18]Report by Juan de Castanedo, New Orleans, December 31, 1797, Miscellaneous Spanish Documents, I, 41–51; Minutes of the New Orleans cabildo, July 13, 1797, IV; Holmes, "Some Economic Problems of Spanish Governors of Louisiana," 541.

ever, a visiting physician was able to write, "The means to be employed in rendering New Orleans healthful, are: 1st, to raise its streets, and to give them a sufficient incline for the drainage of the waters. . . ."[19] Sanitary conditions at the end of the eighteenth century were still in such a deplorable condition that disease, particularly yellow fever, raged in epidemic proportions.[20]

Zoning regulations existed in New Orleans as they did in Natchez, and shortly after Gayoso arrived, the *auditor de guerra* and lieutenant-governor, Nicolás María Vidal, petitioned the new governor-general to disallow construction of buildings on the wharves and levees of the town.[21] Gayoso ordered vehicles, coaches, and horses to stay off the levees.[22]

Other decrees relative to the public safety and health were included in Gayoso's all-inclusive *bando*. He warned the owners of dogs to keep them confined, for within three days of the publication of the decree, all animals wandering in the streets would be killed. No person was allowed to keep gunpowder in excess of twenty-five pounds in his store or warehouse. Dead animals were to be buried, and no one could keep swine within the confines of the town. No one could wash his clothes below the point where vessels were careened, and stiff penalties were meted out to litter-bugs.[23]

Gayoso found that in questions relating to civic order, finances, and public health, he was forced to cooperate with the New Orleans

---

[19]Gayoso's *bando de buen gobierno*, 1798; Carondelet to Aranda, No. 1, New Orleans, November 6, 1792, AHN, ESTADO, leg. 3898; Reflections of Paul Alliot to Jefferson, New York, April 13, 1804, in Robertson (ed.), *Louisiana*, I, 39; Whitaker, *Mississippi Question*, 41.

[20]Laura L. Porteous (trans.), "Sanitary Conditions in New Orleans under the Spanish Régime, 1799–1800," *Louisiana Historical Quarterly*, XV (October, 1932), 610–17. This letter from P. D. Barran, public magistrate of the cabildo, to the membership of that body, January 24, 1800, shows how bad sanitation in New Orleans was at the turn of the century. Governor W. C. C. Claiborne to James Madison, near government house, New Orleans, December 17, 1809, in Carter (ed.), *Territorial Papers of the United States*, IX; *Orleans*, 859–60, shows that conditions had changed little during the decade following.

[21]Petition of Vidal, New Orleans, 1797, and Gayoso's comments, New Orleans, September 25, 1797, AGI, PC, leg. 221-a.

[22]Gayoso's *bando de buen gobierno*, 1798.

[23]*Ibid.*

cabildo. Formed by O'Reilly in 1769 in keeping with Spanish traditions of municipal government, the cabildo was a focal point of
local self-government in New Orleans. The jurisdiction of this
body extended to the far corners of Louisiana, but generally the
six judges confined their attention to local matters. Carondelet
recommended the addition of six members, and on December 23,
1796, the king approved the request. In keeping with the Spanish
tradition of selling posts in the cabildo to the highest bidders,
Gayoso, as head of the council conducted the elections. The price
of the office was as much as $15,000, and the deductions from the
annual salary of $100 did not leave much for the trouble and hard
work of those who had bid successfully for the position. Yet, the
jobs were sought by many who hoped to serve the king, their own
interests, or those of their friends.

Gayoso announced that the successful purchasers in 1797 were
Darby Danycan, Jaime Jordá, Gilberto Andry, José LeBlanc, Juan
de Castanedo, and Francisco Riaño. The following year, upon the
death of Almonester y Roxas, Lieutenant Pedro Denis de la Ronde,
a member of the Regular Louisiana Infantry Regiment, successfully
bid almost $16,000 for the post.[24]

The cabildo considered a host of problems facing the city and,
as presiding officer, Gayoso was forced to spend much of his official time examining complaints and recommending action. Poor
Claudio Francisco Girod denied adulterating his vinegar, and one
of the cabildo members, Nicolás Forstall, had trouble paying the
money he owed to the San Lázaro lepers' hospital. Was Almonester

[24]Minutes of New Orleans cabildo, September 22, 1797, IV, 47–57;
Chambers, Louisiana, I, 378, states that Louis Darby d'Amicaut was appointed
instead of LeBlanc. De la Ronde's commission is signed by Gayoso, New
Orleans, June 6, 1798, Parsons Collection, University of Texas; Danican
resigned his post in 1799 and was replaced by Gabriel Tonbergne, who bought
the regidor's post for $500 on April 30. Document No. 379, Box 80, New
Orleans cabildo Museum Records (in the safe of the Cabildo). The salaries
of the various cabildo members are in AGI, PC, leg. 538-b. Salaries for
1802 are in A. P. Nasatir (ed.), "Government Employees and Salaries in
Spanish Louisiana," Louisiana Historical Quarterly, XXIX (October, 1946),
984–86. The author wishes to express his gratitude to the American Philosophical Society for supporting his research on the New Orleans Cabildo in 1960
with a grant. A preliminary report on the results of the research is in the
Yearbook, 1961 (Philadelphia, 1962), 376–77.

doing the proper job at the Ursuline Convent's building program? Couldn't Gayoso raise the salary of the hangman to fifteen dollars monthly? Had Bartolomé Lafond repaired all the bridges around the city as agreed?[25]

One of Gayoso's concerns was education in New Orleans. Between 1770 and 1774, royal decrees concerning the establishment of proper educational facilities for New Orleans had been granted, but the Spanish schools were not supported by the French population, who preferred to send their children to private schools managed by secular Frenchmen. The classes in the Spanish school hardly exceeded thirty pupils, and in 1788 the schoolhouse was destroyed in the famous fire. Six Franciscans came to Louisiana in 1787, some for the purpose of teaching in the school. By 1791 Father Ubaldo Delgado conducted primary classes. In 1796 a royal order reminded the governor-general that the earlier decrees regarding education should be implemented and that teachers be appointed to instruct the people of Louisiana in the Spanish language. It was Gayoso's first official duty to announce this reemphasis on education to the cabildo.[26]

Girls from good families and orphans alike attended the overcrowded classrooms of the Ursuline Convent, which was the most important school for females in the colony. Young Irene Folch, daughter of Vicente Folch y Juan, commandant at Pensacola, arrived in New Orleans in 1796 from Havana for the purpose of attending the Ursuline school.[27]

[25]Minutes of the New Orleans cabildo, 1797, IV, *passim.*
[26]*Ibid.,* August 5, 1797, IV, 73. The educational history of New Orleans during the Spanish period may be gleaned from Roger Baudier, *The Catholic Church in Louisiana* (New Orleans, 1939), 217; Claiborne to Jefferson, near Natchez, August 24, 1803, and Daniel Clark to Secretary of State (Madison), New Orleans, September 8, 1803, with enclosures, in Carter (ed.), *Territorial Papers of the United States,* IX: *Orleans,* 22, 38; David K. Bjork (trans. & ed.), "Documents Relating to the Establishment of Schools in Louisiana, 1771," *MVHR,* XI (March, 1925), 561–69; Council of Indies to King, February 27, 1772, translated in Louisiana Documents, National Archives, Record Group 59; Berquin-Duvallon, *Vue de la colonie,* 293–95.
[27]Pontalba to his wife, New Orleans, March-July, 1796, *Pontalba's Journal,* 41, 116, 144, 159. An interesting account of the Ursulines is Heloise Hulse Cruzat, "The Ursulines of Louisiana," *Louisiana Historical Quarterly,* II (January, 1919), 5–23. On February 23, 1770, O'Reilly set $120 annually as

In addition to government-supported charitable institutions, Gayoso also supported philanthropy when he found it in individual citizens. Francisco Dunegan Beaurosier, a founder of San Fernando de Florisante in Missouri, had taken in as many orphans as he could, educating them and caring for them in his own home with no subsidy or support from the government. In recognition of his services in this instance, and because of his service to the Crown in repelling Indian attacks while an officer in the militia, Gayoso recommended him for an annual salary of $100 beginning on January 1, 1794.[28]

With a population of almost 10,000 at the end of the eighteenth century, New Orleans was an urban center.[29] In addition to being the political capital and economic *entrepôt* of the provinces, "La Ville" was the cultural and social heart of Spanish Louisiana. Travelers never ceased to marvel at the beauty of the crescent-shaped Mississippi as it formed one flank of the blocklike French Quarter. During Gayoso's term as governor-general, New Orleans society was already formed of the first families who could trace their forebears back to the early eighteenth-century French founders. It was a gay city, ready and eager at the first excuse to attend masked balls and operas. Theater seats were usually reserved for the first families, and even then they were difficult to obtain.[30] Following the disaster at Cap Français and the plight of the royalist emigrés from Paris, theater companies did a thriving business in New Orleans[31]

---

the pay for each of the nuns, plus $30 for each of the twelve orphans. By an order of September 14, 1787, the amount was increased to $216 and $50 respectively. The nuns left for Havana after the retrocession of Louisiana to the French. Pay sheets of Ursulines, AGI, PC, leg. 538-b.

[28]Gayoso to Santa Clara, No. 126, New Orleans, April 26, 1798, AGI, PC, leg. 1501-b.

[29]Population of New Orleans in 1785 was 4,980; in 1788, 5,338; in 1803, almost 9,000. Census accounts in Martin, *Louisiana,* 239–40, 251; *Appendix to an Account of Louisiana,* lxxxv–lxxxvii. The 1803 census shows 3,948 white persons; 1,335 free people of color, and 2,773 Negro slaves. It does not include the free people of color in the second ward of the St. Charles District, which might swell the total to almost 9,000.

[30]Pontalba to his wife, March 19, 20, 1796, and *passim.; Pontalba's Journal,* 37, 41, *passim,* refers to meetings of the local theater's stockholders' organization for the purpose of distributing boxes.

[31]Berquin-Duvallon, *Vue de la colonie,* 29–31, discusses the comedy, "La Mort de César." See also, Minter Wood, "Life in New Orleans in the Spanish

As in the case of economic matters, the comedy was regulated by the governor-general, from the censorship of objectionable plays or the use of indecent language, to the manner in which tickets would be distributed among the public. Traffic outside the theater was also regulated during performances to prevent disturbing the actors and spectators. All shows began at precisely 5:30 in the evening. Spectators were forbidden to stand, wear their hats, or smoke during performances.[32]

Carnival, Mardi Gras, and Fasching are universal explosions of hilarity, intoxication, and last-fling gaiety before the austere period of Lent in most Catholic countries. New Orleans was no exception, and its season during the Spanish domination was hardly less exciting than in modern days. As in the case of the opera and comedy, all balls were strictly regulated as to the time and place, masks, guard duty, musicians, singing, whistling, and the kind of attire permitted or forbidden on certain occasions.[33]

Gayoso stepped into Carondelet's vacated position as the social leader of New Orleans. Convivial and *bon vivant*, Gayoso thoroughly enjoyed a good time and wanted to share the festive celebrations of New Orleans with his friends. He invited Mrs. Stephen Minor to attend the Carnival celebrations, even though he confided to Minor himself, "A million of attentions occupies me just now, the gay time of the Season gives me more trouble than to Command ten thousand men." [34]

Period," *Louisiana Historical Quarterly*, XXII (July, 1939), 692. An article dealing with opera in New Orleans after the Spanish period is Nellie Warner Price, "Le Spectacle de la Rue St. Pierre," *Louisiana Historical Quarterly*, I, (January 8, 1918), 215–23.

[32]Regulation of Carondelet, New Orleans, October 1, 1792, AGI, PC, leg. 30.

[33]Carondelet's regulation, New Orleans, November 1, 1792, AGI, PC, leg. 206; Berquin-Duvallon, *Vue de la colonie*, 31–39; Wood, "Life in New Orleans in the Spanish Period," 688–91. The Council of New Orleans followed the Spanish pattern of governing balls and the use of masks and disguises during the Mardi Gras season. *Moniteur de la Louisiane*, February 4, 1806.

[34]Gayoso to Minor, New Orleans, February 14, 1798, Gayoso Papers, Louisiana State University; Minor to Gayoso, Natchez, December 25, 1798, AGI, PC, leg. 215-a. Gayoso was also interested in the comedy and expressed pleasure at a script sent him by Jean Baptiste Berret, Premiér Cotte Alemande, June 14, 1798, AGI, PC, leg. 215-a.

But Carnival was a mild season by comparison to the wild re-joicing, celebrating, and cheering which took place on the arrival of the Duke of Orléans in February, 1798. Accompanied by the Dukes of Montpensier and Beaujolay, and the Marquis de Montjoye, the Duke of Orléans remained in New Orleans for almost five weeks, during which time they were lodged with Gayoso at the Government House. No stranger to courtly procedure, Gayoso utilized his training as O'Reilly's adjutant at Cádiz when the Comte d'Artois and Duc de Borbón had been there during the joint Franco-Spanish operations directed against Gibraltar in 1780.[35]

Gayoso wrote to Godoy describing the royal visitors and com-plaining about the infinite expense their visit had cost him, in spite of the many banquets, balls, and dinners thrown by the lead-ing inhabitants. Drawing from his own payroll funds, Gayoso spent $3,000 in addition to the $1,100 drawn from other funds. New Orleanians themselves had never opened their hearts and homes in more generous fashion. But for Gayoso the visit presented many problems in addition to the financial ones. He had to arrange the group's transportation to Havana and back to Europe and some-how keep it from being captured by roving corsairs of England or the United States. The princes, who had traveled down the Mis-sissippi incognito, were forced by circumstances to continue the masquerade as far as Havana to avoid detection and possible em-barrassing capture.[36] Moreover, their too frequent contact with the

[35]Gayoso to Prince of Peace, No. 18, Confidential, New Orleans, April 18, 1798, AHN, ESTADO, leg. 3900, draft in AGI, PC, leg. 178-b; Geoffrey T. Garratt, *Gibraltar and the Mediterranean* (New York, 1939), 76–100.

[36]Correspondence concerning the Duke of Orleans and his American tour is in Carlos Martínez de Irujo to Prince of Peace, No. 12, Philadelphia, November 10, 1796; No. 83, December 5, 1797, AHN, ESTADO, leg. 3896 *bis;* Irujo to Prince of Peace, No. 90, Philadelphia, January 19; No. 102, May 4, 1798, *ibid.,* leg. 3897; Gayoso to Prince of Peace, No. 15, New Orleans, February 24, 1798; No. 16, March 1, 1798; No. 18, Confidential, April 18, 1798, *ibid.,* leg. 3900; Morales to Hormazas, No. 214, New Orleans, March 3, 1798, *ibid.,* leg. 3902; Gayoso to Santa Clara, No. 103, New Orleans, February 24, 1798, AGI, PC, leg. 1501-a; No. 108, March 20, 1798; draft, Santa Clara to Gayoso, Havana, March 28, 1798; Gayoso to Santa Clara, San Phelipe de Placaminas, March 21, 1798, *ibid.;* Minor to Ellicott, New Orleans, March 19, 1798, and Ellicott to Pickering, Natchez, February 20, 1798, Southern Boundary MSS., II. Published accounts include Jane Marsh Parker, "Louis Philippe in the United States," *Century Magazine,* LXII (September, 1901),

Negro slaves of Louisiana boded no good to the Spanish policy of careful isolation of their slaves from the infectuous strain of *revolutionitis* which had attacked those in Santo Domingo. Louisiana planters were still mindful of the terrifying revolt of Negro slaves on the Poydras plantation at Punta Cortada in 1795 and the rumbling tremors of lesser movements. The French visitors cheerfully suggested liberation to all Negroes they encountered, and Gayoso had a very ticklish problem on his hands.[37]

By the end of March, however, the royal visitors had embarked for Havana, and Gayoso was able to turn his attention to the growing economic issues which faced his desperate colony. The annual subsidy which Mexico supplied to Louisiana via Havana had grown in the face of mounting defense costs and boundary commission expenses from $500,000 to $800,000 in 1797.[38] Resourceful and not always meticulous in keeping records, Gayoso was able to keep the ship of state from floundering during 1798 when cruising English men-of-war hoped to intercept the rich shipment from Veracruz. Long delayed, the subsidy more often than not was retained in

---

746–57; "Louis Philippe in the United States," *American Pioneer,* I (December, 1842), 414; Gayarré, *Louisiana,* 389–90.

[37]Stephen Minor told Gayoso about the dangerous pro-Negro talk of the Duke of Orleans and his party. Minor to Gayoso, Natchez, February 15, 1798, AGI, PC, leg. 215-a. On the Negro uprising, see Carondelet to Las Casas, No. 140, Confidential, New Orleans, July 30, 1795, AGI, PC, leg. 1441; Guillaume Duparc and Joseph Vázquez Vahamonde, List of the Criminals at Pointe Coupée, May 29, 1795, and supporting documents on the case, AGI, PC, leg. 31; Carondelet to Las Casas, Very Confidential, New Orleans, May 3, 1795, AHN, ESTADO, leg. 3899.

[38]Morales to Marqués de Branciforte, New Orleans, June 28, 1798, copy in AGN, Historia, tomo 334. *Cf.* Holmes, "Some Economic Problems of Spanish Governors in Louisiana," 522, 540; expenses for the province of Louisiana in 1785 were $537,285. Those of North Carolina with almost ten times the population, were $56,930. Martin, *Louisiana,* 240–44. Defense costs were the difference. By 1800 the total subsidy had risen to more than $866,739. With other revenues the total income for the province was in excess of $1,198,-828; the expenses, which included salaries for militia, regular troops, public officials, pensions, Indian expenses, fortifications, hospitals, intrigue, religious affairs, boundary commission, evacuation of the posts, construction of houses, ship repairs, rental of houses, the manufacture of bread, repayment of loans to the treasury, etc., amounted to something more than $1,050,645. Account of Gilbert Leonard, New Orleans, February 4, 1800, AGI, SD, leg. 2638. This covers the year 1799.

Havana for the captain-general's "extraordinary expenses." So obnoxious had this practice become to Gayoso that he suggested Louisiana be placed under the direct supervision of the viceroy of New Spain, especially since Louisiana's security was the key to Mexico's future.[39]

By the end of 1798 Gayoso was in desperate straits. He borrowed from the merchants, appropriated $7,000 belonging to the Ursulines, and wrote pleading letters to the captain-general, viceroy, and numerous Spanish officials. Gayoso's pleas were finally heard and on December 12 the corvette *Ardilla* and the merchant ship *Fidela* left Veracruz bound for New Orleans with a cargo of gunpowder and $100,000. By April, 1799, another convoy had brought an additional $484,239; and the pressure on Gayoso's finances eased somewhat.[40] To his friend, Stephen Minor, he wrote gleefully, "Never such a sum came into this Town at one time since its foundation. Everything is in the greatest plenty therefore at present we do not feel the scourge of War." [41]

Gayoso's somewhat unorthodox handling of government finances at Natchez had involved him with the army accountant and the intendant on numerous occasions. Unfortunately, he did not mend his ways when he advanced to the governor-generalship of the province. He was not the meticulous accountant who jealously watched every cent and rendered complete and unassailable accounts to his sovereign. On the other hand, Gayoso had a broadness of vision that took in the entire spheres of business, politics, and trade with one quick glance. Not content to permit the status quo comfort

[39]Gayoso to Azanza, New Orleans, August 2, 1798, AGN, Historia, tomo 334, folios 30–38, and edited by Jack D. L. Holmes, "La última barrera: la Luisiana y la Nueva España," *Historia Mexicana*, X (abril-junio, 1961), 637–49.

[40]Gayoso to Santa Clara, No. 154 ½, New Orleans, June 7, 1798, AGI, PC, leg. 1501-b; Gayoso to Santa Clara, No. 204, New Orleans, February 15, 1799, *ibid.*, leg. 1502-a; Gayoso to Branciforte, Very Confidential, New Orleans, July 9, 1798, AGI, PC, leg. 2365; Gayoso to Saavedra, No. 1, Confidential, New Orleans, February 24, 1799, AHN, ESTADO, leg. 3901; Gayoso to Saavedra, No. 5, New Orleans, April 21, 1799, AGI, SD, leg. 2638; Azanza to Saavedra, No. 190, Mexico, December 7, 1798, *ibid.*; No. 230, January 5, 1799, *ibid.*; Gayoso to Saavedra, No. 6, New Orleans, April 21, 1799, *ibid.*; Morales to Soler, No. 23, Confidential, New Orleans, March 31, 1799, AGI, SD, leg. 2615.

[41]Gayoso to Minor, New Orleans, April 25, 1799, Gayoso Papers, Louisiana State University.

to dim his vision of the future of New Orleans, Gayoso attempted to intercede with the king on behalf of reducing the duties on western exports to 6 per cent. Gayoso's contacts along the Mississippi knew of and appreciated his efforts. James Garrard of Frankfort praised the governor-general for his forward-looking policy "by which the city of New Orleans must become one of the greatest markets in the world." [42]

Shortly after his arrival at New Orleans, Gayoso received a petition from a resident, Francisco Bermúdez, who proposed he receive a lot of land on which to build a factory and groves of trees for the purpose of keeping bees and manufacturing wax for the use of the church and private individuals of the province. Because the proposed location was too close to the St. Ferdinand and Burgundy redoubts of the New Orleans fortifications, the chief of engineers, Joaquín de la Torre, recommended it be built at a considerable distance away. Two years from the date of his petition, Bermúdez received permission to build the proposed wax factory. [43]

Gayoso also devoted a good deal of attention to the problem of flooding during times of the river's greatest rise in the spring. His first inspection of the province, undertaken shortly after he took the oath of office, was concerned with the condition of the dikes, levees, and bridges which protected the low-lying Louisiana bottom land. On the basis of this reconnaissance, Gayoso issued a circular on March 6, 1798, requiring the various commandants of the province to call together their magistrates, syndics, and major landowners to discuss the question of placing all public levees and other internal improvements in a state of good repair. [44]

Most inhabitants answered the call to duty by offering a self-

[42]James Garrard to Gayoso, Frankfort, Kentucky, April 23, 1799, AGI, PC, leg. 2371.
[43]Petition of Bermúdez to Gayoso, New Orleans, August 7, 1797, and 19 supporting documents, *expediente*, AGI, Indiferente, leg. 1344. The plan in colors, of the proposed factory, is in Planos, Luisiana y Floridas, No. 186.
[44]Gayoso to Santa Clara, No. 8, New Orleans, December 18, 1797, AGI, PC, leg. 1502-b; Gayoso to the Bishop, October 28, 1797, cited in Bishop to Gayoso, New Orleans, October 30, 1797, AGI, PC, leg. 102; Gayoso to J. Armand, New Orleans, August 28, 1797, Remy Papers, Louisiana State University; Minutes of the New Orleans cabildo, August 11, 1797, IV, 26–27; Gayoso's proclamation of March 6, 1798, AGI, PC, leg. 215-b.

imposed tax on the basis of their landholdings for the governor-general to use to hire the necessary workers or to pay the soldiers employed on the works.[45] Sometimes a resident would refuse to serve in the work crews or pay for the repair of essential levees. Because the complete success of the programs depended on the entire cooperation of the people, Gayoso allowed no one to escape his obligations. Jean Baptiste Pechoux of the La Fourche de Cheti-machas District refused and was incarcerated until he quickly changed his mind.[46] Gayoso might have been embarrassed when a syndic reported that the governor's own father-in-law, Stephen Watts, had failed to send slaves to repair breaks in his dikes, so Gay-oso issued the necessary instructions for the work to be done.[47]

Gayoso's relations with the commercial trading firm of William Panton, John Leslie, and Thomas Forbes, operating out of Pensacola and furnishing trade goods to the Indian nations under Spain's protection, continued to be cordial though the intendant ad interim, Juan Ventura Morales, attempted to stop the lucrative trade. Pan-ton, whose original temporary license had been extended since 1790 as a result of the warm support of Carondelet and Gayoso, had considered quitting the Louisiana and West Florida trade in the face of growing competition from the United States, especially after the Treaty of San Lorenzo. Gayoso attempted to placate Panton and intercede with the King on his behalf, but Morales' con-stant interference in any matter which remotely involved finances undid much of Gayoso's work.[48]

[45]Evan Jones to Gayoso, La Fourche, June 14, 1798, AGI, PC, leg. 215-b.

[46]Evan Jones to Gayoso, La Fourche, June 14, 1798; Pechoux to Gayoso, New Orleans, June 19, 1798; and Gayoso to Jones, New Orleans, June 20, 1798, AGI, PC, leg. 215-b.

[47]Gayoso to Carondelet, No. 700, Natchez, October 28, 1796, AGI, PC, leg. 34; Lorenzo Sigur to Gayoso, Iberville, November 28, 1797, AGI, PC, leg. 215-a; Gayoso to Minor, 1797–1798, various letters, Gayoso Papers, Louisiana State University. Dam repairs were also a major concern of Gayoso's successor, the Marqués de Casa-Calvo, who was forced to use royal funds and soldier labor to protect royal lands below New Orleans. Ramón de López y Angulo to Eugenio Llaguno y Amirola, No. 16, New Orleans, April 30, 1800, AGI, SD, leg. 2638. A typical bridge over these levees and dikes is shown in Ponset's petition, March 2, 1796, in AGI, Planos, Luisiana y Floridas, No. 181.

[48]Carondelet to Panton, New Orleans, August 15, 1797; Folch to Panton, Pensacola, January 9, 1798; John Savage to Panton, Leslie, & Co., Madrid, February 25, 1797; Panton to John Forbes, Pensacola, August 15, 1797; Morales to Panton, New Orleans, February 1, 1797; Gayoso to Panton, New Orleans,

The dispute between Gayoso and Morales extended to virtually every aspect of government. The basic cause lay in the nature of the Spanish colonial system of overlapping jurisdiction, which was supposed to maintain centralization and improve the quality of government. The intendant system was a French import, first established by Philip V for Spain in 1718 for the purpose of ironing out the numerous wrinkles of Spanish financial and judicial administration. Temporarily suspended, it was reestablished in 1749, and on December 4, 1786, the king promulgated a lengthy, 306-article regulation governing the conduct of intendants in New Spain. Charles III hoped that this system would replace the inefficiency of American colonial government, and he made the intendant subordinate to no viceroy or governor. Ostensibly, jurisdiction over all matters involving smuggling, trade, collection of revenue, municipal finance, military expenses, agriculture, industry, land grants, and every conceivable aspect of administration belonged solely to this treasury official.[49]

Martín Navarro, first intendant of Louisiana during the Spanish régime, worked closely with Governor-General Miró from 1784 to 1788; and the rare disputes which arose between the two were usually settled amicably. From 1788 to 1793 the intendancy was united to the office of governor-general, but when Carondelet complained about the multiplicity of duties, the two were separated once again. Francisco de Rendón, former Spanish minister to the United States, became intendant on August 26, 1794, but less than two years later he assumed the functions of intendant and *corregidor* at Zacatecas in New Spain.[50]

March 10, 1798; Panton to Robert Leslie, Pensacola, July 18, November 8, 1796, all in Panton-Forbes Papers, Mobile Public Library; Gayoso to Saavedra, New Orleans, May 1, 1799, AGI, PC, leg. 179-a; Morales to Saavedra, No. 282, 283, New Orleans, March 31, 1799, Spanish MSS., Mississippi Valley, New Orleans Museum, IV, 329–30.

[49]Lillian Estelle Fisher, *The Intendant System in Spanish America* (Berkeley, 1929); and Lillian Estelle Fisher, "The Intendant System in Spanish America," *HAHR*, VIII, (February, 1928), 8–13; Luis Navarro García, *Intendencias en Indias* (Sevilla, 1959).

[50]Las Casas to Gardoqui, No. 13, Havana, February 24, 1794, and Carondelet to the King, New Orleans, March 11, 1794, AGI, SD, leg. 2546; decree of October 7, 1794, cited in Carondelet to Gayoso, New Orleans, April 23, 1795, AGI, PC, leg. 22; Burson, *The Stewardship of Miró*, 57–59; Gayarré, *History of Louisiana, The Spanish Dominion*, 334.

Juan Ventura Morales, the army accountant and legal advisor
(*contador*), was appointed intendant ad interim in 1796. Born in
Málaga in 1756, Morales had served for 27 years in various fiscal
posts from assistant to the collector of tobacco revenues at Málaga,
to officer of the Royal Treasury. His pioneer studies of more efficient accounting methods in the Department of Immigration and
Indian Affairs caught the attention of superiors who considered
him an ideal watchdog over the expenditures of governors who were
perhaps, overextravagant in their management of Louisiana affairs.
By 1799 he had become the principal accountant of the army and
royal treasury for Louisiana and West Florida, with virtually dicta-
torial powers over expenses and lands. Long a foe of the political and
military governors and commandants of the province, he made enemies in all places and was on one occasion kicked and struck by a
schoolmaster for larceny and was implicated in an unsavory adulter-
ous affair in which the wronged husband was poisoned.[51]

Although Morales had traveled to Louisiana from Cádiz with
Gayoso in 1788 and had expressed pleasure at seeing him in New
Orleans in 1794, there was little love lost between these two officers,
both jealous of the prerogatives of their respective offices. When
Gayoso assumed the governor-generalship of the province, Morales
wrote the understatement of his long career: "I predict that things
will be stormy for the Intendancy." [52] Gayoso had already had a
run-in concerning the respective powers of a subdelegate of the
treasury, Vicente Folch y Juan, when the latter was commandant
at San Fernando de las Barrancas. On that occasion Gayoso denied
that the treasury department had jurisdiction over military matters.[53]

[51]Biographical data on Morales is in his service record, AGI, PC, leg.
565; his decree of July 17, 1799, AGI, PC, leg. 2366; and paysheet, AGI, PC,
leg. 538-b. The charges against his character were made by Casa-Calvo to
Someruelos, No. 29, New Orleans, September 30, 1805, AGI, PC, leg. 142-a;
on the intendancy in Louisiana, see the critical remarks of Berquin-Duvallon,
Vue de la colonie, 168–71.

[52]See *supra,* Chapter I, note 73; Gutiérrez de Arroyo to Gayoso, New
Orleans, September 30, 1794, AGI, PC, leg. 47; Morales to Azanza, No. 1,
New Orleans, May 2, 1796, AGI, SD, leg. 2565; Morales to Prince of Peace,
No. 1, May 2, 1796, AHN, ESTADO, leg. 3902; Morales to Pedro Varela y
Ulloa, New Orleans, August 18, 1797, AGI, SD, leg. 2546.

[53]Folch to Gayoso, San Fernando de las Barrancas, December 16, 1795, AGI,
PC, leg. 52.

One bone of contention between Morales and Gayoso concerned the governor-general's order permitting Santiago Fletcher to introduce two hundred Negro slaves into the colony in the face of Carondelet's 1795 order suspending their import because of the prevalence of revolutionary sentiments among Louisiana slaves. Gayoso considered Negro slaves essential to the economy of the province, and he rescinded his predecessor's order.[54]

A more serious dispute centered on the question of who had authority to grant lands in the provinces. On September 9, 1797, with the sad experience at Natchez fresh in his mind, Gayoso issued a proclamation regarding the admission of new settlers into Louisiana. Its general purpose was to attract actual farmers and artisans by forbidding unmarried immigrants without slaves to receive land. He also reiterated the exclusion of public worship by the Protestants and clarified the religious provisions of private worship as extending only to the first generation of immigrants.[55]

On October 22, 1798, the king revived Article 81 of the instructions for the intendants of New Spain and applied it to Louisiana. This gave the intendant the exclusive jurisdiction over granting and distribution of lands in Louisiana. Morales accordingly drew up his own ordinance, but Gayoso refused to publish it as the intendant demanded. Splenetic correspondence between the two shattered the shaky truce between intendant and governor-general; and Morales, who was supported by influential ministers in Spain, won the case. Morales' ordinance, which was posted at the usual public places in New Orleans in March, 1799, was clearly anti-American. Anyone living in Louisiana less than two years who could not pro-

[54]Carondelet's proclamation of 1796 on Negro slave trade is in AGI, PC, leg. 23. Morales to Saavedra, No. 284, New Orleans, March 31, 1799, Spanish MSS., Mississippi Valley, IV, 330–32; power of attorney, Ignacio Paz and Ignacio de Acosta, Pensacola, July 2, 1798, Panton-Forbes Papers, Mobile Public Library.

[55]Gayoso's instructions to commandants for admission of new settlers, New Orleans, September 9, 1797, AGI, PC, leg. 2354; a similar ordinance was issued on January 1, 1798, ibid., and leg. 2365; a certified copy dated March 5, 1799, New Orleans, is in the Territorial Papers, Louisiana, National Archives, Record Group 59, with a printed copy in "Documents," in ibid. Translations are also in Gayarré, History of Louisiana, The Spanish Dominion, 386–88; Martin, Louisiana, 276–77; and a summary in Chambers, Louisiana, I, 388.

duce legal title to his land was required to give it up. Those who had more than two years' residence were obligated to pay for their lands at a price set by Morales or the Royal Treasury. Inasmuch as a vast majority of immigrants who had held lands in Louisiana since 1789 had come from the United States, the intent of Morales' regulations proved he was "a headstrong individual with antipathy toward things American." [56] Gayoso recognized that the soft, easygoing policy, which had won so many Americans to Spain for ten years, was now completely upset by Morales; but there was little he could do under the circumstances. He reluctantly accepted Morales' power over land grants, but continued to urge the Spanish ministers to change an obnoxious situation which threatened the very existence of Spanish power in Louisiana.[57]

By 1799, Morales had made Gayoso's life and his official duties completely miserable. The governor-general's hands were virtually tied by the backbiting Morales, who seemed to delight in obstructing every aspect of government from defense to Indian affairs to business matters. Morales blocked the payment of funds to the Spanish boundary commission. He objected to the repair and construction of new cannon emplacements for the galleys. The intendant interfered with the duties of the pilots and guides at the Balize and with the powers of the Captain of the Port, José de Hevia.[58]

[56]A copy of Morales' ordinance dated—de Julio de 1799, is in the Florida Papers, National Archives, Record Group 59. Correspondence on the subject is in Morales to Pedro Varela y Ulloa, No. 174, New Orleans, October 16, 1797, *ibid.*, and includes the correspondence between Morales and Gayoso from February through July, 1799. A brief discussion of the ordinance is in Francis B. Burns, "The Spanish Land Laws of Louisiana," *Louisiana Historical Quarterly*, XI (October, 1928), 557–81.

[57]Gayoso to Guillermo Duparc, New Orleans, March 12, 1798, AGI, PC, leg. 215-a. Gayoso's correspondence on the dispute with Morales is almost as voluminous as that of Morales. An early statement of his opposition to Morales' methods and procedures is Gayoso to Prince of Peace, No. 2, New Orleans, September 5, 1797, AHN, ESTADO, leg. 3900. The best single source for Gayoso's complaints on the entire dispute with Morales is Gayoso to Saavedra, No. 17, New Orleans, May 1, 1799, AGI, PC, leg. 179-a.

[58]Gayoso wrote, "The intendant places more obstacles in my way than the enemy. . . . His unmitigated ambition forces him to intervene in military and political matters which tie my hands, his selfish ambition and indifference

A typical example of the petty character of the intendant is afforded in the "rock matter." Finding twenty tons of stone which several leading inhabitants of New Orleans owned, Gayoso persuaded them to donate it to the government for the use of repairing and paving the streets and sidewalks of the city. Morales learned of the matter and sent the governor-general a bill in the amount of $100 on the grounds that the rock was given to the government and only Morales could decree how it was to be used. "I alone have exclusive right to dispose of the king's materials, no matter how they were obtained," he wrote.[59]

When Morales insisted on written requests for funds involving military activities, such as improving fortifications and the disposition of galleys in the fleet, Gayoso complained that if the request were complied with, it would mean the enemy would learn of the Spaniards' defensive plans and render them useless. Moreover, the maintenance of secret agents in the "conspiracy" of Kentucky and other western American settlements would be out of the question, inasmuch as the success of their activities depended on absolute secrecy.[60]

Gayoso pleaded with Godoy to unite once more the intendancy and governor-general, or at least to replace the ad interim intendant with someone like Rendón, whose cooperative attitude would allow the activities of government to proceed in an orderly manner. Although the Prince of Peace, Gayoso's main contact at court, was in favor of his suggestion, popular resentment toward Godoy as the Queen's favorite resulted in his removal on March 28, 1798. He was replaced with Francisco de Saavedra, described as a "man of firm character, well-organized head, considerable knowledge, great disinterestedness, and incorruptible honesty." Unfortunately, he was in

---

to the true interests of the king, are the causes which he claims in order to pester me and cover his own selfish desires." Gayoso to Santa Clara, No. 22, Confidential, New Orleans, February 17, 1799, AGI, PC, leg. 1502-b.

[59]Gayoso to Prince of Peace, No. 2, New Orleans, August 31, 1797, AGI, SD, leg. 2546.

[60]Gayoso to Santa Clara, New Orleans, August 31, 1797, *ibid.;* Gayoso to Saavedra, No. 17, May 1, 1799; Gayoso to Prince of Peace, New Orleans, August 17, September 4, 5, 1797, AHN, ESTADO, leg. 3900.

sympathy with the intendant, and he refused to change the separation, which he felt would result in economy in government.[61]

Amid these myriad vexations, Gayoso still found time to attend to domestic matters. Fond of fine Madeira wines and justly famed throughout the Mississippi Valley for the extent of his wine cellar and for his openhanded liberality with the wine glasses, Gayoso was unhappy at the relative dryness of New Orleans; and he asked his wife to send him a shipment from the hundreds of bottles he kept at Concord in Natchez.[62] Gayoso also looked for and found, near the Cabildo, a house for his family. Complete with patio and gardens, the house was ideal; and the governor himself supervised the refurnishing. To aid his wife when she arrived, he selected several recommended household Negro slaves. Ever solicitous of his family, Gayoso, in his preserved correspondence with his wife Peggy, frequently asks about his young son and his in-laws.

During his first months in New Orleans, Gayoso borrowed the bishop's coach, an elaborately designed, showy vehicle. He later ordered from William Panton a coach as a present for his wife and

[61]*Ibid.;* Prince of Peace to Saavedra, San Lorenzo, December 20, 1797, AGI, SD, leg. 2546; Cayetano Soler to Mariano Luis de Urquijo, Aranjuez, May 25, 1799, AHN, ESTADO, leg. 3901. A short sketch of Saavedra is in David Humphreys to Pickering, No. 133, Madrid, March 30, 1798, Letters of David Humphreys, National Archives, Record Group 59. Morales' subsequent action in closing New Orleans to the Americans without replacing it with another port as required by the Treaty of San Lorenzo, earned him the enmity of President Adams; Morales was soon replaced by López y Angulo, who called Morales' various activities reprehensible. López y Angulo to Cayetano Soler, New Orleans, August 8, 1801, Spanish MSS., Mississippi Valley, New Orleans, IV, 345; Gayarré, *History of Louisiana, The Spanish Dominion,* 398–99. Ultimately, Morales was again returned to the intendancy of Louisiana and West Florida where he plagued civil governors and commandants.

[62]Gayoso to Peggy, New Orleans, August 22, 1797, Cole Papers. An inventory of Gayoso's wine cellar in 1799 showed a remarkable variety and quantity, including red and white table wines, cherry liqueur, beer, Bordeaux red, 180 bottles of white Madeira, and 75 bottles of port. Gayoso's *causa mortuoria,* 1799, AGI, PC, leg. 169. Gayoso's friend, William Panton, was also fond of good Port, which he sent to his friends with the admonition, "I advise you to let the bottles remain on their bottom for a few weeks & then carefully decant it without shaking, and unless it has had foul play since it left this, you never drank better wine in your life." Panton to William Lawrence, Pensacola, November 20, 1798, and Panton to (unknown recipient) Pensacola, July 19, 1794, Panton-Forbes Papers, Mobile Public Library.

constantly tried to obtain perfectly matched teams of horses for his carriages.

The temporary release afforded by the simple pleasures could not take Gayoso's mind from the constant pressures of his office. His health suffered from the strain of his many obligations, and he often complained of sore, red eyes.[63] In addition to the above mentioned duties, Gayoso also exercised a judicial role in Louisiana government. On several occasions the duties involved were merely perfunctory, such as approving an inventory of the papers of deceased individuals.[64] In several cases, however, Gayoso was expected to use Solomon-like wisdom in rendering justice. Particularly ticklish were cases involving the manumission of slaves belonging to deceased owners. Renato Trahan had willed freedom for his Negro mistress and her mulatto children. When the heirs disputed the will, Gayoso ruled that a fifth part of the estate of the deceased went to the slave because she was the mother of Trahan's children. He added that the purchase price of her freedom would be subtracted from that sum.[65] On another occasion, a Negress, Margarita Josepha, pleaded with Gayoso for her manumission on the grounds that she was half white and her children were sired by a white man. In this instance, Gayoso decreed her freedom.[66]

As vice-patron of the Church, Gayoso fell heir to that interesting arrangement between church and state so typical in colonial Latin America. Spanish kings from the time of the Reconquest had won the right to appoint bishops and other hierarchy posts as well as the privilege of supporting the church financially. After the

[63]Gayoso to Minor, New Orleans, September 22, October 23, 1797, Gayoso Papers, Louisiana State University; Gayoso to Peggy, two dozen letters, August-November, 1797, Cole Papers. The author is presently editing the Gayoso-Minor-Peggy correspondence. Gayoso's house in New Orleans, located at 616 St. Peter Street, is known today as "Le Petit Théâtre du Vieux Carré." A portrait of Gayoso, painted by one of his descendants, Pedro de Lemos, used to hang in the gallery.

[64]*Judge* Manuel de Gayoso conducted an official inventory of the papers of Beltrán Gravier, New Orleans, October 6, 1798, New Orleans Cabildo Museum (safe), file 82.

[65]Gayoso to Luis deBlanc, New Orleans, November 1, 1797, and February 13, 1798, Gayoso Papers, Louisiana State University.

[66]Margarita Josepha to Gayoso, Santa Genoveva, June 20, 1798, and Gayoso's reply, July 7, 1798, AGI, PC, leg. 215-a.

conquest of America in the fifteenth and sixteenth centuries, this *patronato real* power was extended by the monarchs to their viceroys, captains-general, and governors. From the time of O'Reilly, in 1769, Spanish governors in Louisiana showed a keen interest in the work of the church. In 1770 O'Reilly followed the suggestions of the Capuchin Father Dagobert in recommending the formation of eleven parishes supplied with eighteen priests.[67] Father Cirillo de Barcelona, who served as chaplain with the Gálvez expeditions of 1780–81, acted the role of auxiliary bishop of Cuba until 1787 when the Provinces of Louisiana and the Floridas were placed under the jurisdiction of the newly created Diocese of St. Christopher of Havana. In 1787 the pastor of St. Louis Parish Church in New Orleans, Fray Antonio de Sedella, was appointed commissioner of the Holy Inquisition for Louisiana, but the violent opposition of Governor-General Miró resulted in his temporary expulsion and the end of all attempts to establish that institution so opposed by the people of Louisiana.[68]

The little New Orleans church burned to the ground during the 1788 fire, and Andrés Almonester y Roxas offered to loan the king sufficient money to build a new one. It was finished, despite continual bickering and acrimonious charges against Almonester in December, 1794, and the following year it was made a cathedral. In 1791 the king divided the Havana diocese; and on April 25, 1793, Pope Pius VI decreed the establishment of an independent Diocese for Louisiana, the second one in what is today the United States.[69]

When the bishop, Luis Ignacio María de Peñalver y Cárdenas, arrived in New Orleans in July, 1795, he found the moral climate of Louisiana completely depraved. Prostitution, adultery, miscegenation, bastardy, and riotous living were common. Of 11,000 persons

[67]O'Reilly's statement, New Orleans, February 14, 1770, AGI, PC, leg. 2357, and also in Kinnaird (ed.), *Spain in the Mississippi Valley*, Part I, 159–60; Baudier, *Catholic Church in Louisiana*, 179–82. *Recopilación de las leyes de los reinos de las Indias* (5th ed.; 4 vols.; Madrid, 1841), I, 54, shows the duties and obligations of the church and the governors.

[68]Baudier, *Catholic Church in Louisiana*, 200–12; Burson, *The Stewardship of Miró*, 210–32; Royal order of September 14, 1781, cited in Luis Mariano Pérez, *Guide to the Materials for American History in Cuban Archives* (Washington, 1907), 434.

[69]Pérez, *Guide to the Materials for American History*, 448. The royal decree was November 23, 1793; the papal decree is cited in Baudier, *Catholic Church in Louisiana*, 215–30.

in the New Orleans parish, less than 400 ever attended services. In the space of two years, only thirty officers and men from the Louisiana Regiment attended Mass. Published attacks on church and state led to anarchical conditions. Impudent and sacrilegious songs were sung at the dinner table. Fathers proudly recognized their natural children, and mothers were not properly educated to raise their sons and daughters in the ways of righteousness.[70]

The bishop inspected the province and reported a necessity for appointing additional priests and creating new parishes. As vice-patron, Gayoso was responsible for all such appointments. He usually followed the custom of allowing the bishop to recommend the creation of a parish or the appointment of a certain priest to a post. Then the governor-general gave his approval and drew up an official appointment, a copy of which was forwarded to the intendant, where a pay sheet was drawn up for the new priest or funds allotted for a new church or parish. Gayoso was able to expand the money granted for churches' expenses from $694 to $834 annually, exclusive of the salaries of the priests and other religious functionaries.[71] On the recommendation of Bishop Luis, he also appointed chaplains for the various military corps under his jurisdiction.[72] When the bishop and the mother superior of the Ursuline Convent requested additional funds from the government

[70]Luis Peñalver y Cárdenas' report of November 1, 1795, to the Minister of Grace and Justice, Eugenio Llaguno, is in BN, vol. 19,509, folios 24–27; a summary is in Baudier, *Catholic Church in Louisiana*, 229–31. Other complaints on religious laxity and moral depravity in Louisiana and Florida are in Luis to Carondelet, New Orleans, June 17, 1796, AGI, PC, leg. 102; Carondelet to Luis, New Orleans, January 16, March 9, 1796, AGI, PC, leg. 102; and Joseph Antonio Caballero to Antonio Coruel, San Lorenzo, November 13, 1799, in Robertson (ed.), *Louisiana*, I, 355-58.

[71]List of church expenses and suggestions for additions, New Orleans, September 27, 1797, AGI, PC, leg. 538-b; list of chapel expenses, *ibid.*; Morales' statement of church expenses, New Orleans, March 11, 1801, following his recommendation of September 26, 1799 (which is the same as Gayoso's of 1797), AGI, SD, leg. 2638. Following his 1796–1797 inspection of Louisiana, Bishop Luis recommended the expansion of funds for rebuilding the St. Louis church. Luis to Gayoso, New Orleans, February 14, 16, 1798, AGI, PC, leg. 2365. On Gayoso's appointments of clerical officers, see Gregorio White to Gayoso, La Fourche, June 5, 1798, AGI, PC, leg. 215-b; Luis to Gayoso, New Orleans, April 1, 1799, AGI, PC, leg. 102.

[72]Gayoso to Santa Clara, No. 112, New Orleans, April 17, 1798, AGI, PC, leg. 1501-a; Bishop Luis to Gayoso, New Orleans, December 20, 1797, October 23, 1798, March 30, 1799, AGI, PC, leg. 102.

for enlarging classrooms, it was Gayoso who granted the request.[73] Gayoso was also responsible for firing priests or sacristans who were derelict in their duties.[74] Finally, on several occasions Gayoso met with the bishop and the troubled partners of a marriage which was threatened, thus forming a type of marriage council to persuade the couple to adjust their differences.[75] When any inhabitant complained about excessive fees for marrying, baptizing, or burying by the priests, the governor-general was expected to warn the church to charge no more than set by law.[76]

As administrator of the provinces, Gayoso had charge of all the posts from St. Marks, Florida, to Natchitoches in northwestern Louisiana. The governor-general of Louisiana and West Florida was subordinate to the captain-general of Cuba, but in the closing months of Carondelet's term of office, the governor-general acted independently of Cuba. Gayoso was, however, subordinate to the Conde de Santa-Clara, captain-general of Cuba. In 1801 there was a suggestion that Louisiana and West Florida be combined in a separate government, but the retrocession of the province to France ended all hopes of an independent government.[77]

Gayoso continued to supervise the immigration of the French *emigrés* which began under Carondelet's governor-generalship. One ambitious program, initiated by Philippe Enrique Neri, Baron de Bastrop, centered around the Ouachita Valley in 1795. Carondelet supported Bastrop's ambitious plans for a colony of French and Flemish nobility and set aside almost 900,000 acres on the eastern side of the valley in 1796. Gayoso suspected Bastrop of wanting to

[73]Bishop to Gayoso, New Orleans, April 19, 1799, AGI, PC, leg. 102, and cited in Samuel Wilson, Jr., "An Architectural History of the Royal Hospital and the Ursuline Convent of New Orleans," *Louisiana Historical Quarterly*, XXIX (July, 1946), 618.
[74]Luis to Gayoso, New Orleans, March 27, 1799, AGI, PC, leg. 102.
[75]Gayoso to Bishop, New Orleans, May 9, 1799, *ibid.*, asking the bishop to meet with him, Luis de Macarty and the latter's wife, Juana l'Erable, for the purpose of arranging a reconciliation.
[76]Guillermo Duparc to Gayoso, Pointe Coupée, February 6, 1798, AGI, PC, leg. 215-a.
[77]Enrique White to William Panton, St. Augustine, January 2, 1797, Panton-Forbes Papers, Mobile Public Library; Duvon Clough Corbitt, "The Administrative System in the Floridas, 1781-1821," *Tequesta*, I (August, 1942), 41-62.

settle Protestants in Louisiana against his orders and, for once in agreement with Morales, the governor-general suspended Bastrop's contract until the king might decide.[78]

Gayoso also opposed any aid extended to the settlement planned by the Marqués de Maison Rouge, a friend of Bastrop, who envisioned an agricultural paradise also in the Ouachita area, which he described in a glowing flyer intended to attract farmers and artisans to the "promised land." He had been authorized to settle three hundred families from Holland in the Ouachita Valley.[79]

On the other hand, Gayoso favored the establishment of loyal Spanish subjects at the frontier posts along the Mississippi and Missouri rivers. James White had demonstrated his loyalty toward Gayoso during the Natchez revolt of 1797, and the governor-general rewarded him with the command of the newly created Spanish post of New Feliciana. A number of Americans chose to live under Spanish rule, rather than United States jurisdiction, and they followed White. These people were so successful that a number of others made plans to join them the next year.[80] Another group settled

[78]Bastrop's memorial, New Orleans, March 14, 1795, enclosed in Carondelet to Rendón, New Orleans, March 16, 1795, AGI, PC, leg. 2364; *expediente* on the Ouachita, 1796–1800, National Archives of Cuba (Havana), Floridas, 595, leg. 11; Casa-Calvo to Carlos Villemont, New Orleans, March 20, 1801, AGI, PC, leg. 70-b; Charles A. Bacarisse, "Baron de Bastrop," *Southwestern Historical Quarterly*, LVIII (January, 1955), 319–30; Mattie Austin Hatcher, "The Louisiana Background of the Colonization of Texas, 1763–1803," *Southwestern Historical Quarterly*, XXIV (January, 1921), 188, 191. Joseph Piernas, a retired sub-lieutenant, also had dreams of a substantial settlement in western Louisiana, in this case, on the Calcasieu River at the present-day site of Lake Charles. His project and description of the area are in Holmes (ed.), *Documentos de la Luisiana*, 131–69, and the somewhat inaccurate earlier translation by Jack D. L. Holmes, "Joseph Piernas and a Proposed Settlement on the Calcasieu River, 1795," *McNeese Review*, XIII (1962), 59–80.

[79]Maison Rouge's memorial, enclosed in Carondelet to Rendón, New Orleans, March 9, 1795, AGI, PC, leg. 2364; Maison-Rouge's description of the Ouachita, March 17, 1795, printed flier, *ibid.*, leg. 2354; Gayoso to Minor, New Orleans, September 22, 1797, Gayoso Papers, Louisiana State University; Minor to Gayoso, Natchez, October 6, 7, 1797, AGI, PC, leg. 2371. These colonization movements are discussed in Din, "Colonización en la Luisiana española."

[80]This James White may be the same who represented North Carolina in the Continental Congress and was involved in the "Spanish Conspiracy" with Gayoso in 1789, traveling to New Orleans under the name Jacques Dubois.

across the Mississippi from Natchez at a post its commandant, Joseph Vidal, named "Concordia" in honor of the friendly relations between Americans and Spaniards on both sides of the river.[81] Still other Americans settled at Bayou Boeuf.[82] In all these instances Gayoso used extreme caution and allowed no one whose loyalty to Spain had not already been demonstrated to immigrate to Spanish Louisiana.

James Mackay, a Scot in the service first of the Canadian fur traders and later an explorer for the Missouri Company, founded a settlement at St. Andrew (Bonhomme, Missouri) in 1798. He complained to Gayoso that the exclusion order given against introducing Protestants to Upper Louisiana had caused a mortal blow to the nascent community. Lack of sufficient Catholic settlers and the failure of the government to send a priest to the area left it open to incursions of the Indians. Gayoso was interested in populating

---

He later served as judge of the Attakapas District in 1804, and was the father of Chief Justice E. D. White. Abernethy, *The South in the New Nation*, 159; Carter (ed.), *Territorial Papers of the United States*, V: *Mississippi*, 100–101 n; James White to Gayoso, Natchez, October 4, 1798, AGI, PC, leg. 142-a; Gayoso to Minor, New Orleans, November 29, 1798, Gayoso Papers, Louisiana State University; Narsworthy Hunter to the editor of the *Impartial Observer*, Philadelphia, February 4, 1800, and Daniel Clark, Sr., to Claiborne, Clarksville, June 18, 1800, in *Papers in Relation to the Conduct of Governour Sargent*, 5–7, 25. Petitions of inhabitants from New Feliciana asking land include that of Richard Tickell to Gayoso, New Feliciana, September 2, 1797, and Gayoso's approval for 300 arpents, September 23, 1797, in Kuntz Collection, Tulane University. A petition asking for a regulation to prevent stock running wild from a number of settlers (1798) is in AGI, PC, leg. 2354. Regulations, June 26, 1798, by commandant Josef Deville Degoutin are *ibid*. New Feliciana included the old Bayou Sara section of the Natchez District. Gayoso to Santa Clara, No. 99, New Orleans, January 23, 1798, AGI, PC, leg. 1501-a; Gayoso to Isaac Johnson, New Orleans, November 30, 1798, AGI, PC, leg. 215-a, in which the governor asked Johnson to draw up regulations similar to those which governed at Natchez. See also, Minor to Gayoso, Bayou Sara, July 9, 1798, AGI, PC, leg. 215-b.

[81]Concordia was commanded first by Vidal and later by Minor. Minor delivered the post to the French on January 12, 1804, AGI, PC, leg. 70-a. On the early history of the post, see Robert Dabney Calhoun, "A History of Concordia Parish, Louisiana," *Louisiana Historical Quarterly*, XV (January, 1932), 44–67; (April, 1932), 214–33; (July, 1932), 428–52; (October, 1932), 618–45.

[82]Petition of John Tear and Patrick Gurnet, Bayou Boeuf, September 13, 1798, AGI, PC, leg. 215-b. Other Americans asked for lands under Spanish jurisdiction near the Escambia and Pensacola rivers. Memorial to Gayoso, Tensaw, November 8, 1798, and approval, November 20, 1798, AGI, PC, leg. 206.

Upper Louisiana, but only with solid pro-Spanish settlers; therefore, he had decreed that no Americans were to be permitted to settle there.[83]

Gayoso supported the nascent community of Hopefield, née Campo de la Esperanza, which was located opposite the former site of San Fernando de las Barrancas on the Arkansas shore of the Mississippi. He wrote the commandant there, Benjamin Fooy, that as soon as peace was declared he would devote his full attention to making Hopefield a flourishing settlement. As in the case of St. Andrew, however, Gayoso decreed that no Americans be permitted to colonize across the Mississippi.[84]

As complex as his political duties were, no matter how involved he might become with economic and social difficulties in New Orleans and in the province, notwithstanding his numerous arguments with the intendant, and over and above his duties as vice-patron, Gayoso never lost sight of the primary function for which he had been designated governor-general. He was supposed to protect the frontiers of Louisiana and West Florida. He was charged with maintaining the friendship of the Indians and of the Americans on his borders. While the vegetables, sauce, and trimmings related to the domestic political, economic, and social aspects of his complex government, the real meat and potatoes extended to defense and foreign policy.

[83]Mackay to Gayoso, New Orleans, June 8, 1798, AGI, PC, leg. 2365; Houck (ed.), *Spanish Régime in Missouri*, II, 71; part of Mackay's diary is in Carondelet to Prince of Peace, No. 78, Confidential, New Orleans, June 3, 1796, AHN, ESTADO, leg. 3900; Carlos deHault deLassus to Stoddard, March 6, 1804, in Billon (ed.), *St. Louis*, 367; Santiago Mackay to Gayoso, St. Andrew du Missouri, November 28, 1798, AGI, PC, leg. 215-b; Gayoso to Saavedra, New Orleans, November 22, 1798, AGI, PC, leg. 2365; Carondelet to Prince of Peace, No. 8, Confidential, New Orleans, June 3, 1796, and appointment, May 11, 1796, AGI, PC, leg. 2364; A.P. Nasatir, "John Evans, Explorer and Surveyor," *Missouri Historical Review*, XXV (January, 1931), 224–38.

[84]Gayoso to Fooy, New Orleans, July 18, August 14, 1798, March 2, 1799; Gayoso to deHault deLassus, New Orleans, July 18, 1798, certified copies, Hope-field, July 13, 1808, in Missouri Historical Society, St. Louis. Fooy's land holdings are shown in the plats of the Crittenden County (Arkansas) County Clerk's Office, Township Plats, Vol. I. His political activities in Arkansas territorial government are briefly cited in Carter (ed.), *Territorial Papers of the United States*, XIII–XV, XIX: *Louisiana-Missouri, Arkansas, passim*; see index.

CHAPTER IX

Defense and Diplomacy, 1797-1799

FROM THE MOMENT his Majesty loses dominion of the Mississippi, an equal fate will be decreed for the Kingdom of Mexico." *Gayoso to the Prince of Peace, April 19, 1798.*

"I am sufficiently authorized to employ whatever measures I deem necessary to fulfill my responsibility, and I should be derelict in my duty were I not to use them." *Gayoso to Morales, May 31, 1799.*

An old refrain runs, "For want of a nail a shoe was lost; for want of a shoe a horse was lost; for want of a horse a battle was lost; and for want of a battle a kingdom was lost." Louisiana was the nail in the Spanish-American Empire. A parade of governors and governors-general warned of the consequences to Spanish security in the Gulf of Mexico should any other power dominate that *Mare Nostrum*. Of all these capable ministers, none recognized the true importance of Louisiana more than Manuel Gayoso de Lemos.

Although his warning against yielding navigation of the Mississippi and control over the Natchez District to the United States went unheeded in Spain, as governor-general of Louisiana and West Florida, Gayoso continued to urge a positive, long-range program for preserving what remained to the Spanish king of his vast Mississippi Valley possession. In the face of almost unbearable opposition from royal officials in New Orleans, Havana, and Madrid, and with full knowledge of the possibility of war with the United States, Gayoso guided his small ship of state perilously between the Scylla of France and the Charybdis of the United States.

Andrew Ellicott was waiting in Natchez to begin the operations which would determine the thirty-first parallel north latitude, separating the possessions of Spain from those of the United States. For five months after he took possession of the governor-general's office, Gayoso waited for orders from Spain regarding the evacuation of those key posts, Nogales and Natchez. Finally, in January, 1798, Gayoso received the royal order of September 22, 1797, directing him to proceed with the evacuation as originally planned. With no reason to delay any longer, Gayoso immediately prepared to follow orders.[1]

To Ellicott he wrote, "It is with the greatest satisfaction that I have the pleasure to announce to you this agreeable event as it justifies our disposition in complying with our engagements as soon as political circumstances permits it."[2] On the same day he wrote the commander of the galleys, Captain Manuel García, to lead his squadron to Nogales and prepare to load the artillery and troops waiting there. From upper Missouri, Captain Domingo Bontoux de la Blache was ordered to descend with his galleys to aid in the evacuation.[3]

On January 19, Gayoso sent instructions to the commandants of the posts, Captain Elías Beauregard at Nogales, and Captain

[1]Gayoso to Santa Clara, No. 99, New Orleans, January 23, 1798, AGI, PC, leg. 1501-a, and draft *ibid.*, leg. 154-a.

[2]Gayoso to Ellicott, New Orleans, January 10, 1798, Southern Boundary MSS, II; Ellicott's *Journal*, 167–68.

[3]Gayoso to Manuel García, New Orleans, January 10, 1798, draft copy, enclosed in Gayoso to Santa Clara, January, 1798, draft, AGI, PC, leg. 154-a.

Stephen Minor at Natchez.[4] To Minor, Gayoso confided, "I dare say that the wisky Beauregard has at the [Walnut] Hills will offer greater difficulties to dislodge than the King's effects, therefore send him up again the boats as fast as possible; that is one of the reasons I have had to order that post to be evacuated before the Natchez." [5]

Ellicott, who had been more than anxious to see the Spanish Bourbon banner fly no more at Natchez, was not so sure about what was to follow. He warned the secretary of state that if the evacuation took place as planned—before the legal authority of the United States could be established—anarchy and lawlessness would prevail among the lower elements of the people.[6]

Nogales was evacuated without fanfare on March 23, and the troops were transferred to Baton Rouge and other lower posts in Louisiana. Under mounting pressure from the American military commander at Natchez, Captain Isaac Guion, Minor gave the necessary orders for the evacuation of that post on March 30. Just after taps, the troops marched from the abandoned Fort Panmure de Natchez to the waiting boats at the landing. The following day a detachment of American troops marched to the fort and raised the Stars and Stripes; the United States of America had taken its first step in territorial expansion.[7]

The Spaniards had delayed this step for more than a year, and few believed they had finally gone in peace. Secretary of State Pickering read in Brown's Philadelphia *Gazette and Universal Advertiser* the news of evacuation and remarked he hoped it was true. He had heard rumors that Gayoso's orders to evacuate had

[4]Gayoso's instructions to Beauregard, New Orleans, January 19, 1798, AGI, PC, leg. 44, and printed in Serrano y Sanz, *El Brigadier Jaime Wilkinson*, 78–79, n; Gayoso's instructions to Minor, New Orleans, January 19, 1798, AGI, PC, leg. 154-a, and copy enclosed in Morales to Hormazas, No. 208, New Orleans, March 3, 1798, AHN, ESTADO, leg. 3902; Gayoso to Minor, New Orleans, January 18, 22, 1798, Gayoso Papers, Louisiana State University.

[5]Gayoso to Minor, New Orleans, March 2, 1798, Gayoso Papers, Louisiana State University.

[6]Ellicott to Pickering, Natchez, February 10, 1798, Southern Boundary, II.

[7]Ellicott to Secretary of State Pickering, Natchez, April 1, 1798, *ibid.*; Gayoso to Santa Clara, No. 121, New Orleans, April 17, 1798, AGI, PC, leg. 1501-a; Morales to Hormazas, No. 219, New Orleans, April 27, 1798, AHN, ESTADO, leg. 3902.

been countermanded, though the story was without foundation.[8] Samuel Mitchell, American agent to the Choctaws, wrote William Panton he was convinced the Spaniards would evacuate as scheduled and that the boundary line would be drawn soon after.[9] Over in Florida, however, John McQueen, Jr., wrote that he doubted the news of the evacuation.[10]

With the evacuation out of the way, Gayoso turned his attention to meeting with Ellicott to begin observations to set the exact point of the thirty-first parallel. On April 9, Ellicott left Natchez for Clarksville, near the thirty-first parallel. Gayoso had made a diplomatic *faux pas* in writing to Captain Guion to ask about the plans the American officer had made for the escort of the boundary commission. As Minor wrote Gayoso, Guion spread the story about camp and exaggerated his own importance. A captain with an annual salary of $480 was thus placed in a position superior to a special state department commissary earning $3,500. The effect, wrote Minor, was to irritate Ellicott needlessly.[11]

Gayoso planned to meet Ellicott at Clarksville, but the arrival of an English squadron off Havana prevented the captain-general from sending Louisiana's subsidy, so Gayoso had to postpone the date of his departure.[12] In the meantime, the governor-general made appointments to the boundary commission. For the desirable post of commissioner, the counterpart to Ellicott, Gayoso selected his old friend Stephen Minor. As the astronomer for Spain, he chose the well-known scientist, William Dunbar, who had served as surveyor of the Spanish Natchez District under Gayoso. Thomas Power was

[8]Secretary of State Pickering to George Mathews, Philadelphia, April 1, 1798, and Pickering to Ellicott, Philadelphia, April 26, 1798, in Carter (ed.), *Territorial Papers of the United States*, V: *Mississippi*, 16–17, 25.

[9]Mitchell to Panton, at John Pitchlynns (Choctaw Nation), March 13, 1798, Panton-Forbes Papers, Mobile Public Library.

[10]McQueen to Eliza Anne McQueen, Fort George, March 11, 1798, in Walter Charlton Hartridge (ed.), *The Letters of Don Juan McQueen to his Family Written from Spanish East Florida, 1791–1807* (Columbia, 1943), 45–46.

[11]Minor to Gayoso, Natchez, January 27, 1798, AGI, PC, leg. 215-b; Ellicott to Gayoso, Natchez, February 1, 1798, and Ellicott to Pickering, Natchez, February 10, 1798, Southern Boundary MSS., II.

[12]Gayoso to Ellicott, New Orleans, March 14, 1798, Southern Boundary MSS., II.

later selected as secretary. Lesser employees were also chosen, together with a number of Negro workers, regarded by Dunbar and Minor as superior to white workers because of their resistance to the heat and to the fevers that had already struck down many of the workers on both commissions. As a final measure, plans were drawn up for supplying instruments, tents, and rations.[13]

In the interim, Ellicott took his observations at Clarksville with a small zenith sector by shooting the position of Pollux on five consecutive evenings. Minor arrived on May 21, and Dunbar, already ailing, on the 26th. Finally, on May 31, accompanied by a naval ensign, Jayme Janico, who was a skilled astronomer in his own right, Gayoso arrived in the corvette *La Diligencia*. He examined Ellicott's observations, compared them with those of Dunbar, and checked his own findings with Ensign Janico. They all agreed on the initial point of the thirty-first parallel. As an indication of the harmony existing between the Spanish and American camps, Gayoso named the point of beginning "Union Hill." [14]

The ceremony by which Gayoso and Ellicott signed their approval of the initial point was as elaborate as the primitive frontier

[13]Gayoso to Ellicott, New Orleans, February 13, 1798, and Minor to Ellicott, New Orleans, March 19, 1798, *ibid.*; Minor to Gayoso, Natchez, January 20, 1798, AGI, PC, leg. 215-b; Gayoso to Morales, New Orleans, April 11, 1798, draft, AGI, PC, leg. 2365; Morales to Prince of Peace, New Orleans, July 31, 1798, AGI, PC, leg. 2354; Morales to Saavedra, No. 234, New Orleans, July 31, 1798, AHN, ESTADO, leg. 3902; payroll sheets of William Dunbar, Thomas Power, Jayme Scott, Francisco Cabrera, Zadoc Brashears, Ramón de Haras y Hevia, Enrique Flowers, Nicolás Gensak, Felipe Engel, Jr. and Sr., and Juan Bautista Tregnier, in AGI, PC, leg. 538-b. The contract for supplying provisions, Gayoso and George Cochran, was witnessed in New Orleans by Andrés López de Armesto and Militia Captain Roberto McKay, New Orleans, June 1, 1798, AGI, PC, leg. 2365. Thirty thousand dollars was sent from Mexico to pay the costs of the Spanish portion of the boundary commission. Morales to Gardoqui, No. 44, 67, New Orleans, October 31, 1796, December 1, 1796, AGI, SD, leg. 2613. The rations and payscale of the commission members, as well as procedures to be followed, are mentioned in Gayoso to Morales, New Orleans, April 11, 23, 1798, AGI, PC, leg. 590.

[14]Ellicott to Pickering, Camp Bayou Sarah, June 19, 1798, Southern Boundary MSS., II; Ellicott's *Journal*, 179–80; Ellicott's astronomical journal, June 8, 1798, Southern Boundary MSS, III; *Moniteur de la Louisiane* (New Orleans), June 11, 1798, translated and edited by Jack D. L. Holmes, "The *Moniteur de la Louisiane* in 1798," *Louisiana History*, II (Spring, 1961), 234–35.

conditions would allow. Gayoso, following the customary Spanish tradition, gave Ellicott a warm *abrazo*, or embrace, but Ellicott was embarrassed. "I had not been shaved for two days," he wrote his wife, and "Men's kissing I think a most abominable custom." [15] A large table was placed in a clearing, covered with a green cloth. A candle for sealing wax stood beside an ornamental inkstand which was engraved with martial figures. Gayoso jested that the inkstand was in character, "for the matter drawn from the mouth of that vessel often has great destructive power." When the ceremony of signing closed, the Spanish naval guns fired a salute and Gayoso returned to New Orleans. [16]

The southern Indian nations were by no means happy about the boundary line and the evacuation of the Spanish military posts; and soon Gayoso found himself devoting more attention to Indian affairs. No sooner had he arrived in New Orleans than Gayoso learned that the Choctaws of the six villages threatened to massacre the American camp and had warned the Spaniards to form separate camps if they did not wish a similar fate. [17] If the Choctaws were aggressive, the Talapoosa Creeks were even more so. As the commission continued drawing the boundary line, the threats of constant Indian attacks almost stopped their work. On one occasion Ellicott was ordered to withdraw from the line, a step Gayoso interpreted as a prelude to armed attack from the United States. Seminoles near Tallahassee stole horses and plundered a vessel of more than $400. [18]

[15]Ellicott to his wife, Camp Bayou Sarah, June 19, 1798, in Mathews, *Ellicott*, 159.
[16]*Ibid.* Gayoso's report on the line is in Gayoso to Santa Clara, No. 150, New Orleans, June 8, 1798, AGI, PC, leg. 2354; Gayoso to Prince of Peace, No. 21, Confidential, New Orleans, June 6, 1798, AHN, ESTADO, leg. 3900. Minor and Ellicott continued the line into West Florida, descending the Apalachicola River by boat before completing their observations at St. Mary's in East Florida by 1800. The correspondence between Ellicott and the Secretary of State is found in Southern Boundary MSS., III. Minor's reports to Gayoso during 1799 are in AGI, PC, leg. 2355.
[17]Gayoso to Santa Clara, No. 154, New Orleans, June 6, 1798, AGI, PC, leg. 1501-b; Gayoso to Minor, New Orleans, June 6, 1798, copy enclosed in Gayoso to Prince of Peace, No. 22, New Orleans, June 6, 1798, AHN, ESTADO, leg. 3900.
[18]Folch to Gayoso, No. 169, Pensacola, August 20, 1798, and Howard to Gayoso, Pensacola, August 16, 1798, copies enclosed in Gayoso to Prince

Gayoso ordered Minor to be on his guard and, if necessary, join the Americans to repel any Indian insults.[19]

Gayoso had made a sincere effort to keep the Indians within bounds by informing his various Indian agents to work for cooperation. To James DuRouzeaux he wrote, "Experience having completely convinced us that the Indians made it a point to be troublesome either to us, or to the citizens of the United States, according to their own interest and private views, . . . polity and prudence have compelled us to enter into a Treaty with our neighbours the Americans, by which we mutually bind ourselves to exert every faculty in endeavoring to secure their happiness. . . ." This included withholding arms and ammunition from the Indians.[20]

The governor-general realized that the evacuation of the posts would cause considerable ill feeling among those Indians who remembered that the posts had been ceded to the Spaniards on condition they never be delivered over to the Americans. His policy lay in continuing bountiful presents and, especially, barrels of firewater. Unfortunately for the success of this policy, Morales opposed every penny spent to win the Indians' friendship and consistently argued against supplying such leaders as the Cherokee chief, Bloody Fellow, with expensive presents.[21] The firm of William Panton, which had

---

of Peace, No. 29, Confidential, New Orleans, September 26, 1798, AHN, ESTADO, leg. 3900; Ellicott to Pickering, Pensacola, June 18, 1799, and Camp on the Chattahoochee, August 21, 1799, Southern Boundary MSS., III; Hawkins to Panton, Cowetuk Tallahassee, October 14, 1799, Panton-Forbes Papers, Mobile Public Library; Minor to Gayoso, Camp on the Chattahoochee River, August 5, 1799; Minor to Gayoso, No. 81, encampment, Chattahoochee River, August 14, 1799; and Minor to Daunoy, No. 82, Limits, Encampment River Flint, September 6, 1799, all in AGI, PC, leg. 2355. These mention Indian attacks and depredations.

[19]Gayoso to Minor, New Orleans, June 6, 1798.

[20]Gayoso to Pedro Olivier, New Orleans, January 30, 1798, AGI, PC, leg. 2354; Gayoso to James DuRouzeaux, New Orleans, February 16, 1798, AGI, PC, leg. 215-a; Winthrop Sargent to Pickering, Natchez, September 18, 1798, in Rowland (ed.), *Mississippi Territorial Archives*, I, 46–47.

[21]Gayoso to Morales, New Orleans, November 4, 1797, AGI, PC, leg. 590; Morales to Saavedra, No. 228, New Orleans, May 2, 1798, AHN, ESTADO, leg. 3902; Whitaker, "Spain and the Cherokee Indians," 269; Gayoso to Morales, New Orleans, October 25, 1797, and Morales to Prince of Peace, New Orleans, January 20, 1798, AHN, ESTADO, leg. 3902; Irujo to Gayoso, Philadelphia, April 30, 1798, AGI, PC, leg. 1502-b.

kept the Indians supplied with goods, received special permission from an Order in Council from England to continue importing English goods; but there was much unrest among the Indians.[22] Pedro Varela reported that the fort in the Osage country was no longer necessary at a time when Gayoso considered its elimination as false economy. Not only had Fort Carondelet kept the peace in upper Missouri, but many Indians had been persuaded by its commandant, Renato Chouteau, to embrace civilization and cultivate their lands peacefully.[23] Moreover, word filtered down the valley that President Adams had sent a circular letter to the northern Indian tribes denouncing the Spaniards. There was even a rumor that for every Spaniard turned over to the Americans, the Indians would receive fifty dollars and a carbine.[24]

The evacuation of the Natchez District and the running of the boundary line posed new problems of defense for Lower Louisiana, and Gayoso in his characteristic manner endeavored to solve them. He warned Godoy that the surrender had endangered not only Louisiana, but also the rich province and viceroyalty of New Spain. Free use of the Mississippi would lead, undoubtedly, to contraband traffic with the internal provinces of Texas, Coahuila, and other areas in the Southwest. Although it would be expensive to place Louisiana as a true barrier against the Americans, this outlay of funds was absolutely essential to prevent the loss of Mexico. Accordingly, Gayoso prepared an outline for the defense of Louisiana.[25]

First, Baton Rouge must be made the most important military post in Lower Louisiana, not only because it was adjacent to the

[22]British orders in council, St. James, April 25, 1798; proclamation of George III, May 3, 1798, in Panton-Forbes Papers, Mobile Public Library; Gayoso to Santa Clara, No. 199, New Orleans, September 26, 1798, AGI, PC, leg. 1501-b.
[23]Gayoso to Santa Clara, No. 6, Confidential, New Orleans, November 30, 1797, and draft of Santa Clara's reply, January 29, 1798, AGI, PC, leg. 1502-b.
[24]Trudeau to Gayoso, St. Louis, April 29, 1798, AGI, PC, leg. 1502-b; Gayoso to Santa Clara, No. 13, Confidential, New Orleans, July 25, 1798, AGI, PC, leg. 1502-b.
[25]Gayoso to Prince of Peace, No. 19, Confidential, New Orleans, April 19, 1798, AHN, ESTADO, leg. 3900. The points which follow are from this letter.

American frontier, but also because its location allowed easy access to Lakes Pontchartrain, Borgne, and Maurepas, through which the Spaniards communicated with Mobile and Pensacola. Second, the vital post on the Amite River, Galvez-Town, which had been founded by Bernardo de Gálvez in 1779, would be strengthened to preserve communication via the Amite and Iberville channels.[26]

Third, a line of blockhouses, five leagues distant from each other, must be established along the frontier of the Natchez District. Fourth, a strong, well-populated and well-defended settlement should be formed at New Feliciana, opposite Natchez on the southern frontier, in which a governor or commandant would reside, supported by at least a hundred mounted troops to patrol the boundary. Fifth, opposite the city of Natchez, at the former settlement of San Fernando de las Barrancas on the Chickasaw Bluffs, and near the mouth of the Ohio River, Gayoso proposed the establishment of three new military posts. Sixth, he recommended completion of the defenses at St. Louis and sending a strong force from the Louisiana Regiment garnered from the scattered posts in Upper Louisiana.

Seventh, Gayoso felt his government should sustain along the Mississippi and Missouri rivers, a squadron of galleys, galiots, and gunboats, reinforced by fifty-man crews. Gayoso wanted the number of ships in the Mississippi Squadron increased in order to acquire absolute control of the waterways protecting the access to Louisiana.

As his eighth point, Gayoso recommended a full regiment of the Louisiana infantry be stationed at New Orleans and a new battalion be created from troops in Havana or Spain to garrison Pensacola. His ninth proposal called for an increase in the number of artillerymen.

Gayoso's tenth point was, perhaps, the most far-reaching suggestion of his long career. He proposed free trade for New Orleans so that citizens of Louisiana would have equal trading privileges with Americans who, by the terms of the Treaty of San Lorenzo,

[26]Bernardo de Gálvez to Joseph de Gálvez, No. 233, New Orleans, January 15, 1779, copy, in AGI, PC, leg. 223-b; a report on the poor condition of its fort by commandant Francisco Rivas was made at Galvez-town January 2, 1795, AGI, PC, leg. 31. A complete inspection of the post, the Amite and Iberville Rivers, and environs was made by Juan María Perchet from December 27–29, 1796, and is in AGI, PC, leg. 2354.

were able to import and export their goods without paying the 6 per cent duties which Louisiana residents paid. With commission agents' fees amounting to a maximum of 4 per cent, Gayoso recommended the equalization of duties for all using New Orleans as an entrepôt. In order to facilitate mercantile exchange, Gayoso further suggested the creation of a Tribunal of Appeals for the prompt administration of justice in admiralty cases; the appointment of an American consul in New Orleans; and the restoration of the broad, plenary powers which O'Reilly had possessed during his 1769–79 administration of the colony.[27]

A favorite theme in the letters of Gayoso at this juncture was his warning that Louisiana was the protecting barrier to New Spain; should the former be surrendered, the latter would surely follow. So desperate was Gayoso that on one occasion he wrote that it would be better to allow the French to possess Louisiana than to permit it to remain unpopulated and defenseless, an easy prey to rapacious American frontiersmen.[28] For ten years rumors had persisted that Louisiana was to be retroceded to France, but Gayoso did not have to live to see the day when Napoleon would compel a weak Spanish government to return the province.[29]

To prevent the loss of Louisiana by default, Gayoso called together a war council in New Orleans to discuss the best methods of defense. Although the captain-general ordered Gayoso to submit all decisions of the council to Havana before attempting to undertake them himself, Gayoso was able to do things on his own volition in July, 1798, when Cuba itself was besieged by marauding English corsairs.[30]

The war council of July 6 included Gayoso, the intendant Morales, artillery corps director Nicolás D'Aunoy, engineers Gilberto Guillemard and Joaquín de la Torre, Major Juan Gautier,

[27]Gayoso to Prince of Peace, No. 19, Confidential, April 19, 1798.

[28]Gayoso to Azanza, New Orleans, August 2, 1798, AGN, Historia, tomo 334, edited by Holmes in "La última barrera: la Luisiana y la Nueva España," 641. *Cf.* Gayoso to Saavedra, No. 1, Confidential, New Orleans, November 22, 1798, AHN, ESTADO, leg. 3900.

[29]Retrocession was suggested by a memorial of Benjamin Tardiveau, New York, February 20, 1788, enclosed in Gardoqui to Floridablanca, No. 20, Confidential, New York, July 25, 1788, AHN, ESTADO, leg. 3893.

[30]Gayoso to Santa Clara, No. 111, New Orleans, April 17, 1798, AGI, PC, leg. 1501-a.

government secretary Andrés López Armesto, and commander of the squadron Manuel García. Gayoso opened the session by revealing the news he had obtained on American troop movements. At their new post on the Chickasaw Bluffs, Fort Adams, and distributed at Nogales and Natchez, the Americans had more than a thousand troops. Colonel Hamtramck had entered the Mississippi with three companies. General Wilkinson was expected to follow with a galley and reinforcements to fortify the Roche à Davion or Loftus Cliffs, just below Natchez, in what was finally named Fort Adams. Congress had voted two million dollars for fortifications, guns, side arms, naval craft, and funds for raising 20,000 men.

At Fort Pitt shipwrights from Philadelphia were busily constructing galleys and gunboats to challenge Spanish naval power on the Mississippi.[31] Because of the evacuation of Nogales and Natchez, Spanish frontiers were exposed to any attack from above. The United States, on the point of breaking off relations with France and ready and willing to go to war on the high seas, considered Louisiana the weak belly of American defenses. Should war come, France would undoubtedly seize Louisiana and attack the United States. Therefore, it was predicted that American strategy in event of war would be to grab Louisiana first. Either way, Spain stood to lose Louisiana.[32]

In the dispute between the Federalists and the Jeffersonian Republicans, which was fast coming to a climax in the United States during 1798, each foreign power sought to widen the rift for its own aims. The French minister, Pierre Auguste Adet, supported the Jeffersonians against the Federalists and virtually pushed Washington closer to the British.[33] The British utilized the split to further their own commercial ambitions in the Gulf of Mexico.[34]

---

[31]Irujo to Saavedra, No. 109, Philadelphia, August 11, 1798, AHN, ESTADO, leg. 3897; Junta de guerra, New Orleans, July 6, 1798, in AGI, PC, leg. 1502-a.

[32]Junta de guerra, New Orleans, July 6, 1798, AGI, PC, leg. 1502-a; cf. Gayoso to Saavedra, No. 24, New Orleans, June 30, 1798, AHN, ESTADO, leg. 3900.

[33]Alexander de Conde, "Washington's Farewell, the French Alliance, and the Election of 1796," MVHR, XLIII (March, 1957), 641–58; John C. Miller, The Federalist Era, 1789–1801 (New York, 1960).

[34]Irujo to Saavedra, No. 109, August 11, 1798; Gayoso to Saavedro, No. 1, Confidential, New Orleans, February 24, 1799, AHN, ESTADO, leg. 3901.

As Carondelet had employed extraordinary measures and spent money he did not have to guard against the expected English attack from Canada, so Gayoso proposed to protect Louisiana against any attempted invasion from the United States or France. Morales weakly pointed out that there remained in the treasury only $80,000; Pensacola was already broke; $25,000 in letters of credit needed to be redeemed; and the blockade threatened to cut off all financial aid from Mexico. The army had not been paid in months and the Louisiana Regiment was due $30,000. Yet, not being a military man, Morales magnanimously acquiesced to the decision of the council. They were unanimously in favor of Gayoso's suggestions. All possible measures consistent with available funds would be taken to defend Louisiana.[35]

Following the council meeting Gayoso wrote to the captain-general imploring his aid. The colony needed an immediate subsidy of $300,000 to cover costs. He needed hundreds of men from Mexico, Havana, and Spain to complete the rosters of the various regiments. He needed several squadrons of galleys, gunboats, and galiots. He suggested using the French emigré officers such as General Collot, many of whom would be forced to leave the United States because of the newly enacted Alien Acts. Finally, Gayoso asked for funds to keep the militia on a standby state of readiness.[36]

What were the realities of Gayoso's situation? It was certain that Congress had voted to raise 20,000 men, but what were they to be used for? Certainly, the *Aurora's* statement by "Democritus" did nothing to allay Gayoso's fears: ". . . 20,000 men will not be wanted to protect the conquered country, we will make an attempt on Mexico, and our success is certain, for *we have Miranda's plans;* and then, there is no need of conquering; it is enough to divide, and introduce our commerce, once the door open, time will do the rest; and be well assured, cousin, that before twenty years are elapsed, we shall go to China by Acapulco."[37]

From Philadelphia, the Spanish minister Carlos Martínez de Irujo kept Gayoso well informed of political events in the United States, and Gayoso relayed the information to the Viceroy of Mexico,

[35]Minutes of the Junta de guerra, July 6, 1798.
[36]Gayoso to Santa Clara, No. 17, Confidential, New Orleans, July 30, 1798, AGI, PC, leg. 1502-b.
[37]*Aurora and General Advertiser* (Philadelphia), May 27, 1797.

Miguel Joseph de Azanza, from whom the governor-general asked aid.[38] None of the actions taken by the United States seemed favorable to the Spanish officials. The movement of large numbers of American troops to the Mississippi frontier, the numerous newspaper attacks on Spain, the orders for Ellicott to retire from the boundary line, the rumors that Americans were trying to influence the Indians against Spain, and the addition of twelve regiments to the American army and alerting of the militia, all seemed to Gayoso to foretell war against Spain in Louisiana.[39]

As part of his defensive program, Gayoso asked his commandants and the lieutenant-governor of Upper Louisiana to prepare reports on the weak points of the province, and particularly the Indian tribes.[40] Lieutenant Colonel Carlos Howard made voyages of inspection from Missouri to Nogales, and James Mackay, a former agent for the Missouri Company whom Gayoso appointed as a captain in the militia, forwarded his report of conditions along the Missouri River to Gayoso. As a result of these reports, Gayoso ordered the defenses of St. Louis continued and the fort and garrison at Ste. Genèvieve prepared to resist an attack. The galleys were brought into position and their artillery increased. As for permitting Americans to settle in the new Missouri posts, Gayoso was thoroughly opposed to it on the assumption that these settlers would side with the United States in the event of a showdown.[41]

[38]Gayoso to Azanza, August 2, 1798; Philadelphia *Gazette and Universal Daily Advertiser,* March 19, 1798; Irujo to Gayoso, Philadelphia, March 20, 1798, AGI, PC, leg. 1502-a.
    [39]Gayoso to Santa Clara, No. 190, New Orleans, September 26, 1798, AGI, PC, leg. 1501-b; No. 13, Confidential, New Orleans, July 25, 1798, and No. 14, Confidential, New Orleans, July 30, 1798, AGI, PC, leg. 1502-b; Gayoso to Santa Clara, No. 199, New Orleans, September 26, 1798, AGI, PC, leg. 1501-b; Stoddard, *Sketches, Historical and Descriptive of Louisiana,* 101.
    [40]Gayoso to deHault deLassus, Natchez, July 24, 1797, deLassus Papers, Missouri Historical Society; Trudeau to Gayoso, No. 316, St. Louis, January 15, 1798, AGI, PC, leg. 2365; Nasatir (ed.), *Before Lewis and Clark,* II, 534–44.
    [41]Santiago Mackay to Gayoso, St. Andrew du Missouri, November 28, 1798, AGI, PC, leg. 215-b; Trudeau to Gayoso, No. 316, January 15, 1798; Gayoso to Morales, New Orleans, April 16, 1798, Gayoso to Trudeau, New Orleans, April 16, August 14, 1798, in Nasatir (ed.), *Before Lewis and Clark,* II, 554–55, 571, 556 n.; Dunbar Rowland (ed.), "Military Journal of Captain Isaac Guion, 1797–1799," in *Seventh Annual Report, 1907–1908,* Director of the Department of Archives and History, State of Mississippi (Nashville, 1909), 103–104; 42–43,

For settlers, Gayoso wanted serious Canadian farmers and artisans. To encourage them to come to Missouri, he proposed a type of headright system. For each thousand arpents settled by Canadians, the entrepreneur bringing them would receive ten arpents.[42] Recognizing the importance of securing the northern frontier with Canada, Gayoso urged Saavedra to draw a boundary from the Lake of the Woods to the Pacific, in order to keep the Colorado River well within Spanish territory. Since both England and the United States coveted the rich fur trade of the Missouri River, Gayoso felt it was essential to keep their traders out of the region.[43]

Having taken steps to insure the security of Upper Louisiana, Gayoso then turned his attention to his proposed defensive program for the lower areas of the province. Royal approval for rebuilding the small fort near San Phelipe de Placaminas below New Orleans also included permission to construct a post at Galvez-town and a powder magazine at the Pensacola post of San Carlos de Barrancas and to reconstruct Fort Charles in Arkansas.[44] Gayoso ordered his engineers, Juan María Perchet and Joaquín de la Torre, to go to Baton Rouge and draw up the necessary fortification plans and

---

45, 48–50, include Guion to Wilkinson, Pike, and McHenry, September 2, 25, and October 22, 1797; Morales to Hormazas, No. 194, No. 195, New Orleans, January 20, 1798, AHN, ESTADO, leg. 3902; Gayoso's certification, enclosed in Gayoso to Morales, New Orleans, December 28, 1797, *ibid.;* Morales to Gardoqui, No. 88, New Orleans, March 3, 1797, *ibid.;* Howard's service sheet, December 31, 1797, AGS, GM, leg. 7292, X, 2; Howard's report of July 26, 1797, enclosed in Gayoso to Morales, Confidential, New Orleans, August 16, 1797, copy enclosed in Morales to Varela y Ulloa, No. 18, Confidential, New Orleans, October 16, 1797, AHN, ESTADO, leg. 3902; Gayoso to deHault deLassus, New Orleans, February 27, 1799, DeLassus Papers, Missouri Historical Society; appointment of Santiago McKay as captain of militia, New Orleans, May 1, 1798, Gayoso Papers, Missouri Historical Society; Gayoso to deHault deLassus, New Orleans, March 2, 1799, *ibid.;* Gayoso to deHault deLassus, New Orleans, August 4, 1798, AGI, PC, leg. 2365; A. P. Nasatir, "Anglo-Spanish Rivalry in the Iowa Country, 1797–1798," *Iowa Journal of History and Politics,* XXVIII (July, 1930), 351.

[42]Gayoso to Trudeau, April 16, 1798.
[43]Gayoso to Saavedra, No. 1, Confidential, November 22, 1798.
[44]Gayoso to Santa Clara, No. 169, New Orleans, July 19, 1798, acknowledging Santa Clara's dispatch of June 8, 1798, AGI, PC, leg. 1501-b; Santa Clara to Gayoso, Havana, June 8, 1798, AGI, PC, leg. 154-a.

estimates. Perchet, with whom Gayoso had numerous difficulties at San Fernando de las Barrancas in 1795, inspected the site and came to the conclusion that it was not suitable for what Gayoso intended. Accordingly, he prepared his own suggestions which he submitted to the astonished governor-general. Gayoso recalled Perchet, but his dispute with de la Torre also hampered his defensive plans.[45]

Constantly hindered by the lack of adequate, cooperative engineers who were officials in the Royal Engineer Corps, Gayoso turned to foreigners such as Nicolás deFiniels and Louis Van den Bemden. DeFiniels had come to the United States during the Revolution and served with the American army before Irujo hired him, on General Collot's recommendation, and sent him to St. Louis to protect that post from the expected English attack in 1797. When the engineer's pay was cancelled, Gayoso ordered it restored and, on his own authority, called deFiniels to New Orleans to fulfill the functions of engineer extraordinary. DeFiniels drew plans of Baton Rouge, New Orleans, and Mobile before becoming a lieutenant colonel in the Spanish army charged with the defenses of San Carlos de las Barrancas.[46] Van den Bemden, a Dutch engineer with a flair for hydraulics, was one of Carondelet's appointees to direct the fortifications at St. Louis in 1797. Gayoso recommended him for continued service, although he doubted his political loyalty.[47]

The Mississippi Squadron of Galleys had been one of Gayoso's favorites since 1792 when he recommended its creation as a nucleus

[45]Gayoso to Santa Clara, No. 138, New Orleans, May 20, 1798, AGI, PC, leg. 1501-a; Gayoso to Perchet, New Orleans, July 19, September 6, 17, 1798, Gayoso to de la Torre, New Orleans, September 19, 1798; Perchet's military reflections on Baton Rouge, September 5, 1798; Perchet to Gayoso, Baton Rouge, September 6, 10, 1798; all copies enclosed in Gayoso to Santa Clara, No. 191, New Orleans, September 26, 1798, AGI, PC, leg. 1501-b. Perchet's interesting Louisiana career is sketched in Holmes, "Some French Engineers in Spanish Louisiana."

[46]DeFiniels' career is outlined in Holmes, "Some French Engineers in Spanish Louisiana"; and Holmes (ed.), *Documentos de la Luisiana,* 359–420. On Gayoso's role in his career, see Gayoso to Santa Clara, No. 176, 191, July 30, September 26, 1798; draft of Santa Clara to Gayoso, Havana, November 14, 1798, AGI, PC, leg. 1501-b; Morales to Gilberto Leonard, New Orleans, April 11, 1798, AGI, PC, leg. 560.

[47]Holmes (ed.), *Documentos de la Luisiana,* 122–23.

of defensive power on the Mississippi. Learning of American ship-building on the Ohio at Fort Pitt, he was convinced that vigorous measures on the part of the Spaniards must be employed to maintain Spanish naval superiority on the western waters. Accordingly, he recommended the repair of those galleys, galiots, and gunboats not suitable for service and the construction of new vessels. When the captain-general questioned Gayoso's use of the galiot *La Vigilante* for his own service, the governor-general explained that with 500 leagues along the Mississippi under his jurisdiction, the necessity of inspecting fortifications and levees from Punta Cortada to the Gulf, and the needs of the boundary commission, such a craft was absolutely essential.[48]

In 1798 the floating forces consisted of three galleys—*La Luisiana*, *La Venganza*, and *La Phelipa*. *La Leal*, which had been constructed with funds donated by officers of the Louisiana Infantry Regiment, was useless. The cannon ranged in size from simple swivel guns to large 24-pounders. The crews of the galleys did not exceed forty in number for the largest, *La Phelipa*. There were three galiots—*La Vigilante*, which was Gayoso's own boat, *La Activa*, and *La Flecha*. *La Vigilante* carried a crew of twenty-two, but the others had fewer men to man the oars. A bombardier, *La Margarita*, boasted a 9-inch mortar and a crew of seventeen. There were three gunboats, *Tetis*, *Aquiles*, and *Socorro* with 12-pounder guns and crews of twenty men each. The total number of sailors, who enjoyed the same privileges as those in the Royal Armada, with the exception of pay, was 278. The sailors received $15 per month plus their rations.[49]

In the face of almost constant opposition from Morales, Gayoso increased the size of the crews and raised their pay.[50] The squadron

[48]Gayoso to Santa Clara, No. 11, Very Confidential, No. 17, Confidential, and No. 94, New Orleans, June 5, July 30, January 23, 1798, AGI, PC, legs. 1502-b, 1501-a; Trudeau to Gayoso, No. 12, St. Louis, July 12, 1798, in Nasatir, "Anglo-Spanish Rivalry in the Iowa Country," 383–88.

[49]Statement of Gayoso, New Orleans, May 15, 1799, AGI, SD, leg. 2638; Gayoso to Saavedra, No. 19, New Orleans, June 9, 1799, AHN, ESTADO, leg. 3901; Gayoso to Santa Clara, No. 17, Confidential, July 30, 1798.

[50]The dispute between Morales and Gayoso over naval matters stretched from 1798 into 1799. A number of enclosures on the matter is in Morales to Miguel Cayetano Soler, No. 27, Confidential, New Orleans, May 31, 1799, AGI,

proved itself in numerous ways. Roberto McCoy took *La Activa* up river on a two-month voyage to inspect forts and American naval craft in December, 1798.[51] Bernardo Molina took *La Flecha* from St. Louis to Prairie du Chien to acquire information on the English traders in the area.[52]

The most important service rendered by these naval forces was at the entrance to the passes of the Mississippi. Fearing that the convoy carrying the subsidy to Louisiana was in danger from English sea rovers, Gayoso ordered a division of galleys under the commander of the squadron, Manuel García, to the Balize. When the governor-general learned that an English man-of-war with forty cannon had anchored and sent two longboats to examine an American brig anchored nearby, he sailed to the mouth of the river himself, followed by additional ships in the squadron. The English frigate, *La Iris*, had sailed away, however, leaving the astonished American with a handful of bullets and a message to give to Gayoso. The governor-general suspected the English ship was one of Commodore Cochran's squadron, known to be in the area. To insure the safety of the river entrance to New Orleans, Gayoso ordered his galleys to stand guard, and he appointed Captain Antonio Patricio Walsh to command *La Margarita* on guard at the Balize.[53]

During 1798 the so-called undeclared naval war between France and the United States threatened to involve Louisiana. A French

---

SD, leg. 2638; *cf.* Gayoso to Santa Clara, No. 24, Confidential, New Orleans, February 24, 1799, AGI, PC, leg. 1502-b; Gayoso to Santa Clara, No. 183, New Orleans, July 31, 1798, enclosing petition of Manuel García to Gayoso, New Orleans, July 14, 1798, AGI, PC, leg. 1501-b; petition of Vicente Fernández Texeiro, New Orleans, July 23, 1798, enclosed in Gayoso to Santa Clara, No. 183, July 31, 1798; Morales to Cayetano Soler, No. 356, New Orleans, December 22, 1799, AGI, SD, leg. 2638.

[51]Robert McKay to Gayoso, New Madrid, December 14, 1798, AGI, PC, leg. 215-b.

[52]Nasatir, "Anglo-Spanish Rivalry in the Iowa Country," 352–53, 383–88.

[53]García's report, Bayou de los Prácticos (pilots), aboard the galera *Venganza*, April 25, 1798, AGI, PC, leg. 47; García to Gayoso, No. 37, galera *Venganza* at Placaminas, April 29, 1798, AGI, PC, leg. 215-b; Gayoso to Santa Clara, No. 137½, galeota *Vigilante*, Fort at the Balize, May 4, 1798, AGI, PC, leg. 1501-a, with enclosures; Gayoso to Walsh, New Orleans, October 11, 1798, Walsh Papers, Louisiana State University, which also has additional documents relating to Walsh's naval activities.

corsair, *El Hennique,* prowled the Gulf of Mexico capturing English and American vessels. In August, 1798, its captain, Miguel Moreau, brought two American prizes from Honduras Bay to New Orleans to sell in accordance with maritime law. The Royal decree of July 14, 1797, established principles under which Gayoso's admiralty court in New Orleans would judge whether the prizes taken were done in accordance with international law. One ship had been taken in an unauthorized manner, and the French consul at Charleston ordered it released.[54]

An American frigate, *Matilde,* bound from New York via Providence, was halted by the English man-of-war, *Thunder,* and searched on the high seas. Gayoso felt this ship was part of a permanent ambush stationed near Havana and the mouth of the Mississippi where they hoped to intercept the subsidy. For this reason, the viceroy waited until he had a strong convoy before allowing merchant or government ships carrying funds for Cuba and Louisiana to set sail from Veracruz.[55] To protect the vessels once they reached the mouth of the Mississippi, Gayoso sent a division of his galleys to the passes under the command of Manuel García.[56]

The peppery ship captain, Luis Maroteau, commanding the Spanish frigate *El Misisipi,* was met by a convoy three days out of Havana, The British corvet and brig separated and ran when Maroteau pluckily signaled for battle order and the deadly Spanish fire

[54]Bouligny to Santa Clara, No. 255, 266, New Orleans, May 1, 1799, AGI, PC, leg. 1502-a; Gayoso to Santa Clara, No. 186, New Orleans, September 26, 1798, AGI, PC, leg. 1501-b. Spain also permitted an American privateer to capture a British ship carrying Mosquito Coast logs and to dispose of the cargo in New Orleans. Panton indignantly wrote, "This sirs is the Protection that we now receive from the King of Spain & this is the reward we meet with, for preserving these Provinces in peace & quietness for eleven years past." Panton to Robert Leslie, Pensacola, November 8, 1796, Panton-Forbes Papers, Mobile Public Library.

[55]Gayoso to Santa Clara, No. 123, New Orleans, April 20, 1798, AGI, PC, leg. 1502-a; Gayoso to Azanza, New Orleans, November 15, 1798, AGN, Historia, tomo 334; Gayoso to Álvarez, New Orleans, July 10, 1799, AGI, PC, leg. 179; Gayoso to Ellicott, New Orleans, March 14, 1798, Southern Boundary MSS., II.

[56]Gayoso to Manuel García, New Orleans, September 4, 1798, AGI, PC, leg. 147-a.

raked the nearest English ship.[57] Unfortunately, any of these seizures might involve Gayoso in a dispute leading to open war. He wrote William Panton, "I have a distant hope that the affairs between the United States and France will take a favorable turn." [58] But, less than a year later, when the United States was preparing to send its three commissioners to deal with Talleyrand in what was to result in the famous "X-Y-Z Affair," an American warship captured a French vessel near Guadaloupe. The French governor of that island declared war on the United States in the name of the French Republic; and Gayoso feared that if France followed suit, the United States would immediately invade Louisiana.[59]

Perhaps the governor-general would have been more confident had he not seen the muster rolls of the Louisiana Infantry Regiment. Notwithstanding an official recommendation in 1794 that Louisiana be garrisoned with 4,000 regular troops of the veteran line and 8,000 militia,[60] the only thing constant about the number of troops in Louisiana was their declining number. In July, 1793, there were three battalions of the Louisiana Infantry Regiment with a paper strength of 84 officers, 58 drummers, 78 sergeants, 213 corporals, and 1,507 men. Actually, there were only 1,333 soldiers, and a corresponding lack of noncommissioned and regular officers. The paper strength in 1793 was 1,856; the actual force, 1,637.[61]

By 1796, the situation had deteriorated greatly, regarding not only numbers but also quality. When Gayoso asked Carondelet for reinforcements, the terse reply was, "Don't ask me for troops now; I lack 426 men to complete the rosters of the Louisiana Regi-

[57]Gayoso to Santa Clara, No. 204, New Orleans, February 15, 1799, AGI, PC, leg. 1502-a; September 26, 1798, AGI, PC, leg. 1501-b.

[58]Gayoso to Panton, New Orleans, October 16, 1798, *Florida Historical Quarterly*, XV, (April, 1937), 250.

[59]Gayoso to Pedro de Nava, New Orleans, June 10, 1799, Archivo Histórico de Sonora (Hermosillo, Mexico).

[60]Pedro Grimaret's report, with addenda of Pedro Garrido y Durán, Madrid, July 12, 1794, ASHM, 5-1-7-6.

[61]Roster of the regiment by Grand-Pré, New Orleans, June 30, 1793, AGI, PC, leg. 161-a; roster of the regiment approved by Francisco Bouligny, New Orleans, July 22, 1793, enclosed in Carondelet to Alcudia, No. 12, Confidential, New Orleans, July 31, 1793, AHN, ESTADO, leg. 3898. This was an improvement over the 1791 report which showed only 1,345 men and a vacancy of 511. Phelipe Treviño and Francisco Bouligny, Report of the Regiment, New Orleans, September 21, 1791, AHN, ESTADO, leg. 3898.

ment, and am unable to cover even the most essential posts." [62] The lack of troops varied during 1796 from 426 to 460.[63] Although the Louisiana Infantry Regiment had sent recruiting teams to Mexico with the offer of bonuses to men enlisting for up to eight years' terms, the results were not satisfactory. Mexico offered its troops better pay and other privileges; clearly, Louisiana represented to many a hardship post. If the recruitment produced more than seventy troops a year, it was considered remarkable. Unfortunately, these men took the first opportunity to desert and flee through the wilderness by land back to their homes in Mexico. Offal of the prisons; rejects from the Cuban and Havana regiments; men vicious and disposed to murder, larceny, and desertion—these were the replacements for those of the Louisiana Regiment whose period of enlistment had expired.[64]

By 1799, the number of troops in the Louisiana Regiment had shrunk to 1,166; the regular regiment had a constant lack of between 600 and 700 troops.[65] Although reinforced by detachments of the Mexican Infantry Regiment and Mexican dragoons, Gayoso's total military strength, including the Mexican, Louisiana, and militia troops, amounted to 4,708.[66] The only bright point in the

[62]Carondelet to Gayoso, New Orleans, September 16, 1796, AGI, PC, leg. 23.

[63]Carondelet to Gayoso, New Orleans, August 8, November 6, 1796, January 19, 1797, *ibid.*; Carondelet's statement of the force, New Orleans, December 1, 1796, AGI, PC, leg. 178-b.

[64]Gayoso to Saavedra, No. 6, New Orleans, April 21, 1799, AGI, SD, leg. 2638; Bouligny to Carondelet, No. 526, New Orleans, March 22, 1796, AGI, PC, leg. 33.

[65]Account of Gilberto Leonard, New Orleans, February 4, 1800, AGI, SD, leg. 2638, covering the year 1799; statement of the troops for February-April, 1799, enclosed in Bouligny to Santa Clara, No. 252, New Orleans, May 1, 1799, AGI, PC, leg. 1502-a; Gayoso to Santa Clara, No. 173, New Orleans, July 19, 1798, AGI, PC, leg. 1501-b; statement of force in 1798, enclosed in Gayoso to Santa Clara, No. 173, July 19, 1798; and LeBlanc's statement enclosed in Bouligny to Santa Clara, No. 208, New Orleans, March 30, 1799, AGI, PC, leg. 1502-a. The 1797 reports are enclosed in Gayoso to Santa Clara, No. 102, New Orleans, AGI, PC, leg. 1501-a.

[66]Gayoso to Álvarez, No. 4, New Orleans, July 10, 1799, AGI, PC, leg. 179-a; review of the Mexican Regiment, February 8, 1799, AGI, PC, leg. 160-a; review of the Mexican dragoons, November 9, 1799, AGI, PC, leg. 160-a; review of the second battalion of Mexican troops, San Carlos, August 6, 1799, AGI, PC, leg. 161-a.

dismal picture was the annual saving of almost $76,000 in payroll expenses![67]

Conditions in the Louisiana Infantry Regiment left much to be desired, but in some ways their lot was better than that of their American counterparts. A Spanish private earned almost $7 a month; an American, $3. The Spanish captains and their American equals received $40 per month. A royal order of 1790 raised the pay of soldiers serving in the provinces, but many considered themselves underpaid.[68]

However there were certain advantages for those soldiers seriously interested in the military life. They enjoyed the *fuero militar*, that is, a military court instead of a civil one to judge criminal and civil cases. They received the regular premiums given to those whose "continuous duty" without discharge, desertion, or stain on their records entitled them to additional monthly stipends. For example, a sergeant who had completed five hitches, or twenty-five years, was granted an additional monthly pay of ninety reals, or $17.50. Soldiers who had served three five-year terms received between six and nine reals extra each month.[69] Officers were entitled to the *Monte Pío*, a type of pension fund for the widows and orphans of those officers who qualified. A pension for disabled veterans and continued reduced salaries for those officers who took their discharges after a certain period of service were additional privileges.[70]

[67]Gayoso to Santa Clara, No. 22, Confidential, New Orleans, February 17, 1799, AGI, PC, leg. 1502-b.

[68]Salary statement, New Orleans, June 9, 1790, Miscellaneous Spanish Documents, New Orleans Public Library, I, 88; Gayoso's statement of American salaries, 1798, AGI, PC, leg. 2371; petition of Pedro Foucher, New Orleans, March 31, 1797, enclosed in Carondelet to Álvarez, No. 26, April 30, 1797, AHN, ESTADO, leg. 3900.

[69]An example was Fernando Lisoro, first sergeant in the Louisiana Regiment; see his reward, San Ildefonso, August 18, 1785, AGI, PC, leg. 161-b. Those who earned prizes did not always live up to them: Simon Baquero, a soldier in the Louisiana Regiment, was granted a prize of seventy-five cents a month, but never collected it because he deserted from his Illinois post on April 28, 1799, AGI, PC, leg. 161-a. On the *fuero militar*, see Lyle McAlister, "The Reorganization of the Army of New Spain, 1763–1767," *HAHR*, XXXIII (February, 1953), 25–27, and *The "Fuero Militar" in New Spain, 1764-1800* (Gainesville, Florida, 1957).

[70]The regulations for the Monte de Piedad, Madrid, 1761, and amended January 1, 1796, together with matrimonial regulations of 1742 and 1749, are

A regular school was maintained by the regiment for its cadets in which qualified instruction was provided in mathematics and military subjects. One of Gayoso's duties was to supervise examinations on an annual basis and approve the remarks made by the colonel of the regiment.[71]

Even though he had all the best intentions of improving the quality of the Louisiana Regiment, Gayoso was not successful. Ellicott wrote that "nine tenths of the officers of the Louisiana regiment are at this time corrupted and the officers of the Mexican regiment which is now in this country are but little better." [72] Cases involving one soldier killing another, especially at Pensacola where the dregs of the Regiment were stationed, were quite common. Even the threat of hanging failed to deter the murderers.[73] Gayoso was forced to order the arrest of Captain Juan Bautista Macarty in a dispute over proper discipline.[74] Lieutenant Antonio Palao spent most of his time under arrest for various infractions.[75] Even the cadets lacked discipline. Carlos D'Aunoy drew his sword in an

---

printed in Enrique de Ocerín, *Índice de los expedientes matrimoniales de militares y marinos que se conservan en el Archivo General Militar, 1761–1865* (Madrid, 1959), 662–81. This volume gives a partial list of the petitions of officers in Louisiana requesting permission to come under the provisions of the *Monte Pío* when they married.

[71]Gayoso to Santa Clara, No. 140, New Orleans, May 20, 1798, AGI, PC, leg. 1501-a. Some of the commandants of the cadet school were Tomás de Acosta 1773–1774), Josef de la Peña (1774–1777), Francisco Paula Morales (1793), and Ignacio Fernández de Velasco (1794–1795).

[72]Ellicott to Secretary of State (Pickering), Natchez, November 14, 1798, in Mathews, *Ellicott*, 162.

[73]Gayoso to Santa Clara, No. 131, New Orleans, April 30, 1798, AGI, PC, leg. 1502-a; Gayoso to Santa Clara, No. 192, New Orleans, September 26, 1798, *ibid.*, 1501-b, with draft of Santa Clara's answer of November 28, 1798.

[74]Macarty to Gayoso, New Orleans, April 14, 1798, AGI, PC, leg. 215-a. The Macartys, a prominient Creole family, seemed to be involved in numerous disputes on occasion. Luis Macarty's notorious behavior in 1796, when he sought to force his affections on the young daughter of one of his friends (although Luis was married and the father of grown sons at the time), caused Carondelet to jail him. Gayoso attempted to arrange a reconciliation between Luis and his estranged wife. *Supra*, Chapter VIII, note 75; Pontalba to his wife, New Orleans, 1796, in *Pontalba's Journal, passim.*

[75]Palao's petition, New Orleans, December 11, 1803, AGI, PC, leg. 70-b; Bouligny to Santa Clara, No. 236, New Orleans, April 20, 1799, AGI, PC, leg. 1502-a, with enclosures.

altercation at a New Orleans billiard parlor, and the other officers of the regiment testified in his behalf at the courts-martial held in 1792.[76] Captain Juan Antonio Bassot, a German from Lorraine who had been in the Spanish army since 1779, was an erratic officer and thought nothing of plunging into the wilderness to tackle thousands of miles of travel when he was under orders to go by water directly to his new post. Accused of lunacy, he was finally discharged from the service with a monthly pension of $15, but not before he had almost plunged the Spaniards into a war with the Choctaws over stealing their property.[77]

The officers of the Louisiana Regiment were extremely jealous of matters such as their rights of seniority, and Gayoso was often forced to decide complaints that one officer had been promoted out of turn.[78] Even more serious was the attempt of a number of Creole officers to resign or transfer out of Louisiana. Captain Marcos de Villiers had opposed two justices of the peace sent to arrest his young Negro slave for a minor misdemeanor. This incident developed into a major issue when the other Creole officers took Villiers' part as a *cause de corps*. Gayoso blamed the matter on a lack of discipline. The illness of the regiment's colonel, Francisco Bouligny, enabled the officers to act in an insubordinate way. He should be replaced with Lieutenant Colonel Carlos Howard, an able officer from Ireland whom Gayoso supported.[79] Gayoso also rec-

---

[76]The trial is in AGI, PC, leg. 206. Although Gayoso was not involved, the case is mentioned as being typical of the high morale of the Creole officers who cooperated so well when one of them was accused of any crime and of the wildness of certain young members of the regiment. See also the Bishop's report of high living and licentiousness in the regiment. Luis to Eugenio Llaguno, New Orleans, November 1, 1795, BN, vol. 19,509, folios 24–27.

[77]Bassot's pleas are contained in a large *expediente*, AGI, PC, leg. 1659. On his disputes and career, see his service sheet and pay sheets, AGI, PC, legs. 161-a, 538-b; Carondelet to Las Casas, No. 6, New Orleans, March 20, 1797, AGS, Guerra Moderna, leg. 6927; Carlos Howard and Gayoso to Santa Clara, No. 151, New Orleans, June 6, 1798, AGI, PC, leg. 1501-b; Carondelet to Las Casas, January 26, 1795, AGI, PC, leg. 1443-b; Gayoso to Santa Clara, No. 164, New Orleans, July 19, 1798, AGI, PC, leg. 1501-b.

[78]Balderas' petition [Ignacio Balderas, Adjutant Major of the Third Battalion], San Carlos de las Barrancas, March 12, 1798, enclosed in Gayoso to Santa Clara, No. 179, New Orleans, July 19, 1798, AGI, PC, leg. 1501-b.

[79]The interesting career of Carlos Howard is sketched in Holmes, "Some Irish Officers in Spanish Louisiana," 240–43.

ommended the appointment of Maximiliano de St. Maxent as com-
mander of the notoriously rebellious Third Battalion at Pensacola.
In the event that properly qualified officers were not available,
Gayoso suggested that high-ranking European brass be brought to
Louisiana to infuse new life into the sagging morale and discipline
of the provincial troops and officers.[80]

Gayoso's old nemesis, Vicente Folch y Juan, was commandant at
Pensacola, and soon a dispute developed between the two officials.
A proud Asturian, Joseph Noriega, with a distinguished career at
Pensacola, including the post of major of the town and garrison,
had been imprisoned by Folch. Gayoso ordered him released. There
developed a split in the officers and men, some siding with Folch,
and others, including the quartermaster, with Gayoso. As usual,
the dispute was submitted to the captain-general. Gayoso wrote
that Folch was too independent, that he lacked proper military
discipline and subordination. His actions at Pensacola threatened to
provoke the people into rebellion. "Folch," Gayoso concluded,
"has always put difficulties in the way of executing what I've
ordered him to do, even in matters where he is obviously my subordinate." [81]

For all its defects and failings, the Louisiana Regiment was
Gayoso's first line of defense against an invading army; and he
never questioned its loyalty. When a royal order of 1798 asked
all loyal Spaniards to contribute what they could in a voluntary
subscription to help Spain prosecute the war against her enemies,
Gayoso found the officers of the Louisiana Regiment were as

[80]Juan Gautier to Carlos Howard, New Orleans, September 21, 1798, AGI,
PC, leg. 215-b; Gayoso to Santa Clara, No. 16, Confidential, New Orleans,
July 28, 1798, AGI, PC, leg. 1502-b, and draft of Santa Clara's answer of
November 22, 1798.

[81]Gayoso to Santa Clara, No. 175, New Orleans, July 30, 1798, AGI, PC,
leg. 1501-b; service sheet of Noriega, AGI, PC, leg. 30; Gayoso to Santa Clara,
No. 125, New Orleans, April 26, 1798, AGI, PC, leg. 1501-a; Folch to
Santa Clara, Pensacola, August 18, 1798, AGI, PC, leg. 154-a; Gayoso to Santa
Clara, No. 18, Confidential, New Orleans, October 3, 1798, AGI, PC, leg.
1502-b; No. 143, May 20, 1798, AGI, PC, leg. 1501-a; No. 162, March 27, 1798,
AGI, PC, leg. 1501-b. Both Folch and Noriega had subsequent conflicts over
jurisdiction, the former with Carlos Howard, and the latter with Governor
José Callava. Howard to Marqués de Someruelos, Guanabacoa, May 18, 1810,
AGI, PC, leg. 1659; Duvon C. Corbitt, "The Last Spanish Census of Pensacola,
1820," *Florida Historical Quarterly*, XXIV (July, 1945), 31–32.

willing as ever to make sacrifices. The governor-general set an example by offering $700 in behalf of his two sons, Manuel Gayoso Hopman and Fernando Gayoso Watts, and himself. Other officers gave as much as $2,388 in all for the New Orleans area; cadets, non-commissioned officers, and soldiers gave another $1,927. Even the people of Louisiana offered their jewelry, cows, tobacco, and other produce in recognition of the joys of living under Spanish rule—and because it was probably very expedient to do so. The lists of contributors were published, thus shaming those who had not given.[82]

The people of Louisiana also demonstrated their loyalty by joining the militia units. The free mulattoes and free Negroes of New Orleans formed four companies of infantry and two of grenadiers.[83] Carondelet's reorganization of the militia from 1792 to 1796 resulted in a full regiment of German Coast militia, a battalion of New Orleans militia, an artillery company in the capital, a corps of Mississippi volunteers, and a legion of militia taken from the Mississippi River posts. In addition, each post had its own militia units. Gayoso alerted the militia in 1798, and many pledged that they would "shed their last drop of blood in defense of their King and God." Most planters, however, were not willing to fight except to defend their homes during attack. They felt that militia drill in New Orleans during harvest season was not in their best interests.[84]

Gayoso spent much time approving the service sheets on each

[82]Royal order of May 27, 1798, read to the New Orleans cabildo, Minutes, IV, No. 3, 16–17; royal order of June 20, 1798, in French, AGI, PC, leg. 215-a, copy enclosed in Saavedra to Gayoso, June 26, 1798, AGI, PC, leg. 2354; it is printed in Billon (ed.), St. Louis, 288–93. A list of those furnishing gifts from Missouri is in Houck (ed.), History of Missouri, II, 62; those from Avoyelles, listed by commdt. Joseph Joffrion, July 25, 1799, AGI, PC, leg. 215-b; the effect of the proclamation, in Morales to Cayetano Soler, No. 320, New Orleans, July 25, 1799, AGI, SD, leg. 2546; Gautier's lists of officers and men of the regiment who gave money to the cause, New Orleans, April 10, 1799, AGI, PC, leg. 160-a; Gayoso's gifts and pledges, in Morales to Soler, July 25, 1799; Gilberto Leonard's receipt, New Orleans, December 3, 1799, in causa mortuoria of Gayoso, AGI, PC, leg. 169.
[83]Luis deClouet's lists, New Orleans, May 1, 1801, AGI, PC, leg. 160-a; Casa-Calvo to Someruelos, New Orleans, June 30, 1801, AGI, PC, leg. 70-a.
[84]Andrés Bega to Gayoso, Valenzuela, March 6, 1798, AGI, PC, leg. 215-b; service sheets of the various militia units, AGI, PC, leg. 1501-a, 161-a; Archivo de Simancas, Hojas de servicios de América (Valladolid, 1958), 340.

officer of militia. His task was made more difficult with the death of Andrés Almonester y Roxas on April 25, 1798. Almonester had been the colonel of the militia battalion of New Orleans; and to replace him the governor-general recommended Pedro Marigny, "the richest, most prominent and one of those most addicted to the Spanish cause in these Provinces."[85] Gayoso also appointed new militia officers and raised some in rank. Philip Hicky was made a captain in the Feliciana militia;[86] Antonio Patricio Walsh was made a captain in charge of one of the naval vessels defending the mouth of the Mississippi.[87]

In 1797, Gayoso sent Vicente Fernández to Veracruz in the corvette, *La Luisiana*, for the purpose of obtaining gunpowder, flints, and firearms. He predicted he would need 10,000 rifles for the militia and regular troops under his command. Most of his requests to the captain-general at Havana were turned down because Gayoso's superior did not have any munitions to spare.[88]

Not only large details, but the small ones too occupied the attention of Gayoso as commander-in-chief of the regular troops, militia and galley squadron. There were petitions for retirement to be scrutinized and recommendations to be made. Widows claimed benefits under the pension fund, and Gayoso was forced to make his suggestions. The governor-general was the middleman in most military matters, acting between his officers and men and the captain-general. The appointment of military commandants, promotion of officers, retirement decisions, recommendations for advancement, the examination of cadets, the recommendation for rewards for regulars and militia alike, the filling of vacancies in the officers' ranks, and the disposition of forced convict labor at the military presidios—these multifarious military duties were minor in

[85]Gayoso to Santa Clara, No. 145, New Orleans, May 20, 1798, AGI, PC, leg. 1501-a; No. 146, same date, *ibid.*

[86]Appointment of Felipe Hicky by Gayoso, New Orleans, December 24, 1798, Hicky Papers, Louisiana State University.

[87]Appointment of Patricio Antonio Walsh by Gayoso, New Orleans, February 21, 1798, Walsh Papers, Louisiana State University.

[88]Gayoso to Santa Clara, No. 181, New Orleans, July 30, 1798, AGI, PC, leg. 1501-b; Azanza to Saavedra, No. 230, Mexico, January 5, 1799, AGI, SD, leg. 2638; Gayoso to Vicente Fernández Texeiro, New Orleans, August 22, 31, 1797, drafts, AGI, PC, leg. 131-a

nature, but their performance consumed the bulk of Gayoso's time.[89]

In a larger sense, however, it was not the military aspect of Gayoso's command upon which the security of Louisiana depended. The conflict brewing between France and the United States was primarily diplomatic, and the defense of Louisiana in the final analysis would depend on the solution to that question. On the one hand, France continued to press Spain for the retrocession of Louisiana by stating the argument that the best security of Mexico lay in France's firm control of the Mississippi Valley.[90]

On the other hand, the role of Spanish minister to the United States, Carlos Martínez de Irujo, was to offset the growing English influence on the Federalist government. When William Cobbett, an English immigrant who published *Peter Porcupine's Gazette*, printed an attack on Irujo as "another Quixote," the Spanish minister sued the editor and ultimately ruined him. Secretary of State Pickering, a staunch Federalist who leaned toward England, engaged in diplomatic duels with Irujo over the Liston-Blount matter in 1797, and the split between the Federalists and Republicans the following year placed the Spanish minister in another embroglio.[91]

These disputes in Philadelphia were reflected in Natchez, where the Federalist governor, Winthrop Sargent, arrived in 1798 to take control of the Mississippi Territory. Conditions in Natchez following the evacuation of the Spaniards in March left much to be

---

[89]Regulations governing the leaves of militiamen were the same as those for the Cuban militia, as supplemented by royal orders of October 6, 1786, and December 9, 1788. Gayoso to Santa Clara, No. 82, New Orleans, January 23, 1798, AGI, PC, leg. 1501-a. Documents relating to Gayoso's multifarious duties include the following: Gayoso to Santa Clara, Nos. 151, 156, 182, 84, 85–90, 93, 139–142, 116, 118–119, 92, 97, 195–196, 202, 149, 152, with the following respective dates: June 6, July 19, 30, January 23, May 20, April 17, January 23, September 26, 27, 1798, in AGI, PC, legs. 1501-a, 1501-b, 1502-a; Gayoso to Lauretat Sigur, New Orleans, April 17, 1798, AGI, PC, leg. 215-a.

[90]Frederick Jackson Turner (ed.), "Correspondence of the French Ministers to the United States, 1791–1797," American Historical Association *Annual Report, 1903* (2 vols.; Washington, 1904), II, 1010–96; E. Wilson Lyon, *Louisiana in French Diplomacy, 1759–1804* (Norman, Oklahoma, 1934), 94–98.

[91]*Supra,* Chapter VII, note 18; some of the correspondence between Pickering and Irujo was published in the Philadelphia *Aurora,* July 6, 14, 15, and 26, 1797. An interesting account of the dispute and its effects is in Henry J. Ford, "Timothy Pickering," *The American Secretaries of State and their Diplomacy,* ed. Samuel Flagg Bemis (10 vols.; New York, 1927), II, 221–27.

desired. Lawlessness and anarchy prevailed as Colonel Anthony Hutchins and the Green clan attempted to take control of the nascent government before Sargent's arrival. Even after the new governor took the reigns of government, Hutchins and Green continued to trouble the Federalists.[92] President John Adams issued a plea for harmony, particularly with the Spaniards on the frontiers.[93]

Unfortunately, Governor Sargent was little disposed to promote this harmony. He advised Pickering of how a large force of American volunteers might be recruited in Tennessee, Kentucky, and the Northwestern Territory (where Sargent had served as secretary to the governor). In the event that Spain ceded Louisiana back to France, Sargent felt that the Indians and Creoles, aided by their Negro slaves, would make life difficult for the Americans, an eventuality Sargent would avoid by invading Louisiana first.[94]

Sargent arrived in Natchez quite ill and he recovered slowly in Gayoso's home, Concord. It was some time before he recovered sufficiently to use common courtesy in thanking Gayoso for the use of his residence and to court the rich widow of David Williams.[95] One of the first matters to come to Sargent's attention was the movement of Zachariah Cox, a filibustering agent of a land speculation company who was arrested and confined in Natchez. Wilkinson and Sargent both warned Gayoso of Cox;

[92]Information on conditions in Natchez during 1797 is in the numerous, detailed, inside reports from Minor to Gayoso, Natchez, August-December, 1797, AGI, PC, leg. 2371; Ellicott to Secretary of State Pickering, Natchez, Camp, September 12, 24, 1797, Southern Boundary, I, which includes various enclosures on Hutchins and the committees that sought power in Natchez; Ellicott's September 24 letter is also printed in Carter (ed.), *Territorial Papers of the United States, V: Mississippi*, 3–15; cf. *Papers in Relation to the Official Conduct of Governour Sargent*, 5–19 and *passim*.

[93]T. H. Cushing to Gayoso, Mulberry Vale, near Natchez, July 22, 1799, AGI, PC, leg. 2371.

[94]Winthrop Sargent to Secretary of State Pickering, Natchez, September 18, 1798, in Rowland (ed.), *Mississippi Territorial Archives*, I, 46–49.

[95]Gayoso to Minor, New Orleans, September 6, 1798, Gayoso Papers, Louisiana State University; Minor to Gayoso, Boundary Line, Thompson's Creek, October 24, 1798, AGI, PC, leg. 215-a. Mary McIntosh Williams, heiress to Pine Grove and Belmont plantations, was married to Sargent by Judge Pedro Bryan Bruin in a surprisingly swift courtship that had tongues wagging in Natchez.

but when the adventurer escaped, Gayoso declined to return him to American territory.[96]

Gayoso was not opposed to entering into an agreement with the governor or with American military authorities regarding the mutual return of deserters or criminals. He wrote Minor, "I shall always be ready to do any thing from which good may result to our respective Countries." [97] As a temporary expedient, subject to reversal by the Spanish crown, Gayoso signed an agreement with Governor Sargent regarding the mutual return of escaped slaves, criminals, and filibusters.[98]

The problem of desertion plagued both Gayoso and Wilkinson. Sailors and soldiers alike welcomed the opportunity to flee from their assignments into the wilderness of the Mississippi Valley. Carondelet had forwarded the revised regulations concerning desertion and the penalties imposed in 1794, but the stiffer penalties did little to dissuade desertion. By 1797, Irujo issued a new decree, based on royal instructions of November 25, 1796, offering amnesty to all deserters who reported within six months to a qualified Spanish consul. Francisco Bouligny wished to know how to treat those deserters captured by the Americans in Natchez and returned to Gayoso.[99]

[96]Minor to Gayoso, Boundary Line, Thompson's Creek, October 4, 1798, AGI, PC, leg. 215-a; Sargent to Gayoso, Natchez, September 28, 1798, in Rowland (ed.), *Mississippi Territorial Archives*, I, 51–53; Gayoso's passport to Cox, New Orleans, October 31, 1798, Louisiana, Miscellaneous MSS., Library of Congress; Pickering to Sargent, Philadelphia, December 10, 1798, in Carter (ed.), *Territorial Papers of the United States, V: Mississippi*, 53–54; Isaac Joslin Cox (ed.), "Documents relating to Zachariah Cox," *Quarterly Publications in History and Philosophy Society of Ohio*, VIII, 31–114; Whitaker, *Mississippi Question*, 114; Abernethy, *The South in the New Nation*, 159–60.

[97]Gayoso to Minor, New Orleans, January 22, 1798, Gayoso Papers, Louisiana State University.

[98]Sargent to Gayoso, Natchez, September 28, 1798, March 14, April 15, 1799, in Rowland (ed.), *Mississippi Territorial Archives*, I, 50 ff.; minutes of the New Orleans cabildo, 1798, IV, No. 3, 21; Sargent to Gayoso, Natchez, March 14, 1799, AGI, PC, leg. 2371; a reciprocal extradition of slaves, strayed cattle, etc., was signed by Enrique White and James Seagrove, at St. Augustine, May 19, 1797, copy enclosed in Irujo to Godoy, No. 78, Philadelphia, August 16, 1797, AHN, ESTADO, leg. 3896 *bis*.

[99]Documents relating to Spanish deserters are Bouligny to Santa Clara, No. 214, New Orleans, April 20, 1799, AGI, PC, leg. 1502-a; Carondelet to Gayoso, New Orleans, March 31, April 14, 1795, AGI, PC, leg. 22; Santa Clara to

Nor did the Spaniards have a monopoly on desertion. In 1801 William R. Booth sent a list of deserters from the American army to the Spanish governor-general.[100] Pope's impressment of American troops found in Natchez before the evacuation has already been mentioned.[101] In February, 1799, therefore, Gayoso and Major General Lovell of the United States signed an agreement concerning the mutual return of deserters, and this agreement was extended by Gayoso the following month.[102]

In leaving Minor in command at Natchez, Gayoso maintained an important listening post. Any hostile intentions of American troops were quickly reported to New Orleans. Moreover, Gayoso expressed a continued, almost paternal interest in what the people of Natchez did and how they felt toward their new government. Although Wilkinson and Governor Sargent attempted to bribe Minor with on offer of command in an American regiment, Gayoso was happy to report that Minor had refused.[103]

Gayoso watched the arrival of General George Mathews and Judge Arthur Miller in 1797 with some suspicion. Both were implicated in the Yazoo land grants of 1795, which the Georgia legislature had approved for land speculation in the Natchez District. Gayoso met Mathews in New Orleans and learned of his mission,

Gayoso, Havana, November 21, 1797, AGI, PC, leg. 1501-a; No. 200 of Gayoso to Santa Clara, New Orleans, September 26, 1798, AGI, PC, leg. 1501-b, and draft answer of Julián de Campos (Auditor de Guerra of Cuba), December 6, 1798; Proclamation of Carlos Martínez de Irujo, Philadelphia, March 25, 1797, published in the Philadelphia *Aurora*, April 10, 1797; amnesty decree, January 2, 1793, AHN, ESTADO, leg. 3895; Cornel to Urquijo, March 24, 1800; Urquijo to Humphreys, March 26, 1800; and Humphreys to Urquijo, March 28, 1800, *ibid.*, leg. 3892.

[100]AGI, PC, leg. 217; Booth's list of deserters, February 11, 1801, AGI, PC, leg. 2372.

[101]*Supra*, Chapter VII, note 36.

[102]Gayoso to Santa Clara, No. 24, Confidential, New Orleans, February 26, 1799, AGI, PC, leg. 1502-b; Gayoso to Wilkinson, New Orleans, April 15, 1799, draft, AGI, PC, leg. 215-b; Louis Lorimier to deHault deLassus, Cap Girardeau, March 4, 1801, AGI, PC, leg. 2372; Sargent to Wilkinson, Natchez, March 25, 1799, in Rowland (ed.), *Mississippi Territorial Archives*, I, 121-22; Holmes, "The Two Series of the *Moniteur de la Louisiane*," 327-28.

[103]Gayoso to Santa Clara, No. 24, Confidential, New Orleans, February 26, 1799, AGI, PC, leg. 1502-b.

but the Spaniard refused to allow the American to verify the limits of the company lands.[104]

Most activities in Natchez, from the appointment of the militia companies to the description of the American loyalty oath and the popular reaction thereto, were reported fully to Gayoso by Joseph Vidal, Gayoso's former secretary who was appointed consul at Natchez following the evacuation. Vidal's encounters with the irascible Captain Isaac Guion almost precipitated his expulsion from Natchez on several occasions; but when he did leave, it was to take command of the Spanish post opposite Natchez at Concordia.[105]

Gayoso was always on good terms with Wilkinson, and the American's appointment as commander of the army seemed to portend favorable results for the old Spanish dream of disrupting the United States by persuading the Western states to secede and form an independent nation under Spain's protection. Despite Thomas Power's arrest by Wilkinson, Gayoso was convinced this action merely was a cover for the general's growing intrigues. The Federalists suspected Wilkinson's relations with the Spaniards and sent spies to watch his movements, so his arrest of Power might have been to cover his own tracks. Furthermore, with the passage of the Alien and Sedition Acts designed to preserve waning Federalist power in the American government, Kentucky and Virginia both issued strong statements of protest. Kentucky's resolutions were tantamount to nullification, and Gayoso gleefully predicted final success in the eleven-year-old "Spanish Conspiracy" if he could only receive enough funds to utilize the dissatisfaction.[106]

[104]Gayoso to Santa Clara, No. 8, Confidential, New Orleans, December 18, 1797, AGI, PC, leg. 1502-b.
[105]Vidal's instructions from Gayoso, New Orleans, January 19, 1798, AGI, PC, leg. 154-a; Vidal to Gayoso, Natchez, August 24, 1797, AGI, PC, leg. 48; Vidal to Gayoso, Natchez, June 20, 1798; Guion to Vidal, June 20, 1798; Vidal to Gayoso, No. 20, Natchez, July 10, 1798, all in AGI, PC, leg. 1502; Vidal to Gayoso, Natchez, October 8, 10, 11, 1798, copies in Gayoso to Azanza, Confidential, New Orleans, October 20, 1798, AGN, Historia, tomo 334; Sargent to Secretary of State Pickering, Natchez, September 18, 1798, in Rowland (ed.), *Mississippi Territorial Archives*, I, 46–49; Sargent to Gayoso, Natchez, June 13, 1799, *ibid.*, 152–53. A biographical sketch is in Holmes, "Algunos gallegos notables en la Luisiana española," 119–20.
[106]Vidal to Gayoso, Natchez, October 8, 1798; Gayoso to Azanza, October 20, 1798.

While he maintained friendly relations with Wilkinson and invited him to New Orleans to talk matters over, Gayoso was still suspicious of the man's long-range plans. Vidal had reported a rumor that Wilkinson had bragged to his friends at Fort Massac, "I hope things go as they probably will, that this winter I will establish my headquarters in New Orleans." [107] Gayoso was never persuaded that Wilkinson had any but personal ambitions, but he sought throughout the long and stormy history of the intrigues with the Americans to utilize their ambitions to further Spanish aims.

Wilkinson also introduced Philip Nolan to Gayoso. This redoubtable Irishman, one of the most skillful horsewranglers on the Spanish-American frontier, had been one of Wilkinson's friends and agents. Receiving a letter of introduction to Gayoso from Wilkinson, he proposed a speculation scheme to the Spanish governor still at Natchez. If Gayoso would approve a passport and permission to ship $100,000 worth of goods into Texas, Nolan would split the immense expected profits fifty-fifty. Gayoso played along until he learned of Nolan's true designs and plans. Nolan had demonstrated his true loyalties by poking fun at the Catholic religion and warning Ellicott against the Spaniards in 1797.

Nolan learned of Gayoso's dislike and wrote, "a vile man and my implacable enemy" was the governor-general, "I may yet be obliged to shoot the monster with a poisoned arrow." [108] But it was the governor-general who got in the first shot. On June 10, 1799, while Nolan was in Texas with a passport from the Baron de Carondelet, Gayoso wrote to the viceroy and governor of Texas to capture Nolan and imprison him where he would never be seen again. When the Spaniards finally cornered Nolan near present-day Waco, in March, 1801, a gunfight ensued and Nolan was killed by a cannonball.[109]

[107] Vidal to Gayoso, October, 8, 1798.
[108] Nolan to Wilkinson, Natchez, July 21, 1797, in Wilkinson, *Memoirs,* II, appendix, document 2.
[109] The author is presently engaged in writing Nolan's biography. On his activities with Gayoso, see Nolan to Gayoso, Natchez, March 13, 14, 1797, AGI, PC, leg. 213, and Yale University, photostats in the University of Texas; Gayoso to Nolan, Natchez, April 1, 1797, in King, "The Real Philip Nolan,"

Ellicott had written that Gayoso was one of the few Spanish officers never "concerned in traffick, nor in the habit of taking doceurs."[110] But the governor-general wrote that he had spent $13,000 of his own money in dining and wining people at Natchez during the 1794 visit of Prince Edward, the Duke of Kent, and in creating the festivities at New Orleans honoring the Duke of Orleans and his retinue. To avoid expense to the crown in reimbursing him for these expenses, Gayoso suggested he be permitted to send a vessel to Veracruz loaded with 300 tons of merchandise, but pay only the customary duties on the cargo. "I am not in favor of a similar speculation, but it would be desirable to extend this privilege to the merchants of New Orleans and would also help the people of Veracruz who had been denied imports due to the war."[111]

Another speculation project also concerned Gayoso in 1798. Minor suggested that, with $3,000 capital, they could make a profit of $50,000 in five years. Everything depended on having a stable government in Natchez and a friendly government at New Orleans. The nature of the speculation, which Ellicott discovered the following year, involved General Wilkinson and Joseph Collins too. The proposal was to use the rich grasslands across the Mississippi as pasture for beef and pork livestock and then sell animals to the Americans, particularly the military organization.[112]

New Orleans was a hotbed of intrigue, particularly during the Franco-American dispute. Because so many ships were taken on the high seas as prizes and brought to New Orleans for sale and dis-

---

99; Ellicott's *Journal*, 29–30, 35; Gayoso to Pedro de Nava, New Orleans, June 10, 1799; Nava to Azanza, Chihuahua, September 26, 1798; Azanza to de Nava, Confidential, Mexico, September 2, 1798; and Muñoz to de Nava, No. 547, San Antonio, Sept. 4, 1797, Archivo Histórico de Sonora, Hermosillo (Mexico).

[110]Ellicott's *Journal*, 216.

[111]Gayoso to Prince of Peace, No. 18, Confidential, New Orleans, April 18, 1798, AHN, ESTADO, leg. 3900.

[112]Minor to Gayoso, Natchez, January 20, 1798, AGI, PC, leg. 215-b; Gayoso to Minor, New Orleans, January 10, October 23, November 29, 1798, Gayoso Papers, Louisiana State University; Ellicott to Pickering, Pensacola, June 18, 1799, Southern Boundary, III; Jacobs, *Tarnished Warrior*, 186; list of duties on livestock sent from Texas to Louisiana in 1796, Bernardo Fernández to Cristobal de Córdoba, Nacogdoches, January 9, 1796, Bexar Archives, University of Texas.

posal, France demanded a consular agent in the Spanish port. Trubuc, an agent from St. Domingue, was sent on orders from General Hedonville and the French Directorate to New Orleans to collect the 12.5 per cent duty on prizes taken by French corsairs in Louisiana and the Floridas.[113]

The United States also sought to send consular agents to New Orleans. In 1797 President Adams and Secretary of State Pickering wanted Oliver Pollock's son, Procopio Jacinto, named; but the first vice-consul for New Orleans was William Empton Hulings, a former resident of the Crescent City and onetime merchant. He had a commission from President Adams and the secretary of state dated March 19, 1798. In accordance with the Treaty of San Lorenzo, which permitted American consuls at New Orleans, Gayoso approved the appointment.[114]

Another consul was Daniel Clark, Jr., nephew of the influential Natchez planter, who was an intimate friend of Governor Gayoso. Clark was not officially approved, however, until 1802; and during the interim, his place was taken by Evan Jones. Jones, originally from New York, settled in West Florida in 1775 but later joined the Spanish German Coast militia and served as commandant of La Fourche de Chetimachas until 1798. His consular appointment was dated May 11, 1799, but his official recognition by Francisco Bouligny in New Orleans was delayed until approval came from the captain-general.[115]

The general duties of these American consuls and vice-consuls were to protect American commercial rights. Accordingly, they were active in furthering the growing Philadelphia–New Orleans trade that had grown from a trickle to a torrent by 1800. Clark,

---

[113]Trubuc to Gayoso, Havana, November 14, 1798, AGI, PC, leg. 215-a.
[114]Gayoso to Ellicott, New Orleans, March 14, 1798, Southern Boundary, II; Gayoso to Santa Clara, No. 185, New Orleans, September 26, 1798, AGI, PC, leg. 1501-b; Carmelo Richard Arena, "Philadelphia-Spanish New Orleans Trade" (Ph.D. dissertation, University of Pennsylvania, 1959), 107.
[115]Arena, "Philadelphia-Spanish New Orleans Trade," 117–19; C. Richard Arena, "Philadelphia-Spanish New Orleans Trade in the 1790's," *Louisiana History*, II (Fall, 1961), 436–42; Daniel Clark, Jr., to (Minor), New Orleans, January 30, 1798, AGI, PC, leg. 2371; Pickering to Sargent, Philadelphia, December 10, 1798, in Carter (ed.), *Territorial Papers*, V: *Mississippi*, 52–55; Whitaker, *Mississippi Question*, 323, n. 30.

a vigorous partisan, suggested equal duties for American and Spanish ships in New Orleans and the relaxation of Spanish commercial restrictions. Clark was also active in exposing the intrigues of General Wilkinson and, so involved in Louisiana politics did he become, that his opposition to Governor William C. C. Claiborne resulted in a duel.[116]

Gayoso attempted to cooperate with these consuls and to further commercial privileges, for he realized that the future safety and prosperity of Louisiana depended on sound economic and political relations with the United States. Throughout his two years as governor-general he continued to prepare military defenses to the best of his limited means, while at the same time conducting those necessary diplomatic relations with his neighbors which would obviate the necessity of using force to preserve Louisiana for his sovereign.

[116]Gayoso to Santa Clara, No. 187, New Orleans, September 26, 1798, AGI, PC, leg. 1501-b; Questions of Clark, January 30, 1798, AGI, PC, leg. 2371; Isaac Joslin Cox, "Daniel Clark," *Dictionary of American Biography*, IV, 125.

CHAPTER X

Fin del Siglo

As THE SUMMER of 1799 came with its heat waves and recurrence of fever, Gayoso was barely aware that his fate, like that of Louisiana, was rapidly reaching the destiny decreed. The end of the eighteenth century brought with it the end of Louisiana's Spanish dominion. Through three stormy decades, dedicated governors had grown weary with the Herculean task of governing the vast, polyglot provinces and receiving little reward for their efforts. Gayoso was the seventh governor-general of Louisiana. But he was not the last, even though Spain had lost most of her power in the Mississippi Valley long before Gayoso died.[1]

General Wilkinson paid a visit to Gayoso in June, and unkind

[1]Gayoso's predecessors were Antonio de Ulloa, Alexander O'Reilly, Luis de Unzaga y Amezaga, Bernardo de Gálvez, Esteban Miró, and the Baron de Carondelet. He was succeeded by the Marqués de Casa-Calvo and Manuel Juan de Salcedo. While some historians, including A. P. Nasatir, claim O'Reilly was *not* governor of Louisiana, his official communications use the term "gobernador," and O'Reilly's biographers call him that.

gossips wagged their tongues about the known beverage-holding prowess of the two. But Wilkinson sailed from New Orleans for Philadelphia in early July.[2] On July 18, at five o'clock, Gayoso died from a malignant fever, probably the well-known yellow fever which had ravaged New Orleans since 1793. Careless writers have concluded that, since Gayoso died following his parties with Wilkinson, he was debilitated by the debauch and died as a result.[3] Wilkinson's own grandson pointed to the fallacy of this statement: "It is the first time that I ever heard of a malignant fever resulting from a convivial celebration." [4] The end came suddenly—as in most cases of yellow fever—and Gayoso barely had enough time to draw up his will and receive the last rites of the Church before succumbing. On July 19 he was interred beneath the altar of St. Louis Cathedral, though no plaque today commemorates his last resting place.[5]

The cabildo met on July 19 to elect the governors ad interim. Francisco Bouligny, the colonel of the Louisiana Infantry Regiment and highest ranking military officer in the colony, assumed the command of military aspects of Gayoso's late government, while Dr. Nicolás María Vidal, the military judge advocate and lieutenant-

[2]Wilkinson arrived in New Orleans on June 4, 1799; two days later he became ill and moved in with Gayoso. Gayoso to Saavedra, No. 20, New Orleans, June 9, 1799, AHN, ESTADO, leg. 3901. He left during the first week in July. Knoxville *Gazette*, August 7, 1799; Jacobs, *Tarnished Warrior*, 189. Gayarré, *History of Louisiana, The Spanish Dominion*, 405, repeats the rumor that Gayoso died of a drinking bout or its effects. This story is repeated by Royal Ornan Shreve, *The Finished Scoundrel* (Indianapolis, 1933), 105–06; and John R. Spears and A. H. Clark, *A History of the Mississippi Valley* (New York, 1903), 389.

[3]All official reports of Gayoso's death give "malignant fever" as the cause. Francisco Bouligny to Pedro de Nava, New Orleans, August 8, 1799, draft, AGI, PC, leg. 70-a; Morales to Saavedra, No. 320, New Orleans, July 25, 1799, AGI, SD, leg. 2546, and also in Spanish MSS., Mississippi Valley, New Orleans, IV, 336–37. William C. C. Claiborne to James Madison, near New Orleans, December 17, 1809, in Carter (ed.), *Territorial Papers of the United States*, IX: *Orleans*, 860.

[4]James Wilkinson, "General James Wilkinson," *Louisiana Historical Quarterly*, I (September, 1917), 103.

[5]Gayoso's will, dated July 18, 1799, is in the New Orleans Notarial Archives, Pedesclaux, I, folios 612–15; and in his *causa mortuoria*, 1799, AGI, PC, leg. 169. His death certificate telling of his burial on July 19 in St. Louis Cathedral is in the Burial Archives of that building, folio 67.

governor, assumed the political command. Both were soon replaced by Sebastián Calvo de la Puerta y O'Farrill, Marqués de Casa-Calvo.[6]

Even in death Gayoso was not free from the vituperative attacks of Morales. The intendant wrote that Gayoso had died hopelessly in debt, "impoverished by a life spent in extravagant living." He added, "With the product of some slaves and household effects, the only possessions that he had because of his natural propensity to spend, there is hardly enough to pay off the expenses of 2,000 pesos . . . he was advanced in March, 1797, . . . the commissioner of limits expenses . . . and [the] 700 pesos . . . offering and patriotic loan. . . ."[7] As was customary with military and civil officials who died in office, Gayoso's property was inventoried and then sold at public auction. His assets totaled $12,121.44, while his debts exceeded $16,574.[8]

Gayoso's father-in-law, Stephen Watts, wrote that Gayoso died considerably in debt and that his widow's income was very small, but enabled her to live decently.[9] In 1804, prior to her remarriage to Captain James Stille, Gayoso's widow complained about her poverty-stricken condition in asking that her pension be continued following the Spanish evacuation of Louisiana.[10]

On the other hand, Gayoso had possessed considerable holdings of real estate at Natchez and Baton Rouge. Concord was worth at

[6]Holmes (ed.), *Documentos de la Luisiana,* 371 n; Bouligny to Pedro de Nava, draft, New Orleans, August 8, 1799; minutes of the New Orleans cabildo, July 19, 1799, IV, 46.

[7]Morales to Cayetano Soler, No. 320, July 25, 1799.

[8]Compiled from the sale of his estate and documents in the *causa mortuoria.*

[9]Stephen Watts to [unknown correspondent], New Orleans, October 28, 1799, Coles Papers. She drew only $333.25 per year, and that was cut by one-third to pay off some of Gayoso's debts. Statement of Benigno García Calderón, Pensacola, September 1, 1815, AGI, PC, leg. 147-a.

[10]Petition of Margarita Watts, New Orleans, June 6, 1804, Kuntz Collection, Tulane University. Mention of her remarriage, as well as a dispute in 1830 between Fernando Gayoso, son of the governor-general, and his stepbrothers, is in the family history, Cole papers. St. Landry Parish Probate Court Records, Opelousas, Louisiana, transcript furnished by Winston DeVille. When the Spaniards evacuated Louisiana in 1805, Margaret Watts Gayoso Stille was granted permission to remain in Louisiana. Statement of Andrew López Armesto, New Orleans, July 30, 1805, in Carter (ed.), *Territorial Papers of the United States,* IX: *Orleans,* 486–87.

least $10,000, although the widow Gayoso sold it for a mere
$5,000. In addition, Gayoso had held a thousand acres near the
fort of Baton Rouge.[11]

The best description for the emotion Gayoso's subordinates felt
for him is hero-worship. Two humble servants told Vahamonde, the
gallego who commanded Baton Rouge, that they would follow
Gayoso to hell if necessary.[12] The often insincere Wilkinson was
quoted as saying if one of his arms were cut off, he would embrace
Gayoso with the other.[13] Perhaps the reasons for this loyalty lay
in Gayoso's impartiality and keen sense of justice. To Gabriel Cerré,
who had written for special privileges, Gayoso answered, "The
immutable principles of justice, as well as the great interest I
take in you, do not permit me to pronounce a decision other
than that which will be communicated to you officially. . . . The
public servant must never let his affections or sentiments in a personal friendship . . . interfere with his duty to equity and impartiality." [14]

When he was able to give promotions and benefits to those
who served him well, Gayoso always pointed out that this recognition was based on the merit of the recipients. When he promoted
Carlos deHault deLassus to the post of lieutenant-governor of
Illinois, he wrote, "Your promotion to Illinois is due to your own
self, as well as of the high opinion I have of your abilities." [15]
To Stephen Minor, with whom he had an almost Damon-Pythias
relationship, he wrote, "I feel all your difficulties, but I likewise rely

[11]Natchez Court Records, Land Claims, Book B, 364, 634; *American State
Papers*, Class VIII: *Public Lands*, III, 466; Land survey by Carlos Trudeau,
February 10, 1797, Louisiana Miscellaneous Documents, Library of Congress;
Grand-Pré to Morales, Baton Rouge, December 29, 1805, Louisiana Territorial
Papers, National Archives, Record Group 59. A survey of the lands held
by Gayoso and their proximity to the Baton Rouge fort is in AGI, Planos,
Luisiana y Floridas, No. 229.
[12]Vahamonde to Gayoso, Baton Rouge, March 6, 1792, AGI, PC, leg.
47.
[13]Quoted in Whitaker, "Gayoso," *Dictionary of American Biography*,
VII, 202.
[14]Gayoso to Cerré, New Orleans, April 25, 1798, Gabriel Cerré Papers,
Missouri Historical Society, St. Louis.
[15]Gayoso to Carlos deHault deLassus, New Orleans, March 2, 1799, Gayoso
Papers, *ibid.*

on your abilities; I know that you are fitt for the task, a task that will be productive of the greatest satisfaction to you & family, . . . & now that I have the means I shall be proud in making the world sensible of the justice that is due to an officer of merit." [16]

Gayoso was no paragon of virtue, however, and he often quarreled with his subordinates and complained of his equals to his superiors. His dispute with Pedro Favrot, temporarily commander of the troops at Natchez in 1793, resulted in Favrot's recall to New Orleans; but when Favrot lost his son in 1797, Gayoso was one of the first to send a letter of condolences, signing it, "a friend and your servant." [17] On the other hand, when Gayoso found a lack of subservience to his will, he could be as unbending and firm as the rocky hills of Galicia. Juan María Perchet, Vicente Folch y Juan, and Joaquín de la Torre found the governor as unyielding as they were stubborn.

While at Natchez Gayoso used his plenary powers to cut corners of administrative inefficency and to slice yards of red tape from the often time-consuming aspects of judicial procedure. At no time did he seem to forget why he was sent to America. He was a royal servant, dedicated to the proposition that the people of his jurisdiction would show their loyalty to the crown in proportion to the fairness, protection, and continued concern which the governor demonstrated toward them. Dr. James White was able to inform Gayoso that the people of Natchez lamented their loss when he went to New Orleans and called him their "father & their friend." [18] Another resident looked back on halcyon days of Spanish rule under Gayoso: "The mind, paternal rule of the good Governor makes an old man revert with pleasure to the scenes of his youth, and even at times to regret the change of government." [19]

Andrew Ellicott had come to Natchez with a large chip on his shoulder, convinced that all Spaniards, and especially Gayoso, were

---

[16]Gayoso to Minor, New Orleans, September 25, 1797, Gayoso Papers, Louisiana State University.

[17]Gayoso to Favrot, New Orleans, August 7, September 25, 1797, Favrot Papers, V, 92, 97–98.

[18]James White to Gayoso, Natchez, October 4, 1798, AGI, PC, leg. 142-a.

[19]George Willey, "Natchez in the Olden Times," in Claiborne, *Mississippi*, 527.

evil men, depraved by dishonesty and corruption. During his year at Natchez he helped launch a revolt against Gayoso, but withal, learned to admire the proud dignity and *noblesse oblige* of the governor. Before he finished drawing the boundary line Ellicott had come to know and admire Gayoso, if not the government he represented. When he heard of his death, Ellicott wrote:

> We received an account of the death of the late Governor General Gayoso, which I then, and yet consider a great loss to our western citizens concerned in the Mississippi trade, to whom he paid particular attention, and who frequently partook of that hospitality, for which he was so highly esteemed. As the Governor of an arbitrary monarch, he was certainly entitled to great merit, and it appeared in an eminent degree to be his pride, to render the situation of those over whom he was appointed to preside, as easy, and comfortable as possible, and in a particular manner directed his attention to the improvement of the country, by opening roads which he considered the arteries of commerce. He was educated in Great Britian, and retained in a considerable degree the manners, and customs, of that nation until his death, especially in his style of living. In his conversation he was easy and affable, and his politeness was of that superior cast, which showed it to be the effect of early habit, rather than an accomplishment merely intended to render him agreeable. His passions were naturally so strong, and his temper so remarkably quick, that they sometimes hurried him into difficulties, from which he was not easily extricated. It was frequently remarked of him as a singularity, that he was neither concerned in traffick, nor in the habit of taking doceurs, as was too frequently the case with other officers of his Catholic Majesty in that country. He was fond of show and parade, which he indulged to the great injury of his fortune, and not a little to his reputation as a paymaster. This fondness for parade showed itself in all his transactions, but in nothing more than the ordinary business of his government, to which, method and system, were too generally sacrificed. In his domestic character he merited imitation: he was a tender husband, an affectionate parent, and a good master. In his correspondence with me relative to the late treaty, it is presumed he was governed by his instructions, and therefore no conclusion ought to be drawn from

that discussion to his disadvantage as a man, and gentleman.[20]

Gayoso's close friend, Stephen Minor, wrote one of the finest
tributes to the late governor:

> It is with the most painful sensations that I read the account
> of the sudden death of our good friend Gayoso. An excel-
> lent and generous heart, a liberal mind, and an enlightened
> understanding, are the qualities that he has carried off
> with him, the loss of which mankind in general must
> lament; and an ardent desire and unremitting ambition to
> promote the prosperity of this colony must make his
> loss the more severely felt by the inhabitants. It is unfor-
> tunate for us that at the moment we began to be con-
> vinced by experience, that he possessed all the qualities we
> can wish for in a Governor, he should be snatched from us.
> And what must add to our grief is the reflection that now
> there is no rampart between us and the oppression of the
> Intendant. I fear that the number of Candidates for the
> Government there are few calculated to make us forget
> our good Governor Gayoso.[21]

Historians who have followed Gayoso's trail have been unani-
mous in their judgment of his ability and resourcefulness. Joseph
Dunbar Shields, who described the history of Natchez, wrote, "He
was raised by his country to high renown, but death claimed him
while yet in the meridian of life. . . . He was a genial man but
in endeavoring to uphold a tumbling power with an impatient
population surging against it, he had a hard task to perform. He
was known never to take bribes, . . . [was] a good master, an
affectionate father and a tender husband. Such a chaplet placed
by history upon a man's character, is worth more than an emperor's
crown." [22]

Arthur P. Whitaker and Irving Leonard both agree that Gayoso
was regarded as the ablest governor Louisiana ever had because

[20]Ellicott's *Journal*, 215–16.
[21]Minor to William Panton, Boundary Line, Chattahoochee River, [August,
1799], originally owned by María de Vargas, New Orleans, copy in Cole
Papers.
[22]Shields, *Natchez, its Early History*, 26.

of his versatility and his penetrating insight into the American character.[23] Ernest Liljegren contrasted Gayoso with Carondelet: "The governor of the district, Manuel Gayoso de Lemos had a perfect command of the English language and was exceedingly popular. He was well educated, gentlemanly, suave, and tactful. In contrast to Carondelet, he was a good judge of human nature. While Carondelet credited every rumor that came to his attention, Gayoso was able to appraise information and people at their proper value." [24]

With these comments it is difficult for any writer to add something to the stature of this remarkable governor. Gayoso experienced many frustrations in his ten years of duty in the Mississippi Valley, but in 1799 he seemed as dedicated and selfless as he was in 1789 when he stepped off the boat at New Orleans. His ten years had witnessed many significant changes in the Spanish-American frontier. Filibusters, invasion threats, and many immigrants had come and gone; but Spain still retained its hold on Louisiana. Few governors faced more challenges, and none accomplished more.

If he failed to make loyal Spaniards out of the Anglo-Americans of Natchez, he at least succeeded better than a later generation of Mexicans would do with the restless settlers of Texas. Gayoso might have succeeded in his mission had he received the continued support of the Spanish ministers. Had the predictions of Miró, Carondelet, and Gayoso been heeded, Spain would not have yielded control of the Mississippi and the Natchez District. Few responsible officials recognized the relationship between Natchez and Lower Louisiana; fewer still knew that the security of Louisiana was the key to Mexico's future.

As an administrator Gayoso was able to appoint dedicated men to positions of importance. It is no accident that the leaders in the Mississippi Territory and the prominent gentlemen who drew up the Louisiana constitution had been trained in the Spanish service. Gayoso had a major part in appointing many of them. Although he personally expressed his doubts about the anarchical nature of

[23]Whitaker, *Spanish-American Frontier,* 82; Irving Leonard, "A Frontier Library, 1799," *HAHR,* XXIII (February, 1943), 23.
[24]Liljegren, "Jacobism in Spanish Louisiana," 79–80.

democratic politics, in his own political practices he showed a belief in representative government. Paternal republicanism characterized his entire career in the Mississippi Valley.

His military abilities were never given the acid test of battle or campaign, but his belief in a strong defense perhaps prevented a showdown. Under his vigorous leadership forts rose in the valley, staffed by loyal militia and protected by his pet squadron. The friendship of the Indians—a most vital factor in the Spanish-American struggle for the Mississippi frontier—was assured to Spain as long as men like Gayoso could sit and smoke the pipe of peace, give the Indians generous gifts, and prevent Spanish settlers from moving onto Indian hunting lands.

As a municipal planner, Gayoso was far ahead of his time. Believing in zoning, sanitation, highways, fire protection, and the maintenance of law and order he laid the foundations of four cities by his progressive regulations for the governments of New Orleans, Natchez, Nogales, and San Fernando de las Barrancas. Moreover, by permitting the establishment of new settlements at Hopefield, Concordia, New Feliciana, and elsewhere in the province, he could be considered the greatest town planner of his day. In all these actions he did not use arbitrary powers which, by law, he possessed. When making laws, he called together the leading inhabitants and asked their opinions. If the laws needed strengthening, Gayoso called the inhabitants together again and asked for their recommendations. On occasion the settlers would petition Gayoso for regulations, but more often than not, Gayoso would shift the responsibility back to the people.

While maintaining Spanish dignity and honor in difficult times, Gayoso never neglected opportunities to promote friendly relations with his neighbors. He corresponded with governors of the Northwestern and Southwestern Territories and proposed to make voyages to seek friendly relations with his neighbors. With courage and energy Gayoso performed his duties to the best of his ability. Because his abilities were superlative, he was able to accomplish much at Natchez and New Orleans.

For many years it has been popular to wave the "black legend" flag of Spanish cruelty and incompetence. Amos Stoddard, who took possession of portions of Louisiana from Spanish commandants, wrote, "The Spanish history, in particular, for more than two centuries, affords nothing but a series of complicated crimes, the black catalogue of which will continue to excite in every breast, the mingled emotions of pity and indignation." [25] It is fortunate that Gayoso's remarkable career can be placed against this charge. If a large weight were needed to balance the scales of justice, the distinguished, selfless, and dedicated years of service performed by Manuel Gayoso de Lemos would undoubtedly fill the bill.

[25]Stoddard, *Sketches, Historical and Descriptive of Louisiana*, 55.

APPENDIX

Genealogical and Heraldic Notes

SOURCES

Unpublished

Gayoso de Lemos, Manuel. Family Tree. Original MS owned by Mrs. C. Grenes Cole, Gayoso's great-great-granddaughter, New Orleans.

Gayoso's last will and testament, New Orleans, July 18, 1799, New Orleans Notarial Archives, Notary Pedesclaux, I, fols. 612–15; and in the *causa mortuoria*, 1799–1801, AGI, PC, leg. 169.

Gayoso's baptismal certificate, Nostra Senhora de Asunção (Sé Catedral), Oporto, Portugal, June 21, 1747, original in Arquivo do Distrito do Porto (Portugal), fol. 205. A certified copy is in Gayoso's request for permission to marry, 1797, in the Archivo General Militar de Segovia.

Gayoso's *expediente matrimonial*, 1797, in Archivo General Militar de Segovia.

Gayoso's death notice, July 19, 1799, St. Louis Cathedral Archives (New Orleans), Register 4 of Deaths, fol. 67.

Gayoso's marriage and baptism of his son, records, December 10, 1797, *ibid*.

Baptismal and marriage records of the parishes of San Bartolomé de Pontevedra and Santa María de Pontevedra, Galicia, Spain.

Francisco Gayoso de Lemos to Conde de Fernán Núñez, Oporto, March 24, 1787, Archivo Histórico Nacional (Madrid), ESTADO, leg. 4516–2.

Familia Gayosso. Photo-copies of an unidentified manuscript on the genealogy of the Gayoso family, given the author by a descendant of Gayoso, José Mancebo Benfield, in 1959, Mexico City.

List of Passengers leaving Cádiz, September 4, 1788, Archivo General de Indias, Sección de Contratación, leg. 5532.

Pay records of Gayoso, AGI, PC, leg. 538-a

St. Landry Parish Territorial Records, Louisiana State Archives and Records Commission.

St. Landry Parish Probate Court Records, Opelousas, No. 63, Fernando Gayoso v. Heirs of Margaret Watts, Widow James Stille.

Cole Papers. Genealogical Records, correspondence, and family records belonging to Mrs. C. Grenes Cole of New Orleans.

Published

Arthur, Stanley Clisby, and George Campbell Huchet de Kernion (eds.). *Old Families of Louisiana.* New Orleans, 1931.

Holmes, Jack D. L. "Gallegos notables en la Lusiana," *Cuadernos de Estudios Gallegos,* Fascículo LVII (1964), 103–110.

———. (ed.). *Documentos inéditos para la historia de la Luisiana, 1792–1810.* Madrid, 1963.

Leonard, Irving A. "A Frontier Library, 1799." *Hispanic American Historical Review,* XXIII (February, 1943), 21–51.

Lemos, Pedro de. "Don Manuel Gayoso de Lemos, Founder of the City of Natchez." Natchez (Mississippi) *Democrat,* Pilgrimages Edition (March, 1942).

Points, Marie Louise. "Gayoso de Lemos." *The Daily Picayune* (New Orleans), November 20, 1892.

Whitaker, Arthur P. "Gayoso de Lemos, Manuel." *Dictionary of American Biography.* New York, 1928–1936. VII, 201-02.

GENEALOGY

1. *Gregorio Vázquez Gayoso* (1). Born San Martín de Sendaban. Married *María Albenes* (2), who was born in Santiago de Compostela. Their son was *Bartolomé* (3).

2. *Bartolomé Gayoso y Albenes* (3). Born in Santiago de Compostela. Achieved degree of *licenciado* in the university. Married

María Arindez (4), who was born in Caldas. Their son was *Antonio* (5).

3. *Antonio Gayoso y Arindez* (5). Born in Santiago de Compostela. Died June 1, 1650. Married *María de Castro* (6) of Caldas. Their son was *Joseph Francisco* (7).

4. *Joseph Francisco Gayoso de Castro* (7). Married at San Andrés (Santiago de Compostela), October 15, 1669, to *Ana* (8), widow of Sr. *Castro y Aldao*. Their son was *Benito* (9).

5. *Benito Gayoso y Aldao* (9). Born October 30, 1677. Married on May 3, 1701, in Bueu, to *Doña Balthasara de la Rua Freire y Mondragón* (10). She was the daughter of *Joseph de la Rua y Freire* (11), a natural son of *Don Fernando de la Rua* (12), as declared in October, 1697; and of *María Larinta Verosides de Castro y Mondragón* (13), who was born at San Lorenzo de Pousada, January 7, 1658, and married there on October 19, 1682. The son of *Benito* and *Balthasara* was *Andrés Manuel* (14).

6. *Andrés Manuel Gayoso de la Rua Freire* (14). Born at San Martín de Bueu, October 30, 1701. He was married to *María Luisa Rosa de Lemos y Figueroa* (15), who was born at San Bartolomé de Pontevedra, October 19, 1706, the daughter of unmarried parents, *Benito de Lemos y Figueroa* (16), and *María Martínez de Casal* (17). *Benito* (16) was born at San Bartolomé de Pontevedra, December 26, 1674, the son of *Francisco de Lemos* (18), and *Thomesa Figueroa* (19). *Francisco* (18) was born in Pontevedra on May 5, 1644. *Thomesa* (19) was born at San Bartolomé de Pontevedra on January 25, 1650, and was married at San Bartolomé on February 16, 1670. *María* (17) was evidently married to a man named Acuña. She had been born at San Bartolomé de Pontevedra on April 26, 1676, the daughter of *Domingo Martínez* (20), who was born at San Martín de Salzedo, on April 1, 1652, and was married at San Bartolomé de Pontevedra on November 4, 16–, to *María Antonia de Casal* (21), who was born at San Bartolomé on April 9, 16–. The son of *Andrés* (14) and *María* (15) was *Manuel Luis* (22).

7. *Manuel Luis Gayoso de Lemos y Sarmiento* (22). Born and baptized at Santa María de Pontevedra, August 30, 1721. Served many years as Spanish consul-general at Oporto, Portugal. Died there on March 16, 1787. Married to *Theresa Angelica de Amorín y Magallanes* (23), a native of Oporto, who died prior to 1799. Children included *Francisco* (24), who was also consul at Oporto and later a member of the diplomatic corps in Madrid before becoming a governor of a Spanish province

not identified. *Francisco's* son, *Domingo* (26), married *Josefa Corona* (27), and their succession was established in Mexico and Guatemala. Another son of *Manuel* (22) and *Theresa* (23) was *Manuel* (25).

8. *Manuel Gayoso de Lemos y Amorín y Magallanes* (25). Born in Oporto, Portugal, May 30, 1747. Died in New Orleans, July 18, 1799. Married three times.

   A. Married first to *Theresa Margarita Hopman y Pereira* (28), a native of Lisbon. Married in Lisbon *c.* 1787. Children were *Manuel* (31) and *Henriqueta* (32). *Theresa* (28) died at Natchez, September 3, 1790.

   (1) *Manuel* (31) born in Lisbon *c.* 1788. Left with maternal aunt to be raised: *María Hopman y Pereira.* Later raised by an uncle in Italy, known to be a merchant. Among his descendants are *Pedro de Lemos* (33), late director of Stanford's University Art Museum and author of a biographical sketch of his ancestor, *Manuel* (25).

   (2) *Henriqueta Gayoso y Hopman* (32), born during voyage from Cádiz to New Orleans, 1788–1789. Died as an infant in Natchez, *c.* 1790.

   B. Married second to *Elizabeth Watts* (29), daughter of *Stephen Watts* (34), and *Frances Assheton Watts* (35), born in Philadelphia, May 4, 1773. Married at Natchez on April 23, 1792. She died there in July, 1792, without issue.

   C. Married third to *Margaret Cyrilla Watts* (30), fifth child of *Stephen Watts* (34) and *Franches Assheton Watts* (35), born at Belmont Plantation, Natchez District, March 23, 1775, and baptized at La Fourche, Louisiana, in October, 1785. Married soon after marital contract signed on January 14, 1796. Officially blessed matrimony by Bishop of Louisiana, Luis Peñalver y Cárdenas, at St. Louis Cathedral, New Orleans, December 10, 1797. Their only child was *Fernando* (36). *Margaret* (30) married second Captain *James Stille* (37), by whom she had as children, *Frances Telle* (38), who married *Joshua Baker* (39); *Caroline* (40), who married *John Brownson* (41); and *Sarah* (42), who married *Abner Pride* (43). Three sons, *James* (44), *Lewis* (45), and *Edward* (46), died young or without issue.

9. *Fernando Gayoso de Lemos y Watts* (36). Born at Natchez, July 14, 1797, and baptized by Bishop Luis Peñalver y Cárdenas at St. Louis Cathedral, New Orleans, December 10, 1797. Died at Natchitoches, January 14, 1837. Married twice. First

wife, *Julia Ann Wikoff* (47); and second wife, *Victoria Lodoiska Pérez* (48).

A. Married first, *Julia Ann (Juliana) Wikoff* (47), daughter of *William Wikoff* (49), who was not married at the time of her birth. She died in Opelousas in 1823. He was a native of Monmounth County, New Jersey, who migrated to Natchez in 1788. He was married in 1791 to *Susanna Watts* (50), the daughter of *Stephen Watts* (34) and *Frances Assheton Watts* (35). *Susanna* (50) was born on April 4, 1771. Children of *Fernando* (36) and *Julia Ann* (47) who were married at Baton Rouge in 1816, were as follows:

(1) *Elizabeth* (51), who was born in 1817 and died at Baton Rouge in 1819.

(2) *Manuel* (52), who was born at Baton Rouge in 1819 and died at Natchitoches on November 27, 1835.

(3) *James* (53), who was born on September 20, 1821, and died at Natchitoches, July, 1839 without issue.

B. Married second, *Victoria Lodoiska Pérez* (48) at Baton Rouge, June 17, 1825. She was born in New Orleans, April 7, 1807, the daughter of *Manuel Cyrillo Pérez* (54) and *Marie Madeleine Felicité Toutant-Beauregard* (55). *Manuel Cyrillo* (54) was the son of Lieutenant Colonel *Manuel Pérez* (56), of the Louisiana Regular Infantry Regiment, and of *Jeanne Dubois* (57). *Marie Madeleine Felicité* (55) was born on April 8, 1782, and died on June 26, 1817. She married *Manuel* (54) in New Orleans on June 24, 1801. She was the daughter of Captain *Elías Toutant-Beauregard* (58), of the Louisiana Regular Infantry Regiment, who was born in New Orleans on June 17, 1759, and who was married to *Marie Felicité Durel* (59), daughter of *Jean Baptiste Durel* (60), and of *Cecile LeBrun* (61); *Marie* (59) married in 1782, and she died at Baton Rouge, December, 1809. *Victoria* (48) died at Houma, October 7, 1887. Her children were *Caroline* (62), *Marguerite* (63), *Aurora Pepita* (64), *Fernando* (65), and *Felicité Toutant-Beauregard* (66).

(1) *Caroline* (62), born 1826, died on September 7, 1826.

(2) *Marguerite* (63), was born at Opelousas, May 31, 1828, and baptized there on August 18, 1829. She married on May 2, 1845, *Merrit Moore Robinson* (67), of Norfolk, Virginia, who died at Pascagoula, Mississippi, on May 28, 1850. They had two children: *Anne Amelia Robinson* (68), and *Manuel Gayoso Robinson* (69), both

unmarried. *Marguerite* (63) died in New Orleans on August 14, 1867.

(3) *Aurora Pepita Gayoso de Lemos* (64), was born August 20, 1831, and died September 19, 1882. She married *Thomas Benton Hart* (70) of Lexington, Kentucky, who died in San Antonio, Texas, on January 8, 1875. Six children formed matrimonial alliances with the Froneberger, Prescott, and West families, the last two of whom were from Waco and Houston, Texas.

(4) *Fernando Gayoso de Lemos* (65), born at St. Martinville, Louisiana, October 6 or 9, 1833, died in Dallas, Texas, April 9, 1906. He married on January 18, 1871, in Quitman, Texas, *Silphia Sunedrecker* (71). Their eight children married into the Frazer, Leath, Huber, Hyskell, Kammann, and Gowen families.

10. *Felicité Toutant-Beauregard Gayoso de Lemos* (66), the daughter of *Fernando* (36) and *Victoria* (48), was born at Natchitoches, Louisiana, on February 1, 1836, and died in New Orleans, on December 31, 1917. She was married in Terrebonne Parish, on August 28, 1856, to *Charles Tennent* (72). He was born at Seafold, Delaware, on March 4, 1822, the son of *John Tennent* (73) and *Sarah Polk Hooper* (74). *Charles* (72) was a lieutenant in General John Coffee's division at the Battle of New Orleans in 1815. Their children were *Mary Pérez* (75), *Jennie Lodoiska* (76), and *Fernando* (77).

   A. *Mary Pérez Tennent* (75) died unmarried.

   B. *Fernando Tennent* (77) died unmarried.

11. *Jennie Lodoiska Tennent* (76) married *Robert Ruffin Barrow* (78), who was born on Residence Plantation, Houma, Louisiana, on February 28, 1858, and died on Roberta Grove Plantation at Houma, on March 24, 1926. Their children were as follows:

   A. *Volumnia Hunley Barrow* (79), who died young.

   B. *Robert Ruffin Barrow* (80), who died young.

   C. *Irene Felicité Barrow* (81), unmarried.

   D. *Zoé Gayoso Tennent Barrow* (82), wife of Dr. *Robert S. Topping* (85), who died in 1939.

   E. *Jennie Tennent Barrow* (83), who married Dr. *Harris Pickens Dawson* (86), and is a resident of Montgomery, Alabama.

   F. *Hallette Mary Tennent Barrow* (84), who married Dr. *Christian Grenes Cole* (87) of New Orleans.

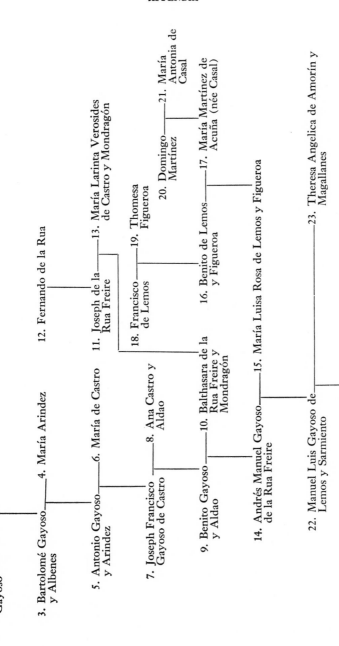

1. Gregorio Vázquez Gayoso ——— 2. María Albenes

3. Bartolomé Gayoso y Albenes ——— 4. María Arindez

5. Antonio Gayoso y Arindez ——— 6. María de Castro

7. Joseph Francisco Gayoso de Castro ——— 8. Ana Castro y Aldao

9. Benito Gayoso y Aldao ——— 10. Balthasara de la Rua Freire y Mondragón

11. Joseph de la Rua Freire ——— 12. Fernando de la Rua / 13. María Larinta Verosides de Castro y Mondragón

14. Andrés Manuel Gayoso de la Rua Freire ——— 15. María Luisa Rosa de Lemos y Figueroa

16. Benito de Lemos y Figueroa ——— 17. María Martínez de Acuña (née Casal)

18. Francisco de Lemos ——— 19. Thomesa Figueroa

20. Domingo Martínez ——— 21. María Antonia de Casal

22. Manuel Luis Gayoso de Lemos y Sarmiento ——— 23. Theresa Angelica de Amorín y Magallanes

25. Manuel Gayoso de Lemos y Amorín y Magallanes

HERALDRY[1]

The de Lemos family

There are various legends and facts surrounding the de Lemos family, of which Manuel Gayoso de Lemos was a distinguished descendant. An early account refers to the Roman invasion of Spain during the second, third and fourth centuries before Christ. When the Romans established the town of *Lucus* (now Lugo) in Galicia, two of the forty-eight Roman judges brought to this area were of the family of "de Leimus." When the Roman legions withdrew, the de Leimus family hispanicized their name and remained to continue their popular and liberal rule. Many old Spanish maps of the sixteenth century show a section of Galicia marked "Territory of de Lemos." The patronymic home, Montforte de Lemos, produced one of Spain's leading colonial administrators in Peru, Pedro Antonio Fernández de Castro, Tenth Count of Lemos.[2]

The heraldry of the de Lemos family consists of a shield of silver, surmounted by thirteen blue discs.[3] The source of this heraldry is interesting; it varies considerably from the Spanish accounts to the more inaccurate "legends" about Gayoso de Lemos heraldry in the United States. During the Moorish occupation of Galicia it was customary for the Galician nobles to provide their masters with an annual tribute of fifty of their more comely daughters. At one point, the nobles of Galicia joined forces and refused to pay the tribute. Moreover, they rescued fifty of their daughters and returned them to their homes. In recognition of this valorous and chivalrous deed, the shields of those who had participated in the campaign were emblazoned with marks of the encounter. This heraldric reward extended to the families of Figueroa, Somoças, Mirandas, Quiros, and de Lemos. The last received a shield surmounted by thirteen blue circles or discs on a silver background, in memory of the thirteen young girls rescued by the de Lemos nobles from the Moors.[4] One of the earliest nobles of this family was the Conde de Amarente, Alonzo López de Lemos.[5]

[1]This information on Gayoso's heraldry is based on Galician sources and not on imaginative or suggestive American accounts.

[2]Guillermo Lohmann Villena, *El Conde de Lemos, Virrey del Perú* (Madrid, 1946), 1–17; Pedro de Lemos, "Don Manuel Gayoso de Lemos," Natchez *Democrat*, Pilgrimages Edition, March, 1942, 10, 12.

[3]José S. Crespo Pozo, *Heráldica de Galicia* (Santiago de Compostela, 1957), 339.

[4]Fray Felipe de la Gándara, *Armas i triunfos, hechos heróicos, de los hijos de Galicia* (Madrid, 1662), 62. Cf. Pedro de Lemos, "Don Manuel Gayoso de Lemos," 10; heraldry of Gayoso, MS, in possession of Mrs. C. Grenes Cole of

The Gayoso family

Like the de Lemos family, the Gayosos belong to a branch of the house in Lugo, Galicia, and originate, apparently, from the descendants of Pedro López de Lugo, a royal official in the service of Alfonso XI. The small village of Gayoso is the patronymic center of the family with an ancient chapel located amid the rolling farmsteads. The Gayoso family is one of the oldest in Galicia. One of its distinguished members, Alfonso de Gayoso, comendador of Estriana, a member of the Royal Order of Santiago, and governor of the city of Sienna, was a hero of the Italian wars. In the Battle of Pavia, where he fought as a captain, he was captured by French troops under Francis I and imprisoned. Upon his release, he returned to Spain where he commanded a section of Spanish troops at Tunis and died at Valladolid. His brother, Juan de Gayoso, served with Carlos V with distinction, and later fought for Pope Clement VII. He endowed the hospital of the city of Santiago de Compostela in Galicia. Descendants of the Gayosos served as members of the Santa Oficio or Holy Inquisition. The family was intimate with royalty and served the various monarchs in numerous capacities. The lord of the villiage of Ocá, Don Andrés de Gayoso, married Doña Constanza Arias Ozores Lemos y Ulloa, another distinguished family of Galicia.[6] Among the distinguished correspondence of the eighteenth century, the name Gayoso appears often.[7]

Contrary to what has appeared in print about the Gayoso coat of arms in the United States,[8] the central shield of his coat of arms does *not* represent his wife's family, but rather, the Gayoso arms, and appears on the ancestral home in Rajó in Galicia.[9]

New Orleans, upon which was based the account in Stanley Clisby Arthur and George Campbell Huchet de Kernion (eds.), *Old Families of Louisiana* (New Orleans, 1931), 280–81.

[5]Gándara, *Armas i triunfos*, 71.

[6]Ignacio Fernández de Henestrosa Gayoso de los Cobos, *Apuntes para el historial de la Casa de Camarasa* (San Sebastián, 1934), 244–45.

[7]For example, see the *Cartas familiares del P. Joseph Francisco de Isla, escritas á su hermana Doña María Francisca de Isla y Losada y á su cuñado D. Nicolás de Ayala* (2nd ed.; 3 vols.; Madrid, 1790), *passim*.

[8]A most imaginative account is in Arthur and Kernion (eds.), *Old Families of Louisiana*, 280–81.

[9]See my illustration in "Gallegos notables en la Luisiana," *Cuadernos de Estudios Gallegos*, LVII (1964), opposite 105.

Bibliography of Manuscript Sources

CUBA

Archivo Nacional de Cuba (Havana).
1. Sección de Floridas.
   Legajos 2, 11.
2. Reales Cédulas.
   Tomo IX.

FRANCE

Bibliothèque Nationale.
1. Manuscripts Nouvelles. Louisiane.
   No. 9510.
2. Manuscrits espagnoles.
   Vol. 363–64.
3. Cartes de la Louisiane.

Archives Nationales.
1. Collection D'Anville (Maps); Cartes de la Louisiane.
2. Colonies, 13-A, 51.

Bibliothèque, Ministre du Marine (Service Hydrographique).
1. Cartes, Amèrique Septentrionale, Cours d'Eau.
2. Cartes, Amèrique Septentrionale, Cartes Anciennes.

3. Cartes, Amèrique Septentrionale, Canada.
4. Cartes, Cartes Particulières, Etats-Unis.

Archives Etrangères (Foreign Ministry), Etats-Unis, VII.

GUATEMALA

Archivo Nacional de Guatemala (Guatemala).
1. Sección A 1–40.
Legajo 4797.

MEXICO

Archivo General de la Nación (Mexico, D. F.).
1. Sección de Historia.
Tomo 334, 430.

Archivo Histórico de Sonora (Hermosillo).
1. *Expediente* on Philip Nolan.

PORTUGAL

Arquivo do Distrito do Porto, Baptismal Records (Oporto).

SPAIN

Archivo General de Indias (Sevilla).
1. Papeles procedentes de la Isla de Cuba.
Legajos 6, 9, 12–14, 16–18, 21–23, 30–34, 41–43, 47–48, 64, 70-a,
70-b, 102, 108, 110, 113, 116 131-a, 140, 142-a, 147-a, 152, 154-a,
159-a, 159-b, 160-a, 160-b, 161-a, 161-b, 163-a, 169, 170-a, 170-b,
173, 175, 176-b, 177–79-b, 184-a, 187-a, 190, 193-a, 193-b, 195-
96, 198, 200–204, 206, 208, 210–13, 215-a, 215-b, 217, 221-a,
223-b, 481, 533-a, 533-b, 538-a, 538-b, 560, 565, 569, 590,
671, 684, 1304, 1376, 1394, 1440-a–1447-b, 1484, 1501-a–1502-b,
1659, 1839, 2317-a, 2317-b, 2352–55, 2357, 2359–60, 2362–68,
2370–72.
2. Contratación.
Legajo 5532.

3. Audiencia de Santo Domingo.
   Legajos 1145, 2543, 2546, 2553, 2556, 2565, 2588, 2613–15, 2638, 2643.
4. Indiferente.
   Legajo 1344.

Archivo Histórico Nacional (Madrid).
1. Sección de Estado.
   Legajos 3883–3902, 4360, 4402, 4467-I, 4475-I, 4475-II, 4492, 4492 *bis.*, 4516-II, 4537-II, 4541-II, 5549.
2. Consejo de Indias.
   Legajos 20900, 20925, 20927, 21055.

Biblioteca Nacional (Madrid).
1. Sección de Manuscritos de Ultramar.
   Tomos 19,246–48
2. Colección de Documentos para la Historia de Florida (1709–1819).
   Tomos 19,508–09.
3. Sección de Mapas.

Archivo del Servicio Histórico Militar (Madrid).
1. Sección de San Luis de Potosí.
2. Sección de Méjico.
3. Sección de Florida.
4. Sección de Mapas.

Museo Naval (Madrid).
1. Sección de Mapas, Grupo VI, Carpeta A.
2. Manuscritos.
   Tomos 133, 140, 291, 315, 323, 325, 469, 476, 567, 569, 1036.

Biblioteca del Archivo del Ministerio de Asuntos Exteriores.
Tomo 27.

Archivo Municipal de Cádiz (Cádiz).
Actas de Cabildo, Vol. CXLII.

Archivo General Militar de Segovia.
Expedientes Matrimoniales y Hojas de Servicio.

Archivo General de Simancas.
1. Sección Guerra Moderna.
   Legajos 6912–28, 6930–32, 7245, 7291–92.
2. Sección de Mapas.

Archivo y Museo Álvaro y Bazán Marina de Guerra (El Viso del Marqués).
Sección de Indiferente.

ALABAMA

Mobile Public Library.
1. Panton-Forbes Papers.

ARKANSAS

Crittenden County Clerk's Office.
1. Plat Book, Vol. I.

LOUISIANA

Louisiana State University Archives (Baton Rouge).
1. Hicky, Daniel and Philip. Papers. 33 items (1762–1846).
2. Gayoso de Lemos, Manuel. Papers. 3 folders (1792–1805).
3. Remy, Henry. Papers, 2 vols. & 1 item (1799).
4. Walsh, Antonio Patricio. Papers. 4 letters (1798–1799).
5. W.P.A. Survey of Federal Archives in Louisiana. Dispatches of the Spanish Governors. 11 vols.
6. Minor Papers.

St. Landry Parish Records (Opelousas, now in Baton Rouge).

Howard-Tilton Memorial Library (New Orleans).
1. Rosemonde E. and Emile Kuntz Collection.
2. Gayoso papers.

New Orleans Public Library (New Orleans).
1. Census of 1791.
2. Miscellaneous Spanish and French Documents. 4 vols.
3. Records and Deliberations of the Cabildo. 5 vols.

Louisiana State Museum Library (New Orleans).
1. Spanish MSS., Mississippi Valley. 4 vols. (1765–1808).
2. Map Collection.

Cabildo Museum Safe Records (New Orleans).
1. Various records uncatalogued in the Cabildo.

Private Collection of Mrs. C. Grenes Cole (New Orleans).
1. Family records and correspondence of Gayoso.

St. Louis Cathedral Archives: Baptisms, Deaths and Marriages.

MISSISSIPPI

State Department of Archives and History (Jackson).
1. Correspondence of Gayoso to his wife.
2. Mississippi Provincial Archives, Spanish Dominion. 9 vols. (1759–1820).

Natchez Chancery Court
1. Records. 40 vols. (*c.* 1781-1797).
2. Will Book. Vol. I.
3. Miscellaneous Court Records.

MISSOURI

Missouri Historical Society (St. Louis).
1. Pierce Smith Pope Papers.
2. Gayoso Papers.
3. deLassus Papers.
4. Gabriel Cerré Papers.

NEW YORK

New York Public Library.
1. Louisiana, Governors. Dispatches of the Spanish Governors of Louisiana to the Captains-General of Cuba. 30 vols. (1766–1791), photostats.
2. Gayoso's *Bando de Buen Gobierno*, 1798. Photostat, Rare Books Room.

3. Carondelet's Proclamation, May 31, 1797. Photostat.
4. Chalmers Papers, MSS. Collection.

Collection of Lloyd Robertson (private) in New Hyde Park.

NORTH CAROLINA

Department of Archives and History (Raleigh).
1. Transcripts and photostats of Spanish archival material.

TENNESSEE

Gayoso Scrapbook. Formerly owned by Gayoso Hotel, now in the possession of the West Tennessee Historical Society, Memphis.

McClung Historical Collection. Lawson McGhee Library (Knoxville).
1. Transcripts and photostats of Spanish archival material. (18 boxes).

TEXAS

University of Texas (Austin).
1. Bexar Archives.
2. Parsons Collection (Humanities Research Center).

WASHINGTON, D.C.

Library of Congress.
1. Louisiana, Miscellaneous Documents, 1790–1799.
2. Transcripts and photostats from the Archivo General de Indias and the Archivo General de Simancas.

National Archives.
1. Florida Archives, General Records of the Department of State, Record Group 59.
2. Letters of David Humphreys, Madrid, 1797–1799, General Record Group 59.

3. Southern Boundary MSS, U.S. and Spain, Andrew Ellicott, 3 vols., correspondence (1796–1804), Record Group 76.
4. Territorial Papers, Florida, I (1777–1811), Record Group 59.
5. Territorial Papers, Louisiana, I (1796–1812), Record Group 59.

INDEX

structs houses, 206; mentioned, 173, 201, 224, 238, 265n
Gálvez, José de, Marqués de Sonora, 40, 69
Gálvez-Town, 238, 243
Gambling, 62, 127, 204
García, Manuel, 231, 240, 246, 247
García de Fernández, Manuel, 112n
García de Texada, Manuel, 135
Gardoqui, Diego de: Spanish *chargé d'affaires* to U.S., 22; speaks to Dr. James White, 28; ideas on Natchez tobacco, 92n, 95; negotiations with John Jay, 138
Garrard, James, 215
Gates, Horatio, 25
Gautier, Juan, 239
Gayoso de Lemos y Amorín, Francisco, 9, 277-278
Gayoso de Lemos y Amorín, Manuel Luis: arrives at New Orleans, 3, 30-31; birth and early life, 4, 278; early military and diplomatic career, 4-10; appointed governor of Natchez, 10, 26-27, 29-30; fluency in languages, 10, 29, 110, 201; arrives at Natchez, 31, 33; administrative powers, 33-54 *passim*; issues land grants, 34-38; role in "Spanish Conspiracy," 39, 40, 139-40, 175-76, 221, 260-61; interim governor of Louisiana, 40; draws town plans for Natchez, 41-43; establishes town on Cole's Creek, 44-45; urges road construction, 45-48, 270; political theories, 48-49, 52-54, 98; attempts to establish Natchez cabildo, 49-50; organizes Natchez police, 57-58; attempts to check crime, 58-61; judicial functions, 63-68, 84-85; duties towards church, 73-77, 223, 225-26; attitudes towards religion, 78-81, 128-29, 223-27, 228-29; economic policies, 87-89, 264; encourages tobacco culture, 93-96; urges moratorium for planters, 96-99, 129, 189; encourages cattle industry, 101-104; conducts census of Natchez, 114-16; slave holdings, 118; seeks permission to marry, 122-24; style of entertaining, 124-26, 211-13, 222; indebtedness, 125-26, 267; policy towards education, 128-29, 209-210; aids hospital, 132-34; Indian policy, 141-42, 144-61 *passim*, 235-37; suggests naval squadron for Mississippi, 162-

63, 244-46; urges construction of forts, 163-67; forms Natchez militia, 169-71; named as boundary commissioner, 176; opposes Treaty of San Lorenzo, 178-80; learns of Blount Conspiracy, 181; relations with Andrew Ellicott, 183-89, 231-35; commands Fort Panmure during Natchez revolt, 191-94; promoted to brigadier general, 197; named governor-general of Louisiana and West Florida, 198, 200; farewell address to Natchez, 198; conducts *residencia* of Carondelet, 202; issues *Bando de Buen Gobierno*, 203-204; regulates New Orleans city affairs, 205-209; economic policies in Louisiana, 213-15; quarrels with intendant Morales, 216-22; policy towards immigration, 226-29, 243; orders evacuation of Natchez and Nogales, 231-33; supervises 31st parallel point, 233-35; military policies, 237-56 *passim*; relations with Governor Sargent, 257-59; relations with American military officers, 258-59; involved in speculation schemes, 261-62; dies of yellow fever, 266; appraisal of career, 268-74
Gayoso de Lemos y Hopman, Henriqueta, 30, 31, 38, 278
Gayoso de Lemos y Hopman, Manuel, 27, 38, 254, 278
Gayoso de Lemos y Sarmiento, Manuel Luis, 4, 9, 277-78, 281
Gayoso de Lemos y Watts, Fernando, 124, 199, 254, 278-79
Genêt, Edmond, 172
Gil, Andrés, 135
Girault, John, 105, 152
Girod, Claudio Francisco, 208
Godoy Álvarez de Faria Ríos Sánchez y Zaragoza, Manuel de: attitude towards America, 31, 174; praises Gayoso, 150; Prince of Peace for Treaty of Basel, 174; tries to delay execution of Treaty of San Lorenzo, 179; mentioned, 159, 165, 167, 186, 212, 221
Government expenses: for Natchez post, 20; for Natchez church, 73-76; Indian relations, 142n, 154; for Natchez Treaty, 150; on fortifications, 164; for boundary commission, 177, 234n; for defense, 172;

Mardi Gras, 211
Margarita, 245, 246
Marigny, Bernard, 121–22
Marigny, Pedro de, 192*n*, 255
Marmillon, Antonio, 152
Maroteau, Luis, 247
Marriage: royal families of Spain and Portugal, 7–8; Gayoso to Margarita Hopman y Pereira, 27; regulations on, 77–78; performed by Baptists, 82–83; Gayoso to Elizabeth Watts, 122; Gayoso to Margaret Cyrilla Watts, 123–24; common between Spaniards and Louisiana families, 124; irregularities in, 224–25; Gayoso serves as counselor of, 226. *See also* Morals; Miscegenation
Marschalk, Andrew, 130
Marshal, Humphrey, 140
Marshal, Thomas, 140
Martínez de Irujo, Carlos: warns Carondelet of impending British attack, 186; informs Gayoso of U.S. moves, 241; mentioned, 244
Mather, James, 141
Mathews, George, 259–60
Matilde, 247
Maurepas, Lake, 182–83, 238
Mayne, Father, 9
Mayo, Josef Antonio, 28
Meat: rations for troops at Natchez, 104; contracts for supply of, 112–13, 113*n*; taxes on in New Orleans, 206
Medicine: state of in Natchez, 130–35. *See also* Hospitals; Illness; Remedies; Surgeons
Merchants, in Natchez, 96–98
Mexico. *See* New Spain
Mexico, Gulf of, 240, 247
Militia: used for defense of Louisiana, 138; history of, 168–69, 254–55; use of in Natchez, 169–71, 192; Spanish in Louisiana mentioned, 210, 242, 273; American organization of, 242
Miller, Arthur, 259–60
Mills, 101, 104, 113*n*
Mills, John, 73–74
Mingo Pincus, 152
Minor, Stephen: sells land to government, 41, 51; post adjutant at Natchez, 50; early life and career, 51, 147*n*; litigation with Anthony Hutchins, 64; supports horse racing, 126; sent by Gayoso to Choctaws, 146–47; role in Treaty of Natchez, 150; proposes militia for Natchez,

169–70; appointed interim governor of Natchez, 199; ordered to evacuate Natchez, 232; boundary commissioner, 233; suggests speculation to Gayoso, 262; Gayoso praises work of, 268–69; praises memory of Gayoso, 271; mentioned, 128, 151, 197, 214, 233, 258, 259
Minors, status of, 68
Miró y Sabater, Esteban Rodríguez: service in Lisbon Regiment, 4–5; commandant of Natchez, 18; interim-governor of Louisiana, 18; relaxes commercial restrictions, 23; immigration policy, 24; connection with "Spanish Conspiracy," 25–26; displeasure with Gayoso, 39–40; recommendation of Gayoso, 40, 197; favors schools for Natchez, 128; supports hospital for Natchez, 133; Indian policy, 153; *residencia* of, 202; cooperates with Navarro, 217; opposes Inquisition in Louisiana, 224; mentioned, 265*n*
Miscegenation, 223, 224
Misisipi, 247–48
Mississippi River, Spain's control of, 138, 140, 173
Mississippi, Squadron of. *See* Squadron
Missouri, Company of Explorers of, 180–81, 228, 242
Missouri, Spanish settlements in, 175, 237, 242
Mistechico, 152
Mitchell, Samuel, 233
Mobile, town of, 141, 153, 238
Mobile, Treaty of, 142, 150, 152, 154
Molina, Bernardo, 246
Monge, Antonio, 104
Monge, Juan, 134
Moñino y Redondo, José, Conde de Floridablanca, 8, 21, 95, 139
Moniteur de la Louisiane, 129–30, 204
Monsanto, Benjamin, 78
Monte Pío, 250–51
Montjoye, Marquis de, 212–13
Morales, Juan Ventura: arrives in Louisiana, 28; quarrels with Gayoso, 216–22, 245; member of war council, 239, 241; says Gayoso died in poverty, 267; mentioned, 227
Morals: alleged promiscuity of Gayoso, 123; conduct of Luis Macarty, 251*n*
Moratorium, 96–99, 129, 189